DECOLONIZING FOREIGN LANGUAGE EDUCATION

Decolonizing Foreign Language Education interrogates current foreign language and second language education approaches that prioritize white, western thought. Edited by acclaimed critical theorist and linguist Donaldo Macedo, this volume includes cutting-edge work by a select group of critical language scholars working to rigorously challenge the marginalization of foreign language education and the displacement of indigenous and non-standard language varieties through the reification of colonial languages. Each chapter confronts the hold of colonialism and imperialism that informs and shapes the relationship between foreign language education and literary studies by asserting that a critical approach to applied linguistics is just as important a tool for FL/ESL/EFL educators as literature or linguistic theory.

Donaldo Macedo, Distinguished Professor of Liberal Arts and Education, is a critical theorist, expert on critical language studies, and founder and former chair of the Applied Linguistics Master Program at the University of Massachusetts Boston.

Macedo was one of the pioneers of critical pedagogy in North America in the early 1980s along with Paulo Freire, Henry Giroux, Ira Shaw, Michelle Fine, bell hooks, Roger Simon, Stanley Aronowitz, and Linda Brodkey and has been a central figure in the field for more than 35 years. His co-published work with Paulo Freire broke new theoretical ground, as it helped develop a critical understanding of the ways in which language, power, and culture contribute to the positioning and formation of human experience and learning. In addition to his work with Freire, Macedo collaborated in book projects with Noam Chomsky (*Noam Chomsky on MisEducation*) and Howard Zinn (*Howard Zinn on Democratic Education*). Macedo's published work has been translated into seven languages.

Series in Critical Narrative

Series Editor:
Donaldo Macedo, *University of Massachusetts Boston*

Dear Paulo: Letters from Those Who Dare Teach
Sonia Nieto

Uncommon Sense: From the Writings of Howard Zinn
Dean Birkenkamp and Wanda Rhudy

Paulo Freire and the Curriculum
Georgios Grollios

Freedom at Work: Language, Professional, and Intellectual Development in Schools
Maria E. Torres-Guzman with Ruth Swinney

The Latinization of U.S. Schools: Successful Teaching and Learning in Shifting Cultural Contexts
Jason G. Irizarry

Culture and Power in the Classroom: Educational Foundations for the Schooling of Bicultural Students
Antonia Darder

Changing Lives: Working with Literature in an Alternative Sentencing Program
Taylor Stoehr

Seeds of Freedom: Liberating Education in Guatemala
Clark Taylor

Pedagogy of Commitment
Paulo Freire

Latino Civil Rights in Education: La Lucha Sigue
edited by Anaida Colón-Muñiz and Magaly Lavadenz

Decolonizing Educational Research: From Ownership to Answerability
Lisa Patel

Decolonizing Foreign Language Education: The Misteaching of English and Other Imperial Languages
edited by Donaldo Macedo

For more information about this series, please visit: https://www.routledge.com/Series-in-Critical-Narrative/book-series/SCN

DECOLONIZING FOREIGN LANGUAGE EDUCATION

The Misteaching of English and Other Colonial Languages

Edited by Donaldo Macedo
UNIVERSITY OF MASSACHUSETTS BOSTON

Foreword by Michel DeGraff
MASSACHUSETTS INSTITUTE OF TECHNOLOGY

Routledge
Taylor & Francis Group
NEW YORK AND LONDON

First published 2019
by Routledge
52 Vanderbilt Avenue, New York, NY 10017

and by Routledge
2 Park Square, Milton Park, Abingdon, Oxon, OX14 4RN

Routledge is an imprint of the Taylor & Francis Group, an informa business

Library of Congress Cataloging-in-Publication Data
A catalog record for this title has been requested

ISBN: 978-1-138-32068-0 (hbk)
ISBN: 978-1-138-32069-7 (pbk)
ISBN: 978-0-429-45311-3 (ebk)

Typeset in Bembo
by Apex CoVantage, LLC
Printed by CPI Group (UK) Ltd, Croydon CR0 4YY

DEDICATION

to **Lilia Isabel Bartolomé**

whose humanity, compassion, and resilience to withstand, at a very early age, the blows of racism against her psyche and her brown Mexican body radicalized her resistance while emboldening her courage to denounce the *a priori* institutional trumpism in the form of systemic racism now normalized by President Trump, aided and abetted by the sanguinary white supremacy etched in the ethos of its institutions, including educational institutions, that varnish their racism through a politically correct language of diversity and humanism only to be hollowed-out by their *othering* of those whom they typecast as less human so that they can be silenced, subjugated, and dehumanized. Lilia Isabel never buckled under the infliction of disparate treatment for the "crime" of being born Mexican and brown nor allowed her human dignity to be trampled by the weight of careerism, greed, and cynicism as she steadily, and with conviction, promoted her always humane pedagogy by co-learning, motivating, and inspiring thousands of teachers, particularly language teachers, to create pedagogical spaces that enable subjugated and submerged voices to emerge in a cacophony of languages that decry the cries of brown Latinx children being cruelly yanked from their parents and jailed in chain-link cages at the border so as to protect the old, beaten, empty slogan of American family values.

CONTENTS

FOREWORD

Against Apartheid in Education and in Linguistics: The Case of Haitian Creole in Neo-Colonial Haiti[1]

Michel DeGraff
Massachusetts Institute of Technology
MIT-Haiti Initiative
Akademi Kreyòl Ayisyen

In Donaldo Macedo's words, this volume on *Decolonizing Foreign Language Education* instantiates "engaged and militant scholarship" against colonial methods in our classrooms. I write this Foreword firstly as a rallying call for educators throughout the world, but especially in the Global South, to join forces for the promotion of "linguistic human rights [as] instruments of decolonization opposing hegemonic aggression" (François Victor Torchon, this volume, p. 261–281). Here I write from the perspective of a linguist who has been engaged in a protracted anti-colonial struggle in my native Haiti, which is yet another post-colony where "linguicism has taken over from racism as a more subtle way of hierarchizing social groups" (cf. Phillipson, 1992, as quoted in Hatice Çelebi, this volume, p. 247).

Against Linguicism as the New Racism

Reading Macedo's fiery introduction to this volume I found the perfect quotation to summarize my Foreword, namely an important reflection from bell hooks on Adrienne Rich's insights on the *colonial* uses of the English language by the oppressed—"This is the oppressor's language yet I need it to talk to you," to which bell hooks added:

> ". . . it is not the English language that hurts me, but what the oppressors do with it, how they shape it to become a territory that limits and defines, how they make it a weapon that can shame, humiliate, and colonize."
>
> *(hooks, 1994: 167, as quoted in Macedo, this volume, p. 29)*

bell hooks' caveat brings to mind how British, then US, imperialism enlisted the English language as a weapon to control and dehumanize Native Americans, throughout North America and as far as Hawai'i, forcing them into assimilation through English-only academic programs that contributed to destroying their languages and cultures (Grenoble & Whaley, 2006; Wilson, 2014; Wilson and Kanamā, 2006, 2011; McCarty, 2011) while their lands were being stolen (Zinn, 1980). Like schoolchildren in Haiti and other post-colonies throughout the world, Native American children were physically and psychologically abused for speaking their home languages.

In my own experience as a speaker of Haitian Creole (known as "Kreyòl" in Haiti) and as a linguist interested in Caribbean Creole and other non-colonial languages, bell hooks' quotation also applies to the colonial uses of European languages in the Caribbean, Latin America, Africa, etc. Taken together, these post-colonial language-related predicaments can serve as paradigmatic cases for the struggle that this volume exhorts educators to engage in throughout the world. These predicaments add urgency to Macedo's invitation for language teachers to become "agents of history" by "engaging in critical reflection followed by knowledgeable action."

In the particular case of my native Haiti it's French that "limits and defines" as "a weapon that can shame, humiliate, and colonize," starting as early as in kindergarten when Kreyòl-speaking children are often silenced through the imposition of a former colonial language that even the teachers, by and large, do not speak fluently. Even deputies and senators in Haiti's Parliament are "shamed, humiliated and colonized," through recurrent ridicule on social media and other public venues, for any perceived deviance in their French—or for unwittingly engaging in Kreyòl-French "translanguaging" à la García (this volume). In other words, even authority figures can be silenced and made relatively powerless[2] through the (self-)imposition of French as sole "legitimate" language (cf. Saint-Fort, 2014; Charles, 2015), notwithstanding the fact that since 1987 both French and Kreyòl are, by law, Haiti's co-official languages, with Kreyòl legally recognized as our sole national language.

In effect, then, neo-colonization and class domination through French have become part and parcel of every corner of Haitian society, relegating monolingual Kreyòl speakers to second-class citizenship even though they constitute the numerical majority and should have the most influence in political matters. It is thus that the use of French in Haiti not only cements "elite closure" (à la

Myers-Scotton, 1993) but it fatally undermines the very foundations of freedom and democracy in a country that, ironically, freed itself of French colonial rule, then promised liberty and equality to its population of formerly enslaved Africans. Another dream deferred . . .

The rest of my Foreword will, then, focus on Haiti and its unfinished revolution. My plan is to highlight the formidable potential of this volume toward breaking these neo-colonial intellectual, ideological and political chains that, through language and education, still poison my native country while imprisoning it in a state of "arrested development" (Doucet, 2012) with schools that are "upside down in an upside down country" (Dejean, 2006).

A Key Distinction for Students in Haiti: Learning IN French vs Learning OF French

My work as linguist and educator has convinced me that Kreyòl is an indispensable tool for deep learning, human rights, social justice and economic development in Haiti. From that perspective, bell hooks' quotation will help me clarify that my aim is not to ban the learning *of* French in Haiti. Instead my aim is to eliminate the colonial barriers that are imposed on these millions of Kreyòl-speaking children who, generation after generation, are forced, from the earliest grades onward, to "learn" *in* French, a language that they do not speak. Such use of French as language of instruction among Kreyòl-only speakers amounts to a strategy of "élite closure" (cf. Myers-Scotton, 1993), a pedagogical mis-practice that excludes the majority of Haiti's population (the monolingual Kreyòl speakers) from access to quality education, *including the adequate learning of French and other foreign languages.*

This issue of access warrants a crucial, but apparently ill-understood, distinction *vis-à-vis* the status of French in Haitian classrooms. Indeed, there's a fundamental, but often neglected, difference between "the learning *of* French" vs. "learning *in* French." The former (i.e., the learning *of* French in Haiti) is certainly a worthy academic endeavor, alongside the learning of any other language—but, especially, Spanish and English given Haiti's location in the Americas. But failed attempts at learning *in* French from the earliest grades bring along a host of pedagogical, psychological and sociological hurdles that trap most Haitians in a persistent colonial state of "linguistic apartheid" (i.e., segregation on the basis of language, with roots in the French colonial system). This linguicism becomes even more challenging when learning *in* French is expected without any prior learning *of* French and within a context where participation in state affairs and in formal administrative and legal matters *requires* fluency in French even though the vast majority of the population speaks Kreyòl only.

These patterns of linguistic discrimination are yet another reason why I feel so privileged to have been invited to write this Foreword to this volume on decolonizing foreign language education. Indeed, though my native Haiti has been independent for more than two centuries, it remains, more than most other countries, in utmost need of decolonization when it comes to the fact that most Haitians are still being educated *in* what amounts to a foreign language (i.e., they are being *mis*-educated through the colonial use of the French language).

The use of French in Haitian classrooms (and beyond) is, thus, not a mere technical and neutral pedagogical endeavor. Educators in Haiti who uncritically teach French and, especially, those who uncritically teach *in* French are complicit in the reproduction of the colonial ideology that excludes millions of monolingual Kreyòl speakers from education, administration, justice, etc. In other words, French, like English in the analysis of Alastair Pennycook (this volume, p. 169–185), cannot be "disconnected from culture, politics, and its colonial history." So teachers in Haiti too should heed Pennycook's plea (this volume, p. 178) for the sort of activism that:

> ". . . brings the notion of resourceful speakers into conversation with a longer history of critical practice, with a perspective that acknowledges the politics of language and education and seeks to address and transform social, cultural, and economic inequalities."

Decolonization is Even More Urgent When the MEDIUM of Education is a Foreign Language that Disenfranchises Most of the Population

The title of this volume is "Decolonizing Foreign Language Education"—referring to coloniality in the teaching *of* foreign languages. But the need to decolonize is even more urgent in school systems where the very *medium* of education (and of formal administration, justice, etc.) is a foreign language—or when the medium of education (for example, English among Native Americans) was purposefully chosen as a tool to annihilate Indigenous languages such as Wampanoag, Mohawk, Navajo, Ojibwe, Hawaiian, etc., and when such a medium of instruction still exerts oppressive control over the speakers of these Indigenous languages. More generally, the urgent need to decolonize formal education is a global one if we consider that 40 percent of the world's population (more than 2 billion people, in mostly non-white communities in post-colonial nation-states in the Americas, Africa and Asia) are being "educated" in a language that is, in effect, a foreign language (Walter & Benson, 2012, UNESCO, 2016), to the detriment of these children's intellectual and psycho-social development. As UNESCO's (2016) white paper so aptly puts it, "If you don't understand, how can you learn?"

Consider, again, my native Haiti. Until its independence in 1804 Haiti was France's wealthiest colony. Though it's been more than two centuries since Haitians liberated themselves, at least administratively, from the French empire, we yet have to break the intellectual, cultural and political chains of neo-colonialism. The imposition of French as the primary language of formal education and administration has, since colonial times, dominated and devalued most of the African-derived and local ("Creole") ingredients of Haitian culture, including our Creole language (hereafter, "Kreyòl"). Hence, as Albert Memmi so correctly highlighted, "[a]ll the efforts of the colonialist are directed toward maintaining this social immobility [i.e., the immutable oppression of the colonized by the colonizer], and racism is the surest weapon for this aim . . . Racism appears then, not as an incidental detail, but as a consubstantial part of colonialism" (Memmi, 1991, p. 118).

From this perspective, the role of French as a tool of linguicism in Haiti is somewhat similar to that of English in Turkey, as described by Hatice Çelebi (this volume, p. 241), to the extent that French in Haiti, like English in Turkey,

> ". . . provides privileges to some people (primarily those in the 'core') while being harmful in both obvious and subtle ways in the social, economic, and political spheres of [. . .] people of the 'periphery' . . . "

In Haiti the people at the outer edge of the "periphery" are the numerical majority and are typically monolingual Kreyòl speakers in rural areas, and they are often called, in Kreyòl, "moun an deyò," which translates, literally, as "the people on the outside" (!).

Before leaving the topic of coloniality *vis-à-vis* the language of instruction, one more caveat is warranted concerning the teaching *of* foreign languages vs. teaching *in* foreign languages. This caveat is particularly important for the many educators (practitioners, policy-makers and researchers, including myself) who favor language-immersion and dual-language programs—*when appropriate*. We advocate these programs because we believe that, in certain well-defined contexts, teaching *in* a non-native language does contribute to the teaching *of* that language without incurring the sort of pedagogical, sociological and ideological pitfalls that are associated with teaching *in* French in Haiti. Here what I have in mind are these language-immersion or dual-language programs where the target non-native language is often a minority or non-colonial language (for example, Spanish or Native American languages in the US). In the US cases that I understand the best, the teaching in/of a non-native language as part of (one- or two-way) language immersion programs effectively promotes multilingualism and multiculturalism while boosting learning gains, including fluency in English, among recent immigrants from the Global South.

One familiar case in point, which I know first-hand, is the teaching in/of Haitian Creole in a recently launched English/Haitian Creole dual-language program in a Boston neighborhood with a large percentage of Haitian immigrants. This program, started in 2017–2018 with its first cohort of kindergarteners and first graders (with either Kreyòl or English or both spoken at home), offers a much-needed boost for Kreyòl-speaking children whose native language used to be treated as a deficit rather than the asset that it actually is. This program offers win-win opportunities in light of the fact that the English-speaking children, as well, will benefit from growing up bilingual and bi-cultural, thus enriching their humanity—while Kreyòl-speaking children become fluent in English (and bi-cultural too) and retain and deepen their fluency and literacy skills in Kreyòl along with their roots in Haitian culture (García Mathewson, 2017; Vaznis, 2017).

Another case in point is Hawai'i: the Hawaiian language is one of the many Indigenous languages previously endangered by genocidal US imperialism. Since 1978 Hawaiian has been an official language in Hawai'i. In Hawai'i's language-immersion programs, Hawaiian now successfully doubles as both the *medium* of instruction and the *subject* of instruction in successful language revitalization programs ("language nests and survival schools") that have managed to revive a language that was previously banned and threatened with extinction (Grenoble & Whaley, 2006; McCarty, 2011; Wilson, 2014; Wilson & Kanamā, 2006, 2011, 2017).[3] These language-immersion programs are now embedded in university-based teacher education curricula promoting the Hawaiian language as the medium of education.[4] The University of Hawai'i offers the first academic program in a Native American language, including a PhD in Hawaiian and Indigenous Language and Culture Revitalization. This program has been contributing innovative insights to language-immersion programs for the revitalization of Indigenous languages throughout the US.[5] In this vein it's good news that recent US legislation promotes the expansion of language-immersion and dual-language education in Native American and other minority languages.[6]

There is another key demographic and socio-linguistic difference between the target language in such language-immersion/dual-language programs in the US (be it Haitian Creole, Hawaiian, etc.) vs. French as language of instruction in Haiti: generally the former, unlike the latter, is the native, home, community, heritage or ancestral language of a substantial proportion of the students involved in such a program. In most schools in Haiti, French is not a native or home (or even a comfortable) language for anyone in the classrooms—be they students or teachers. Recall that the vast majority in Haiti, including most teachers, are fluent in Kreyòl only. Therefore, in most Haitian schools there's no real opportunity for any immersion in fluently spoken French. The only adequate immersion available is in Kreyòl.

Another key difference between US language-immersion programs vs. teaching in French in Haiti is that the former, unlike the latter, neither threaten the human rights and cultural integrity of, nor disenfranchise and impoverish, the majority. On the contrary, such programs honor their students' diverse identities and cultures, contribute to the well-being of communities previously victimized by colonial dehumanizing practices, and create academic environments where both English-speakers and their non-English-speaking counterparts can equitably share their home languages and cultures to their mutual benefit. Indeed, such programs aim at positive social transformation toward equal opportunity in academic and socioeconomic terms—a far cry from elitist French-based education in Haiti where access and opportunity are denied to the disenfranchised majority. In this comparison, only the circumstances of French in Haiti instantiate "the tortures of colonial bilingualism" decried by Albert Memmi (1991, p. 150). Only in Haiti do we have one language (French) cast as the "'superior" or "pure" language, "elaborated" language, or "cultured' language" (Macedo, this volume, p. 1) against the inferior, impure, primitive and uncultured lesser language (Kreyòl) of the so-called uncouth masses.

Haiti as a Paradigmatic Case of Linguistic Apartheid in Utmost Need of Decolonization

What makes this volume on *Decolonizing Foreign Language Education* at once unique and powerful is the political clarity it offers about its plea that foreign-language teachers question the assumption that the former colonizers' languages can be used to save people from their (quasi-)colonized status. Or, as Macedo (this volume) asks in the case of English, can English-language teachers save people from their subaltern status as stigmatized non-English speakers?

It is with passion and commitment that each author in this courageous volume, through multiple strategies, unveils the colonial ideology that is hidden in foreign-language curricula, materials and methods. These contributing authors seek a much-needed paradigm shift where foreign-language teachers can be asked to challenge and eventually undermine what Memmi has called the "fundamental discrimination between colonizer and colonized," that "*sine qua non* of colonial life [that] also lays the foundation for the immutability of this life" (Memmi, 1991, p. 118). The authors of *Decolonizing Foreign Language Education* share a common drive to "fracture [once and for all] the yoke of linguistic imperialism" in foreign-language classrooms, as the subtitle of this important volume so defiantly puts it—a defiance informed by analysis and hope.

While the arguments in my Foreword showcase mostly the ravages of "linguistic apartheid" in Haiti, I believe that my analysis applies, perhaps in more subtle or indirect fashion, to all people who have been conquered or oppressed linguistically and culturally for the economic and political advantages of the élite few against the impoverished majority. In this vein, Haiti represents a spectacular case study of a global predicament—all the more spectacular that, in Haiti, the language that is excluded from the discourse of formal education, official administration and other formal institutions is the one single language that is fluently spoken by the entire population and that is recognized as such in the country's 1987 Constitution. Having one single well-established national language spoken by an entire population would constitute a formidable asset for any country. Yet this is an advantage that Haiti's linguistic apartheid keeps laying to waste. Meanwhile the country is so impoverished and so dependent on foreign aid that it has become known as "the Republic of NGOs." Such a spectacular predicament becomes all the more challenging when we consider the odds of gaining full cultural, intellectual and political autonomy when colonialism becomes neo-colonialism, and when foreign organizations such as the Organisation Internationale de la Francophonie (OIF) and global financial institutions such as the International Monetary Fund (IMF) and the World Bank replace colonial armies. Here Haiti becomes a paradigmatic case of the neo-colonial predicament decried by Timothy Reagan and Terry Osborn (this volume, p. 83):

> "The end of the colonial era, and of formal colonial relations, did not mean the end of western imperialism. Colonialism was replaced by neo-colonialism and neo-imperialism, which, although no longer formal and somewhat less blatant, nevertheless resulted in the continuing subjugation of peoples around the world. In essence, neo-colonialism refers to the efforts of European powers (including, for the purposes of this discussion, the United States as a 'neo-European' power) to continue to maintain influence in and even domination of former colonial areas (as well as other developing societies) through alternative means . . ."

These "alternative means" include the use of a (former) colonial language—for example, French in Haiti—as primary language of education and administration.

The Yoke of Francophonie in Haiti[7]

Let's consider two recent and related events at the Élysée (the official residence of French presidents) involving two pairs of French and Haitian presidents: French President François Hollande and Haitian President Michel Martelly in October 2014; then, in December 2016, French President Emmanuel Macron and Haitian President Jovenel Moïse. Both events illustrate contemporary instances of "the yoke of imperialism" as a neo-colonization strategy that uses language and education for advancing the political and socio-economic advantages (the "national interests" à la Claire Kamsch, this volume, p. 57) of powerful countries over impoverished ones—and, within the latter, of the relatively privileged few over the disenfranchised majority.

Before delving into these recent language-related neo-colonial struggles at the Élysée, a bit of historical background is in order. The details of these struggles—on both the national and international scenes—have been documented by an unlikely source: WikiLeaks' release of US Department of State cables, where both local and foreign authorities openly express concern over the use of Creole languages as tools for education and liberation. For example, back in 1979 confidential cables from the US Department of State, as disclosed by WikiLeaks,[8] discussed a popular Martinican "campaign against the growing number of metropolitan teachers coming into Martinique [. . .] the influx [of whom] poses serious learning problems for the [Martinican] students [due to] the [French] teachers having little sympathy for the Creole language and consequently the child is seriously handicapped." Moreover, these US Department of State cables describe a "French assimilationist policy" whereby "Martinican children learn about 'our ancestors, the Gauls' but nothing about their African ancestry or about local Creole culture, which is denigrated."

In the case of Haiti, we also find US cables that document the suppression of Kreyòl. These cables, too, are dated 1979 which, as it turns out, is the year when the Haitian government inaugurated a radical reform to promote Kreyòl as the language of instruction. This reform was vigorously contested by anti-democratic forces, from both within and without the government (Alexandre, 2013). So it is not surprising that US State Department cables of that same period document "the imposition of cultural censorship" against theater and radio broadcasting in Kreyòl with the potential to educate the population about the government's "failings and abuses"—such broadcasting in Kreyòl makes the masses "less politically predictable"(!)

That the use of Kreyòl is indispensable for educating the masses about "failings and abuses" has become most evident in the current "PetroCaribe Challenge" social media campaign against state corruption in Haiti: the entire campaign, now gone viral, is being conducted in Kreyòl—an important fact that's barely mentioned in mainstream media, both in Haiti and abroad.[9] Yet Gilbert Mirambeau Jr., who launched the *#PetroCaribeChallenge* campaign on August 14, 2018, with a single tweet in Kreyòl asking "*Kot kòb PetroCaribe a?*" ("Where is the PetroCaribe money?"), was quick to tell me that his choice of using Kreyòl on social media had been a deliberate and consistent decision coupled with a conscious and consciousness-raising act of identity and patriotism against neo-colonization and massive state-sponsored corruption—financial and intellectual (personal communication with Gilbert Mirambeau Jr. via WhatsApp, September 22nd, 2018).

As for the role of language in Haiti's geo-political struggles with France, historian Webert Arthus's 2014 book (pp. 109–115) has documented the French government's persistent anti-Kreyòl and anti-development neo-colonial policies over the years, in collaboration with certain quarters of Haiti's leadership. France's well-entrenched neo-colonial stance against Haiti, in complicity with local Haitian élites, was revealed quite clearly on October 31, 2014, when President Hollande of France, during his meeting at the Élysée with President Martelly of Haiti, unambiguously stated that:

> "the French language is a major link between France and Haiti. So we're making sure that the high schools that are being built today in Haiti offer the most teaching in French, by French teachers when possible, otherwise by Francophones, because we do not want that Haiti lose the French language which makes its identity."
>
> *(cited and rebuked in DeGraff, 2015—also see DeGraff & Stump, 2018, pp. 150–151[10])*

In essence, under the banner of a "do-gooder," President Hollande proposed the reinforcement of Haiti's elitist French-based educational system, which alienates Haitians from their own local culture and national Kreyòl language and which routinely discriminates against those who don't speak French—which is the vast majority of the population. Furthermore, President Hollande's speech tendentiously makes the French language the exclusive privilege of *French* citizens, with "*Francophone*" speakers (i.e., speakers of French who are not French and who, by and large, are not white) ranked second in terms of their capacity to teach French. François Hollande's self-serving ranking of who can best teach French is a racist rebuke to those "Francophone" writers who seem so proud of their awards from the Francophonie movement, including prestigious chairs at the Académie Française and Collège de France![11]

On December 11, 2017, at the same Élysée in Paris, President Moïse of Haiti declared French to be Haiti's "official language" (*in the singular!*) contrary to fact. This declaration was part of a meeting during which French President Macron sketched a multi-million dollar plan to help "improve" Haiti's education system; then President Moïse (in return?) promised that he would do his utmost to promote French as a working language in CARICOM—an association of 15 Caribbean countries working toward economic development (Haiti Libre, 2017).

As it turns out, it's *both* Kreyòl and French that are official languages in Haiti, and it's Kreyòl, *not French*, that is constitutionally recognized as the country's sole *national* language; that is, as the sole language that can guarantee universal access to quality education in Haiti. As for CARICOM, there are more Kreyòl speakers than French speakers in the Caribbean (Mathieu, 2005; Komite pou tabli Akademi Kreyòl Ayisyen, 2013; Belfort, 2013). When President Moïse or any CARICOM leaders make speeches in French, there's a majority of interested individuals, both in Haiti and, more generally, in the Caribbean, who are left out. In effect, making French a "working language" of CARICOM works against the national interests of Caribbean countries. Instead, such a decision serves France's economic and political domination, to the detriment of local Caribbean needs such as those of Creole speakers in Haiti, Dominica and Saint Lucia who have long asked, unsuccessfully to date, that Kreyòl be a working language of CARICOM (Mathieu, 2006; Komite pou tabli Akademi Kreyòl Ayisyen, 2013; Belfort, 2013).[12]

At both these meetings at the Élysée, three years apart, all four presidents converged on one objective whose implementation would further the intellectual and economic domination of France, alongside that of a small Haitian élite, over the general population of Haiti. Such meetings illustrate, at the highest levels of governance in both countries, the continuation of a practice that has, for centuries, betrayed best practice in education and respect of human rights. Indeed, one must stress, again and again, that teaching in children's home languages—such as Kreyòl, instead of French, in Haiti—is of crucial importance for children's rights, anti-discrimination, quality education and equal opportunity for all. Yet it also bears highlighting, again, this paradoxical fact that Haiti still stands out as one of the rare nations in which there is one single language spoken by all citizens (i.e., Kreyòl), while the school system, by and large, uses another language (i.e., French) as the main language of instruction and examination.

Symbolic and Structural Violence in the Guise of a "Balanced Bilingualism" Chimera

In the 2010–2015 Operational Plan of Haiti's Ministry of National Education and Professional Training (*Groupe de Travail sur l'Éducation et la Formation*, 2010), the government announced, without any realistic means for implementation, the goal of "balanced bilingualism"—whereby the whole country should become equally fluent in both French and Kreyòl. Scientific findings from language-acquisition and language-teaching research (e.g., Reagan & Osborn and Ortega, this volume) would suggest that such an objective of nation-wide balanced bilingualism is an insurmountable task, given that the country is mostly monolingual in Kreyòl and suffers from extreme forms of economic impoverishment, of the sort that excludes any possibility of giving every Haitian access to competent and fluent French teachers and high-quality language-learning equipment. Teachers themselves often do not speak French fluently, and most Haitians have no opportunity to be regularly immersed in any community that speaks fluent French, be it at home or at school—a situation that makes "balanced bilingualism" on a national scale a socially and economically costly pipe dream (a *chimera*, indeed!). So Haitian schools should heed the paradigm shift proposed by Timothy Reagan and Terry Osborn (this volume) for foreign-language education. Reagan and Osborn draw a sharp and important methodological distinction between foreign-language *study* as part of general education and the attainment of foreign-language *fluency* for a smaller subset of students (I return to their proposal below).

Meanwhile, virtually every Haitian in Haiti speaks Kreyòl as their native language, while no more than 10 percent speak French, perhaps as few as 3 percent if we only count those who effortlessly speak fluent French, having learnt French as a native language at home amongst French-speaking relatives and peers. Given such a demographic profile, the systematic use of Kreyòl at all levels of education, government, administration, justice, etc., is indispensable for ensuring fair treatment and equality of opportunity among all Haitians (DeGraff, 2016b). More broadly, the systematic use of a community's home language by the state and by schools is an indispensable ingredient for the respect of human rights and for the most sustainable and optimal foundations to develop children's human capacity for problem solving and socio-economic development in Haiti and everywhere else (DeGraff & Ruggles, 2014; DeGraff, 2018b; DeGraff & Stump, 2018; Devonish, 2007; Milson-Whyte, 2018; Brock-Utne, 2000).[13] As I argue below, any use of French in Haitian schools should, then, consider French as a language that, in effect, is *foreign* to most students. Kreyòl must, then, be given its due as the full-fledged native language at the core of Haitian identity and as a sound basis for active learning in all academic disciplines, including foreign-language education.

Such a decolonial approach to education in Haiti is deeply germane to the contributions to this volume, especially when we consider the aforementioned discussion in Reagan and Osborn (this volume, p. 83) where it is reported that, even in the US, "less than 1 percent of American adults are proficient in the language that they studied in a US classroom." In Reagan and Osborn's chapter, one recommendation is for US teachers to clearly separate two objectives regarding foreign languages: (i) *studying* a language in the context of "the general enlightenment goals of education" vs. (ii) becoming *fluent* in that language "as an option to some students who are so inclined." Fluency in a foreign language (objective ii) is more ambitious than simply studying a language (objective i) and needs not be assigned to every student studying a foreign language.

Be that as it may, despite multiple plans and documents promoting the use of Kreyòl in Haitian education, most schools and universities there continue to impose French as the primary language of instruction and examination, thus devaluing Haiti's national language and perpetuating a long history of (neo-)colonial structural violence against the majority of the population. In many places in Haiti, official exams are offered almost exclusively in French, except the exams *on* Kreyòl. When students do have access to exams in both French and Kreyòl, many prefer to take the French version because they have already rote-memorized, often with little if any comprehension, the corresponding materials in French. Typically, students do not have access to a full range of books in Kreyòl, and especially not in science and mathematics at the more advanced levels. Worse yet, in too many Haitian classrooms students are still punished, humiliated and even expelled for speaking Kreyòl at school.

It's as if most teachers in Haiti remain oblivious to the central role they play against equal opportunity and against human rights while they continue promoting French as the primary language of formal education—as if French could magically open the doors to Haitians who have been imprisoned in a protracted state of mis-education through the ongoing exclusion and stigmatization of their native Kreyòl. I must recall that such abuses, in schools and beyond, are not unique to Haiti. They are endemic to the Caribbean (Devonish, 2007; Milson-Whyte, 2018) and to other former European colonies in the Global South (Brock-Utne, 2000; DeGraff, 2018b). Recently we have been reminded of similar structural linguistic violence in the US, as documented in videos showing children being reprimanded for using their native Spanish in the classroom (Zehr, 2003; Benavides, 2017; Edwards, 2017).

This practice of punishing children for using their mother tongue interferes with their skills, creativity and well-being. In Haiti, among every ten children who enter first grade, only one (i.e., 10 percent) will finish school, as reported in 2010 by the state-sponsored Groupe de Travail sur l'Éducation et la Formation (2010). Interestingly, approximately 10 percent of Haitians speak French to various degrees, in addition to Kreyòl. If this 10 percent substantially overlaps with the 10 percent that finish school, Haiti's school system could indeed be playing a very powerful role in producing and reproducing socio-economic inequalities through exclusionary linguistic practices. Such practices, coupled with a brutally unequal distribution of resources, amount to systemic discrimination and violations of human rights—a type of "linguistic apartheid" that undermines the excluded majority's mental health and sense of identity while blocking both academic progress and socio-economic development.

"A Population of Degenerate Types" Condemned to Silence and Alienation?

The successes of school systems in countries such as Finland suggest that children are most successful at learning foreign languages, and all else at school, when they can build strong academic foundations, including literacy, in their home and community languages (Pinnock & Vijayakumar, 2009). Such comparative data add to our ongoing argument that the use of Kreyòl as the language of instruction among Haitian children is indispensable for developing literacy and other academic skills, including the learning (or the *study,* à la Reagan & Osborn, this volume) *of* foreign languages such as French, English, or Spanish. This is exactly what works in successful Kreyòl-based education, as in the Lekòl Kominotè Matènwa (LKM) in La Gonâve, which—partly thanks to funding from US institutions such as the National Science Foundation and World Vision—has now become a model for other schools in that area (Dizikes, 2015). The children at LKM read, on average, three times better than children in schools that still favor French-based education (DeGraff, 2016c; DeGraff & Stump, 2018).

Clearly the use of local vernacular languages in education worldwide has transformative potential (DeGraff, 2018a,b). As advocated in this volume, the teaching of foreign languages should not relegate local native languages or other home or community speech varieties to second-class status. On the contrary, foreign-language teaching should incorporate the value and history of children's entire linguistic repertoires as determinants of students' identities and as fundamental tools for active learning.

Indeed, I now better understand, thanks to this volume, the reasons for students' learning gains when teachers allow "code-switching" (viewed at the level of *internal* grammars, à la Jeff McSwann, this volume) or "translanguaging" (i.e., "the deployment of a speaker's *full linguistic repertoire* without regard for watchful adherence to the socially and politically defined boundaries of named (and usually national and state) languages," as defined, at the level of *utterances*, by Ofelia García, this volume). In Pennycook's analysis, teachers need to "look at translingual practices where communication transcends both individual languages, thus involving 'diverse semiotic resources and ecological affordances.'"

Similar acceptance should be promoted *vis-à-vis* students' diverse "accents" instead of using such accents to tendentiously index degrees of intelligence or humanity (see the chapters by Claire Kramsh and Theresa Austin, this volume, and related work by Smitherman, 2000; Charity Hudley & Madison, 2014; Rickford & King, 2016; and Baugh, 2018 on African American vernacular English in US schools and other institutions). In the current academic climate of Haiti, code-switching between Kreyòl and French (and non-standard varieties of French with various degrees of Kreyòl influence) is anathema to most teachers. The latter are quick at penalizing the slightest transfer from Kreyòl into the French spoken by Haitian students. This prescriptive purism is somewhat reminiscent of Austin's (this volume) analysis of Spanish-language programs' preference for standardized Peninsular Spanish over non-Peninsular varieties.

In effect, such norms in Haiti (for example, stigmas against Kreyòl-French translanguaging and against Kreyòl-influenced varieties of French) render Kreyòl-speaking students virtually speechless, as predicted by García's indictment of "nation-states [that] have co-opted the human potential of language as a meaning-making semiotic tool, relegating many speakers to a position of speechlessness." In fact, Haitian teachers often use French as a tool of control in their classrooms, knowing very well that students, and even adults, would rather remain silent instead of running the risk of being shamed and humiliated for the slightest French mistakes. The latter are often misinterpreted, in brutally prejudiced fashion, as reflexes of stupidity or markers of the lowest rungs of the social-class hierarchy (DeGraff & Stump, 2018, p. 146).[14] It is thus that the Haitian school system, with French as the main language of instruction, renders Kreyòl-dominant speakers "at risk" or, worse yet, "as a population of degenerate types" (in the terminology of Hemphill & Blakely, this volume, p. 220). Here, too, Haiti becomes a paradigmatic case of this brand of "colonization [that] occurs in large part through mandating a standardized and commodified 'academic language,' and devaluing other language varieties" (again, Hemphill & Blakely, this volume, p. 224).

"Fracturing the Yoke of Linguistic Imperialism"—in Education, Development and Linguistics

This volume is a loud and valiant call for institutions, educators and scholars worldwide to concretely honor linguistic diversity by enlisting it as a means of promoting equitable access to quality education and for protecting children's rights. Given the geo-politics and the social-class correlates of language- and education-related choices at both the group and individual levels (DeGraff, 2005, 2014, 2017, 2018a,b), this call should be transmitted as well to international organizations such as the United Nations, alongside their member states, which should check whether their documentation and pedagogical materials (websites, social media, memos, syllabi, textbooks, examinations, etc.) are delivered in the corresponding local languages. Such monitoring could also provide longitudinal data to evaluate progress in the use of local languages. All levels of human rights organizations should pay systematic attention to actual language and education practices on the ground.

In Haiti, for example, the vast majority of administrative, legal and educational documents are still written exclusively in French—including documents being produced by the very organizations whose official objectives include the promotion of children's rights and education. One UNICEF site, titled "Timoun yo! The Voice of Haiti's Children,"[15] is an example of that ambivalence toward the use of Kreyòl, notwithstanding UNICEF's pro-Kreyòl advocacy elsewhere. The site's home page prominently displays the UN Convention on the Rights of the Child, but the site itself is in French and English and not in Kreyòl—the only language spoken by most Haitian children (and adults). Worse yet, most publications by the Haitian state, including the Ministry of Culture and Communication,[16] the Ministry of National Education,[17] the State University,[18] and human rights institutions such as the Office de la Protection du Citoyen,[19] are in French, thus they routinely violate Haiti's 1987 Constitution, which mandates the use of French and Kreyòl as co-official languages, with Kreyòl deemed the one single language that bonds the entire nation. Similar abuses are apparent in Haiti's court system, which functions primarily in French even though judges, lawyers, audiences, etc. are, by and large, most fluent in Kreyòl while the contending parties (accusers, accused, witnesses, etc.) most often speak Kreyòl *only*. Thus most Haitians "have no real access to justice" (Carew Craft, 2015). In effect, such linguistic practices, even among local and international human-rights organizations, discriminate against the majority of the population and violate their . . . human rights!

Even the UN violates its own Universal Declaration of Human Rights, which grants[20]

> "rights and freedoms . . . without distinction of any kind such as race, colour, sex, *language*, religion, political or other opinion, national or social origin, property, birth or other status."
>
> *[emphases added]*

The UN routinely violates such "rights and freedoms"; for example, UN authorities in Haiti have used French to conduct meetings with Haitians who speak Kreyòl only. French has even been used in UN meetings with Kreyòl-speaking communities that are being decimated by the cholera epidemic that was introduced in October 2010 by UN troops disposing of their feces in a major river and killing thousands, with nearly a million sick and the illness spreading to other countries (Frerichs *et al,* 2012), not even a year after Haiti's catastrophic earthquake of January 12, 2010.[21]

Now, let's move toward the bright side, with a more personal perspective rooted in my own work as linguist, educator and activist at MIT and in Haiti. Acknowledging the primacy of native languages as foundations for knowledge and human rights is the fundamental premise that underlies the workings of the MIT-Haiti Initiative[22] that I co-founded with Dr. Vijay Kumar at MIT in 2010 and that has been funded by the US National Science Foundation since 2012. By providing state-of-the-art teacher training and pedagogical resources in Kreyòl to faculty in Haiti, the Initiative is directly contributing to universal access to quality education (Miller, 2016; DeGraff, 2016a, 2018a,b; DeGraff & Stump, 2018). Furthermore, this Initiative—which enlists the collaboration of educators, humanists, scientists, engineers, mathematicians, politicians, activists, artists, etc., both in the US and in Haiti—seems a perfect example of the sort of "transdisciplinarity" advocated by Lourdes Ortega (this volume, p. 112) whereby

> ". . . scholarly communities attempt to solve complex knowledge problems with social impact by working across multiple disciplinary boundaries as well as with social actors outside academia, willing to integrate diverse and often discipline-internal perspectives into more than the sum of each discipline-specific fund of knowledge . . . Broadening knowledge bases in this way increases experts' capacities to meet complex contemporary demands for socially useful knowledge."

Before the MIT-Haiti Initiative began there were no substantial Kreyòl-language online materials and digital learning tools for university-level science and mathematics. The Initiative now provides resources that can help teach science and mathematics in Kreyòl beyond linguistic and social-class barriers, thus joining the still too small number of organizations that work to increase access to quality education through the use of Haiti's national language. Since 2012 the Initiative has also provided teacher-training workshops to enhance high school and university teachers' skills in Kreyòl-based active-learning pedagogy and in hands-on technology for education (Miller, 2016; DeGraff & Stump, 2018).

In order to succeed, this paradigm shift requires the participation of local and international institutions—governments and courts, schools and universities, research centers, telecommunication companies, funding agencies and NGOs, among other institutions and activities that create and transmit knowledge and power. It's especially important that linguists, as well, distance themselves from the colonial foundations of subfields such as Creole studies whose very foundations were part of Europe's *mission civilisatrice,* whereby non-Whites and their languages and cultures had to be ranked as inferior to their counterparts among European Whites (DeGraff, 2005). It is such beliefs that led to the age-old prejudices at the core of "Creole Exceptionalism" dogmas even among contemporary linguists. These dogmas (or "linguists' most dangerous fallacies," as described in DeGraff, 2005) have, for far too long, assumed Creoles to be developmentally or structurally "exceptional" (i.e., freakish) languages originating from mythical (and undocumented!) pidgins qua spectacularly impoverished (quasi-) languages.[23] It it thus that these dogmas have (directly or indirectly) contributed to excluding Creole languages both from the family of "normal" human languages and from their use in classrooms, courts, formal administration, etc. (see DeGraff, 2001, 2005 for extended surveys and critiques of Creole Exceptionalism dogmas).

DeGraff (2009) and Aboh and DeGraff (2017) present analyses of Creole formation whereby the history and structures of Creole languages are on a par with their counterparts in non-Creole languages, thus confirming Mufwene's (2008, pp. 40–58) argument that the notion "Creole" can only be defined in socio-historical and ethnographic terms without any specific linguistic structural traits that would define what a Creole language is. In other words, Creole languages are just . . . languages! And like any other languages, they help format their native speakers' minds/brains from the womb and are the most adapted linguistic tools for building solid foundations for their speakers' cognitive, social and academic needs.

From Colonial Alienation to Liberation

In Haiti, like in most nations still struggling against neo-colonial powers from both within and without, social justice and equal opportunity for all will remain figments of our imagination as long as we have not decolonized our research and teaching practices, our views of ourselves and of our languages, cultures, etc., and our relationships with foreign powers. Regretfully, in the case of Haiti, like elsewhere in the Global South, there are formidable geo-political forces—which Claire Kamsch (this volume, p. 57) calls the "national interests" of foreign powers such as the US and Europe—that have historically plundered our human and natural resources, reproduced colonial dependency, and disparaged our languages and cultures. In Haiti these foreign interests, alongside internal social-class struggles with linguistic and other cultural correlates, have caused what Jean Price-Mars (1928 [1983: 8]) has called Haiti's "collective bovarism"—the belief on the part of many educated Haitians that they are "colored Frenchmen" (sigh . . .). In a related vein, various contributions to Blanc and Madhère's (2017) volume on Afro-Caribbean epistemology consider the possibility, à la Frantz Fanon (1967), that the tragic post-traumatic effects of colonization and slavery on the Haitian collective psyche are partly responsible for at least two pathologies: (i) the neo-colonial aspects of Haitian society, especially the predatory nature of its political apparatus, and (ii) the ongoing ambivalence of the population, especially Haitian leaders and intellectuals, vis-à-vis Haiti's national culture and identity, including our national language of Kreyòl.

Unless Haitian political and socio-economic leaders, policy-makers and educators decolonize their minds and rid themselves of this persistent belief in the superiority of the French language and culture—a belief still being promoted by schools' curricula, educational materials and teaching methods (see DeGraff & Stump, 2018)—they will unreflectively and uncritically perpetuate the self-debilitating myth that "it's the French language that constitutes Haitian identity," along the line of François Hollande's propaganda (as discussed above—regarding "the yoke of Francophonie" in Haiti; also see notes 10 and 11). These Francophile myths concerning French superiority and Haiti's (pseudo-) French identity are found even among the most "progressive" and "liberal" Haitian intellectuals. One most unfortunate corollary of these myths is that they turn most Haitians (i.e., those who speak Kreyòl only) into refuse of humanity who have no "identity" to speak of and thus can be relegated and forgotten in the dustbins of academic and socio-economic progress.

This is how Haiti has become a paradigmatic case of the dangerous epistemological, pedagogical and societal defects that the contributors in this volume are trying to denounce so as to correct. These defects are rooted in the mistaken colonial belief that certain foreign languages (i.e., from Europe's neo-colonial powers) can increase the degree of humanity of those who have, for far too long, been considered lesser humans with lesser languages. US imperialism took this colonial belief to its most brutal logical conclusion, namely the genocide of North America's Indigenous peoples whose languages were decimated in the course of Native American children becoming victims of forced assimilation in English-only schools that banned the use of their ancestral languages (Grenoble & Whaley, 2006; Wilson & Kanamā, 2006, 2011; McCarty, 2011). Native Americans' cultures, overall autonomy and wellbeing were decimated as well:

> Besides outright oppression, indigenous language endangerment is tied to the loss of traditional economies and autonomy based in hunting and gathering, fishing, subsistence agriculture, and herding, all of which are conducted through the indigenous languages.
>
> *(Wilson & Kanamā, 2011, p. 37; also see Zinn, 1980 for the larger historical context around European and US imperialism)*

Fortunately the groundbreaking example traced by Hawaiian-language immersion schools in Hawaiʻi—"the most successful effort in language revitalization efforts in the United States" (Wilson, 2014; cf. Grenoble & Whaley, 2006)—suggests a hopeful way forward, one where a new sort of anti-colonial linguistics can reverse the effect of linguicide in imperialist conquests and play a key role in the human right to education (DeGraff, 2018a,b) as we strive for linguistic and cultural diversity to enrich our humanity.[24] Closer to us, in Massachusetts, the inspiring story of Jessie Little Doe Baird and her Wampanoag people reviving their ancestral language (Baird *et al*, 2010) beautifully exemplifies the role that linguistics as well can play in this anti-colonial struggle. These examples from Indigenous communities in the US, alongside this volume's case studies, show the potential of foreign-language education *and* linguistics toward social transformation (see DeGraff, 2018a for related examples among Creole speakers and in Creole studies).

It is thus crucial for our own wellbeing as scholars, educators and parents, for the wellbeing of children worldwide, for mutually respectful and enriching North-South relations and for a more just and humane world that the teaching of/in "foreign" or "ancestral" or "heritage" or "indigenous" or "local" or "vernacular" or "native" languages—and *all* teaching for that matter—"fracture the yoke of linguistic imperialism" at long last. So let's carefully read this volume together and take its message to heart . . . and to our classrooms throughout the world.

Notes

1 I am most thankful to my dear friend and colleague Donaldo Macedo for all his inspiring work helping us become better at "reading the word and the world," for inviting me to this project, and for his generous feedback on this Foreword. And special thanks to my "chouchous" Elena and Nuriel for always sharing feedback and encouragements on so many aspects of my work (and more!). For this paper, Nuriel saved me, at the last minute, from one grossly embarrassing factual mistake.

2 In the US as well, stigmatized speech varieties have rendered certain populations, including authority figures, relatively speechless—even in the case of Judge Clarence Thomas on the Supreme Court who once reported suffering from linguistic insecurity due to his "having grown up speaking a kind of [Geechee/Gullah] dialect" (Thomas, 2000, cf. DeGraff, 2016b). Prejudices against vernacular varieties are an obstacle to social justice as well (Rickford & King, 2016; Baugh, 2018).

3 I am indebted to William "Pila" Wilson for insightful discussion of Hawai'i and related cases that bring important nuances to the notion "teaching *in*" vs. "teaching *of*" a language, especially in decolonial language-immersion contexts. Unfortunately and unlike Hawaiian nowadays, Hawaiian Creole (known as "Pidgin" in Hawai'i) still has no official status; it remains, by and large, stigmatized as "improper" or "broken" English. In other words, the decolonization of Hawaiian Creole is far behind that of Hawaiian. But efforts are being made on that front as well, especially among the linguists at the University of Hawai'i. Heartfelt thanks to Jason Cabral, Scott Saft and Pila Wilson (at the University of Hawai'i at Hilo) for showing me the way forward, and in person, on both the Hawaiian and Creole anti-colonial fronts.

4 https://hilo.hawaii.edu/catalog/kahuawaiola-indigenous-teacher-education-program.

5 https://hilo.hawaii.edu/catalog/ma_hll, https://hilo.hawaii.edu/catalog/phd_hilcr, https://hilo.hawaii.edu/news/stories/2017/03/03/international-group-meets-at-uh-hilo/, https://hilo.hawaii.edu/keaohou/2012/10/17/william-wilson-hawaiian-language/.

6 Every Student Succeeds Act (2015): http://www.congress.gov/amendment/114th-congress/senate-amendment/2240/text.

7 The paragraphs below expand DeGraff's (2017) plea against "linguistic apartheid" in Haiti, which was initially submitted to the United Nations' High Commissioner for Human Rights.

8 https://www.facebook.com/michel.degraff/posts/10154805918923872. https://www.facebook.com/michel.degraff/posts/10154805985218872. https://www.facebook.com/michel.degraff/posts/10154805996838872. https://www.facebook.com/michel.degraff/posts/10154805978543872. https://www.facebook.com/michel.degraff/posts/10154805942788872.

9 For example, in one *Miami Herald* article about the "PetroCaribe Challenge" campaign, all the quoted social media postings about the campaign are in Kreyòl, but the fact that this viral campaign is being waged almost exclusively in Kreyòl is not noted, even though the author (Jacqueline Charles) is a veteran Haitian journalist: https://www.miamiherald.com/news/nation-world/world/americas/haiti/article217110220.html. The prominence of Kreyòl on social media in Haiti is quantified in DeGraff (2016a, pp. 178–179).

10 President François Hollande's speech about Haitian identity, education and development, alongside the response by President Michel Martelly, is available online at: http://www.boursorama.com/actualites/france-haiti-martelly-evoque-un-partenariat-pour-l-education-ae69f38cb59bf8a08f286a1949fc4165, with an English translation at https://www.facebook.com/michel.degraff/videos/10156132035733872/.

11 Hollande's notion that "Francophone" teachers cannot teach French as well as French-born teachers is reminiscent of this Turkish university president, in Hatice Çelebi's paper in this volume (p. 241–281), who believes that non-native speakers of English cannot

teach English: "As he [this university president] handed over the [English-teaching] contract for me to sign, he congratulated me on my new job and, without further comment, said he did not believe that 'Turkish people can teach English' . . . "

12 There has been one positive update since the initial writing of this Foreword. After that December 2017 meeting between Presidents Macron and Moïse, President Moïse revised his declaration at the Élysée and, instead, proposed to CARICOM that Kreyòl as well, alongside French, be made into an official language of CARICOM (Haiti Libre, 2018). As of this writing, this demand has not yet been granted.

13 See Mufwene 2018 for related questions regarding the economic implications of linguistic diversity in the Global South. Mufwene constructively problematizes the "chicken-and-egg" link between formal education and economic development. One key question concerns the classroom use of regional lingua francas (e.g., Wolof, Swahili, Lingala in sub-Saharan Africa) in cases where the students speak such lingua franca(s) alongside their home/community language(s). In personal communication (September 27, 2018) Mufwene stresses the important fact that in many parts of sub-Saharan Africa these lingua francas double as home and community languages (i.e., as mother tongues) for children in these areas. Mufwene also makes the important point that highly multilingual ecologies make different economic and pedagogical demands on school systems as compared to ecologies with fewer languages to contend with. But, still, a caveat seems needed: if some of these lingua francas are, in effect, *second* or (quasi) *foreign* languages for many of these children (see, for example, Brock-Utne 2000, p. 200), then the initial investment that is required to produce materials in the relevant Indigenous languages may well be worth the effort, keeping in mind the now familiar risk of maintaining certain children (those less fluent in the lingua franca) in a pedagogically challenging situation with dire psycho-social and economic consequences for themselves and their communities.

14 Here are social-media examples of French mistakes on the part of two Haitian senators. These senators' French caused them to be called "ignoramus," "stupid," "illiterate," etc.: https://www.facebook.com/michel.degraff/posts/10155588908963872 https://www.facebook.com/michel.degraff/posts/10155589602853872.

15 http://timounyo.com/ accessed on July 17, 2018.

16 https://www.communication.gouv.ht/. Accessed on July 17, 2018.

17 http://menfp.gouv.ht/ accessed on July 17, 2018.

18 http://www.ueh.edu.ht/ accessed on July 17, 2018.

19 https://www.facebook.com/OPC-Ha%C3%AFti-Office-de-la-Protection-du-Citoyen-dHa%C3%AFti-217050851679230. Accessed on July 17, 2018.

20 http://www.un.org/en/universal-declaration-human-rights/.

21 Brian Concannon Jr., personal communication. See the Institute for Justice & Democracy website at http://ijdh.org for more details about the UN's violations of human rights in Haiti.

22 https://haiti.mit.edu.

23 In some of the scenarios that treat Creoles as extraordinarily simple languages, such utmost simplicity is due to their hypothetical origins in structurally impoverished interlanguages in peculiar instances of second-language acquisition. Here, prejudices against Creole languages converge with what seem like prejudices against adult language learners. One such area of theoretical convergence is the hypothesis that pidgin languages, presumably because they originate in adult learners' early interlanguages, would instantiate some sort of "basic variety" that lacks some of the fundamental design features of truly human languages. See DeGraff 2001, especially pages 249–250, for one extended critique of this "basic variety" hypothesis in the context of a long series of erroneous claims to the effect that Creole languages are among the world's most primitive languages (also see DeGraff, 2005, 2009; and DeGraff & Aboh, 2017 for counter-arguments).

24 A note to foreign-language teachers among our readers: one striking fact about the Hawaiian language-immersion programs is that the average competency in English of students graduating from these programs exceeds that of their counterparts in non-immersion programs (Wilson & Kanamā, 2017).

Bibliography

Aboh, Enoch & Michel DeGraff (2017) "A null theory of Creole formation." In Ian Roberts (Ed.), *Oxford Handbook of Universal Grammar* (pp. 401–458). New York: Oxford University Press [http://linguistics.mit.edu/wp-content/uploads/aboh-and-degraff-2017-null-theory-of-creole-formation.pdf].

Alexandre, Guy (2013) "La politique éducative du Jean-Claudisme: Chronique de l'échec 'organisé' d'un projet de réforme". In Pierre Buteau and Lyonel Trouillot (Eds.), *Le Prix du Jean-Claudisme: Arbitraire, parodie, désocialisation.* Port-au-Prince: C3 Éditions.

Arthus, Wien Weibert (2014) Duvalier à l'ombre de la guerre froide: Les dessous de la politique étrangère d'Haïti (1957–1963). Port-au-Prince: Imprimeur S.A.

Baird, Jessie Little Doe, Anne Makepeace, Jennifer Weston, Mary Lampson, Stephen McCarthy & Joel Goodman (2010) *Âs Nutayuneân = We still live here.* Oley, PA: Bullfrog Films.

Baugh, John (2018) *Linguistics in pursuit of justice.* Cambridge, UK: Cambridge University Press.

Belfort, Jocelyn (2013) "Suze Mathieu opte pour la création d'un bloc créolophone à la CARICOM." *Le Nouvelliste,* February 19, 2013. [http://lenouvelliste.com/article/113575/suze-mathieu-opte-pour-la-creation-dun-bloc-creolophone-a-la-caricom]

bell hooks (1996) *Teaching to Transgress.* New York: Routledge.

Benavides, Cristian (2017) "Students walk out after teacher orders 'Speak American'." *NBC News,* October 16, 2017. [https://www.nbcnews.com/news/latino/students-walk-out-after-teacher-tells-students-speak-american-n811256]

Blanc, Judith & Serge Madhère (Eds.) (2017) *Pensée afro-caribéenne et (psycho)traumatismes de l'esclavage et de la colonisation / Toubiyon twoma lesklavaj ak kolonizasyon: Dangoyaj panse afro-karayibeyen.* Port-au-Prince: Collection Ayiti. [https://scienceetbiencommun.pressbooks.pub/psychologieafricaine/]

Brock-Utne, Birgit (2000) *Whose Education For All? The Recolonization of the African Mind.* New York and London: Falmer Press, Taylor & Francis Group.

Carew Craft, Jessica (2015). "Establishing the rule of law in a country where justice hardly exists." *The Atlantic,* April 22, 2015. [https://www.theatlantic.com/education/archive/2015/04/establishing-the-rule-of-law-in-a-country-where-justice-hardly-exists/391113/]

Charity Hudley, Anne & Christine Mallinson (2014) *We do language: English language variation in the secondary English classroom.* New York: Teachers College Press.

Charles, Fabian (2015) "Ki sa pale vle di ann Ayiti?" *Potomitan: Site de promotion des cultures et des langues créoles,* avril [www.potomitan.info/ayiti/charles/pale.php]; *AyiboPost,* avril [http://ayibopost.com/ki-sa-pale-vle-di-ann-ayiti/]

DeGraff, Michel (2001) "On the Origin of Creoles: A Cartesian Critique of Neo-Darwinian Linguistics." *Linguistics Typology,* vol. 5, nos. 2 and 3, pp. 213–310. [http://lingphil.mit.edu/papers/degraff/degraff-lt-2001.pdf]

DeGraff, Michel (2005) "Linguists' Most Dangerous Myth: The Fallacy of Creole Exceptionalism." *Language in Society,* 34.4, pp. 53–591.

DeGraff, Michel (2009) "Language acquisition in creolization and, thus, language change: Some Cartesian-Uniformitarian boundary conditions." *Language and Linguistics Compass*, 3.4, pp. 888–971. [http://lingphil.mit.edu/papers/degraff/degraff2009language_acquisition_in_creolization.pdf]

DeGraff, Michel (2014) "The Ecology of Language Evolution in Latin America: A Haitian Postscript Toward a Postcolonial Sequel." In Salikoko Mufwene (Ed.), *Iberian Imperialism and Language Evolution in Latin America* (pp. 274–327). Chicago, IL: University of Chicago Press. [http://lingphil.mit.edu/papers/degraff/degraff_2014_ecology_of_language_evolution_in_latin_america.pdf]

DeGraff, Michel (2015) "France's *misconceived* 'Marshall Plan' for Haiti." *Le Monde Diplomatique*, May 26, 2015. [http://mondediplo.com/blogs/france-s-misconceived-marshall-plan-for-haiti].

DeGraff, Michel (2016a) La langue maternelle comme fondement du savoir: L'Initiative MIT-Haiti: Vers une éducation en créole efficace et inclusive. *Revue transatlantique d'études suisses*. 6/7, 177–197. [http://linguistics.mit.edu/wp-content/uploads/degraff-2017-langue-maternelle-comme-fondement-du-savoir-MIT-Haiti.pdf]

DeGraff, Michel (2016a) Lang matènèl, pedagoji entèraktif, lojisyèl edikatif nan Inisyativ MIT-Ayiti : « Twa wòch dife » pou bon jan edikasyon ak inovasyon alawonnbadè ann Ayiti. *Journal of Haitian Studies*. 22.2.128–141. [http://linguistics.mit.edu/wp-content/uploads/DeGraff-20170310-JoHS-two-woch-dife.pdf]

DeGraff, Michel (2016b) "Linguistic equality as a condition for economic and political equality." *The Boston Review*, May 9, 2016. [http://bostonreview.net/forum/what-education/michel-degraff-michel-degraff-responds-danielle-allen]

DeGraff, Michel (2016c) "Mother-tongue books in Haiti: The power of Kreyòl in learning to read and in reading to learn." *Prospects: Comparative Journal of Curriculum, Learning and Assessment*. [http://rdcu.be/IyEG]

DeGraff, Michel (2017) "Haiti's '*linguistic* apartheid' violates *children's* rights and hampers development." [https://opendemocracy.net/openglobalrights/michel-degraff/haiti-s-linguistic-apartheid-violates-children-s-rights-and-hampers-]

DeGraff, Michel (2018a) "Error correction and social transformation in Creole studies and among Creole speakers: The case of Haiti." *Language in Society* 47:3, pp. 354–360. [http://lingphil.scripts.mit.edu/papers/degraff/DeGraff_2018_Error_correction_and_social_transformation_in_Haiti.pdf]

DeGraff, Michel (2018b) "Linguistics' role in the right to education." *Science Magazine* volume 360, issue 6388, p. 502, May 2018. [http://lingphil.scripts.mit.edu/papers/degraff/DeGraff_in_Science_Magazine_20180504_Linguistics_in%20right_to_education.pdf]

DeGraff, Michel & Molly Ruggles (2014) "A Creole solution for Haiti's woes." *New York Times*, August 1, 2014. [https://www.nytimes.com/2014/08/02/opinion/a-creole-solution-for-haitis-woes.html]

DeGraff, Michel & Glenda S. Stump (2018) "Kreyòl, pedagogy, and technology for opening up quality education in Haiti: Changes in teachers' meta-linguistic attitudes as first steps in a paradigm shift." *Language* 94.2, 127–157. [https://www.linguisticsociety.org/sites/default/files/e3_94.2DeGraff.pdf]

Dejean, Yves (2006) *Yon lekòl tèt anba nan yon peyi tèt anba*. Port-au Prince: FOKAL.

Devonish, Hubert (2007) *Language and liberation : Creole language politics in the Caribbean*. Kingston, Jamaica: Arawak.

Dizikes, Peter (2015) "Three questions: Michel DeGraff on Haiti's new policy for teaching in Kreyòl." *MIT News*, July 20, 2015. [http://newsoffice.mit.edu/2015/3-questions-michel-degraff-haiti-teaching-kreyol-0720]

Doucet, Fabienne (2012). "Arrested development: How lack of will cripples educational reform in Haiti." *Journal of Haitian Studies* vol. 19, no. 1, pp. 120–150.

Edwards, Breanna (2017) "NJ teacher asks students to 'Speak American,' but who's gonna tell her that 'American' is not a language." *The Root,* October 25, 2017. [https://www.theroot.com/nj-teacher-tells-students-to-speak-american-but-who-1819499808]

Fanon, Frantz (1967) *Black Skins, White Masks.* New York: Grove Press.

Frerichs, R.R., P.S. Keim, R. Barrais & R. Piarroux (2012) "Nepalese origin of cholera epidemic in Haiti." *Clinical Microbiology and Infection,* Volume 18, Issue 6, pp. E158–E163. [https://www.clinicalmicrobiologyandinfection.com/article/S1198-743X(14)64134-3/fulltext]

García Mathewson, Tara (2017) "How discrimination nearly stalled a dual-language program." *The Atlantic,* April 7, 2017. [https://www.theatlantic.com/education/archive/2017/04/how-discrimination-nearly-prevented-a-dual-language-program-in-boston/522174/]

Grenoble, Lenore A. & Lindsay J. Whaley (2006) *Saving Languages: An Introduction to Language Revitalization.* Cambridge, UK: Cambridge University Press.

Groupe de Travail sur l'Éducation et la Formation (2010) *Pour un Pacte National pour l'Éducation en Haïti,* Port-au-Prince: Bibliothèque Nationale. [http://planipolis.iiep.unesco.org/sites/planipolis/files/ressources/haiti_pacte_national_education.pdf]

Haiti Libre (2017) "Haiti—Flash: Promises of Macron to President Jovenel Moïse." *Haiti Libre,* December 12, 2017. [http://www.haitilibre.com/en/news-22959-haiti-flash-promises-of-macron-to-president-jovenel-moise.html, accessed on July 17, 2018]

Haiti Libre (2018) "Haiti—Politics: End of the 29th conference of heads of states of CARICOM." *Haiti Libre,* February 28, 2018. [http://www.haitilibre.com/en/news-23684-haiti-politic-end-of-the-29th-conference-of-heads-of-state-of-caricom.html, accessed on July 17, 2018]

Komite pou tabli Akademi Kreyòl Ayisyen (2013) "Lang kreyòl: Dezyèm lang ofisyèl CARICOM." *Potomitan: Site de promotion des cultures et des langues créoles.* [http://www.potomitan.info/ayiti/akademi_kreyol8.php]

Mathieu, Suze (2005) *Depi nan Ginen nèg renmen nèg. Kreyòl ak demokrasi ann Ayiti.* Pòtoprens: Près nasyonal peyi d Ayiti.

McCarty, Teresa. L. (2011) State of the field: The role of Native languages and cultures in American Indian, Alaska Native, and Native Hawaiian student achievement. Policy paper prepared for: *The Promising Practices and Partnerships in Indian Education Working Group* and the *U.S. Department of Education Office of Indian Education Programs under contract to Kauffman Associates, Inc. Spokane, WA.* Phoenix, Ariz. [https://static1.squarespace.com/static/52cf1070e4b048ae22d972b2/t/54aac6b3e4b0c309d027948a/1420478131256/McCarty+%282011%29.+Role+and+Impact+of+Native+Languages+and+Cultural+Context.pdf]

Memmi, Albert (1991). *The Colonizer and the Colonized.* Boston, MA: Beacon Press.

Miller, Haynes (2016) "The MIT-Haiti Initiative. An international engagement." MIT Faculty Newsletter. Vol XXIX, No. 1, September/October 2016. [http://web.mit.edu/fnl/volume/291/miller.html]

Milson-Whyte, Vivette (2018) "Caribbean Creole-speaking cultures, language and identities. In John Liontas (editor), Margo DelliCarpini (project editor) and Shondel Nero (volume editor), *The TESOL Encyclopedia of English Language Teaching.* Volume VI, pp. 3483–3489. Oxford, UK: John Wiley & Sons.

Mufwene, Salikoko (2008). *Language evolution: Contact, competition and change.* London, UK: Continuum.

Mufwene, Salikoko (2018). "Linguistic diversity, formal education, and economic development: The sub-Saharan African chicken-and-egg dilemma?" Written version of keynote lecture presented at the *12th International Language & Development Conference*, Senegal, December 27–29, 2017.

Myers-Scotton, Carol (1993) "Elite closure as a powerful language strategy: the African case." *International Journal of the Sociology of Language*, 103.1, pp. 149–164.

Phillipson, Robert (1992) *Linguistic imperialism*. Oxford, UK: Oxford University Press.

Pinnock, Helen & Gowri Vijayakumar (2009) *Language and education: The missing link: How the language used in schools threatens the achievement of Education for All*. Reading, UK: CFBT Education Trust. [http://www.unesco.org/education/EFAWG2009/Language-Education.pdf]

Price-Mars, Louis (1928 [1983]) *Ainsi parla l'oncle: Essais d'ethnographie*. Port-au-Prince: Imprimerie de Compiegne. Eng. ed., *So spoke the uncle*. Trans. Magdaline Shannon. Washington, DC: Three Continents.

Rickford, John R. & Sharese King (2016) Language and linguistics on trial: Hearing Rachel Jeantel and other vernacular speakers in the courtroom and beyond. *Language* 92(4), pp. 948–988.

Saint-Fort, Hugues (2014) "Le 'marché linguistique' haïtien: Fonctionnement, idéologie et avenir." *Potomitan: Site de promotion des cultures et des langues creoles*. [http://ww.potomitan.info/ayiti/saint-fort/marche.php].

Smitherman, Geneva (2000). *Talkin that talk: Language, culture, and education in African America*. New York: Routledge.

UNESCO (2016) *If you don't understand how can you learn*. *Policy Paper 24*, Paris: Global Education Monitoring Report. [http://unesdoc.unesco.org/images/0024/002437/243713E.pdf]

Vaznis, James (2017) "A Haitian Creole program arrives in Mattapan." *Boston Globe*. September 7, 2017. [http://www.bostonglobe.com/metro/2017/09/06/mattapan-haitian-creole-program-for-preschoolers/O6PydlII1WWoaOGdqlYYZJ/story.html]

Walter, Stephen & Carol Benson (2012) Language policy and medium of instruction in formal education. In Bernard Spolsky (Ed.), *The Cambridge handbook of language policy* (pp. 278–300). Cambridge: Cambridge University Press.

Wilson, William (2014) "Hawaiian: A Native American language official for a State". In Terrence G. Wiley, Joy Kreeft Peyton, Donna Christian, Sarah Catherine K. Moore and Na Liu (Eds.), *Handbook of Heritage. Research, Policy, and Educational Practice Wiley, Wiley* (pp. 219–228). New York: Routledge.

Wilson, William H. & Kauanoe Kanamā (2006) "'For the interests of the Hawaiians themselves': Reclaiming the benefits of Hawaiian-medium education." *Hūlili: Multidisciplinary research on Hawaiian well-being*, Volume 3, Number 1, pp. 153–181. [http://www.kpublishing.org/_assets/publishing/hulili/Hulili_Vol3_9.pdf]

Wilson, William H. & Kauanoe Kanamā (2011) "Insights from Indigenous Language Immersion in Hawai'i: The Case of Nāwahī School." In Diane J. Tedick, Donna Christian and Tara Williams Fortune (Eds.), *Immersion Education, Practices, Policies, Possibilities* (pp. 36–57). Clevedon, UK: Multilingual Matters.

Wilson, William H. & Kauanoe Kanamā (2017) "The Hakalama: The 'Aha Pūnana Leo's Syllabic Hawaiian Reading Program." In C. McLachlan and A. Arrow (Eds.), *Literacy in the Early Years. International Perspectives on Early Childhood Education and Development*, Vol 17. Singapore: Springer.

Zehr, Mary Ann (2003). "Classroom ban on Spanish protested." *Education Week* October 29, 2003. [https://www.edweek.org/ew/articles/2003/10/29/09spanish.h23.html]

Zinn, Howard (1980) *A People's History of the United States, 1492–Present*. New York: HarperCollins Publishers.

CREDITS

The following chapters have been previously published and their publication details are given below.

Chapter 4: SLA for the 21st Century: Disciplinary Progress, Transdisciplinary Relevance, and the Bi/multilingual Turn, by Lourdes Ortega
Ortega, L. (2013). SLA for the 21st Century: Disciplinary Progress, Transdisciplinary Relevance, and the Bi/multilingual Turn. *Language Learning*, 63 (s1), 1–24 (Taylor & Francis)

Chapter 8: A Multilingual Perspective on Translanguaging, by Jeff MacSwan
MacSwan, J. (2017). A Multilingual Perspective on Translanguaging. *American Educational Research Journal*, 54 (1), 167–201 (SAGE)

1

RUPTURING THE YOKE OF COLONIALISM IN FOREIGN LANGUAGE EDUCATION

An Introduction

Donaldo Macedo

UNIVERSITY OF MASSACHUSETTS BOSTON

> "We should not hire any more critical pedagogues. We should hire 'pure' applied linguists"

I have been extremely fortunate to have had the opportunity to visit, evaluate, and help in the development of many Bilingual Education (BE), English as Second Language (ESL), Dual Language (DL), and Foreign Language (FL) programs throughout the country from elementary to university graduate levels. As a result, I have been exposed to a multiplicity of (mis)interpretations and (mis)conceptions regarding what constitutes a good language teaching and learning curriculum, ranging from an elementary French/English program in Northern Vermont that I evaluated for six years to a graduate language teacher preparation program that I evaluated for three years in the Northwestern part of the country. In the former program the debate typically centered on to what variety of French the school system should adopt. Administrators tended to argue that the Parisian French would bring parents and their children greater pride in their ethnic background, whereas the "dialectal" variety spoken in the Québécois borderland with Canada would continue to pigeonhole its speakers as culturally and linguistically less sophisticated. The parents had a mixture of feelings regarding the language of instruction but they were united by a common denominator: They were unanimously happy that their children would have the opportunity to be fluent and literate in French, the language of their ancestors, even though the French variety spoken in Northern Vermont provides its speakers with the experience of subordination and sometimes shame *vis à vis* the Parisian accented speech which is generally used as "the yoke of Francophonie . . . to tendentiously index degrees of intelligence or humanity" (DeGraff, this volume). In other words, a Parisian accented speaker can be as dumb as a door nail and ethically challenged but, nevertheless, is generally viewed as scoring higher in the "index of intelligence or humanity" than a Québécois or Haitian accented French speaker (Lambert, 1969, 1972; Macedo, 1981; DeGraff & Stump, 2018; DeGraff, this volume).

As for the language teacher preparation in the Northwest, the argument consistently pointed to the underlying racism camouflaged in elitist educational posturing that wanted to ascertain that the Spanish-speaking teachers who were enrolled in the program and graduating from the university should demonstrate high and near native proficiency in English, whereas their native proficiency and literacy in Spanish was generally ignored. Thus the competence of Dual Language teachers (Spanish/English) graduating from this university was linked to his/her competency in English and other skill sets, while native fluency and high literacy in Spanish were generally minimized and, in some instances, routinely dismissed. The English-dominant teachers did not, however, have to show high fluency and literacy in Spanish. The end result of these on-going debates, centered on what criteria should be used to prepare language teachers, yielded little consensus in spite of excellent data available to guide policy decision-making and the existence of a multiplicity of models concerning language teacher preparation in many parts of the country and abroad. By never reaching a consensus, what continued to undergird policy decision-making in this language teacher preparation was the erroneous assumption that views English proficiency as education itself, while high proficiency in Spanish was summarily dismissed (many graduate students were literate native speakers of Spanish). Their cultural "funds of knowledge" and their organic relationship with the community were generally minimized and swept under the rug.

Given my more than three decades of observation, evaluation, and participation in language program development throughout the country, I have heard many absurd arguments to support language education programs that loosely fit under the denomination of applied linguistics, an area of linguistics studies that, in turn, is paralyzed by its own insecurities regarding its standing against linguistics departments in most research universities. Hence I was not at all surprised with the statement in the epigraph that begins this introductory chapter that falsely claims the existence of "pure applied linguists." Not only is the statement an oxymoron, but it also reflects the deep-seated insecurity among applied linguists who are caught in a false elitist binarism that pervades most theoretically oriented linguistic departments. Given the paralyzing insecurities suffered by many applied linguists, their defense mechanism is to call for "scientific" methods of teaching, meaning technical in its orientation and, as Lilia Bartolomé so clearly pointed out, the "solutions to [the general failures of the field of language education] . . . are also expected to be technical in nature" (Bartolomé, 1994). The requirement that the applied linguist must be "pure" is very much ingrained in a positivistic method of inquiry where "theory and knowledge are subordinated to the imperatives of efficiency and technical mastery, and history is reduced to a minor footnote in the priorities of 'empirical' scientific inquiry'" (Giroux, 1983: 87)—a posture that, according to Paulo Freire, reduces science to scientism (Freire, 2018). In other words, the blind celebration of a "pure" and "technical" approach to language studies and teaching hides the limitations of empiricism that has created a culture in which pseudoscientists, particularly in schools of education and language teacher preparation programs, can engage in a form of "naïve empiricism," believing "that facts are not human statements about the world but aspects of the world itself" (Schudson, 1978).

In this introductory chapter I discuss the conundrum of foreign language teaching that produces a high level of arrogant elitism which, in my view, constitutes a defense mechanism to hide the fact that, with all the preparation that language teachers receive and the billions of dollars spent on foreign language education in the United States, the field produces a mere "**1% of American adults** [my emphasis] who become proficient in the foreign language they study in a U.S. classroom" (Friedman, 2015, cited by Reagan & Osborn, this volume). I then propose that the general failure of foreign language education is, at least, partly due to a baseless elitism derived from what DeGraff calls "Neo-Darwinian linguists . . . [who measured the worth of a language in terms of 'young vs. old' [read classic], 'simple' vs. complex,' etc.]." According to DeGraff, "these terms, although perhaps useful as atheoretical heuristics and socio-historical approximations, cannot serve as theoretically grounded linguistic-structural taxa" (DeGraff, 2001). The false assumption that "old" languages are more complex, thus less simple, still informs and shapes views that hold that Latin and old Greek are superior languages, which leads to the following question: "For the child who was born in the Homeric age, who became aware of the speech forms of his linguistic community by hearing them, and then reproduced them in order to make himself understood by his fellow man – for that child were these speech ancient?" (Osthoff & Brugman, 1878, cited in DeGraff, 2001).

Although the answer to the above question is so obvious as to make the "young vs. old" proposition silly, to say the least, the folk theory generated by this Western-centric linguistic postulation continues to shape, for instance, tense sequencing in foreign language textbooks (i.e., present tense is considered simple and thus taught first, while the subjunctive mood is deemed to be more complex and is usually taught last). The false elitist binarism of "young" vs. "old" has given rise also to an artificial hierarchy of foreign languages taught in schools and universities that are, in turn, intimately tied to the imposition of imperial and colonial languages. Other linguistic realizations such as translanguaging, pidgins, and creoles, and languages in contact that are considered "inferior" are summarily classified as mere simplifications of the "superstrate" language due to the absence of marked features—features that are often used as a kind of yardstick to substantiate, for example, the notion of simplification proposed by Coelho (1880), Hall (1966), Naro (1971), Bickerton (1977), among others, who claim that the new linguistic system that arises from languages in contact is always reduced to a "hybridized and unstable linguistic system" (Macedo & D'Introno, 1998; DeGraff, 2001).

I also make the case that this atheoretical posture that emphasizes a top-to-bottom mode of linguistic analysis, with colonial languages at the top (superstrate), removes, for instance, the native languages (substrate) from any meaningful participation in either the construction or the development of what has been characterized as a "hybridized and unstable linguistic system." Hence the simplification model is very limited in nature since it fails to fully capture the (un)marked dynamics of languages in contact, dismissing almost entirely the role that the substrate may play in language formation (DeGraff, 2001). The simplification model that emerges from the "pre- and neo-Darwinian claims about language evolution" (DeGraff, 2001) is partly responsible for how foreign language syllabi are constructed and the hierarchy of foreign languages offered by educational institutions. That is, it dogmatizes the reductionist view of languages in contact by taking what is claimed to be the "upper-languages" (always colonial) as a point of reference and postulates that the omission of marked features of "upper-languages (i.e., verbal inflections) in the "hybridized and unstable linguistic system" proves the simplification claim. Given the a-theoretical nature that prevailed in the neo-Darwinian tradition of linguistic analysis (DeGraff, 2001), a tradition steeped in racial animus and which still informs and shapes a large sector of language study and language education, I propose that language educators as well as many linguists need to differentiate the factors that are purely socio-cultural in nature from those that are part of the language organism guided and shaped by principles of Universal Grammar.

My interest in this chapter is not to add fuel to the present debate concerning "simple" languages which, in my view, has given rise to conceptual gaps and obfuscates the true nature of the linguistic system that develops in language contact contexts, including the interlanguage in foreign languages classroom. Rather, my main interest is to invite language educators to embrace the "Neogrammarians' stated goal to understand Language . . . [in which] . . . grammars live in speakers' mind, not society; thus the study of individual grammars as manifestations of a 'physical [i.e., psychological] organism' should take epistemological priority over 'Historical Grammar' (i.e., 'descriptive grammars of different periods [. . .] tacked together'" (DeGraff, 2001).

By embracing the Neogrammarian goal of linguistic theory in their language teaching preparation, language educators are able to develop critical skills that keep them from confusing learning from acquisition, from being seduced by the imperial supremacy ethos that the "old" is more "complex," thus superior, while also being able to expurgate the "folk" from theory. Simply put, I believe that language educators should be exposed to as much theory as necessary so that their practice reflects a deeper understanding that language acquisition (L1 and L2) within "generative linguistics is 'internalist biolinguistic inquiry'" (Chomsky, 1995: 1–11, 2001: 4142, cited in DeGraff, 2001: 222).

In order to achieve this very important goal I will follow DeGraff's suggestion that "[g]iven Universal Grammar and its Cartesian-Uniformitarian foundations (Chomsky, 1966, 1981, 1986, 1995, etc.) there cannot be any invariant and *sui generis* set of structures and processes that fall under labels" (DeGraff, 2001) that are socio-historically constructed without an iota of empirical evidence to support these labels. Thus I posit that the challenge for applied linguistics is to develop a language teacher preparation that is truly interdisciplinary in nature where neither theory nor practice is sacrificed at the altar of expediency.

The Arrogance of the Learned Ignoramus' Elitism

The elite binarism is frequently and unwisely divided into what is considered "purely" theoretical linguistics versus applied linguistics, which is, generally speaking, the least valued branch of linguistics studies to the degree that it implicates teaching, which is also hugely devalued by the academic enterprise. The former involves linguists who specialize in linguistic theory and consider themselves "pure" linguists and have little appreciation or tolerance for issues of language pedagogy and the role of language in society, particularly along the lines of gender, class, race, culture, and ethnicity, including the linguistic hybridity that results from languages in contact that, invariably, gives rise to new language practices—language practices that must also be rule governed, no matter how messy that linguistic data may appear and how far removed they appear to be from the "ideal" speaker model used both in linguistic theory and in foreign language education. In fact, it is through these linguistic practices that speakers of non-Standard varieties make meaning so as to more effectively communicate with one another (García, Pennycook, Kramsch, MacSwan, and Hemphill & Blakely, in this volume). In addition, the tendency to reduce critical pedagogy to a method is reductionistic in that it disarticulates the essence of criticality from the overall academic endeavors. For instance, hard sciences would not survive and evolve without a robust dose of built-in self-criticism, skepticism, and contestation. Thus criticality should inform all fields of study.

Critical pedagogy as it was conceived by Paulo Freire, Henry Giroux, bell hooks, Lilia Bartolomé, and Antónia Darder, among others, is a way of being critically in the world where common sense presuppositions are interrogated and not viewed as given and predetermined by the inevitability of history. Hence the academic challenge of applied linguistics programs is not to hire more or less critical applied linguists but to hire applied linguists who are committed to infusing criticality into the intellectual content of what is commonly identified as applied linguistics. That is, applied linguists should teach their courses in linguistics critically, particularly since the fields applied linguistics borders are so porous given its interdisciplinary nature.

Applied linguistics is a catch-all term that includes linguistics studies, language acquisition studies, foreign language teaching (FLT), heritage language education (HL), English as a foreign language (EFL), discourse analysis (DA), English as a second language (ESL), and bilingual education (BE), including the multiplicity of approaches that fall under the rubric of bilingual education, including dual language instruction. The panoply of terms under applied linguistics are not innocent and they are generated and pigeonholed along a power hierarchy where bilingual education programs are always the least valued by both the schools and the U.S. society within which these schools exist, even though empirical data demonstrate that bilingual education is an effective approach to creating balanced bilinguals who are also bi-literate. Nevertheless, the effectiveness of bilingual education proven from empirical data by researchers such as Virginia Collier (1992), David Ramirez (1986, 1989), Kelly Rolstad (1997), Cazabon, Lambert and Hall (1993), Greene (1997), and Cenoz (1996), among others, is either ignored or buried in the endless debate over research design, which serves a fundamental purpose: to hide the racist inequalities that inform and shape most bilingual programs in the United States. It is important to note that not all bilingual education programs are effective, but their lack of success can be attributed to socio-political and economic issues such as poverty, inequality of resource distribution, poorly prepared teachers, and overall abandonment of quality education from the school system within which the bilingual education program exists. In these schools, not only bilingual education fails to meet the expected benchmarks, but Math and English programs for mainstream students also fail to meet the state-mandated benchmarks.

It is the same racism that propelled the state of Massachusetts to abolish instruction in content areas in languages other than English. It is also the same racism that operates in some applied linguistics programs that creates a concentration hierarchy and falsely ranks the foreign language track as the most prestigious, while the bilingual education area of study is routinely viewed by faculty and administrators as an inferior, disciplineless area of study.

Although both foreign language programs and bilingual programs may be dealing with the same colonial language (i.e., Spanish), the foreign language programs usually reap prestige from the mere fact that they serve mostly white, middle-class students even when they produce colossal failures (Reagan & Osborn, this volume). Given that bilingual education programs in the United States serve mostly minoritized working class and working poor students, particularly in major urban centers, they do not escape the wrath of racist acts exacted against lower-class minoritized students, including their teachers. Even a white, middle-class teacher who works in a bilingual program (both K-12 and graduate teacher preparation) is not immune from racist disparate treatment. In other words, such teachers subsume their students' subordinate and inferior status as well. It does not matter that, by and large, most effective bilingual programs produce impressive results that far surpass most foreign language programs. What matters most in a highly racist society is the constitution of the student population being (mis)educated to become fluent in two languages and bi-literate. The white, middle-class student population wins handily, even though these students continue to exponentially fail in becoming fluent in two languages and becoming bi-literate. Yet we have had no state or federal referenda calling for the closing of foreign language departments due to their generalized failure.

In the U.S. context, the misguided elitism that borders on racism, which generates the false notion of "pure" linguistics, also seeps through the field of applied linguistics, which, in turn, gives rise to a hierarchy as mentioned above and which is demarcated by sub-specializations such as foreign language (considered more prestigious), heritage language studies (even though teachers and students in this program are seldom asked how the language they are currently studying became a heritage language in the first place), English as a foreign language (EFL), English as second language (ESL), bilingualism studies that are global and involve research, and bilingual education. The latter, as mentioned earlier, has the least prestige in the U.S. context given the class, race, and ethnicity status of the student population it serves—students who are mostly enrolled in urban schools' bilingual programs (with the exception of dual language programs that also enroll white, middle-class students) and belong to lower-class immigrant populations who have been minoritized and, with the advent of Trumpism, are under constant attack as they find themselves studying under siege; often fearing they will be arrested in schools or may return home to an empty house if their parents were to be arrested and summarily deported, or traumatized after being torn from their mothers and sent to different parts of the country and detained in chain-link cages.

The pretentiousness over language "purity" is exemplified by the tensions and contradictions in heritage language instruction; for example, when, as told by Theresa Austin: "Yvonne recounts her experience as increasingly 'tension-filled' as she was positioned as inferior through day-to-day interactions of her school. As a 'native' speaker of Spanish she faced challenges from her senior White colleagues who learned a Peninsular variety (from Spain) and who perceived their variety as more prestigious to hers" (Austin, this volume). Given the ever-present tensions infused by racism and classism, heritage language teachers, in general, and foreign language teachers, in particular, need to first denude the cruel fact that heritage speakers exist because of the institutional failed attempts to (a) outright kill non-English language varieties that abound in the U.S. and are considered "inferior," and (b) limit the opportunities for literacy development in multiple non-English varieties—a process that leads to "alienation from our heritage languages [which] happens even in a class that is [in] 'our' language [and] is exacerbated by the dominant ideology of 'English only instruction for immigrant children'" (Austin, this volume). Thus heritage language teachers who lack political clarity and jump on the bandwagon of heritage language "*vogueness*" and "*sexiness*," even with good intentions, end up creating spaces for the colonial appropriation of the linguistic wounds that characterize heritage speakers "as survivors" of attempted *linguicism* (Austin, this volume).

In addition to the various sub-disciplines, many applied linguistics programs have pedagogical concerns and intersections with social and political interests that go beyond teaching about the correctness of grammatical structures, as my former Spanish professor warned me: "En esta clase solamente enseñamos la lengua de Cervantes. Aqui hay que hablar con la "*ceta*" [*θeta*]" (In this class we only teach Cervantes' language. Here everyone must speak with *"ceta"*—a distinct phonological characteristic of Castilian Spanish). Even though my former college Spanish professor lacked fluency in Spanish, he delighted himself in pronouncing "*θeta*" whenever he could. He proceeded to explain all the Spanish grammatical rules that we were expected to memorize in English throughout the semester. Because of the pretentiousness that is often linked with speaking the Standard variety that borders on linguistic ignorance, both the applied linguistics program emphasis, as well as would-be language teachers' interests who are seeking preparation in both theory and practice, must embrace competency in theoretical linguistics as it applies to pedagogical orientation. A rigorous applied linguistics teacher preparation program guided by criticality would avoid cases where being a native speaker suffices to be hired as a language teacher, as is the case, for instance, of many Americans who go abroad to teach English and whose qualifications stem solely from their ability to speak English as native speakers.

A similar situation occurs with bilingual teachers who are hired to teach in bilingual programs and whose only credentials are, like the EFL teacher abroad, that they speak the target language as a native speaker. Initially when bilingual education programs were being implemented in the early 1970s by state mandate, a Spanish surname might be considered sufficient qualification, which already points to the total lack of respect for immigrant students and the field of bilingual education. I am reminded of a story told by the director of a very large school district who was called by a school principal who was seeking help because he could not understand a student who wanted to enroll in his school. The Bilingual/ESL director casually asked the school principal: "In what languages is the student bilingual." The response was quick and without hesitation: "Spanish." Here we have a case where bilingual education does not necessarily mean the ability to speak in two languages. The label "bilingual" in this particular instance serves to typecast Latinx ethnically so as to devalue their human worth. Their bilingualism, unlike the bilingualism achieved through foreign language instruction, represents vestiges of colonialism in which the minoritized speakers experience subordination in speaking both their mother tongues, that are devalued by the dominant ideology, and the dominant language they are learning, often under coercive conditions.

Class Reproduction in Foreign Language Education

As a result of association with lower-class students who are victims of constant discrimination in a society that remains largely racist, many applied linguists suffer from the ravages of professional insecurity disguised, at times, as elitism on at least two fundamental fronts: (1) the misguided arrogance in "purely" theoretical linguistics departments that dismisses any language application consideration, particularly teaching; and (2) the misappropriated and undeserved elitism that emanates from literature departments within which a large proportion of foreign language teaching still takes place—departments whose main *raison d'être* is the perpetuation of colonial ideology through the study of literature designed mainly for a white, middle-class student population. College track students are required to study a foreign language, whereas non-college track students (mostly lower-class minoritized students) are not require to take foreign language courses as a precondition for high school graduation. As for the first front, I am reminded of a former classmate of mine in linguistics whom I met while doing research as a visiting scholar in the Linguistics and Philosophy Department at MIT. When she learned I was working with pidgin and creole languages within the Government and Binding Theoretical Paradigm that Noam Chomsky had at the time introduced, she curiously asked me, "What's a pidgin language?" At first I thought she was joking, but soon I realized that her question was genuine. Here we had a perfect case of a technician of linguistics doing the highest level of syntactic theory available at the time in the field of linguistics without any clue about historical linguistics. It is not difficult to find other examples of such narrow specialization because, more and more, specialists turned "experts" dominate institutions of learning and other institutional structures of our society. Thus the social organization of knowledge via rigidly defined disciplinary boundaries further contributes to the formation of the specialist class that, in turn, gives rise to a noxious elitism—an elitism that licenses the specialist to rationalize the narrowness of his or her specialization and dismiss or devalue any other related area of his or her specialization. Subsequently, a specialist in linguistic theory may dismiss any form of study regarding practice as a means to achieve higher status within the field. As a reaction, many practitioners will reject any form of theory, which in the field of foreign language teaching gives rise to the *fetishization* of methods (Bartolomé, 1994, Macedo & Bartolomé, 2001) that almost always disarticulate theory from practice, even though there is no practice that does not take a detour through theory. That is, every practice is imbued in a theory that guides and shapes it, acknowledged or not. Nevertheless, the field of language teaching is populated by many practitioners who abhor both theory and critical language analysis that is heavily based on theory. They dismiss theory and critical language analysis by falsely labeling it as frontal, caustic, and with having little to do with practice. They sometimes categorize critical language analysis as too theoretical (meaning not practical enough), choosing instead "a method that works." I had a FL student approach me once stating: "I agree with your politics but I don't see how it's going to help me with my 30 students on Monday morning. Just give me a method that works."

As for the second front, regarding the misguided arrogance and elitism that emanate from literature departments under which a large proportion of foreign language teaching still takes place, foreign literature departments have traditionally relegated foreign language teaching to a sub-disciplinary low status in the academy. Unfortunately, most literature professors, who are also mostly middle-class and white, make decisions about the curriculum while knowing little about the very complex nature of the foreign language they teach. They know even less about the multitude of language varieties that surround their university (particularly in urban centers) as they often characterize these varieties as sub-standard and needing to be eradicated. Since a large proportion of foreign language teaching at universities still takes place within foreign literature departments, these professors traditionally have relegated foreign language teaching to a sub-disciplinary low status in the academy. Most literature professors who make decisions about the curriculum know little about the very complex grammar nature of the foreign language they have learned to read and write primarily to gain access to literary texts in the target language. These foreign literature professors know even less about the multifaceted processes of second language acquisition (SLA) (see Lourdes Ortega, in this volume) and how universal principles of grammar determine and predict certain linguistic realizations. The result is that foreign literature students, too, learn a specific language mainly to access original-language literary texts and they are seldom encouraged to take courses in linguistics and SLA courses of the target language they are leaning. Consequently they will never have the opportunity to avail themselves of the complex processes in second language acquisition, as pointedly illuminated, analyzed, and discussed by Ortega (this volume).

By and large, the asymmetrical power relations that inform the co-existence between foreign language studies and the corresponding literatures result in the marginalization of foreign language education. Either way, the uncritical and unreflective teaching of foreign language contributes to what Robert Phillipson accurately labeled as *linguicism*—the killing of indigenous, minoritized, or non-colonial languages through the teaching of imperial languages (Phillipson, 2008; Ngũgĩ, 1986, 1993). A perfunctory review of foreign languages offered in most U.S. universities will readily show the colonial nature of the language teaching offerings, even though in the past decade or so there have been some attempts to include non-European languages such as Mandarin and Arabic, among others (see Kramsch's chapter in this volume). Hence "the imposition of an imperialist cultural tradition [including its languages] whose dire effects are still being felt today . . . [and] under colonialism this took the form of destroying people's languages, history, dances, education, religions, naming systems, and other social institutions that were the basis of their self-conception as people" (Ngũgĩ, 1993: 42). In addition, the imperial languages that are imposed reflect class biases where the foreign language curricula are geared toward white, middle-class realities. For example, even though many urban universities are surrounded by immigrant communities that speak the languages being taught in their foreign language and literature departments, seldom are students encouraged to go to these language communities to practice, say, the Spanish they are currently learning. The expectation is that they will go to Spain to be fully immersed in the "model Spanish" reflected in the curriculum, visit the Prado Museum in Madrid, and admire the ruins of Roman monuments left behind in Spain.

The Rupture of the Colonialism Yoke

Accordingly, the challenge in the field of applied linguistics is to go beyond the usual straitjacket teaching of up-to-date methodologies and to rupture the yoke of colonialism and imperialism that informs and shapes the relationship between foreign language education and literary studies—a relationship unavoidably tainted by colonization since, to a great extent, most foreign language programs in the U.S., as mentioned, continue to be housed in foreign literature departments that, with rare exception, reproduce Western-centric dominant and imperial values—values that often devalue the "funds" of knowledge students bring to the classroom (i.e., a Latinx student who speaks a variety of Spanish deemed a dialect—thus considered inferior—by the establishment is often encouraged to eradicate her Spanish dialect so that she can learn the Standard Spanish, preferably Castilian).

The problem with this present arrangement is two-fold: (1) most senior literature professors, who are largely responsible for designing and implementing the foreign language curriculum and adopting textbooks in their respective departments, have little knowledge of either linguistics or second language acquisition (SLA) theories (see Ortega, this volume); and (2) given the arrogant and elitist nature of most literature departments, particularly those that resist critical theory and view literature as art for art's sake, literature professors in these traditional departments tend to disdain language teaching and often dismiss the field of applied linguistics as unworthy of "rigorous" scholarship. For example, in many foreign language and literature departments the publication of textbooks, regardless of how groundbreaking they may be, is not always credited toward tenure. Consequently, one of the many challenges faced by applied linguistics departments is to sever the colonial legacies that continue to shape and mold most foreign language education programs.

Furthermore, the inability of most language educators to de-fetishize methods and re-historicize the imperialistic desires that give rise to the totalization of the object of knowledge that we call "language" presents another difficult and ongoing challenge for these language programs—a challenge that results in ideologically making the standard colonial language they teach distinct from its inevitable varieties, which are derogatorily labeled as "dialect," "patois," "pidgin," "creole," and "Spanglish," among other labels that are socially created by the dominant ruling class with the mere intent to create an ideological distinction so as to devalue, dismiss, and dehumanize. Once the distinction is achieved, its sole purpose is to devalue the corresponding cultures that engender speakers of the multiplicity of variations spoken in the world, which are scientifically neither superior nor inferior (see chapters in this volume by Ofelia García, Claire Kramsch, David Hemphill and Erin Blakely, Timothy Reagan and Terry Osborn, and Alastair Pennycook).

Such derogatory labels as those cited above are used mainly to categorize linguistic realizations and are primarily social labels designed to typecast them so as to devalue their corresponding speakers' cultures, races, ethnicities, and class—a process characterized by Paulo Freire as "cultural invasion, which like divisive tactics and manipulation also serves the ends of [colonial] conquest. In this phenomenon, the invaders penetrate the cultural context of another group, in disrespect of the latter's potentialities; they impose their own view of the world upon those they invade and inhibit the creativity of the invaded by curbing their expression" (Freire, 2000: 152).

EFL teachers working in countries that were colonized by the British Empire can, if they teach uncritically and reflexively, expand the "curbing of [the invaded] expression" if they engage in displacement of indigenous, minoritized, and colonial languages that, as cultural invasion, "is thus always an act of violence against the persons of the invaded culture, who lose their originality or face the threat of losing it" (Freire, 2000: 152). EFL teachers need to find ways to teach English as an *additional* language rather than feed the "imperialist cultural tradition in its colonial form [which] was meant to undermine peoples' belief in themselves and make them look to the European cultures, languages and the arts, for a measurement of themselves and their abilities" (Ngũgĩ, 1993: 43–44).

The critical approach to EFL teaching required to avoid imposition of a neo-colonialism perspective also applies to the internal colonialism experienced by minoritized persons who live in the U.S. Hence the zeal to save these persons from their non-English-speaking status must include colonialist methods used by many dominant schools that function to legitimize Anglocentric values and meaning while at the same time negating the history, culture, and language practices of the minoritized students that populate most urban schools (García, Austin, Hemphill & Blakely, and Pennycook, this volume). The need to decolonize foreign language teaching is not limited to EFL. It also applies to the teaching of other colonial languages that over-celebrate Eurocentric values while sacrificing ways of being and speaking of people who do not fit the white, middle-class mold and are always excluded from this mold no matter how hard they try to fit in. In order to avoid the violence of cultural invasion, foreign language teaching must move beyond the false and racist notion of "purity" and be informed by a radical language pedagogy that respects and celebrates the language practices that students bring to school and makes concrete such values as solidarity, social responsibility, and creativity (García, Pennycook, Reagan & Osborn, MacSwan, and Austin, this volume).

Even many language researchers fall prey to a form of neo-colonialism while defending non-standard varieties of colonial languages. For example, the very term "restricted code" used by Basil Bernstein to situate his language studies in a class-analysis framework is, on the one hand, commendable and rarely done in the U.S., but it may also end up reducing speakers of "restricted codes" to a societal view that they have "restricted intelligence" and other "less-than-desirable" attributes.

Bernstein and others, for example, fail to realize that it is not the language that is necessarily restricted. All languages have the capacity for highly developed peripheries in the Chomskyan sense. What we label as "restricted" relates to the *a priori* restriction of institutional functions in which a language is or is not used—functions that could enable the language to expand its periphery in order to fulfill the demands of multiple social, economic, legal, commercial, and religious functions. In other words, since technology is, by and large, dominated by the English language, terms such as *input, output, website*, and *Facebook* are simply borrowed by many nation-state languages such as French, Spanish and Portuguese that are considered by folk theory to be "superior" or "elaborated" (these languages were in certain points of their development labeled bastardized and corrupted forms of Latin). These English technological terms are often adjusted to the underlying phonological rules of the borrowing languages. This is a form of language penetration through technology that has existed throughout the history of humankind—a penetration that also brings with it cultural values, readjustments of these values, and different ways of being in the world and with the world. It is an invasion that ultimately gives the languages involved in this process their creative force, which emanates from both their fluidity and hybridity. What would English look like if we had stripped it of its Latinized penetration during the course of its historical evolution? Hence, to speak of a fixed standard language that does not include fluidity and hybridity is a figment of the imagination supported mostly by racist attitudes rather than scientific evidence.

The question that still escapes most applied linguistics departments is how to prepare future language teachers to apply the explicatory theory of the Language Acquisition Device (LAD), also referred to as the "black box," that accounts for languages' creativity, fluidity, and hybridity and allows the incorporation of the translanguaging that invariably will occur in all instances of language acquisition and languages in contact and which must be included as part of foreign language teachers' pedagogy (see García, Pennycook, and MacSwan, this volume).

The Challenge to Decolonize Foreign Language Teaching

Thus far my discussion of the decolonization of foreign language education suggests that the issue at hand is much more complex than the mere adoption of *au courant* methods and sexy labels that critique past practices in the field of applied linguistics. As Kramsch (this volume) observes, post-colonialism embraced only at the level of discourse and that advocates the "decoupling of [foreign languages] from their colonial past," cannot but reproduce neo-colonial globalism to the extent that, for most people, including policymakers and language educators, they "have not [yet] 'decolonized' the view of the world that fueled the desire for American FL education in the first place, which we could call the 'national interest'" (Kramsch, this volume). In other words, here "national interest" has an almost one-to-one correspondence with corporate interest, while it hardly addresses the language and cultural needs of the people subsumed under the euphemism of "national interest"—a national interest that is skewed toward a tiny, white, middle- and upper-class student population who "'take' French, or Spanish, or German . . . for three, four, or five years before entering college, only to discover there that they cannot read, speak, or understand it" (Jacques Barzun, cited by Reagan & Osborn, this volume).

It is no wonder then that "although roughly 18% of the U.S. population report speaking a second language (in comparison to 26% of Canadians and 54% of Europeans), less than **1% of American adults** (emphasis mine) are proficient in the language that they studied in a U.S. classroom" (Friedman, 2015, cited by Reagan & Osborn, this volume). It is important to highlight that there have been significant positive shifts in foreign language education in the past decade or so and the chapters in this volume provide ample evidence for a more hopeful and effective experience in foreign language classrooms. However, we must also remain cognizant that for the vast majority of lower-class white students and minoritized students who are not considered college material, their presence and subsequent success in foreign language classes are negligible, to say the least. To reiterate, the preparation of foreign language teachers is enormously more complex than the mere mechanical manner with which it has been treated in the past—a complexity that requires "a paradigm shift" (Reagan & Osborn, this volume) that radically moves foreign language education from a colonial model historically designed *not* to educate in the true sense of the term; particularly not those students who are victims of internal colonialism, as is the case with minoritized students who now populate "majority-minority" (a euphemism for subordinate students) urban schools while the field of foreign language and its teaching force remain largely white and middle-class. How can the field of foreign language education decolonize itself and, at the same time, justify its vast whiteness as reflected in classrooms, teacher preparation programs, and national and international language teaching organizations such as ACTFL (American Council on the Teaching of Foreign Languages), TESOL (Teaching English to Speakers of Other Languages), AAAL (American Association of Applied Linguistics), among other language organizations, in the globalized world of the twenty-first century?

The Genesis of Linguistic Racism Under Linguistic Colonialism

The not-so-hidden racism that guides and shapes language policy and teaching institutions sabotages the many claims being made for a twenty-first century multilingual and multicultural globalized world. The current attacks ushered in by President Donald Trump on minoritized cultures, particularly Muslim and Mexican cultures in the U.S. (for example, the claim that Mexicans are rapists), are reminiscent of the nineteenth and twentieth centuries when colonizers were merciless imposing, through cultural invasion, "cultural and hence mental and spiritual subjugation" (Ngũgĩ, 1993: 42). Language was, and continues to be, a pivotal vehicle for cultural invasion and cultural genocide as the colonizers "yanked" their conquered subjects' native tongues, without which they were forced to experience their culture through an imposed and, sometimes, borrowed dominant language, as many American Indian nations had to endure. As a tool of domination and subjugation, dominant languages remain the last refuge that one can continue to be racist in, with impunity, in both liberal and illiberal democracies. Hence to forbid, by law, instruction in one's native language is, as in the case in Massachusetts for instance, a cause for celebration even for those individuals who view themselves as progressive citizens who fight otherwise for equality, so long as the struggle is done in English only. The purpose to forbid instruction in public schools in languages other than English is, it is claimed, to guarantee "English for all Children," as the slogan puts it. That is, to impose standard colonial languages on minoritized groups while sacrificing their way of being in the world linguistically is viewed not as racism, but as progress. Consequently the framing of *linguicism* as progress makes even the well-intentioned citizen complicit with the very anti-democratic proposition that, in order to be fully human, one must allow one's language to be *yanked,* as Gloria Anzaldúa so painfully put it, so that one can be reconstituted as human in the oppressors' language.

In view of the lack of critical postures in most foreign language, ESL, EFL, and BE programs due to their emphasis on the technical teaching of grammar and the development of superficial communication skills, most teachers, even those with good intentions, fall prey to a paternalistic zeal to save their students from their non-colonial language-speaker's status in the same manner that the colonialists of the past attempted to inculcate the conquered people with myths and beliefs about their inherent inferiority and sub-human status (Ngũgĩ, 1993; Freire, 2000; Macedo, 2006).

To a large degree the intelligence of the colonized has been always measured by their ability to speak fluently the language of the colonizer while experiencing subordination in speaking their mother tongue, which has been defined by the colonizer as primitive, lacking a grammar, and unable to be written. Since language is a huge part of the culture of a people, by devaluing, disparaging, and engaging in practices of *linguicism*, their cultures are also targeted for destruction due, so the colonizers claim, to their "savageness," "primitiveness," and "utter backwardness." Subsequently the colonial policy of "cultural purity," which also includes "language purity"—a form of white supremacy modeled on Western cultures' supposed superiority—was to eradicate all vestiges of the subjugated and conquered cultures and their respective languages. This was tried unsuccessfully by the Nazis against the Jews until they realized they could not achieve their goal of cultural purity unless they "destroy[ed] a people's culture completely only by destroying the people themselves" (Ngũgĩ, 1993: 42).

Given the complexity involved in language education, in general, and foreign language teaching, in particular, it is not mere coincidence that applied linguists who have accommodated the simplistic and mechanistic model of language teacher preparation would reject hiring faculty members who might raise questions about coloniality and the reproduction of false myths regarding colonial languages and their corresponding and alleged cultural superiority in applied linguistics departments. A language of critique exposes enormous contradictions through the articulation of multiple bodies of knowledge so as to gain a more critical understanding of the foreign language classroom reality that attempts to force the view that language (colonial in this sense) is apolitical, a mere tool of communication, and that it is honorable to celebrate it, seducing students with Western civilization's "great deeds" while simultaneously hiding the carnage, cruelty, and savageness of the colonial racist past. Thus it would be a rarity to find students in German classrooms or English learners in EFL classrooms reading about and analyzing the necessary linkages between the great architecture that students of foreign languages are invariably invited to admire and the blood, sweat, and tears of individuals (sometimes in chains) who built these fabulous monuments used to display the greatness and the victorious past of empires. Bertolt Brecht (1935) captures this reification brilliantly, yet painfully, in his poem "A Worker Reads History":

> Great Rome is full of triumphal arches.
> Who erected them?
> Over whom did the Caesars triumph?
> Had Byzantium, much praised in song, only palaces for its inhabitants?
> Even in fabled Atlantis, the night that the ocean engulfed it,
> The drowning still cried out for their slaves.

The "people's" history, along the lines of Howard Zinn's proposals (2005), is almost never found in foreign language classrooms and teachers seldom urge their students to interrogate the human costs that led to the victorious past and the subsequent building of commemorative monuments to empires' greatness often found in their textbooks; although that is changing along with teachers' development of political clarity, albeit at a snail's pace. The celebration of empires' greatness is usually presented as common sense, as in *of course* they should be celebrated (i.e., Christopher Columbus discovered America. Was America lost?), and a language of critique is usually absent from foreign language classrooms, curricula, and textbooks.

The Cult of Monuments as Erasure of People's History

Most foreign language textbooks celebrate the great deeds of empires and colonial powers. Thus it is not surprising, for instance, that most Spanish language textbooks would highlight Christopher Columbus's "religious feeling, his desire to convert the natives, his reverence for the Bible . . . erected crosses." However, most Spanish textbook writers fail to inform students that Columbus also "built gallows all over the island [of Hispaniola]—340 of them by the year 1500. Crosses and gallows—that deadly historic juxtaposition" (Zinn & Macedo, 2005). By keeping dangerous historical memories out of students' reach, foreign language textbook writers and teacher trainers engage in an Orwellian presentation of history that serves at least two functions: (1) to engage in myth making with the sole objective of monumentalizing Columbus as a stupendous hero and courageous navigator who discovered America; and (2) to astutely and dishonestly suppress the fact that Columbus engaged in savage practices such as "order[ing] the natives to find gold within a certain period of time. And if they did not meet their quota, their arms were hacked off" (Zinn & Macedo, 2005). By suppressing the genocidal goals of Columbus, most students learning Spanish as a foreign language will never know that Columbus, in addition to being a great and valiant navigator, was also the architect of horrendous genocide that practically wiped out all the Indians in Hispaniola; as Harvard historian Samuel Eliot Morrison acknowledged, "the policy and acts of Columbus for which he alone was responsible began the depopulation of the terrestrial paradise that was Hispaniola in 1492. Of the original natives, estimated by modern ethnologists at 300,000 in number, one third were killed off between 1494 and 1496. By 1508, an enumeration showed only 60,000 alive . . . In 1548 Oviedo [Morrison is referring to Fernández de

Oviedo, the official Spanish historian of the conquest] doubted whether 500 Indians remained" (Zinn & Macedo, 2005).

The erasure of dangerous historical memories constitutes not only a historical malpractice but is also part of the blueprint of dominant ideologies which George Orwell keenly understood when he wrote: "Who controls the past controls the future. And who controls the present controls the past" (cited in Zinn & Macedo, 2005). Consequently most foreign language textbook writers and those responsible for foreign language teacher preparation understand too well that their roles, as part of the dominant establishment, should not be concerned with the creation of critical pedagogical spaces where students and teachers, together, unpack Columbus's suppressed history of generalized genocide in the Americas. In other words, the establishment textbook writers and foreign language teacher trainers whose role is to "control the past" will unlikely engage Spanish as a foreign language learners in critical inquiries that could lead them to comprehend why it is, paraphrasing Minder, that "there are no monuments to Adolf Hitler in Germany or in Austria, nor to Benito Mussolini in Italy" while there are monuments and statues all over the Western world celebrating Columbus's great deeds.

Let's take, as an example, one Spanish textbook that attempts to be innovative and integrate culture into the classroom. If you open the section labeled "Vocabúlario 1" as part of *Cultura* (Culture) there is a beautiful picture of "El famoso acueducto romano de Segovia, España, construido a fines del primer siglo despúes de Cristo" (The famous aqueduct of Segovia, Spain, built toward the end of the first century after Christ) that is presented as the ingenuity of the civilized Romans and as an illustration of art combined with utility.

I remember taking part in a summer program in Spain during my undergraduate years to improve my Spanish. The students in the program had an excursion to Segovia and an art professor from the University of Madrid took us to the aqueduct so we could marvel at the Romans' engineering, their ingenuity, and to celebrate the deeds of their great civilization. The art professor was so enamored of his subject matter that we, as students, could not help but be seduced by both the beauty and the technical ingenuity of the Romans. Most of us left Segovia in awe and in love with Roman architecture. What the art professor failed to do was to invite students to ask *à la* Brecht, "Who built the Segovia aqueduct?" Had he asked the question, we would have learned that during the first century, when the Segovia aqueduct was built, there were various social classes within the Roman Empire and that slaves, freemen, and plebeians played a critical role in its day-to-day operations. Students were deprived of an opportunity to become aware of the life experiences of people at various levels of Roman society. To further deepen their cultural awareness of the era, a final activity might have been an assignment that addressed how the Roman class structure and its use of slavery affected the rise or downfall of its empire (for more, see www.pbs.org/empires/romans).

Since the trip to Segovia was centered on the aqueduct and the greatness of "Roman traditions," the art professor could also have, as part of his lesson objectives, incorporated activities to add equilibrium to the history of Romans in Segovia. For instance, the class could have participated in discussion and reading activities related to the social classes of the Roman Empire and the resultant oppressive conditions (www.pbs.or/empire/romans). It could have:

- Viewed video clips and website content that illustrate the differences between the Roman social classes and provide clues about how lower-class citizens and slaves were treated by the upper class.
- Viewed a map of products and trade routes used by the Roman Empire and use the information from the map to draw conclusions about the importance of slave labor.
- Completed a study guide by using primary sources such as the companion website to answer a number of questions about the Roman labor force.
- Participated in a discussion about the long-term effects of a slavery-driven economy on the Roman Empire.
- Completed a creative writing assignment about life in the lower social classes and the significance of the jobs they performed.

Another case in point is the approach used by Conrad J. Schmitt in his textbook *¡Así se dice!* to introduce new vocabulary via *el banco de palabras* (word bank) to prepare students for a trip to Spain. The same *banco de palabras* approach could have been used in the Segovia example to present, in a historical context, words that would have allowed students to critically examine both sides of Roman Empire colonization and its underbelly. For example, Schmitt's textbook introduces students to the four new vocabulary words in the exercise below:

LEER • ESCRIBIR (Read • Write)

Pone (put) sale (leave) trae (bring) hace (make)

1. Eduardo ________ un viaje a España (Eduardo ________ a trip to Spain).
2. Él ________su ropa en la maleta (He ________ his clothes in the suitcase).
3. Eduardo no ________ mucho equipaje (Eduardo does not ________ much luggage).
4. A ________ solamente una maleta y una mochila (________ only a suitcase and a backpack).
5. A________el equipaje en la maletera del taxi (________ the luggage in the taxi's trunk).

FIGURE 1.1 Completa. Escoge del banco de palabras (Complete. Choose from the word bank)

6. ________ para el aeropuerto (________ to the airport).
7. Su vuelo para España ________ a las ocho y media de tarde (His flight to Spain ________ at eight-thity at night).
8. Eduardo ________ un viaje a España (Eduardo ________ a trip to Spain).
9. Él ________ su ropa en la maleta (He ________ his clothes in the suitcase).
10. Eduardo no ________ mucho equipaje (Eduardo does not ________ much luggage).
11. ________ solamente una maleta y una mochila (________ only a suitcase and a backpack)
12. ____________el equipaje en la maletera del taxi (________ the luggage in the taxi's trunk).
13. ________ para el aeropuerto (________ to the airport).
14. Su vuelo para España ________ a las ocho y media de tarde (His flight to Spain________at eight-thirty at night).

FIGURE 1.1 (Continued)

IMAGE 1.1 El famoso acueducto romano de Segovia, España, construído a fines del primer siglo después de Cristo (The famous Roman aqueduct of Segovia, Spain, built toward the end of the first century after Christ)

LEER • ESCRIBIR (Read • Write)

Pone (put) sale (leave) trae (bring) hace (make)

1. El jefe romano ________ cadenas en los pies del esclavo (The Roman chief ________ chains on the slave's feet).
2. Él no ________ equipaje porque los esclavos no tienen nada y son propriedade de los romanos (He does not ________ baggage because slaves have nothing. They are the property of the Romans).
3. El jefe romano ________ cadenas en los pies del esclavo (The Roman chief ________chains on the slave's feet).
4. El jefe romano no ________ justicia pues los esclavo son su propriedad (The Roman chief does not ________ since the slaves are his property).
5. El esclavo no ________ comida y trabaja hasta morir. (The slave does not ________ food and works until he drops dead).
6. El jefe romano ________ todos los esclavos a trabajar con hambre y sin salario (The Roman chief ________ all the slaves to work hungry and without pay).
7. El jefe romano ________ todo, hasta matar a los esclavos como castigo, para construir su famoso acueducto en Segovia (The Roman chief ________ all he can, even killing the slaves, so as to build his famous aqueduct in Segovia).

FIGURE 1.2 Completa. Escoge del banco de palabras (Complete. Choose from the word bank.)

Using the same bank of words, Schmitt could have provided a sense of historical balance. Instead of integrating the aqueduct of Segovia in this lesson as an unproblematized phenomenon of Roman colonization, the author overly romanticizes the ingenuity of Roman architecture and engineering culture, which, in turn, can lead to students blindly embracing "the Great Traditions of what they called Western Civilization" (Aronowitz, 1998: 6). The same word bank used in a different and problematized context based on historical facts would give students critical tools to assess for themselves the underbelly of the monuments designed to reflect the "Great Traditions" of empires and the carnage, human misery, and dehumanization that constituted the foundation of their greatness. This foundation could also be examined with respect to other empires, including the Spanish Empire and its genocide of the Aztec and Inca civilizations, among others. For example, Schmitt could have engaged students in an exercise such as the following, which problematizes the history of the Roman Empire and highlights its dependence on slavery and on the obscene exploitation of human beings to build monuments that celebrate its "Great Traditions."

The questions that are never raised in the preparation of foreign language teachers is why textbooks never delve more deeply into certain contexts, often leaving inconvenient facts out so that students come away with less than a fully nuanced comprehension. In fact, teachers who risk engaging their students to historically understand the meaning of slavery, the subsequent racism, and other less attractive aspects of Western civilization—to interrogate, for example, the *animalification* of humans in order to satisfy the goals of colonialism—will certainly lose their teaching jobs. A shocking illustration of this point occurred in 2010 when

> the [Arizona state] legislature passed a four-part law forbidding any public school classes designed for a specific ethnicity or promoting 'the overthrow of the United States government,' 'resentment toward a race or class of people,' or 'ethnic solidarity' instead of 'treatment of pupils as individuals.' Then-state Superintendent of Public Instruction Tom Horn and then-state Sen. John Huppenthal, both Republicans, crafted the bill to outlaw Mexican-American studies classes specifically. (http://www.huffingtonpost.com/entry/ruling-arizona-mexican-studies_us_5988f8)

The closing of the Mexican-American studies program in Arizona also banned Rodolfo Acuña's classic *Chicano history, Occupied America* because, according to Tom Horne, "the mere title shows what kind of propaganda it is" (http://www.huffingtonpost.com/entry/ruling-arizona-mexican-studies_us_5988f8). Paulo Freire's *Pedagogy of the Oppressed* was also outlawed and, as John Huppenthal reportedly testified in court, "discussions of 'oppression' have no place in classrooms if they delve too far into the subject of the privileged place of white Americans or the marginalized place of Hispanics in the United States." Doing so, he argued, would only "undermine students' ability to succeed in life" (http://www.huffingtonpost.com/entry/ruling-arizona-mexican-studies_us_5988f8).

Against the ever-increasing neo-fascism in society in general, and in the academy in particular, it will require gargantuan efforts on the part of applied linguistics programs and foreign language teachers to implement the courageous and academically rigorous pedagogical proposals contained in each chapter of *Decolonizing Foreign Language Education: The Misteaching of English and Other Colonial Languages.* Hence it is not at all surprising that an applied linguist who has accommodated to a domesticating pedagogy would want to oppose hiring faculty members that are critically oriented and who raise new questions that could propel foreign language education into a paradigm shift (Reagan & Osborn, this volume) and could catapult foreign language education to new heights. This would be an ambitious goal given that the field of linguistics in general, and applied linguistics in particular, still operates under the weight of the school of positivism with its purported call for absolute objectivity, and any insertion of factors such as the unequal distribution of economic and cultural resources, racism, sexism, class stratification, and sexual orientation can be viewed as ideological and considered "an interventionist approach" (Wardhaugh & Fuller, 2015). Elaborating on this perspective, Wardhaugh and Fuller argue that Fairclough's perspective is

> very much an ideological view. Its proponents maintain that all language use is ideological as are all investigations, that is, that there is no hope of an "objective" or "neutral" sociolinguistics. Consequently, critical discourse analysis claims the high ground on issues; it is for people who are struggling against domination and oppression in its linguistic forms.
>
> *(Fairclough, cited by Wardhaugh & Fuller, 2015: 16–17)*

Blommaert (2005: 25), on the other hand, proposes "it is not enough to uncover the social dimensions of language use. These dimensions are the object of moral and political evaluation, and analyzing them should have effects in society: empowering the powerless, giving voices to the voiceless, exposing power abuse, and mobilizing people to remedy social wrongs" (cited in Wardhaugh & Fuller, 2015: 16–17).

Imperial Desires: The Latin Delirium

The asymmetrical value and cultural goods distribution inherent in the current hierarchies of languages and their multiples varieties cannot be truly understood without a historical comprehension of the genesis of these hierarchies in the first place. That is, part of the problem with the field of foreign language education is its denial of historicity that would have shown that the entire architecture of the language teaching enterprise is built on a house of cards that cannot withstand rigorous examination, neither through theory nor through an ideological deconstruction. Thus the animus on the part of domesticated applied linguists against critical language pedagogy and theory. Consequently we should not be surprised that Wardhaugh and Fuller (2015) aggressively caution readers against adopting an ideological view of language analysis unless one is willing to forfeit objectivity. What these two authors fail to acknowledge is that their very claim of objectivity is already infused with a dose of subjectivity. Thus the claim of objectivity is always in dialectical relationship with subjectivity. Furthermore, the false call for objectivity is deeply ingrained in a positivistic method of inquiry that falsely celebrates methodological elegance over history and the pursuit of scientific truth. In effect, the overemphasis on methodological "objectivity" within the school of positivism, as Wardhaugh and Fuller suggest, has resulted in an epistemological stance in which *scientism* rather than science and methodological refinement are celebrated, while "theory and knowledge are subordinated to the imperatives of efficiency and technical mastery, and history is reduced to a minor footnote in the priorities of 'empirical' scientific inquiry" (Giroux, 1983: 87).

A cursory review of doctoral dissertations in language education supports the claim of over-celebration, if not reification, of the methodology sections of these dissertations that occupy an unduly large space while the significance of the study is often secondary to the eloquence of the methodology. For example, one may read countless dissertations on the stages of second language acquisition of English morphology but remain unable to know the *why* regarding these stages and what universal grammar principles are involved in the realization of these different stages. In other words, the very empirical nature of this "scientific" study renders it descriptively uninsightful with respect to how the innate language acquisition device (LAD) really works in the production of novel language structures in defiance of the evidence in the input data.

The down side of the obsession with empiricism in language education concerns a total disregard for history, which serves to undermine what any true language scientist can never refute: that no language variety is superior or inferior. Nevertheless, since the Middle Ages the academy falsely promoted the superiority of Latin while it engaged, through pseudoscientists, in a social construction of not seeing the counter evidence—a willful blindness that, at once, proves the old French adage: "Il n'y a pas de plus sourd que celui qui ne ne veut pas entendre, n'y de plus aveugle que celui ne vent pas voir" (There is no one more deaf than the one who does not want to hear, there is no one more blind than the one who does not want to see). However, the willful blindness to ignore evidence of these so-called scientific claims (i.e., superior language) would indeed have a very short shelf-life in natural sciences. Nevertheless, the folk theory regarding the superiority of Latin has withstood the test of time, as most academics have wrongly believed that,

> in order to acquire any knowledge whatsoever, it was necessary to learn Latin and Greek as it was indispensable to the Basques and the Bas-Bretons to begin learning French.
>
> Living languages were not fixed; printing had not been invented; the human mind had not applied itself to penetrating the secrets of Nature. To be educated was to know what Epicurus and Aristotle had thought. People of the upper classes boasted of not being able to read. The only class that possessed and transmitted knowledge was the clergy. What, then, could that knowledge be? Evidently it had to be limited to the knowledge of dead languages, and principally Latin; Latin was the language of religion; the clergy could teach only what they had learned—Latin.
>
> *(Bastiat, 1995)*

Subsequently, without an iota of scientific evidence, theories held that Latin is a superior language, giving rise to a mythology believed only by non-scientists—a folk theory that views the highly regarded study of Latin as a path to intellectual development:

> This is purely a conventional judgement. The Greeks, who did not learn Latin, were not lacking for intelligence . . . Will it never be understood that the altogether problematic advantage that is alleged to exist in a classical education, if it exists at all, is very dearly paid for by the terrible consequence of having allowed the soul of France to be penetrated, along with the language of the Romans, by their ideas, their sentiments, their opinions, and a caricature of their manners and customs?
>
> *(Bastiat, 1995)*

Thus the claim that Latin enhances intellectual capacity is truly an expression of racism, par excellence, to the degree that the hidden assumption is that the billions of people on earth who, by the accident of birth in the non-Western side of the world, had no exposure to Latin must be intellectually less developed due to innate predispositions found only in Latin speakers. Imperial powers understood all too well the power of language and its role in cultural invasion and the colonization of the mind—a colonization that reduces the conquered people to mere "caricature of their manners and customs" (Bastiat, 1995). Once Latin, as the only written language during the Roman Empire reign, "penetrated the deepest crevices of the French soul" (one could say the same about other territories conquered by the powerful Roman Imperial army), the middle and upper French classes became, in some strange manner, militant defenders of Latin as the *"language"* of civilization and culture while speakers of French (and its multiplicity of varieties) were subject to ridicule, devaluation, and exclusion from the Roman privileges selectively apportioned by the imperial power to its supporters. It was not until 1539 in the town of "Villers-Cotterêts an hour northeast of Paris . . . that Francis I made French rather than Latin the language of all legal acts" (Douthat, 2017). While Francis I made French legal, scholars and intellectuals of the time continued to write in Latin until Descartes published his book, *Discours de la méthode,* entirely in French, in which his famous philosophical proposition "Je pense, donc je suis" first appeared. What Descartes did for the French language in 1637 is to demonstrate that "Cogito ergo sum" was no better, superior, or more clearly stated than "Je pense, donc je suis," with one significant difference: the French version reached a much wider French-speaking audience that had been excluded from literacy in Latin. As he so correctly and courageously stated:

> If I write in French, which is the language of my country, rather than Latin, which is that of my teachers, it is because I hope that those who use only unalloyed natural reason will be better judges of my opinions than those who swear by the books of the ancients. And for those who combine good sense with application, whom alone I wish to have as my judges, I am sure they will not be so partial to Latin that they will refuse to grasp my arguments because I express them in the vernacular."
>
> *(Bastiat, 1995)*

History Repeats Itself: French as the New "Latin" in Haiti

Accordingly, Memmi stoically states that "colonial bilingualism is neither a purely bilingual situation, in which an indigenous tongue coexists with a purist's language (both belonging to the same world of feeling), nor a simple polyglot richness benefiting from an extra but relatively neuter alphabet; it is a linguistic drama" (1991: 107).

Foreign language teachers who teach mostly languages of colonizers—such as EFL teachers in former British colonies in Africa, for example, or ESL teachers in internal colonialism contexts like the United States —must fully comprehend how languages are weaponized to generate, shape, and sustain linguistic dramas (Memmi, 1991) that have psychologically adverse effects and can aggressively wound the cultural souls of speakers whose "tongues are yanked" (Anzaldúa, 1989).

Invariably, as the old adage accurately states, "the more things change, the more they stay the same." The colonization of the French mind through the imposition of Latin in all legal functions of the country did not prevent history from repeating itself and, when France began to practice its own imperialistic desires, its methods and tactics differed little from the policies that Rome had imposed on France, particularly with respect to language. For example, as mentioned earlier, the colonization of Haiti employed the same imperial language policy that gave France total monopoly over all aspects of Haitian institutional life. Kreyòl was summarily demonized and characterized as a primitive language without a grammar, without a written system, making it, in essence, a bastardized form of French—the official language spoken only by a tiny percentage of Haitian elite. Those elite, as colonized people, reap the prestige accorded to French speakers in Haiti—a "prestige [that] has long made Haitian Creole relatively unattractive in the eyes of Haiti's neo-colonial élites anxious to gain respect in a Western world that has often looked down on Haitians for one reason or another. As impeccable speakers of 'good' French, the Haitian élites felt that they would stand a better chance" (DeGraff, 1999: 1; DeGraff, 2005: 570; DeGraff & Stump, 2018).

The inability of most applied linguists to make historical linkages with past language practices and policies creates a large open ground for folk theories to abound and for ignorance to fester. Such ignorance is hardly innocent since those who exhibit the arrogance of language ignorance are often the beneficiaries of privileges awarded to those who willfully embrace the colonization of the mind as it is reflected in the policies and teaching practices they adopt and support. If it had not been for historical amnesia, the folk theory that propagates the false notion that the study of Latin would significantly expand one's intellect would not be reproduced in the twenty-first century even as empirical research points to the contrary. To clarify, research into the topic did not find any differences in the science and mathematics achievement of higher education students who learned Latin at school and those who did not (Thorndike, 1923).

> In the Nuremberg longitudinal study on learning Latin, Haag and Stern (2000) intended to find out whether these findings could be confirmed in Germany 70 years later . . . No differences were found in either verbal and nonverbal IQ or grades in German and mathematics between the 115 students who started with Latin as their foreign language in Grade 5 and the 93 students whose first foreign language was English.
>
> *(Caplan, 2011: 1)*

The researchers cited above and their respective findings only reinforce the adage that the eyes do not see, the mind does. Hence facts do not matter if they counter the mind shaped by prevailing dominant ideology. For language educators who continue to embrace the superiority of Latin in a futile attempt to expand one's intellect, they must also willfully refuse to expose the Romans, who have been said to have "so glorious a veil over their crimes as to transform them into virtues" (Bastiat, 1995)—virtues turned into a blind patriotism that is best characterized by their "hatred of foreigners, the destruction of all civilization, the stifling of all progress, the scourging of the world with fire and sword, the chaining of women, children, and old men to triumphal chariots—this was glory, this was virtue. It was to these atrocities that the marble of the sculptors and the songs of the poets were dedicated," all done in Latin (Bastiat, 1995).

The ideology that extols the "Great Traditions" and creates a false narrative of Latin superiority, unlike the live language, is far from dead. That is, the death of Latin is a gift from the dead that continues to give. It guides and shapes a significant portion of foreign language teaching to the extent that it continues to influence its descendent colonial languages through similar *linguicism* tactics. That is, we are taught in most U.S. schools colonial languages that, in turn, propagate their superiority to other languages as Latin once did and, in some respects, continues to do. Its relation to its colonial descendants provides colonizers with the mechanisms to rationalize their past language policy in the colonies administratively under their control (and now economically and culturally so) through neo-colonialism in the form of neoliberalism.

The uncritical and unreflective teaching of colonial languages also serves to justify the killing of languages whose speakers are not allowed to develop literacy in their own expressive tongues. Institutional and societal functions are always geared toward the study of colonial languages that are rigidly and artificially fixed by nation-states that put tremendous amounts of resources into the spread of their national languages, just as French President François Hollande unabashedly proposed that Haiti remain a French-speaking country even though approximately 95 percent of Haitians do not speak French (DeGraff, 2017; DeGraff & Stump, 2018). During his meeting with Haitian President Michel Martelly at the Élysée in Paris in October 31, 2014, President Hollande stated that, "[f]inally, there is Francophonie. That's a major link that the French language gives us with Haiti. We're making sure that the high schools that are being built today in Haiti offer the most teaching in French, by French teachers when possible, otherwise by Francophones, because we do not want what makes the identity of Haiti, the French language, to disappear" (DeGraff, 2017; DeGraff & Stump, 2018).

Along the same lines of imperial thinking, President Hollande appears clueless about the racism that has characterized French domination of Haiti, even after political independence, by imposing and linking a foreign language with the nation's identity, while Krèyol is never taken into consideration even though it is the mother tongue of practically all Haitians. His comments reflect a deep-seated racist ideology that discriminates linguistically (and also culturally) by advocating that the teaching of French should be carried out by native French speakers and, if this is not possible, by Francophones (seemingly individuals who learned French as an additional language). The same ideology with respect to native speakers as better models for teachers is also very prominent in the EFL programs abroad and in ESL programs in the United States. It is unlikely that an English speaker with an accent would be hired to teach English in the U.S., and many non-English speaking countries also show greater preference for English native speakers regardless of the teachers' qualifications. In some respects, speaking English natively constitutes qualification itself. However, it is quite normal in dominant countries to find teachers teaching foreign languages they barely speak and, if they speak it half fluently, they do so with a heavy accent that almost never disqualifies them from teaching the target language.

Even in countries that were not touched directly by edicts of the Roman Empire, such as Turkey, the overreach of the English hegemony has rendered the Turkish "foreign language education policy to mainly focus on the teaching of English" (Çelebi, 2017, this volume).

Consequently the overreach of English hegemony is spreading outward through economic, cultural, and political neo-colonialism in the form of neoliberalism—a theocracy of the market that has manifold consequences for language policy in countries such as Turkey that were, by and large, untouched "until the 18th century [by] Western languages [in that they] were not given much attention due to a focus on religious education" (Çelebi, 2017, this volume). In Malta, the Maltese language, spoken by all, is now being considered as a "foreign language" object of study, with English becoming more and more popular among students there (Gruppetta, 2018).

Colonial Languages as Linguistic Imperialism

Against a historical landscape that has always promoted *linguicism* by the ruling conquerors, it is important that teachers of foreign language critically engage the history of linguistic imperialism (Phillipson, 2008) so that they can prevent themselves from becoming unreflective linguistic vigilantes whose major role is (1) to expand the colonial language at the expense of minoritized languages, and (2) to reproduce the blatant linguistic racism that attempts to denigrate other peoples' languages and their corresponding cultures (Dendrinos, 2001; Macedo & Bartolomé, 2001; Rosa, 2016; Flores & Rosa, 2015; Meijer & Muysken, 1977, cited by Kramsch, this volume). For example, the same devaluation of French experienced by what Descartes called "vernacular" in 1637 applies to what is now labeled Creole languages, minoritized languages, and translanguaging through various language practices. In other words, these are languages that are truncated through the elimination of their functions in the official and institutional life of society by dominant forces. This is no different from what happened to English when "post 1066, Norman French speakers and the Norman French language dominated the law and the power structure [in England] for a few hundred years" (cited in Caplan, 2011: 1). Had the French dominance continued until today, one would have to assume that Shakespeare's plays would probably have been written in French, and English would have been labeled a dialect, pidgin, or creole. At the same time, these dominant forces create mechanisms designed to convince the speakers of minoritized languages of the primitive and corrupt nature of their language practices—language practices in which "for most of the nineteenth century [and subsequently] views of Creoles were shaped by the same racism that characterized slavery" (cited in DeGraff, 2005). One could say the same for Ebonics and translanguaging. A very similar linguistic phenomenon occurred with the spread of the Roman Empire:

> the languages and customs of the Romans spread to peoples who already had their own languages and cultures. The growing empire required soldiers be positioned at all outposts. These soldiers came from all over the empire and spoke Latin diluted by their native tongues . . . Vulgar Latin was spoken differently in different countries where, over time, it became such familiar modern languages as Spanish, Italian, French, Catalan, Romanian, and Portuguese.
>
> *(Gill, 2017)*

The pejorative treatment of these languages had little to do with their linguistic superiority or inferiority. They later became colonial languages when the nation-states where these languages were spoken became conquerors in the same manner that Romans were conquerors (García, Kramsch, in this volume. The role of conquerors is to subjugate and declare the conquered people racially inferior. Thus these conquered peoples were viewed as less *vis à vis* Classical Latin spoken by the aristocrats of the Roman Empire, in the same manner that people conquered in Africa and in the Americas by European colonialism were considered savages, primitives, and sub-humans. Since those who racialize human beings are always those in power to sub-divide humans along the lines of culture, ethnicity, gender, and race, "it becomes difficult to recognize, let alone admit, your own ethical failings" (McDonald, 2017: A11) when you are a member of the imperial white-supremacy cult that generates, shapes, and sustains racism.

This is also the same racism that, when practiced overtly, promulgates laws that forbid literacy in minoritized languages (for example, in Massachusetts it is against the law to provide instruction in content areas in languages other than English) and, when covert, sees educators and policymakers call for the hiring of "pure applied linguists"(technicists who believe that foreign language teaching should be politically neutral) who will ascertain the "purity" of fixed colonial languages (i.e., the tradition of hiring mostly native speakers as model language teachers: read white teachers, as the former President of France left no doubt when he stated that Haiti should offer the most teaching in French, by French teachers . . .) even though linguists know that when a language is left to its own devices it is always porous, fluid, and hybrid— characteristics that capture the essence of languaging practices discussed by García, MacSwan, Hemphill and Blakely, and Pennycook as translanguaging (this volume).

In a sense, all of the language practices in Vulgar Latin in the Roman Empire that eventually were standardized through nation-state power had undergone a form of translanguaging, particularly in conquered territories that were geographically far from Rome and Latin was in contact with multiple local languages. It is a process that not only upends the rigidity of artificially fixed language boundaries by nation-states (the linguistics landscape in Africa is a case in point, where languages do not respect administrative borders artificially created by past colonial powers). In addition, administrative language rules and regulations are always subverted by universal grammar whose principles generate, guide, and shape all linguistic realizations regardless of the social and institutional constraints falsely framed as "superior" or "pure" language, "elaborated" language, or "cultured" language. Given that these socially constructed labels often have their own counterpart labels, albeit derogatorily, the major purpose of language naming and labeling is to establish ideological distinction (Butler, 1977) with the sole purpose of signaling to speakers of minoritized languages that what they speak is inferior and impure, restricted, and uncultured. The correlate also signals to the minoritized speakers that their culture, too, is inferior and impure, restricted, and less desirable.

These issues can only be truly understood through critical reflection and action as the dominant language ideologies are deconstructed and the intertwined factors such as class, ethnicity, gender, and sexual orientation are unveiled, problematized, and made an integral part of the applied linguistics curriculum. For instance, EFL teachers need to apprehend the target language as the object of knowledge in order to comprehend the paradox in Adrienne Rich's poem, "The Burning of Paper Instead of Children," when she wrote the poignant verse, "This is the oppressor's language yet I need it to talk to you" (cited in hooks, 1994: 167). bell hooks further and wisely cautions us that "it is not the English language that hurts me, but what the oppressors do with it, how they shape it to become a territory that limits and defines, how they make it a weapon that can shame, humiliate, and colonize" (hooks, 1994: 167).

The Dialectical Relationship Between Theory and Practice

The insightful chapters included in this edited volume attempt to transcend the arrogance that has traditionally permeated foreign language literature studies that, with rare exceptions, relegate foreign language teaching to a sub-disciplinary status in the academy. Unfortunately, as I mentioned earlier, most literature professors who continue to make decisions about the foreign language curriculum know little about the very complex nature of the foreign language they have learned to read and write primarily to gain access to that language's literary texts. Most foreign-literature professors know even less about the multifaceted processes of SLA (see Ortega's chapter, this volume) and how universal principles of grammar determine and predict most linguistic realizations (see Ortega's chapter in this volume). I am reminded of a seminar organized decades ago by the late Wilga Rivers,[1,2] a former professor of foreign language education at Harvard University—a seminar that focused on the principles of textbook sequencing. After listening to her prescriptive rationale as to why grammatical concepts needed to follow specific sequencing (i.e., the present tense is followed by the perfect tense which, in turn, is followed by the imperfect tense, the future tense, and so on), I felt unconvinced and politely asked her to reconcile her conclusions with the current emerging research on second-language acquisition spearheaded by Michael Long, Lydia White, Suzanne Flynn, Stephen Krashen, Roger Anderson, John Schumann, John Cummins, and Wallace Lambert, among others—studies that suggested convincingly that the stages of second-language acquisition, like first-language acquisition, are determined by universal principles that must meet at least one fundamental condition: maximal learnability.

It was not my intent to engage Professor Rivers in a debate regarding the theoretical status of learnability, as some have suggested. I simply felt it would be rewarding to engage her and the audience in a discussion that considered the role of Universal Grammar (UG) in determining accessibility to structures. She abruptly interrupted me, suggesting that the second-language acquisition literature was tentative and inconclusive. Given my youth at the time and my enthusiasm for the important insights that the second-language acquisition studies were reporting, I pushed the issue further by insisting that stages of second-language acquisition were governed by UG principles, thus predictable. I more aggressively suggested she would have to consider, for instance, the role of *markedness* theory and other UG principles may play in her determination of tense sequencing in foreign language textbook development and syllibi design. My foray into debating a senior professor of Harvard who commanded undivided and uncritical attention from an audience made up largely of literature professors, with little to no understanding of linguistics and language acquisition theories, was quickly cut short as she interrupted me for a second time: "Young man, you are out of order. We are not going to wait for second-language research findings to write foreign language textbooks." Clueless about academic protocols at the time, I ventured to have the last word by saying, "Thank goodness the medical field does not prescribe cancer treatments in the same manner, without scientific evidence to support their medical interventions!" Needless to say, I was never invited back.

The arrogance of ignorance in the dismissal of theory in the field of language teaching was not unique to Professor Rivers. Neither was it innocent, since ignorance is never innocent.

That is, her lack of knowledge of current trends and development in L2 acquisition research should not be a justification for Professor Rivers' offhand dismissal of my question. Fortunately, the field of language teaching in the United States is changing, albeit slowly, through the insistence and theoretical insights of many scholars' research in second-language acquisition, critical language studies, and critical language pedagogy. The latter study as an area of research did not take hold in the U.S. until the 1980s with the advent of keen interest in the work of Paulo Freire by scholars such as Henry Giroux, Michelle Fine, Linda Brodkey, Donaldo Macedo, Stanley Aronowitz, bell hooks, Roger Simon, and Ira Shaw—all of whom represented the first generation of critical pedagogues starting in the early eighties. As critical pedagogy caught fire and enthusiasm it was embraced by Peter McLaren, Antonia Darder, Lilia Bartolomé, and Joe Kincheloe, among others, who are considered second-generation critical pedagogues. The enthusiasm for criticality in language studies was further promoted in the 1990s with Alastair Pennycook's pioneering critical applied linguistics (Kubota & Lin, 2009). In essence, critical theory from various strands (Marxist, feminist, postmodern constructionism, and post-colonial analysis) began to have an enormous influence on language studies: with Norman Fairclough in critical discourse analysis; Judith Butler in language and feminist theory; Robert Phillipson writing on linguistic imperialism; Tove Skutnabb-Kangas and Robert Phillipson's work on language ecology and language rights; Bessie Dendrinos, Ngũgĩ Wa Thiong'o, and bell hooks' analysis of the intersection of language and race, which is being carried on through the last decade or so by Lilia Bartolomé, Antonia Darder, Donaldo Macedo, Michel DeGraff, and now, more recently, by Jonathan Rosa and Nelson Flores, among others.

The authors included in this edited volume, *Decolonizing Foreign Language Education: The Misteaching of English and Other Colonial Languages,* have all made enormous and insightful contributions in infusing criticality into language studies and pedagogy in foreign language education (see the work of Claire Kramsch, Theresa Austin, and François Tochon). The same dose of criticality also informs the work of Ofelia García, Jeff MacSwan, Theresa Austin, David Hemphill and Erin Blakely, and Alastair Pennycook on bilingualism, heritage language studies, and translanguaging. Even with the great leap by many language scholars toward embracing the many forms of critical theory in their work, the field of language teaching, in general, and foreign language teaching, in particular, still feels the weight of imperial history that can be traced all the way to the Roman Empire and the hegemony of Latin. That weight is often ignored in the curriculum of language teacher preparation even though imperial dogmas constitute the basis for policymaking, including language policy, as when, in 2002, "one of President George W. Bush's top advisers mocked a *New York Times* reporter as living in the 'reality-based community'" (Kramsch, this volume). Bush's top advisor further noted,

> That's not the way the world really works anymore . . . We're an empire now, and when we act, we create our own reality. And while you're studying that reality—judiciously, as you will—we'll act again, creating other new realities, which you can study too, and that's how things will sort out. We're history's actors . . . and you, all of you, will be left to just study what we do *(Suskind, 2016: 10, cited in Kramsch, this volume).*

While most language educators, including foreign language teachers, dismiss history in their practice, President Bush's top advisor took history seriously by acknowledging the paramount importance of imperial legacy appetites that inform U.S. policies while acknowledging that the role of educators (a reporter is also an educator) in reductionistic studies is almost futile given their irrelevancy due to the prevalent disarticulation of most language studies from the historical sources and events that generate, shape, and sustain these studies in the first place. Thus the uncritical language educator who insists on teaching the target language without understanding its link to a colonial past is bound to reproduce the colonial ideology of cultural penetration and language eradication. That is, a French teacher teaching French in Haiti with the sole purpose of saving Haitians from their lack of knowledge of Parisian French may think that he or she is magnanimously helping Haitians gain access to the "civilized" world, with the unspoken caveat that the Haitian students must negate his or her Krèyol and his or her cultural identity in the process of acquiring French. This unreflective and uncritical teacher may claim that teaching should be apolitical and fail to realize what the former French President Hollande hides in his false generosity of building new high schools in Haiti and suggesting that most of the instruction must be done in French by French native speakers so that Haitians maintain a French identity (read remain colonized) and the French language continues to maintain its dominant position in Haitian society as it did during colonial times, even though all Haitians speak their Haitian language and less than 10 percent of Haitians speak French fluently (DeGraff, 2017; DeGraff & Stump, 2018). That is, Haitians are forced to give up their cultural identity so they may access content knowledge in the new high schools gifted to Haiti by France.

While most French teachers cannot see the linkage between French learning and the veiled French hegemony former French President Hollande presented, he is unabashed in his proposal to culturally and linguistically continue to colonize Haitians under rubrics such as globalization, cooperation, and Francophonie—a Francophonie that exudes white supremacy, given the hostility and disdain with which most individuals from former French colonies are treated in France; a subject that remains taboo in French language textbooks. Simply put, French is a tool for continued colonization of minds in contemporary Haiti, as Latin was used as an instrument to expand the Roman Empire and its Latin hegemony to what is today known as the nation-state of France.

The Hegemony of English

In like manner, English plays the same role as other imperial languages of the past in empire building and colonial expansion which, conveniently, is ignored by most English language educators (EFL and ESL). However, the role of English is taken seriously by U.S. policymakers, who make no bones about the current English hegemony being central to empire building and "fake" reality creation. As an empire, the U.S. requires "the ideological monolingualism of the society as well as the hegemony of English in the United States and the marginalization of other languages" (Planas, quoted in Reagan & Osborn, this volume). The strict requirement of ideological monolingualism is one of the major reasons why Americans are said to be poor second-language learners. However, I do not believe that the low aptitude for learning languages other than their own is due to Americans being born with an anti-foreign language-learning gene, a false conception that has led some to believe that "Americans are not good at language learning." This folk theory serves as an apology for the general failure of foreign language education in the United States and is generally reinforced by policymakers who oppose foreign language education—such as the first female governor in the state of Texas, Miriam "Ma" Ferguson, who is claimed to have said, while waving her Bible, "If English was good enough for Jesus Christ, it's good enough for the children of Texas" (Planas, quoted in Reagan & Osborn, this volume) in her opposition to the proposal to teach Spanish in Texas to all children.

Given the anti-Spanish language sentiment in Texas and in most states throughout the nation, Spanish as a foreign language teachers, heritage language teachers, bilingual teachers, and dual language teachers need to also link the expanding *linguophobia* with the colonial legacies (the linguistic drama of Latinx in the United States is a case of internal colonialism that functions primarily to exclude Latinx from full citizenry, even if it requires Latinx children to be yanked from their parents and jailed in chain-link cages). Hence language teachers working with Latinx children cannot ignore the obscene racism exacted against children at the border as they engage in a social construction of not seeing while pretending to remain "pure" applied linguists who only implement policies and apply methodological techniques that determine what happens in Spanish language classrooms. Against the draconian racism with which Latinx students are treated in schools and society, Spanish language educators cannot remain neutral in their classrooms, regardless of the progressive teaching methods that they may propose and embrace. Thus the very proclamation that language education should be apolitical constitutes, in my view, a political act that supports the status quo that must be acknowledged by all educators.

As a linguist and language educator I remain a firm believer in the important role that language teachers can play in reversing the fast-forward movement of the world into a very dark new age. Leading intellectuals such as Noam Chomsky, the late Zygmunt Bauman, Henry Giroux, Arundhati Roy, Amy Goodman, and Thomas Piketty have wisely alerted people around the world to the dire consequences of denying such realities as climate change, obscene economic inequality, or potential nuclear catastrophe as promoted by the far-right power hegemony. These realities, if left unchecked, may potentially result in the end of humanity as we know it. Thus language teachers, including foreign language teachers, can play a pivotal role in helping reverse the current political course and can do so by problematizing statements like that of former President George W. Bush's top advisor who said that, as policymakers, "[w]e're history's actors" (Suskind, 2016: 10, cited by Kramsch, this volume). Instead of just accepting the role assigned to educators, reporters, and people in general by the dominant ideology, educators in particular must reject being relegated to the mere role of observers who study what policymakers do. Beyond studies, educators must engage in praxis where their critical reflection is concretized in knowledgeable action. That is, rather than being complacent observers they must become agents of history. Otherwise they will tragically "be left out to just study what we do," as former President Bush's top advisor proclaimed. (Suskind, 2016: 10, cited by Kramsch, this volume).

However, to engage in praxis in language classrooms means that teacher preparation needs to militantly problematize the false notion of "pure" applied linguists, the major role of which is to disarticulate teacher preparation from political awareness and theory while relegating language teachers to mere technicians who can manipulate, to various degrees, methods that are, in most instances, technically oriented and divorced from the social forces that ultimately determine what happens in a language classroom. By this I mean that, no matter how sophisticated the methods may be, they never explain why only **1% of Americans** (emphasis mine—Reagan & Osborn, this volume) succeed in learning an additional language in school or why, for example, there is a dearth of African Americans in foreign language classrooms. The absence of African Americans and other minoritized groups in foreign language classrooms either as students or as teachers cannot be comprehended fully without a rigorous analysis of white supremacy from slavery time to the current racialized explosion in Charlottesville, North Carolina, where white supremacy asserted itself as being alive and backed by policymakers at all levels, including in the academy where systemic racism is propagated by viewing racism as an individual act and not a systemic policy. Even the usual denial of racism in higher education constitutes already a form of racism. However, given that the Civil Rights Act has been systematically defanged in regards to racial discrimination, it is very difficult to prove racism in the academy since most academics know how to be politically correct and hide their racial animus by avoiding language that would unveil their racist ideology. By not making institutional racism central to all racial discrimination investigations, institutions remain largely racist to the extent that, short of shouting the "N" word to a non-white individual, systemic racism runs amok in institutions with impunity.

What the academy and its policymakers willfully neglect to acknowledge is that, while one can whitewash racist language through political correctness, it does little or nothing to eradicate the systemic racism that keeps African Americans from U.S. foreign language classrooms and keeps them from faculty positions at the university level, either as foreign language teachers or foreign language teacher educators. For example, ask yourself why you never or seldom meet an African American foreign language professor. Why are there so few African Americans majoring in Classics? However, it is claimed that to interrogate the demographic of foreign language classrooms is to politicize education or, as Wardhaugh and Fuller (2015) suggest, to embrace a posture that "is very much ideological" (Wardhaugh & Fuller, 2015), which, in their view, taints the objectivity of the methodologies used in either instruction or research. What both authors fail to understand is that the claim that a person or a position is ideological is also an ideological act. That is, the very claim is already infused and shaped by ideology.

"That's Why I Don't Do Theory"

As I attempted to argue earlier, applied linguists are doubly cursed. They have, on one hand, to deal with the indignities thrown at them by most theoretical linguists' arrogance who find the discipline of language teaching almost sacrilegious, and, on the other, most applied linguists have to co-exist in literature departments that still house a significant percentage of foreign language teaching programs. In many instances, a visceral self-defense is to dismiss theory as they reproduce a cult of methodology that Lilia Bartolomé aptly characterized as a "methods fetish" by arguing that

> educators [also language educators] need to reject the present methods fetish so as to create learning environments informed by both action and reflection. In freeing themselves from the blind adoption of so-called effective (and sometimes "teacher-proof") strategies, teachers can begin the reflective process, which allows them to recreate and reinvent teaching methods and materials by always taking into consideration the sociocultural realities that can either limit or expand the possibilities to humanize [language] education.
>
> *(Bartolomé, 1996: 234)*

However, to engage in both action and reflection the foreign language teacher must first take a detour through "theoretical praxis [that] is only authentic when it maintains the dialectic movement between itself and that praxis which is carried out in a particular context. These two forms of praxis are two inseparable moments of the process by which we reach critical understanding" (Freire &

Macedo, 1995: 377–402). Such a proposal is difficult to implement in a foreign language teaching context since most foreign language teachers have an aversion to critical theory and viscerally dismiss its use of linguistic theory as "too theoretical," meaning not practical enough. This was evident during a discussion with a colleague some decades ago concerning the role of language in class demarcation (i.e., the academic discourse is middle-class marked) when, after exhausting her arguments to deny the existence of class in the United States, she proclaimed: "That's why I don't do theory"—a remark that forced me to point out to her that she, in fact, does do theory. Her problem does not lie with theory *per se* but with the fact that she does bad theory. That is, there are no language teaching practices that can be executed without theory. Bad theory involves its denial by those who falsely claim to be engaged in practice only, particularly when the denial of theory truncates questions that could unveil the *raison d'être* of the very denial of theory so as to keep hidden the enormous contradiction inherent in the claim that "I am a devout activist and I have no need for the theoretical blah, blah, blah."

The theory aversion held by most foreign language teachers and many language teachers' trainers is directly linked to the *fetishization* of methods that is designed to domesticate the mind so as to avoid unpacking "any analysis of the social [which] is imbued with subjective interpretation and ideological stands" (Tochon, this volume). While there has been significant progress in foreign language teaching research and studies in second language acquisition (Lenzing, 2013: 67; Ortega, this volume), many of these studies are adversely impacted by the religiosity of research methodologies, a religiosity that constitutes another curse in applied linguistics due to its over reliance on empiricism that claims to be guided solely by "scientific" objectivity—a cult of absolute objectivity that not only provides the language researcher with a safe haven from which he or she can attempt to prevent the emergence of counter discourses which can interrogate "the hegemony of positivism and empiricism" (Brodkey, 1996: 8), but also generates a narrative about theory believed only by non-scientists. It is important to note that I am not arguing against objectivity. Scientists and researchers need to always strive toward maximum objectivity. The challenge for scientists and researchers is to keenly comprehend that, for every claim of "scientific" and absolute objectivity, there is also a dose of subjectivity. Thus objectivity and subjectivity are always in a dialectal relationship. In other words, a second language study such as the Strategies Approach, which is predicated on "the course of L2 development [in which] the learners are able to produce increasingly complex structures by removing different strategies one after the other in a predicable sequence" (Lenzing, 2013: 65), still remains shackled by the cult of "methodology for empirical study and data analysis" (Lenzing, 2013: 67). That is, a Word Order Acquisition study and the resultant sequence of word order that emerges tells little about the UG internal structures dynamics that generate and shape the development of the sequence in the first place—a fact accurately critiqued by Larsen-Freeman and Michael Long (cited in Lenzing, 2013). Hence, as Linda Brodkey put it, "any and all knowledge, including that arrived at empirically, is necessarily partial, that is, both an incomplete and an interested account of whatever is envisioned" (Brodkey, 1996: 8).

While Suzanne Flynn, Wayne O'Neil, L. Travis, Harald Clahsen, Fred Newmeyer, Lydia White, Fred Eckman, Michel DeGraff, Suzanne Gass, Lourdes Ortega, Ellen Broselow, Barbara Lust, and Jürgen Meisel, among others, have provided illuminating theoretical insights in language acquisition research, very little of their theoretical proposals have been translated into foreign language classrooms. Given the multiplicity and competing theoretical perspectives in L2 research, my focus is not to engage in a debate regarding the ever-increasing theoretical linguistic proposals, but to highlight the importance of theory in language pedagogy, including English as a foreign language. Rather, my main interest is to invite language educators and researchers to move beyond the theory vs. practice false binarism usually produced by neo-Darwinian descriptive and historical and prescriptive grammars (DeGraff, 2001) and, as I had mentioned earlier but it is worth repeating, foreign language teachers and research need to develop theoretical tools that will enable them to identify the limitations of some forms of empiricism that only catalog, for example, the sequence of tense acquisition in English as a second or foreign language but fail to explain the role of the "internal biolinguistic" mechanisms in the linguistic realization process. In other words, it is only through theoretical lenses that foreign language teachers and foreign language researchers can (1) explain the nature of interlanguage, (2) predict, for example, the order of English past tense acquisition, and (3) provide the explicatory power of the internal grammar structures that are implicated in the following interlanguage developmental sequence of the English past tense acquisition of the irregular verb ***to go***:

1. Yesterday me no go movie
2. Yesterday Mary no go***ed*** movie
3. Yesterday Jane no went movie
4. Yesterday Jane and Mary no went***ed*** movie

FIGURE 1.3

A healthier approach for applied linguists is to avoid false dichotomies that, on the one hand, license the silly posture of language research and practice that claim "That's why I don't do theory." On the other hand, applied linguists need to unshackle themselves from the seduction to pretend to adopt "hard science" modes of analysis as part of their research in language studies and analyses which, in my view, has given rise to a form of *scientism* rather than science. By *scientism* I refer to the mechanization of the intellectual work cultivated by language specialists, which often leads to the fragmentation of knowledge: "A fair amount of things that have to be done in physics or in biology is mechanical work of the mind which can be done by anyone, or almost anyone . . . to divide science into small sections, to enclose oneself in one of these, and leave out all consideration of the rest" (Ortega y Gasset, 1932: 111). The fields of general linguistics and, in particular, applied linguistics are preponderantly supportive of language specialists of this sort, who hide their ideology behind a facile call for "scientific rigor" and "absolute objectivity." These "scientific" language specialists have often contributed to further fragmentation of knowledge because of their reductionistic view of the act of knowing. They repeatedly refuse to admit to themselves and to others that the claim of "absolute objectivity" is, in reality, an ideological act. Along the same line, DeGraff has argued succinctly against the myth creation through the proliferation of language labels to satisfy the unquenchable need to classify languages—a process that serves the purpose to create distinction that over valorizes Western white colonial languages as more "elaborated" and "complex," with the resultant designation of non-white languages as "simple," therefore inferior: "In the 17th to 19th centuries, such orthodoxy had explicitly race-based underpinnings. One often taken-for-granted piece of 'normal science' revolves around the notion that non-whites were inferior human beings, and so was non-whites' speech considered inferior to whites' speech" (DeGraff, 2001: 220). Sadly these same myths implicated in language labels continue to determine, shape and guide the field of foreign education that, while proclaiming that colonialism is over, remains chained to coloniality. Why is it that learning institutions continue to restrict their offerings to imperial and colonial languages? The obvious answer to this question is that the field of applied linguistics, by supporting a type of research and language teaching, has and continues to reproduce the colonization of the mind to the degree that the many attempts to democratize language studies, language analyses, and language teaching remain cursed in the ever-present "postpone arrival."[3]

Regardless of the continued reproduction of imperial and colonial myths regarding language superiority and inferiority, all foreign language practice and research must always take a detour to theory. To do otherwise, the promised shift to a paradigm change in applied linguistics will continue to be a mere chimera.

Recommendations

Among many theoretical hypotheses currently being proposed—for example, see an overview in Lenzing, 2013, and Ortega, in this volume—most language educators, including foreign language teachers, do not use theory to explain why language learners defy the input data and adhere to a preference of structure that leads, in most cases, to the defiance of the input data, even if this means the construction of novel structures.

While reviewing several French, Portuguese, and Spanish textbooks, I failed to come across a single language teaching lesson covering any grammatical features that emphasize the construction of novel structures, which, I assume, is dependent on the internal structure dynamics which, in turn, are guided by UG principles. On the contrary, these textbooks presume a sequence hierarchy of verbal inflections to mark tense and mood and almost always fail to even acknowledge the potential that novel structures have pedagogically to facilitate access to structures being taught by these textbooks. On the contrary, even though empirical data indicate that a preponderance of learners gravitate toward the defiance of input data, the resultant output due to the defiance is often considered "errors" that need to be eradicated. At the same time, much energy and attention is spent on many chapters that emphasize irregular past tense verbs, followed by, for example, a chapter, such as in C. J. Smith, which delineates imperfect tense verbs:

> Gramática:
> Imperfecto de los verbos en –**ar**, (-ar imperfect tense verbs)
> Imperfect de los verbos en –er, -ir, (-**er**, -**ir**, imperfect verbs)
> Imperfecto de los verbos irregulares (imperfect tense of irregular verbs)
> (Schmitt, 2012: 7)

FIGURE 1.4

The exercises and drills that follow are designed to reinforce the "correct" form of native standard speech and little attention is given to the fact that "errors" that may occur are part and parcel of the process that is guided by UG principles. To the extent that "errors" are rule governed, the knowledge of such a fact would accomplish at least two important pedagogical requirements: (1) it would lower the social filter, thus lowering learning anxiety; and (2) it would allow learners to focus on authentic communication rather than the memorization of a hierarchy of marked structures of the target language being taught in the unreasonably short period of time allotted to the teaching of the grammatical concept in question.

In addition to a lack of theoretical understanding of L1 acquisition and particularly L2 development, most foreign language teachers follow textbooks that drive their teaching of marked structures (i.e., verbal inflection) of the target language. Teachers are encouraged through their preparation, methods, and the curricula to truncate the centrifugal force generated by UG principles that give rise to so-called "errors," while drilling and over-drilling students using correct structures of the ideal white, middle-class model speaker of the target language, even if it means teaching against the grain. That is, most applied linguistics programs fail to provide foreign language teachers-in-preparation with the adequate and comprehensive knowledge of how the innately internal structures work to pull learners in foreign language classrooms into a tug of war between what is natural acquisition of grammatical structures guided by UG principles and the obsession with teaching the model, standard, white, middle-class target language (the academic discourse) which is defied, at least initially, by learners. This misplaced emphasis on the ideal white, middle-class model speaker brooks no space for "error-making" and experimentation through translanguaging or other development found in non-white, lower-class immigrant students which, more and more, represent the majority of students in public schools, particularly in urban areas.

Among the multiplicity of complex factors that adversely impact foreign language teaching in the United States—which produces, by and large, scandalous failures (Reagan & Osborn, this volume) with students rarely reaching the desirable fluency in the target language they study—applied linguistics and foreign language programs need to tease out the colonial legacy that continues to shape and guide foreign language teacher preparation programs in spite of significant advances in applied linguistics research and practice. Most foreign language teachers struggle to bring their students to a communicative level in the target language that is passable and acceptable, and often do not realize that they were cheated of a meaningful educative experience in their teacher-preparation programs—programs that still are chained to the cult of methods (both teaching and research methods) that don't work and maintain the delirious notion of "superior" languages. Often these methods are disarticulated from the very theory that informs the methodological tool box that foreign language teachers have uncritically and reflexively embraced while dismissing both linguistic theory and social critical theory. By sacrificing critical pedagogy theory, applied linguistics programs cannot help foreign language teachers comprehend, for example, why it is that most of their U.S. colleagues (as well as the majority of their students) are also white and middle-class. Hence a successful language teaching preparation program must be, by its composition, interdisciplinary, so that teachers and students understand the intersections of multiple disciplines that inform and shape applied linguistics.

At the same time, as the field of foreign language moves way from the rigidity of discipline-based departments that are often turned into silos of "fake neutrality" and "objectivity," it should not revert into watered-down disciplines and sub-disciplines that pretend to cross-fertilize under the rubric of freedom of inquiry in interdisciplinary studies. In other words, while the borders of discipline-based departments begin to be more flexible in order to incorporate important elements that were factored out in disciplinary studies so as to preserve the "purity" of the field, interdisciplinarity should never allow for the cannibalization of disciplinary content in the name of expediency.

That is, for instance, teacher preparation programs should never allow educators in applied linguistics to teach in subject areas where they claim to have "expertise," if their "expertise" is based merely on one or two courses that they took in their doctoral program and they have never conducted any serious and significant research in the subject matter they claim to have expertise in. Hence a course in theoretical linguistics should be taught by a specialist in the field who publishes in refereed linguistic theory journals and belongs to professional organizations that reflect the current trends in the field of linguistic theory. A faculty member in an applied linguistics department should not be teaching a graduate level theoretical linguistics course just because he or she possesses a Ph.D. in general linguistics and happened to have taken one course in linguistic theory as a Ph.D. student.

By the same token, just because the theoretical linguist in the department took a course or two in research methodologies (quantitative and/or qualitative), it does not qualify him or her to teach graduate-level courses in research methodologies, particularly when his or her research expertise lies outside the field of research methodologies. Regrettably, the thinking that if one has a Ph.D. one can teach anything pervades many applied linguistics programs, particularly those that are housed in schools of education and literature departments. However, literature departments would never allow a faculty member whose Ph.D. focus and expertise were the contemporary French novel to teach courses in French Medieval literature. Thus a double standard ultimately relegates the field of applied linguistics to a series of watered-down disciplinary contents linked to a semi-emptied-out interdisciplinary framework. This watering-down process often leads even those faculty members with the best of intentions to reproduce the curses that befall applied linguistics, generally referred to in the field of linguistics studies as "light" linguistics or "baby" linguistics, which, in turn, characterizes anyone with an applied Ph.D. as a generalist in linguistics and teaching methodology who can teach almost anything under the "applied linguistics" umbrella, even if this means sacrificing rigor while boasting about the rigor and the "scientific" approach with which they teach their classes.

I argue aggressively against this generalist model and suggest that a rigorous program in applied linguistics must be staffed by experts in the area they teach and research. In other words, an applied linguistics program should be modeled after innovative and creative solutions in interdisciplinary programs in science and technology where students learn from experts in their field of inquiry "in an environment that is intentionally unbound . . . [where] . . . its faculty hold joint appointments in other schools and departments. These organizational structures encourage openness and enable success in ambitious and collaborative areas of inquiry such as bioengineering, nanotechnology, and robotics" (Faust, 2017: 3). The interdisciplinary study that brings biology and engineering together never sacrifices content in either biology or engineering, and rigor is preserved by peer vigilance and peer review. It would be unthinkable to have a non-biologist and a non-engineer evaluate a bioengineering faculty's candidacy for tenure. In fact, to do so would be considered an academic travesty since peer review serves as the backbone to the development and rigor of any scientific endeavor.

Consequently I argue that programs in applied linguistics need to draw from a multiplicity of expertise, which includes the list below but is not limited by it:

- Experts in linguistic theory who specialize in first and second language acquisition and also conduct research in these fields and publish in linguistic and language acquisition theoretical journals (only then does peer review make sense); language methodologists who can align their teaching methods with SLA theories so students can make sense of how theories inform their practice and vice versa and whose research is recognized and published in peer reviewed journals.

- Research methodologists (both qualitative and quantitative) whose specialization is research methodology and whose research is published in peer-reviewed research methodology journals.
- Critical sociolinguistics experts who study and deconstruct the folk theory of "pure applied linguist," language superiority and inferiority so that all language varieties are accorded the dignity and respect they deserve and whose research is informed by social critical theory frameworks and published in critical theory and sociolinguistics journals (also peer reviewed).
- Faculty whose specialization is linguistic ethics so as to help create pedagogical spaces where students are armed with theoretical and practical skills to accelerate the decolonization of foreign language education through a process that denounces the dehumanization involved in *linguicism* (Phillipson, 2008) while announcing humanization by the celebration of all languages. Otherwise, to just denounce colonialism in foreign language education only at the level of written critical discourse analysis that is disarticulated from action will, invariably, reproduce colonial values that often dehumanize the very students who aspire to learn a foreign language as a form of self-liberation. That is, non-bourgeoisie "belief in the emancipation of men and women [that] is rooted in an 'existential' commitment to an ethical idea rather than to historical inevitability" (Aronowitz, 1998: 7) In other words teaching is fundamentally an ethical endeavor (isn't it ironic that most teacher preparation programs do not require students to take a course in ethics?), given the dehumanization to which speakers of thousands of languages are subjugated in these dark times when, according to John Kenneth Galbraith, "the modern conservative [read Far Right] is engaged in one of man's oldest exercises in moral philosophy; that is, the search for a superior moral justification for selfishness" (McDonald, 2017: A11).

  This odious "selfishness" often surfaces through crass careerism where the careerist's main political project is the advancement of his or her career even if this means trampling and sacrificing the academic culture that pronounces the need for ethics, rigor, excellence, and humane pedagogy. When a careerist's advancement is at stake, these laudable pronouncements become, at once, pure blah, blah, and blah, particularly when the critical pedagogue denounces the power structure at the level of written discourse while, simultaneously, voting and supporting reactionary administrators and colleagues.
- Multiculturalists who go beyond the folkloristic anthropologist approach to contrastive cross-cultural communication and whose goal is to interrogate the paternalism imbued in the teaching of multicultural tolerance that, in itself, breeds xenophobia that borders on racism (i.e., "I tolerate you even though your culture is repugnant because we need to go along so that we can get along"—cited in Macedo and Bartolomé, 1999).

- Multiculturalists who study the complexity of the twenty-first century multicultural world and who should situate their scholarly work and research within a cultural studies theoretical framework, not only to avoid the expansion of academic cultural tourism but to consider themselves organic intellectuals and not cultural "facilitators" of common sense wisdom and values clarifications (Aronowitz, 1998).
- They must exhibit intellectual coherence that forces them to walk their talk. That is, it is not enough to denounce multicultural malpractices without a process of divestment in one's privilege. It is chic to be known as the Marxist-in-Residence professor who critiques the evil of capitalism while, simultaneously, engaging in egregious discriminatory practices against students and professors who have been minoritized by the power structure. The announcement of a less discriminatory and more humane world must be accompanied by transformative actions that make amends for past cultural exploitation, cultural malpractices, and cultural subjugation by colonial powers in order to seed hope for more equitable society where equity gains a new meaning and when cultural and material goods are distributed more equally and democratically. Such amends, while rare, are possible. Take the case of Christine Sleeter, the critical multiculturalist, whose unyielding coherence prompted her to give $250,000 she inherited from her ancestors and that, according to her, was "her family inheritance—generated by her great-grandparents selling off American Indian land more than a century ago and then investing the profits" (*The Salt Lake Tribune,* 2017: 2). In keeping with her always present intellectual coherence, Sleeter avoided falling into the usual "false generosity" of a charitable act. To her "it's simply returning what was stolen" from the Ute Indians. (*The Salt Lake Tribune,* 2017: 2)

It is only through the intellectual rigor of key disciplines interacting in a convergent course of study that we can develop rigorous interdisciplinary approaches to language education that will allow applied linguistics graduate programs to transcend the common and facile practice that, because a faculty member has taken a graduate course in a particular area of study during his or her doctoral studies, he or she can teach that course even though he or she never conducts research in the discipline, will never publish in rigorous peer-reviewed journals representing the discipline, and will not be invited to speak to an academic organization made up of peers who represent the field of study. The propensity in social sciences, humanities, and education to water down the content in interdisciplinary studies results in the licensing of unethical faculty members to teach in areas they have little to no expertise—a pedagogical *laissez-faire* that would never be allowed, for example, in the interdisciplinary field of biochemistry. As I mentioned earlier and it is worth repeating, peers in the natural sciences are so vigilant that rigor would never allow itself to be sacrificed for expediency. Therefore, applied linguists who consider themselves "scientific," "pure," and "progressive" need to also be more vigilant and denounce when a peer who receives, for example, a doctoral degree in curriculum and instruction later transmogrifies herself or himself into a cultural studies expert without ever taking a single Ph.D.-level course in cultural studies. I also am reminded of a medieval specialist who, tired of not having enough students to teach and venues to publish, over one summer transformed herself into a literacy expert teaching graduate courses in literacy in the following fall semester. The opposite would never be allowed. A literacy specialist would never be allowed to teach in the medieval literature program at any level.

Against the complexity and complacency in the preparation of language teachers and, in particular, foreign language teachers, applied linguistics programs need to understand the deeper meaning of "Who is to say that robbing a people of its language is less violent than war?" (Smith, cited in Anzaldúa, 1989). Applied linguistics programs should also instill in students the belief in "the learner's capacity to situate herself in historicity . . . [to debunk, for example, the Latin delirium that] . . . education [which] was confined to the study of dead languages [Latin], quite improperly called the learned languages . . . [and which celebrates] . . . the grandeur of [Romans and] their enterprise and the immensity of their success has thrown so glorious a veil over their crimes as to transform them into virtues. And this is precisely why [the] school [that proclaims Latin as a superior language] is so pernicious. It is not abject vice, it is vice crowned with splendor that seduces men's souls" (Bastiat, 1995).

Any form of education that lies so as to seduce the young minds under its care is pure propaganda. It is reflective of a society that lives in the past, ignores the present, and loses its moral compass to forge a future—a future that should be less cruel, more just, less dehumanizing, and more humane. It is a society that proudly spends billions of dollars attempting to make robots more humane by making them speak, obey orders, and carry on a conversation, such as Alexa, while dehumanizing speakers of thousands of natural languages by "deslenguar mujeres y hombres, niñas y niños" (de-tonguing women and men, girls and boys) of their expressive native tongues, wrongly labeled as "bastardized" languages so they can, as it is claimed, become more fully human by acquiring the imposed "civilized" colonial languages.

It is a society that, by ignoring history, including its own, runs the risk of resurrecting the savagery of the past, as was recently done by a professor of political science in Portland state who believes that "[c]olonialism could be resurrected without the usual cries of oppression, occupation, and exploitation" (as cited in Prado, 2017, Yahoo News). Hence the blind and unproblematic teaching of the imperial and colonial past through foreign language education prevents students from becoming "knowers" (Aronowitz, 1998: 14) who interrogate, reject, and announce "with the language of fire" (Anzaldúa, 1989) that the superiority of Latin and its descendant pidgins that we now teach and study as nation-state-sanctioned colonial languages (also considered superior) are a mere figment of imperial imagination. In fact, the hybridity of language practices derived from Vulgar Latin in contact with a multitude of other language varieties are not too dissimilar from the language practices that are sociologically lumped into language categories which, in turn, serve to devalue and dehumanize speakers of Haitian

Creole, Capeverdean Creole, Tok Pisin, and Papiamentu, and non-white, lower!-class language practices (DeGraff, 2017, DeGraff & Stump, 2018)—language practices through which their speakers receive and transmit their cultural mores and values. In sum, the dominant ruling class uses these claimed "inferior" linguistic expressions to intentionally typecast racially, culturally, and ethnically with the sole purpose of devaluing the speakers of these languages and their correspondent cultures. As such, for instance, neither should Spanish teachers be allowed to devalue the language practices that students bring to the classroom. Regrettably, for instance, because translanguaging is considered inferior, Anzaldúa (1989) reports, "even our own people *nos quieren poner candados en la boca* (want to shut our mouths with padlocks). They would hold us back with their bag of '*reglas de academia*' (with rules of the academy)" in a colonizing attempt 'to yank wild tongues [that] can't be tamed, [thus] they are cut out'" (Anzaldúa, 1989).

The authors in this significant edited volume have created pedagogical spaces so that the learners of foreign languages and the teachers who teach them become "knowers" in order to comprehend the real meaning of "*hablar pa' 'trás*" (talking back) and "*repelar*" (fighting back) (Anzaldúa, 1989) so as to prevent current and future generations of foreign language teachers from teaching *de rodillas* (on one's knees) (see Emiliano Zapata quotation).[4] On the contrary, foreign language teachers should teach "standing up" to keep students who were and continue to be dehumanized by the savageness of colonialism from experiencing subordination and shame for speaking their mother tongue or translanguaging so as to make meaning that matters to them. Teaching "standing up" means to protect the cultural and linguistic dignity of millions of students in the United States who, like Gloria Anzaldúa, stoically proclaimed, "I will no longer be made to feel ashamed of existing. I will have a voice: Indian, Spanish, white. I will have my serpent's tongue—my woman's voice, my sexual voice, my poet's voice. I will overcome the tradition of silence" (Anzaldúa, 1993: 81) imposed by imperial and colonial hacking of non-white people's tongues in the name of saving "civilization."

Critical foreign language teachers who embrace both social critical theory and linguistic theory can create spaces through a non-banking form of teaching that unleashes the language potential with which, as humans, we are all endowed to create and recreate our own ways of speaking that correspond to our resistance and rejection of any and all forms of colonial subjugation that is still imbued in many foreign language teaching contexts. In a much-needed advocacy, if not militancy, for translanguaging—a linguistic realization that is supported by our endowed capacity to learn languages, to transform them, to make art with them, as well as weaponize them—Anzaldúa (1989) ruptures the centuries-old imperial and colonial tongue-tying of thousands of languages when she proclaims, "Until I am free to write bilingually and to switch codes without having always to translate, while I still have to speak English or Spanish when I would rather speak Spanglish, and as long as I have to accommodate the English speakers rather than having them accommodate me, my tongue will be illegitimate" (81).

Most foreign language teachers ignore the view that a socially subordinate language, as a repressed language, could, if spoken, challenge the privileged linguistic dominance of the colonial standard language. It is precisely these dimensions that foreign language educators must demystify in order to question dominant colonial standard languages and the old assumptions about their inherent superiority (Donald, cited in Freire & Macedo, 1987: 153). Consequently, foreign language teachers, in order to succeed and democratize their pedagogical practices, must first decolonize the dominant colonial languages so that translanguaging and other subordinated linguistic expressions cease to be repressed and begin to insert and assert themselves in multiple societal spheres such as music (i.e., jazz, rap, etc.), art, commerce, science, and also education. Translanguaging as linguistic practice is not a random selection of chunks of multiple languages woven together by ungrammatical rules. On the contrary, translanguaging is rule-governed and obeys, like all other languages, the principles of the Universal Grammar. On a social dimension, translanguaging represents the future as the world shrinks through technology and demographic shifts, and as the need to communicate deeply and effectively as multiple linguistic groups expands and interpenetrates the linguistic soul and geography of others without the need of "*othering*."

Simply put, while foreign language teaching programs still have not fully cut the yoke of colonialism that generates linguistic oppression, the colonized speakers are using their language practices to defy and interrogate artificial linguistic borders whose major purpose is to exclude so as to exploit, to devalue, and to dehumanize. This defiance—truly a testimony of what it means to come to voice—is eloquently captured in Alzaldúa's "tongue of fire!" *y con rabia* (with anger) which refuses to be "tamed" as it poetically, and with a just ire as Freire would say, denounces the cruel, painful, and inhumane manner in which imperial and colonial powers of the past and the present use the linguistic guillotine to prevent humans from being fully humans:

> *Deslenguadas.* (We are de-tongued.) *Somos los del español deficiente.* (We are those with deficient Spanish.) We are your linguistic nightmare, your linguistic aberration, your linguistic *mestizaje* (your linguistic miscegenation), the subject of your *burla* (the subject of your derision). Because we speak with tongues of fire, we are culturally crucified. Racially, culturally, and linguistically *somos huérfanos* (we are orphans)—we speak an orphan tongue.
>
> *(Anzaldúa, 1989: 58)*

Notes

1 The late Wilga Rivers taught language teaching methodology for many years that coincided with the dearth of research in second language acquisition. Given Harvard's institutional prestige, Professor Rivers commanded a very high status in the field of foreign language education.

2 Linguists characterize this process with different labels that are purely social and not scientific. I am also assuming that all language acquisition undergoes some form of pidginization that mirrors closely the UG principles in language acquisition in general.
3 See Stuart Hall: *Critical Dialogues in Cultural Studies*, edited by David Morley and Kuan-Hsing Chen. Routledge, 1996.
4 Emiliano Zapata quotes (showing 1–17 of 17) "It is better to die on your feet than to live on your knees." "Es mejor morir de pie que vivir de rodillas." *https://www.goodreads.com/author/quotes/1627776.Emiliano_Zapata.*

References

Anzaldúa, G. (1989). *Borderlands: The New Mestiza.* San Francisco, CA: Aunt Lute Press.

Aronowitz, S., (1998). "Introduction" in Freire, P., *Pedagogy of Freedom.* Boulder, CO: Rowman and Littlefield Publishers.

Baptista, M. (2002). *The Syntax of Cape Verdean Creole: The Sotavento Varieties.* Amsterdam/Philadelphia: John Benjamins Publishing Company.

Baptista, M. and Guéron, J. (2007). *Noun Phrases in Creole Languages: A Multi-faceted Approach.* Amsterdam/Philadelphia: John Benjamins Publishing Company.

Bartolomé, L. I. (1994). "Beyond the Methods Fetish: Toward a Humanizing Pedagogy." *Harvard Educational Review,* Vol. 64, No. 2, Summer.

Bastiat, F. (1995). *Selected Essays on Political Economy.* New York: The Foundation for Economic Education.

bell hooks (1996). Teaching to Transgress. New York: Routledge.

Blommaert, J. (2005). *Discourse.* Cambridge, UK: Cambridge University Press.

Brecht, Bertolt, "A Worker Reads History" (poem).

Brodkey, L. (1996). *Writing Permitted in Designated Areas Only.* Minneapolis, MN: Minnesota Press.

Butler, J. (1977). *Excitable speech. A politics of the performance.* New York: Routledge.

Caplan, B. (2011). "The Case Against Latin." Library of Economics and Liberty.

Cazabon, M., Lambert, W. and Hall, G. (1993). Two-way bilingual education: A progress report on the Amigos Program. Santa Cruz, CA: National Center for Research on Cultural Diversity and Second Language Learning.

Cenoz, J. (1996). "Learning a third language: Basque, Spanish and English." In A. Roca and J. B. Jensen (Eds.), *Spanish in Contact: Issues in Bilingualism*, Somerville, MA: Cascadilla Press.

Chomsky, N. (1981). *Lectures on Government and Biding: The Pisa Lectures.* Dordrecht, Holland: Foris Publication.

Christian, D., Montone, C., Lindholm, K. J. and Carranza, I. (1997). Profiles in Two-Way Immersion, Washington, DC.

Collier, V. (1992). "How Long? A Synthesis of Research on Academic Achievement in a Second Language." *TESOL Quarterly,* Vol. 23, No. 3 (Sept. 1989), pp. 509–531.

Darder, A. (2012). *Culture and Power in the Classroom: Educational Foundations for Schooling of Bicultural Students.* New York: Routledge.

DeGraff, M. (1999). "Creolization, Language Change, and Language Acquisition: A Prolegomenon." In M. DeGraff (Ed.), *Language Creation and Language Change: Creolization, Diachrony, and Development.* Cambridge, MA: MIT Press.

DeGraff, M. (2001). "On the Origin of Creoles: A Cartesian critique of Neo-Darwinian linguistics." *Linguistics Typology*, Vol. 5, Nos. 2 and 3, pp. 213–310.

DeGraff, M. (2005). "Linguists' most dangerous myth: The fallacy of Creole Exceptionalism." *Language and Society,* 34.

DeGraff, M. (2017). "Language. Human rights and equal opportunity: Haiti as a case study." *The Syntax of Justice: Law, Language, Access and Exclusion.* Boston, MA: Northeastern University.

DeGraff, M. and Stump, G. (2018). "Kreyòl, pedagogy, and technology for opening up quality education in Haiti: Changes in teachers' metalinguistic attitudes as first steps in a paradigm shift." *Teaching Linguistics and Language and Public Policy.* http://lingphil.scripts.mit.edu/papers/degraff/DeGraff_and_Stump_2018_Kreyol_pedagogy_and_technology_for_education_in_Haiti.pdf.

Dendrinos, B. (2001). The Politics of ELT. Athens: The University of Athens Publications.

Descartes, R. (1887). *Discours de la méthode.* France: Librarie des Bibliophiles.

D'Introno, F. (1992). Teoria Linguística. Variación Paramétrica y Español de América. Typewritten paper. University of Massachusetts Amherst.

Douthat, R. (2017). "Is There a Case for Le Pen." *The New York Times.*

Faust, D. (2017). "An Engine of Ingenuity." *Harvard Magazine,* September–October.

Flores, N. and Rosa, J. (2015). "Undoing appropriateness: Raciolinguistic ideologies and language diversity in education. *Harvard Educational Review,* 85(2), pp. 149–171.

Freire, P. (2000). *Pedagogy of the Oppressed.* New York: Continuum International.

Freire, P. (2018). *Pedagogy of the Oppressed.* 50th Anniversary Edition. London: Bloomsbury Academic.

Freire, P. and Macedo, D. (1987). *Literacy: Reading the Word and the World.* South Hadley, MA: Bergin and Garvey Publishers.

Freire, P. and Macedo, D. (1995). "A Dialogue: Culture, Language, and Race." *Harvard Educational Review,* Vol. 65, No. 3, Fall.

Gill, N. S. (2017). "Vulgar Latin – Learn Why Late Latin Was Called Vulgar." https://www.thoughtco.com.

Giroux, H. A. (1983). Theory and Resistance: A Pedagogy for the Opposition. South Hadley, MA: J. F. Bergin Press.

Greene, J. P. (1997). "A meta-analysis of the Rossell and Baker review of bilingual education research", *Bilingual Research Journal,* 21, pp. 2–3.

Gruppetta, C. (2018) "No. Maltese is not a foreign language." *Times of Malta,* March 18.

hooks, b. (1994). *Teaching to Transgress* (p. 167). New York: Routledge.

Kay, P. and Sankoff, G. (1974). *Pidgin and Creole Languages.* Ithaca, NY: Cornell University Press.

Kubota, T. and Lin, R. (2009). *Race, culture and identities in second language education: Exploring critically engaged practice.* London: Routledge.

Kubota, T. and Miller, E. R. (2017). "Re-Examining and Re-Envisioning Criticality." *Linguistics Inquiry in Language Studies.* Vol. 14, Nos. 2–3, April–September.

Lambert, W. E. and Tucker, R. (1969). "White and Negro Listeners' Reactions to Various American-English Dialects," *Social Forces,* Vol. 47, No. 4, June.

Lambert, W. E. and Tucker, R. G. (1972). *Bilingual Education of Children: The St. Lambert Experiment* (p. 3). New York: Newbury House Publisher.

Lenzing, A. (2013). *The Development of Grammatical System in Early Second Language Acquistion: The Multiple Constraints Hypothesis.* Amsterdam: John Benjamins Publishing Company.

Macedo, D. (1981). "Stereotyped attitudes towards various Portuguese accents." National Clearinghouse for Bilingual Education, Rosslyn, Virginia.

Macedo, D. (2006). *Literacies of Power: What Americans Are Not Allowed to Know*. Boulder, CO: Westview Press.Macedo, D. and Bartolomé, L. I. (1999). *Dancing with Bigotry: Beyond the Politics of Tolerance*. New York: Palgrave.

Macedo, D. and D'Introno, F. (1998). "Pidginization as Language Acquisition." In S. Flynn and W. O'Neil (Eds.), *Linguistic Theory in Second Language Acquisition*. The Netherlands: Kluwer Academic Publishers.

McDonald, D. (2017). "Harvard Business School earns an incomplete in ethics," in *The Boston Globe*, September 25, 2017.

Memmi, A. (1991). *The Colonizer and the Colonized*. Boston, MA: Beacon Press.

Naro, A. J. (1971). "The Origin of West African Pidgin. Papers from the 9th Regional Meeting, Chicago Linguistic Society, 442–9. [Reprinted in *Sociolinguistics Newsletter* 5:8–11, 1974].

Ngũgĩ, W. T. (1986). *Decolonizing the Mind; The Politics of Language in African Literature*. Portsmouth, NH: Heinemann Press.

Ngũgĩ, W. T. (1993). *Moving the Center: The Struggle for Cultural Freedoms*. Portsmouth, NH: Heinemann Press.

Ortega y Gasset, J. (1932). *The Revolt of the Masses* (republished 1964). New York: W. W. Norton.

Phillipson, R. (2004). *Linguistic Imperialism*. Oxford, UK: Oxford University Press.

Phillipson, R. (2009). *Linguistic Imperialism Continued*. New York: Routledge

Ramirez, J. D., Yuen, S. D., Ramey, R. and Pasta, D. J. (1991). Longitudinal study of
Structure-English immersion strategy, early-exit and late-exit transitional bilingual
programs for language-minority children. Final Report to the U.S. Department of Education. Executive Summary and Vols. I and II, San Mateo, CA.

Rosa, J. (2016). Standardization, Racialization, Languagelessness: Raciolinguistic Ideologies across Communicative Contexts. *Journal of Linguistic Anthropology*, 26(2), pp. 162–183.

Schmitt, C. J. (2012). *¡Así se dice!* Columbus, OH: McGraw-Hill Companies.

Schudson, M. (978). *Discovering the News: A Social History of American Newspapers*, (p. 6). New York: Basic Books.

Salt Lake Tribune (2017). "Professor gives $250K to Ute Indian Tribe to compensate for her great-grandparents profiting off tribal land sales."

Skutnabb-Kangas, T. and Phillipson, R. (2008). "A Human Rights Perspective on Language Ecology." In A. Creese, P. Martin & N. Hornberger (Eds.), *Volume 9, Ecology of Language., Encyclopedia of Language and Education* (2nd edition) (pp. 3–14). New York: Springer.

Wardhaugh, R. and Fuller, J. M., (2015). *An Introduction to Sociolinguistics*. Chichester, UK: Blackwell Publishing.

Zinn, H. and Macedo, D. (2005). *Howard Zinn on Democratic Education*. Boulder, CO: Paradigm Publishers.

2

BETWEEN GLOBALIZATION AND DECOLONIZATION

Foreign Languages in the Cross-Fire

Claire Kramsch

UNIVERSITY OF CALIFORNIA BERKELEY

Foreign language education today is positioned between national and global world orders. On the one hand, attempts to decolonize the teaching of national languages through translanguaging (García & Li Wei, 2014), translingual practices (Canagarajah, 2013), and multilingual pedagogies (Cenoz & Gorter, 2015) are weakening the traditional link between standard languages and national cultures and opening up foreign language education to other language varieties and alternative cultures. On the other hand, attempts to respond to the needs of learners in a global economy are instrumentalizing foreign languages and contributing to the commodification of education. Thus, by decolonizing the teaching of foreign languages and decoupling them from their national colonial past, educators run the risk of falling prey to another neo-colonial, neoliberal world order in which languages are mere resources used not for their cultural value, but for their exchange value (Heller & Duchene, 2012). This chapter discusses this dilemma, taking as an example the current debate in Germany on which kind of language and literacy education to promote in an era of globalization (Rosenbrock & Bertschi-Kaufmann, 2013). It strongly argues in favor of promoting critical applied linguistics and, in particular, cultural translation as a field that can bridge the humanities and the social sciences and reclaim foreign language education from the clutches of both colonialism and neoliberalism.

No field of education has been subjected more frequently to the ebbs and flows of global geopolitics than foreign language (FL) education. Wars and displays of military strength, economic and technological power, and claims to cultural superiority can enhance the prestige of one language over another; perceptions of a language's social significance or of its exchange value on the market of symbolic goods can affect people's desire to learn that language. For example, the First World War seriously reduced the demand for German in the United States, the collapse of the Soviet Union at the end of the Cold War wiped out enrollments in Russian, while the victory of the English-speaking Allies in the Second World War promoted the learning of English around the globe. The decision in 2008 by the UC Berkeley administration to severely cut the Japanese, Korean, and Chinese programs for budgetary reasons was reversed not because of the protests by the foreign language departments, but because it mobilized the Asian-American community, which turned the issue into one of civil rights. Heritage language learners and the geopolitical ties they represent came to the rescue of foreign languages. With the increased mobility brought about by globalization, the increased diversity of academic environments, and the hegemonic spread of English as a lingua franca, foreign language education has become at once more necessary and more controversial than it was fifty years ago.

While in the "classical paradigm" (Trim, 2012: 16) foreign languages have traditionally been part of the well-rounded humanistic education provided by nation-states to their citizens to enable them to gain access to higher culture, in the "modern paradigm" under the influence of English as a lingua franca, language education has become diversified into foreign, second, and heritage languages; languages for academic, business, and professional purposes; commonly and less commonly taught languages—the goal being to develop communicative ability and to become a member of a language community. The pressure on FL education to contribute to the social and economic well-being of society by improving communication among people from different cultures has led to the spectacular rise of research in Second Language Acquisition/Applied Linguistics since the 1970s (Kramsch, 2000). While FL educators might not have realized it at the time, communicative language teaching was already paving the way for the globalization of capital, goods, and people that characterize our present era.

Today globalization has taken center stage in discussions of FL education. The old grammar translation method, associated with the literate culture of national elites, has given way to the communicative, interactional, or intercultural approach associated with the oral culture of everyday encounters across cultures and their avowedly democratic turns at talk. As classrooms have become culturally more diverse and more multilingual, and the job market has become more global and thus more unpredictable, English has become the indispensable foreign/second language of the planet and the importance of learning languages other than English has waned. In non-English speaking countries, the first and often the only foreign language learned in schools is English. In the English-speaking world, learning a foreign language has remained an elite occupation, in the United States still at only 8 percent of all school children. In the following I describe how FL education in the United States has been so intent on meeting the needs of students in a "globalized, interdependent world" (Kramsch, 2014) that it has not paid enough attention to the colonial attitudes it continues to convey, from its nationalistic past to its current global orientation. I then discuss what it would take to decolonize FL education and reinstate the learning and teaching of foreign languages for bringing about peace and mutual understanding, rather than for enhancing one's status among the national elites or for gaining a competitive edge in the global market.

FL Education Embraces Globalization

Ever since the Perkins report of 1979 that decried the pitiful state of education in the United States and how it was putting "the nation at risk" (National Commission, 1983), American foreign language education has been framed as an issue of national security and economic prosperity (President's Commission, 1980). The following two passages give a flavor of the way education, and FL education in particular, have been seen in this country in exclusively competitive and expansionist terms.

> Nothing less is at issue than the nation's security. At a time when the resurgent forces of nationalism and of ethnic and linguistic consciousness so directly affect global realities, the United States requires far more reliable capacities to communicate with its allies, analyze the behavior of potential adversaries, and earn the trust and the sympathies of the uncommitted. Yet, there is a widening gap between these needs and the American competence to understand and deal successfully with other peoples in a world in flux.
>
> *(President's Commission, 1980: 11)*

> History is not kind to idlers. The time is long past when America's destiny was assured simply by an abundance of natural resources and inexhaustible human enthusiasm, and by our relative isolation from the malignant problems of older civilizations. The world is indeed one global village. We live among determined, well-educated, and strongly motivated competitors. We compete with them for international standing and markets, not only with products but also with the ideas of our laboratories and neighborhood workshops. America's position in the world may once have been reasonably secure with only a few exceptionally well-trained men and women. It is no longer.
>
> *(National Commission, 1983)*

These two texts capture well what globalization meant for the President's Commission with regard to foreign language education in the United States. Knowledge of foreign languages was meant not to lead to a better understanding of one's own and others' cultures *on their own terms*, but to push back other countries' national ambitions and ethnic identity claims, to increase American economic competitiveness on the world market, and secure its No.1 position in the world. This Cold War rhetoric has continued since the 1980s, bringing with it an ever-increasing awareness of the "global realities" ushered in on the one hand by the internet, economic deregulation, social media, and the global spread of English, and, on the other, 9/11 and the rise of global terrorism (Kramsch, 2005). In FL education this rhetoric has been accompanied by a strong push away from national cultures, national languages as cultural icons, native speakers, national traditions, and national institutions toward a more pragmatic view of language expressed in economic terms. The urge to embrace globalization and thus dismantle the traditionally national underpinnings of FL education manifests itself in various ways.

First, the push to make use of computer technology to teach foreign languages has no equal in any of the other subjects taught at secondary and post-secondary levels in the United States. Students are exposed to authentic materials taken from the internet, they have access to standard and non-standard varieties of the language, they are encouraged to communicate with other learners and with native speakers using electronic chatrooms, blogs, and Facebook, and to take advantage of myriad other ways to use the language outside of institutional demands and textbook constraints. Computer-aided language learning technology serves to individualize learning according to learners' interests, learning styles, modality preferences, and schedule availability.

Second, the focus now is on the here-and-now of online and face-to-face individual encounters, and the negotiation of meaning that goes on in real time between individuals who are increasingly affiliated not just with one national citizenship but with several languages and cultures. Task-based, content-based, action-based, performance-based language learning are all terms used to characterize an a-historical approach to current FL education that, by striving to make the learner into an active participant in a present speech community, shows less interest in understanding national history and its shaping of national identity.

Third, in many parts of the world (for example, Australia, Europe, Latin America) FL education has become interested in intercultural learning and the development of intercultural communicative competence, as captured by Michael Byram and his five competencies or *savoirs* (Byram, 1997), which include, besides knowing how to use the language, also "critical cultural awareness" (*savoir s'engager*) and a willingness to value the other (*savoir être*). In this view, which is also heavily advocated by the Council of Europe, FL education becomes an education to intercultural citizenship (Byram, 2008), with a moral and political agenda that is seen by some as clashing with the purely functional goals of globalization. Indeed, Byram's critics point to the neo-colonial aspects of intercultural communicative competence, which in these last two *savoirs* shows evidence, they say, of "a thick and invasive morality" (*une morale épaisse et envahissante*) (e.g., Antier, 2011).

Second Language Acquisition Research Embraces Post-Colonial Efforts and Identity Politics

While FL education has been keen on jumping onto the globalization bandwagon and capturing the attention of politicians and school administrators regarding the need to prepare youngsters for the "global realities" of tomorrow, second language acquisition (SLA) research has been eager to develop concepts for FL education that support the post-colonial efforts of other scholars in literary and cultural studies. Thus we have seen in recent years the following post-colonial research trends.

First, a move from structuralist to post-structuralist views on language and language learning. Rather than focusing on the acquisition of a linguistic code, scholars have stressed the social turn in second language acquisition research (Block, 2003). Learning a second language doesn't mean only mastering its forms; it means gaining access to the linguistic resources of speech communities (Canagarajah, 2013) even if these are imagined or aspirational communities (Pavlenko & Norton, 2007), participating in sociocultural activities (Pavlenko & Lantolf, 2000), being given a voice that is not only heard but listened to and respected (Norton, 2013a), aligning oneself with others, and negotiating power relationships (Canagarajah, 2013).

Such post-structuralist views are accompanied by efforts to de-institutionalize FL education. SLA research advocates diversifying the sources of knowledge from textbooks and language teachers, whose job it is to teach the forms of the language, to content-based instruction, content-and-language-integrated-learning (CLIL), and service learning that teach language use. Language itself ceases to be the object of instruction; instead it is used as a resource to mediate other activities within communities of practice. This mediation occurs through multiple channels and modalities; for example, verbal, visual, filmic, electronic, musical, and gestural (Lantolf & Thorne, 2006; Kern, 2000). It is not uncommon to contrast the artificial world of language learning in classrooms with the "real world" of workplaces and professional activities. What Canagarajah writes regarding English applies also to FL education:

> To be literate now requires competence not only in multiple modalities of communication (sound, speech, video, and photographs, in addition to writing) and multiple symbol systems (icons, images, color, and charts, in addition to words) but also in multiple registers, discourses, and language. In such a context, we readily recognize that teaching literacy in a single language (English or vernacular) or a single dialect of that language ('Standard English' or nativised varieties of English) fails to equip our students for real-world needs.
>
> *(Canagarajah, 2005: 196–197)*

Task-based learning is meant to precisely provide the learner with real-world challenges to overcome (e.g., Kramsch & Narcy-Combes, 2017).

In the same manner as cultural studies have sought to adopt a post-colonial perspective by giving a voice to writers outside the classical metropolitan canon, SLA scholars have sought to include in their data voices from the colonial periphery or from minority speakers representing other language speakers than the ideal white, heterosexual male native speaker of early SLA research. FL textbooks now include readings by foreign literary authors writing in French, German, or Italian, bilingual texts by Latino writers in the United States, and writings by ethnic minorities, and they make sure that women writers are also well represented in the FL curriculum. These post-colonial concerns find their expression in the spectacular rise of heritage language education that has become a vibrant field of SLA research. No doubt Ronald Walton, the founding member of the National Foreign Language Center in Washington, D.C., in 1986, played a major role in putting heritage languages on the scholarly map. A Chinese scholar and FL educator, he was well connected to the Foreign Service and Defense Language Institutes. He made the case around the time of the Perkins report (see above) that the United States was squandering valuable resources by not drawing on the already available capacities of hyphenated Americans who had native command of less commonly taught and strategically important languages, and whose loyalties to the United States could not be put in doubt because they were U.S. citizens. Since then, heritage language educators have their own professional conferences, their own journal, and their own teacher recruitment pipelines. They ensure that less commonly taught national languages, such as Vietnamese and Swahili, but also regional languages such as Breton, Kurdish, or Navajo, are funded by Title VI and supported by the International Studies Centers around the country.

We must see current efforts to "disinvent" (Makoni & Pennycook, 2007) the traditional boundaries between linguistic systems as so many attempts at further wresting FL education away from its national colonial past. Makoni and Pennycook made the forceful argument that the codification and standardization of languages that took place during the consolidation of nation-states were a creation of missionaries (as in Africa), revolutionaries (as in France), or reformers (as in Luther's Germany). In the nineteenth century the national languages that were inculcated in national educational systems and through grammar books and dictionaries reinforced the power of the dominant national educated elite, but reduced to silence or eradicated altogether the other languages that continued to be spoken among the less well-educated, such as the French patois during the French Revolution or American Indian languages. Efforts to revitalize "endangered languages" in the United States (e.g., Hinton, 1994) and the multilingual turn in SLA research (May, 2011) have led FL education to become sensitive to the increasingly multilingual nature of American FL classrooms (due to the increased number of immigrants and international students).

This multilingual turn has led to current efforts in FL education to validate the languages the students bring with them to the language classroom by allowing them to switch from one code to another (for example, from English to Spanish) or to engage in what García has called "translanguaging" (García, 2009). García proposed the term to refer to the code-meshing practices of bilingual speakers and the way they blend the structures of two languages to form a new language, or "structural coupling" (6). García and Li Wei (2014) suggest that bilingual speakers have one bilingual repertoire from which they draw the elements that enable them to communicate in the most effective way possible, depending on the situation. These bilingual practices constitute the norm for bilingual speakers. In a recent article, García and Leiva (2014) expand this translanguaging from a mere linguistic practice to outright political action.

> Translanguaging, resting on the concept of transculturación, is about a new language reality, original and independent from any of the "parents" or codes, a new way of being, acting and languaging in a different social, cultural, and political context . . . Translanguaging refers to social practices and actions that enact a political process of social and subjectivity transformations.
>
> *(204)*

For example, through translanguaging the teacher "helps students construct a Latino pan-ethnicity . . . where fluid identities are being brought forth with others in a process of continuous becoming" (211). While García and Leiva are keen on validating bilingual minorities for political and economic reasons, Canagarajah (2013) has advocated the generalized use of "translingual practices" in FL education, by which he means the free interaction of linguistic systems according to the situation and the negotiation of linguistic, social, and cultural norms within daily intercultural encounters. Translingual practice represents a frontal assault against the norms of correct speech imposed by the academic and bureaucratic institutions of the nation-state and thus falls under the post-colonial efforts to resist the dominant colonial order. Similarly, the multilingual turn in SLA has spawned efforts to treat the language classroom not as a monolingual realm in which total immersion in the one foreign language is mandatory, but as a multilingual context in which various activities can take place in various languages (Cenoz & Gorter, 2015), including translation from and into the foreign language (e.g., Kramsch & Huffmaster, 2015).

Lastly, in a most recent attempt to contest the disciplinary monopoly of linguistics on SLA research, a multidisciplinary group of scholars, calling themselves the Douglas Fir Group (2016), has called for a "transdisciplinary framework for SLA in a multilingual world" that urges SLA researchers not only to draw on a variety of theoretical strands such as sociocultural theory, language socialization theory, complexity and dynamic systems theory, biocultural perspectives, variationist sociolinguistics, and others, but also to investigate FL education "across private and public, material and digital social contexts in a multilingual world" (20). The Douglas Fir Group has been particularly keen on blurring the boundaries between the academic and the "real" world in a distinct attempt to fight against the colonization of FL education by an academically educated elite. But in so doing it risks ignoring the colonizing role North American academia itself plays in a global economy.

A Changed Political Landscape: From Post-Colonialism to Neo-Colonial Globalism

The post-national and post-colonial efforts to make FL education more open to the global world of multilingual, multicultural encounters and to the needs of real people in the real world have not "decolonized" the view of the world that fueled the desire for American FL education in the first place and which we could call the "national interest." Two developments have changed the context in which this national interest is pursued. The first has to do with the change in our definition of "national interest'." After 9/11, an anguished Ron Scollon asked:

> Are we working in the service of the national state, a domain in which the dominant ideology of the modern period is an equation of the tripartite entity, state, language, and culture, or are we working in the service of ordinary people throughout the world for whom language and culture are diverse, multifarious, complex, continuous, semiotic resources which do not parse out into neat formal and structural entities?
>
> *(Scollon, 2004: 271)*

In this quote, Scollon seemed to suggest that the modern era of nation-states with their national languages and cultures put to the service of national elites had given way to a post-modern, post-structuralist era of semiotic diversity and fluidity. Language is no longer a single cultural heritage, reserved for the few, but a "multifarious resource" available to ordinary people according to their needs—a welcomed democratic development. Scollon continues, however, with a warning:

> Scholars and students of language who take a multiple and variable resource view of language and culture are most often those who also take a socio-political position of opposition to the hegemony of the First World, its nation-state apparatuses, and its monolingual/monocultural views of human life. When their work begins to fall within the ever-searching spotlight of hegemonic attention, they are sometimes startled to discover that what can be used for the good of encouraging diversity, grassroots opposition, and genuine democracy can also be used for surveillance and hegemonic intervention. Their knowledge is in danger of being a classified national security secret.
>
> *(274)*

The post-colonial movement toward more democracy, he warns, has in fact been used to extend the reach of the nation-state within and beyond its borders for surveillance and for economic and military hegemony. The colonial dominance of nation-states has given way to the neo-colonial dominance of business and multinational corporate interests. The monolingual and monocultural colonial practices of state imperialism have merged with the multilingual and multicultural practices of private imperialism.

The second change in the context in which national interests are pursued has to do with a fundamental restructuring of reality itself, which has occurred through the combined forces of the internet and social media, the threat of global terrorism, and the large-scale migrations caused by never-ending wars. While the attack against the World Trade Center was a direct attack against one nation-state, it was also an attack against global capitalism masquerading as global democracy. If the First World has become the global world of private multinational corporations, the business model of human relations now uses the colonial practices of nation-states in the name of freedom and opportunity, but without the protections offered by national institutions. For example, here is how one pundit captures the current Exxon situation:

> Exxon, though headquartered in Irving, Texas, near Dallas, is a sprawling "private empire" with assets spread across the globe. When asked about building more U.S. refineries to protect the U.S. economy and consumers from fuel shortages, former CEO and chairman Lee Raymond put Exxon's view of itself and its loyalty to the U.S. bluntly. "I'm not a U.S. company, and I don't make decisions based on what's good for the U.S," Raymond is quoted as saying in the 2012 book *Private Empire: ExxonMobil and American Power* by Steve Coll.

Such a corporate view, based on the neo-colonial ambitions of privately owned companies, has an additional power. Democracy was still built on fact, rationality, and scientific evidence; crony capitalism is based not just on economic power, but on the power to create reality and manipulate perceptions and beliefs, as we can see today with the proliferation of fake news, global propaganda, and disinformation campaigns. In 2002, one of President George W. Bush's top advisers mocked a *New York Times* reporter as living in the "reality-based community."

> He said that guys like me were "in what we call the reality-based community," which he defined as people who "believe that solutions emerge from your judicious study of discernible reality." I nodded and murmured something about enlightenment principles and empiricism. He cut me off. "That's not the way the world really works anymore," he continued. "We're an empire now, and when we act, we create our own reality. And while you're studying that reality—judiciously, as you will—we'll act again, creating other new realities, which you can study too, and that's how things will sort out. We're history's actors . . . and you, all of you, will be left to just study what we do."
>
> *(Suskind, 2016: 10)*

That new reality is what could be called neo-colonial globalism, which is seen as ubiquitous, natural, unavoidable, and beneficial. While globalization is an economic fact, globalism is an ideology that believes that what is good for the global North is good for the rest of the planet. FL education research has been among the first academic fields to rally behind the banner of globalism, in part in order to secure its precarious position in the North American academic landscape (Kramsch, 2014; Douglas Fir Group, 2016). When the 2007 MLA report on foreign languages decried the two-tiered system of foreign language departments and advocated raising students' historical and political consciousness at all levels of the FL curriculum, it was still thinking in international rather than global terms. It still upheld the notion of the nation-based educated native speaker and enjoined Americans to "see themselves as Americans, that is, as members of a society that is foreign to others" (MLA AdHoc Committee, 2007: 237). Ten years later such an injunction sounds almost quaint. In a United States that is more divided than ever, who are the "Americans," and in an interconnected global world who is really "foreign" to whom? The MLA report of 2007 is no longer a point of reference for the Douglas Fir Group (2016) that seeks to go beyond educational institutions and broaden the mission of SLA research to serve, besides learners themselves, a constituency of various "stakeholders, including teachers, administrators, appointed and elected officials, parents, community members, business leaders, and educational, business, and health organizations." (39) A distrust of state institutions and the push to address directly individuals and groups on the internet, Twitter, Facebook or other social media are some of the hallmarks of globalism.

Globalism is more subtle than the traditional colonialism of the hierarchical elite. It claims to be the voice of the real people in the real world and to be sensitive to cultural difference. It seeks to embrace the world in a common interest in global peace and prosperity. For example, the American Council for the Teaching of Foreign Languages (ACTFL, 2014) now no longer has communicative nor even intercultural competence as its goal but, instead, global competence. Global competence is the ability to:

- Communicate in the language of the people with whom one is interacting.
- Interact with awareness, sensitivity, empathy, and knowledge of the perspectives of others.
- Withhold judgment, examining one's own perspectives as similar to or different from the perspectives of people with whom one is interacting.
- Be alert to cultural differences in situations outside of one's culture, including noticing cues indicating miscommunication or causing an inappropriate action or response in a situation.
- Act respectfully according to what is appropriate in the culture and the situation where everyone is not of the same culture or language background, including gestures, expressions, and behaviors.
- Increase knowledge about the products, practices, and perspectives of other cultures.

While the five Cs of the 2006 National Standards underscored communicating with others, getting to know other cultures, making connections, drawing comparisons, and joining communities, the focus is now exclusively on communicating with people and developing sensitivity to cultural difference. Behind the desire to respond to the interests of the large majority of foreign language learners who, according to the survey by Sally Magnan and her team (Magnan et al., 2014), claimed to be interested only in communication and communities, not in any of the additional three Cs, one senses the fear of globalization and the uncertain future it presages. That fear manifests itself in the overwhelming interest in digital technologies as the panacea for solving educational challenges, as well as in the desire to acquire FL functional competencies in order to better compete in an uncertain global market (Hellmich, 2017). This globalist attitude is reflected in FL educational curricular practice and in SLA/Applied linguistics research.

Neo-Colonial Practices in Foreign Language Education

Curricular Practices

Foreign language and literature departments have tried to respond to the changed circumstances by capitalizing on both the national and the global opportunities offered to them.

On the one hand, despite the rhetoric of transdisciplinarity and post-colonial rhetoric, FL departments are still heavily nationally oriented and are often seen by their national sponsors as colonial outposts. Native speakers are still recruited and prized as language teachers. Under dwindling support from their universities, foreign language departments rely on foreign nationals and native speakers to staff their graduate seminars and on foreign support for their graduate students. Conversely, scholars and native language instructors from European and East Asian countries increasingly seek employment in American foreign language departments, hoping for permanent resettlement in the United States and a green card. The fact that many of these individuals have Ph.D.s in fields that often have nothing to do with language, that many were trained abroad (DaF, FLe, etc.) and might have different educational values from the values promoted by the American institution, doesn't seem to bother these departments, which are mainly concerned about keeping the students happy and holding up enrollments. This they do by exploiting the lure of high culture to enhance their undergraduates' experience and enrich their academic record. In turn, students increasingly view FLs merely as a supplementary feather in their cap for future employment or for tourism purposes; they don't seek to gain a deeper understanding of and empathy for the worldview of speakers of other languages.

On the other hand, the language programs in FL departments are being subjected to a pervasive global neoliberal discourse that has crept into academic institutions and is particularly pronounced in FL education. This neoliberal globalese is recognizable by its econometric metaphors and euphemisms; for example, language as *resource* and *strategy*, language learners as *stakeholders* and *communities of practice*, language learning as *participation* and *investment,* language teaching as *effectiveness* and *accountability*, educational success as *measurable outcome* and *sustainable growth*. The heavy push for the use of computer technology together with the push for ever-greater accountability, that is, testability, and the increasing demands of other subjects in the curriculum, combine to instrumentalize FL education and eventually squeeze foreign languages out of college-level curricula. One way for FLs to keep up enrollments is to publicize their link to the rich humanistic cultures of national communities and their prestigious historical heritage, even when this humanistic cultural aspect is not really focused on. In this sense one could say that FL education is being recolonized by the forces of globalization that reduce national cultures to tourist attractions from the Travel section of the *New York Times* (Vinall, 2012).

FL departments could benefit from a field such as (critical) applied linguistics whose mission is precisely to deal with real-world problems where language is the main focus. And, indeed, we see them increasingly hiring language program directors with a background in SLA/Applied Linguistics and giving them tenure-track appointments. However, in most cases the field of Applied Linguistics itself, located as it is in the social sciences, is still not really integrated into the intellectual life of foreign language departments. Professors in the humanities still have difficulty understanding the difference between Applied Linguistics, SLA, FL education, and FL teaching methodology (Kramsch, 2000). Most graduate student instructors in literature or linguistics don't really understand language (Holquist, 2007: 4) and what it means to acquire someone else's language. Their knowledge of second language acquisition often does not go beyond a one or two semester-long "methods course." In that sense one could say that FL education at the college level is still under the hegemony of the linguistics and literature professoriate. By trivializing applied linguistics, most of the literature/cultural studies scholars are missing an opportunity to contribute to the hotly debated questions that are asked in a critically oriented applied linguistics: what are we teaching FLs for? How can foreign literature help youngsters understand themselves and the complex reality they live in? How can we decolonize FL education from both the esoteric practices of a national cultural elite and the instrumentalized practices of global experts?

Research in FL education, that is, SLA/Applied Linguistics, that heavily draws on Anglo-American research on the teaching of English, remains deeply hostage to language learning concepts and theories born in the global North. It is itself engaged in subtle and pervasive neo-colonial practices of an epistemological kind.

SLA/Applied Linguistic Research

In his well-known classic, *Culture and Imperialism* (1993), Edward Said wrote:

> Just as none of us is outside or beyond geography, none of us is completely free from the struggle over geography. That struggle is complex and inter-

> esting because it is not only about soldiers and cannons but also about ideas, about forms, about images and imaginings (7) . . . In our times, direct colonialism has largely ended, but imperialism lingers where it has always been, in a kind of general cultural sphere as well as in specific political, ideological, economic and social practices (9) . . . Rarely before in human history has there been so massive an intervention of force and ideas from one culture to another as there is today from America to the rest of the world.
>
> *(319)*

As a field that emerged in the 1950s from the need to teach English around the world (Kramsch, 2005), SLA/Applied Linguistics research has retained its Anglo-American claim to universality with regard to FL education. The large numbers of researchers trained at U.K., U.S. and Australian universities disseminate their research questions, their research methodologies, findings, and pedagogical recommendations around the globe; these in turn spawn global theories that find their empirical validation in local settings. These theories then become the unmarked case that does not need to be named. For example, applied linguistics publications that deal exclusively with the teaching of English often don't feel the need to mention their English or American local origin in their titles, whereas work done on the teaching of other languages and published in English cannot assume the same universal relevance. An American professional association such as the American Association for Applied Linguistics (AAAL) with its 53 percent of international members assumes an ambiguous role as both a local and a global association, and its annual meeting with its remarkable success both sustains and decries the neocolonial scholarly practices of its members.

The problem is not just a linguistic one (the obligation to publish in English) but a cultural and epistemological one that is much more pervasive than just English grammar and vocabulary. It has to do with what Walter Mignolo has called "the geopolitics of knowledge" (Mignolo, 2002), and that Tom Ricento and others in Applied Linguistics have described at length (Ricento, 2000). For example, in order to be published in an English-speaking journal, scholars in other languages must make reference to and take a position toward theories, concepts, methods, or ideas born in the Anglo sphere (e.g., Douglas Fir Group or Sociocultural Theory). For instance, U.S. publications constantly make reference to "real-world needs," and thus seem to assume that the institutional world of the classroom is not the real world; worse still, they seem to assume that academia is an elite, self-serving world. In itself this could be seen as an effort to decolonize foreign languages from the artificial environment of academic institutions. But it assumes that academic institutions are intrinsically obstacles to progress when, in many parts of the world, state institutions are the only guarantee of equal access and equal opportunity. It also assumes that the real world of an English-dominant global economy is the only real world that exists. But in many countries FL education has other goals than merely economic goals; for instance, the development of a student's personality, historical and political consciousness, and the development of imagination and empathy through the study of a foreign literature (see the German case of *Bildung*[1] below).

The questions framed by applied linguistics in the global North, such as the relationship of language and identity, global vs. local, multilingualism, or bilingual education determine the current hot topics in the field. They get to dictate the terms of the conversation in FL education. Anglo-American scholars do want to hear subjugated voices, but in terms of their own Anglo-American theories. For example, Bourdieu's (1991) sociological notions of *right to speak* or *investment*, Weedon's (1987) post-modern feminist notion of *subjectivity*, and Anderson's (1983) anthropological notion of *imagined community* have been reappropriated in North American ESL education to suit a particular ideological cause. Bourdieu's right to speak and investment concepts have been recast to serve a liberal civil rights agenda (Norton, 2013a; Kramsch, 2013: 195), Weedon's subjectivity has been made to serve the goals of identity politics (ibid.), and Anderson's imagined community has been coopted to serve a global anti-nationalist/anti-colonialist agenda (ibid.). As Allan Luke wrote, "One of the most robust and suspect theoretical moves of Western philosophy is to assume historical, temporal and spatial synchronicity—that indeed we might live in a 'universal' world where singular theoretical constructs and textual conceits might have generalizable explanatory and practicable power" (Luke, 2005: xv).

There is, of course, nothing wrong in borrowing concepts from other fields, and the production of new knowledge depends on such transdisciplinary and transcultural transfers. But when these concepts are unmoored from their original theoretical contexts they risk being used for political purposes, however well-intended these purposes are. They no longer describe what is, they prescribe what should be. In an afterword to the second edition of Norton's popular book *Identity and Language Learning* (2013a), I wrote:

> [By using the French term *investissement*,] Bourdieu is not enunciating a moral imperative but rather, as a sociologist, spelling out the rules of the game of cultural reproduction as social destiny (196) . . . [and] Anderson's phrase "imagined community" reminds readers today of the overwhelming power of nations to control the imagination of their citizens, both directly through political speeches and indirectly through mass forms of communication."
>
> *(197)*

However, Norton uses "investment" and "imagined community" in a sense that is exactly contrary to what their two original authors had intended. Her social and political agenda, characterized by her firm belief in individual autonomy, personal investment, and entrepreneurship, and her strong trust in the power of "communities" (as opposed to "civic societies"), is an attempt to weaken the dominance of the nation-state and its nefarious colonial practices as she herself experienced them in South Africa (Kramsch, 2013: 192). However, such an attempt risks exercising its own form of neo-colonialism. By viewing FL education as predominantly a tool of sociocultural emancipation from national institutions, traditions, and histories, it ignores or trivializes other questions raised in other educational contexts—for example, in Germany the role of written culture in the development of a national identity and of FL education in the integration of migrants into German society (Ohm, in press), as I discuss in the next section.

An Example of Cultural Neo-Colonialism

The relationship between local and global knowledge and the passage from the institutional context of the classroom to the real world of global communities of practice is a complex transdisciplinary issue. To explore this complexity I trace a concrete example of local/global knowledge transfer taken from Norton's literacy education research.

In 2009 Bonny Norton gave a plenary at the IATEFL conference in Cardiff (U.K.) that was subsequently published in B. Beaven *IATEFL 2009 Cardiff Conference Selections* (Canterbury, U.K.: IATEFL 2010) under the title "Identity, Literacy, and English Language Teaching." This plenary was then translated into German under the title "Identität, Literalität und das multilinguale Klassenzimmer" for a volume edited by Cornelia Rosebrock and Andrea Bertschi-Kaufmann, *Literalität erfassen: bildungspolitisch, kulturell, individuell* [*What is literacy? Educational, Cultural, and Individual* [perspectives], my trsl.], that appeared in Germany with the German publisher Beltz Juventa (Rosebrock & Bertschi-Kaufmann, 2013). In this article Norton reports on her work on English literacy practices in Uganda and she applies her signature concepts—*investment, imagined communities,* and *imagined identities,* borrowed from Bourdieu and Anderson respectively—to the teaching of English in Uganda. The original plenary, conceived for teachers of English, was retitled for a German readership by changing "English Language Teaching" to "Multilingual Classroom" and dropping any mention of English language teaching. Jessica Fischer, the German translator of Norton's English text, retained the first-person narrator of the original paper, but she also retained Norton's signature concepts untranslated within a matrix of German, even though the published translations of Bourdieu and Anderson into German were readily available. Norton writes in the German translation: "Das *investment* eines Lerners in eine *imagined community* setzt ein *investment* in eine *imagined identity* voraus und kann eine beachtliche Wirkung auf Literalität und Sprachentwicklung haben" (italics in the translation) [The investment of a learner in an imagined community presupposes an investment in an imagined identity and can have a remarkable effect on the development of language and literacy] (Norton, 2013b: 4). However, in their published German versions, Pierre Bourdieu's *investissement* is translated as Ger. *Investition* (Dirksmeier, 2009: 208), and Benedict Anderson's notion of imagined community is translated as *vorgestellte Gemeinschaft* (Anderson, 1993). All of this poses the question, why were the German terms not used to translate Norton's terms? Why were her English terms maintained?

One answer might be that, since Norton had put her own spin on those terms, they no longer had the meanings intended by their original authors. But then, why refer to Bourdieu and Anderson at all? Why did the Norton terms not get translated? I would like to argue that, by retaining Norton's English terms without translating them into German, the translator reinforced the prestige of North American literacy research as the lingua franca of global social science with universal validity. This kind of neo-colonialism is subtle and is promoted with the best of intentions. Indeed, it is part of what Brian Street called "the hidden features of [English] academic writing": "Hidden features of academic writing establish the fiction of a single, globalised society in which social processes and change are comparable in all locations, and may be understood from a single, bird's eye perspective." (Street, 2009: 1). The German translator gave this article the enhanced prestige of English terms—one (Bourdieu) from the French original in an English translation, the other (Anderson) in the English original—from two prominent scholars with high disciplinary pedigrees. The English concepts mediated subtly but hegemonically Norton's ideas now presented in German for a German readership eager to adopt the findings of North American literacy research and apply them to the teaching of German literacy (now called *Literalität*) at German schools, in particular to teach German or *Deutsch als Fremd/Zweitsprache* to migrants and refugees. The fact that these refugees might come from (among other places) Uganda is one of the ironies of globalization. Refugees from Uganda might now acquire FL literacy skills in German according to educational principles developed by Bonny Norton for the teaching of English literacy in Canada. These principles are not only academic but claim to have applications in the real world.

But the real world of German literacy education has not been a blank slate. Germany has a long tradition of an eminently literate educational system, built on an age-old national script culture or *Schriftkultur* (Ohm, in press) that goes back to Luther's translation of the Bible into German in the sixteenth century and to the Lutheran respect for reader autonomy in its interpretation. It is also steeped in the eighteenth-century Humboldtian humanistic ideal of *Bildung* (education) as development of the personality, moral and political awareness, imagination, and tolerance. This tradition is still alive and well in the educational efforts to integrate the thousands of migrants that Germany has taken in in recent years, even though such an integration is raising soul-searching debates in Germany about the best way to integrate these migrants both into the national community and into the global economy.

German educators have historically been called upon to teach immigrants the educated High German written culture that will gain them respectability in German society. This is the literate use of German that is taught by the German Federal Ministry of Foreign Affairs through the Goethe institutes in Germany and around the world. This is the kind of literacy education that teaches not only how to read and write, but how to respect German law and institutions and how to abide by the cultural value of *Bildung* (literate education) in German society.[1] Up to now, such a literate education did not use the term "literacy." In fact, the field of literacy research was so unknown among German-speaking educators that the Rosebrock and Bertschi-Kaufmann (2013) edited volume had to have the following explanation on its back cover:

> Mit dem Begriff "Literacy" werden nicht nur die Fähigkeiten des Lesens und Schreibens bezeichnet, sondern auch Text- und Sinnverständnis, Erfahrungen mit der Lese- und Erzählkultur der jeweiligen Gesellschaft, Vertrautheit mit Literatur und anderen schriftbezogenen Medien (inkl. Internet) sowie Kompetenzen im Umgang mit der Schriftsprache. Literalität ist das zentrale Medium der Kommunikation. In Diskussion sind nicht nur die Defizite, sondern auch die Vielfalt der Praktiken, mit denen Schrift und Medien genutzt werden. Ethnographie, Lesesozialisationsforschung und Psychologie bemühen sich darum, sowohl die individuelle Entwicklungen als auch den sozial geprägten Gebrauch von Schrift zu erfassen."
>
> [The notion of "literacy" refers not only to the ability to read and write, but also to understanding the meaning of texts, experiencing the reading and narrative culture of a given society, being familiar with its literature and other written media (including the internet) as well as competence in dealing with the written language. Literacy is the central medium of communication. It has to do not only with the deficits, but also with the diversity of practices that use writing and the media. Ethnography, reading socialization research and psychology attempt to understand individual literacy development but also the use of written language in society. (my translation)]

The new kind of literacy promoted by scholars such as Norton is now calling on immigrants to "invest" in the German language and to claim the "right to speak" and participate in "imagined communities" in that language. But it is not clear which imagined community Norton-in-translation is encouraging them to participate in: a global community of various media users that hardly uses academic German, but instead vernacular varieties permeated with English as a lingua franca, or German society, with its German cultural values and traditions, including the *gebildetes Deutsch* ("academic" German) of German FL educators.

This example is but one illustration of the complex cultural influence of SLA research from the Anglo-American "center" to the global "periphery." Such influence is insidious and, as shown, it is not the work of a single individual. Nor is it only detrimental to local practices; it also brings in new ideas. Decolonizing foreign language education research would require a collective effort to question notions taken from one language into another, reconstruct their historical meanings, and engage with other theories produced elsewhere without judging them less progressive, less relevant, or less important than those produced in the Anglo-American center.

Decolonizing Foreign Language Education: An Exercise in Cultural Translation

The move to borrow notions from other disciplines abstracted from their original historical context and resignify them to promote a different educational and political agenda is precisely what Said and others have called "colonial practices"—practices that extract local resources, transplant them to the metropole, and reship them to the global market as a theoretical brand that accrues a profit of distinction for the colonizer. The colonized in turn are often eager to engage, critically or uncritically, with these linguistically engineered resources. For instance, in the example above, well-respected German and Swiss scholars such as Cornelia Rosebrock and Andrea Bertschi-Kaufmann, writing in German, include in their book the work of American, British, and Canadian literacy scholars such as Catherine Snow, Brian Street, and Bonny Norton, in order to engage in critical dialogue with a conception of literacy that might even go against the *Bildungstradition* of their own country. Theirs is a good example of an effort to decolonize both the class-biased *Bildungsideal* and the Anglo-American colonial imports. In their introductory chapter, Bertschi-Kaufmann and Rosebrock (2013) capture the essence of the debate going on in Germany:

> Man darf aber fragen, wessen Schriftgebrauch und wessen Vorstellung von Schriftgebrauch in das Konzept Literalität aufgenommen werden soll: der konventionell-normativ, am Bildungsideal einer sozialen Gruppe (der bildungsbürgerlichen) orientierte Begriff, oder eine auf Alltagsfunktionalität und soziale Anschlussfähigkeit ausgerichtete und in diesem Sinne ihrerseits normative Vorstellung (sensu PISA und messtechnisch geprägt), oder jene sich mit der Beobachtung von Praktiken, von Funktionen und Funktionalisierungen in sozialen Kontexten und im Laufe individueller Schriftentwicklungen herausbildende Vorstellung. Diese dritte Art, Literalität zu fassen ist stark situativ orientiert, gebunden also an die literalen Situationen, die in ethnographischer Perspektive ausgeleuchtet werden und in anderer Weise in die Diskussion eingebracht werden als dies zum Beispiel für Ergebnisse literalitätsbezogener Leistungsmessung der Fall ist.
>
> *(9)*

> [We may ask whose written language use and whose concept of written language use should be included in the concept of literacy: the conventional/normative concept, oriented toward the educational ideal of one social group (the educated middle class), or a concept oriented toward everyday functionality and socialization and in this sense also normative (according to PISA and its requirement of measurable outcomes), or a concept that focuses on the observation of practices, functions, and functionalizing processes in social contexts and in the course of individual literacy development. This

> third way of conceiving literacy is strongly situational, associated with literacy situations that are illuminated through an ethnographic approach and are discussed differently from the way literacy education outcomes are usually assessed.
>
> *(my translation)]*

By juxtaposing in this edited volume the voices of twenty-one German and Swiss literacy scholars and six scholars from the U.K., U.S., and Canada, the editors lay out the stakes for the debate about the future of *Bildung,* or literacy education in Germany. Since *Bildung* is also what is at stake in German foreign language education, including the teaching of German as a second language to immigrants, those stakes could be formulated as follows: how much of FL education must be assessed according to normative forms of measurement? To what extent must the goals of FL education be functional? To what extent is upward mobility linked to the values of the educated middle class? And, finally, what does "integration" mean for Germany with regard to the enormous influx of migrants and refugees it has taken in from various parts of the world? The Rosebrock and Bertschi-Kaufmann volume is a response to Allan Luke's question regarding Anglo-American neocolonial educational practices.

> What kinds of educational and linguistic practice, what kinds of text and discourse, and what kinds of educated subject can and should be constructed to forge new critical and contingent relationship with globalizing economies and mass cultures—long after the departure of colonial masters, and well after decades of reconstruction of postcolonial curricula and educational infrastructures?
>
> *(Luke, 2005: xviii)*

The volume offers a good example of the way global theories can be put into dialogue with the real world of local educational practice and historical national continuity. However, such a dialogue is conducted here in German for a German readership that knows English and is able to consult the many references to Anglo-American literacy and applied linguistics theory included in the volume. Such a dialogue is not possible for most Anglo-American scholars who are not able to read German literacy theory in the original, nor willing to engage with it if translated into English because they don't feel that the German *Bildungsdebatte* is relevant to their own concerns. Decolonizing FL literacy theory would entail engaging in the difficult two-way bilingual dialogue necessary to decenter Anglo-American theory and open it up to different epistemological perspectives. One could imagine, for example, a dialogue between Anglo-American and German FL educators who know both contexts and who could engage in what Bhabha called "cultural translation" (1994/2004), a process of conceiving of one cultural phenomenon—for example, FL education in the United States—in terms of another—for example, FL education in Germany. Such a translation, which includes also linguistic translation, can decolonize both global and local colonial practices. The challenge is how can we get North American educators to engage enough with German educational theory that they can respond to German FL educational publications in English language journals?[2] How can we get German educators, who all know English, to engage enough with North American educational theory that they respond critically to English language publications, both in English and in German language journals? How can we foster the co-authorship of papers by North American and German scholars who share common interests but come from different cultural and scientific traditions? And, finally, how can we encourage German teachers, say, in the United States to be interested not only in topics of German literature, but in the current debates regarding FL education policies and their relevance to FL education in the United States?

Conclusion

The concept of decolonization has been rendered inordinately more complex by globalization. There are no longer any clear-cut distinctions between colonizers and colonized, but various spheres of influence that require critical dialogue and political engagement. In the field of FL education, where language plays an intrinsic and central role, and where the stakes are both political and ethical, there is a real risk that FL education research gets politicized and becomes prey to the global interests of English-speaking countries. Those interests that were mostly national in nature at the time of the Perkins report in the 1980s have become more and more global as economic deregulation has spread at a brisk pace in the last three decades. The example of the debates going on in Germany about whose language and literacy education should be provided to the thousands of migrants seeking integration in German society offers a glimpse of the complex efforts to decolonize FL education from both the colonial practices of class-based national institutions and the global neo-colonial practices of individual entrepreneurship. Decolonizing FL education requires more than ever the ethical and political capacity to engage in dialogue with speakers from other educational cultures *on their own terms*, and the willingness to enter the slow and difficult process of linguistic and cultural translation. The increased presence of applied linguists within foreign language departments should be a first step toward initiating such dialogues.

Notes

1 *Bildung*, which means "formation," is the term used to denote a general humanistic education based on the mastery of literate language (both academic and non-academic) and a knowledge of the classics of German literature. It is associated with the education received by children of the middle class (*Bildungsbürgertum*). *Literalität*, by contrast, is the translation of the English concept "literacy," seen as a much more functionally oriented ability to read, understand, and use various texts in various media in everyday life.

2 The belief that one can conduct such a dialogue exclusively in English is seen by many as counterproductive as it runs the risk of assimilating all cultures into one monolingual global culture. In his discussion of cultural translation, Anthony Pym (2010: 161) reminds us that "the risk of reduction is perhaps inherent in all theorizing." And yet real decolonization depends on our ability to rethink FL education in the United States in light of the German concept of *Bildung* now recast into our English vocabulary, and the Germans' ability to rethink FL education in Germany in light of the English concept of literacy now recast into the German *Literalität*. The heated debates currently going on in Germany show how difficult such a dialogue can be, even when both sides share the same code.

References

American Council for the Teaching of Foreign Languages (ACTFL). 2014. GlobalCompetencePositionStatement0814.pdf http://www.actfl.org/news/position-statements/global-competence-position-statement#sthash.tzx4zMjH.dpuf. *Approved by the ACTFL Board of Directors, Monday, August 25, 2014.*

Anderson, B. 1983. *Imagined Communities. Reflections on the origins and spread of nationalism.* London: Verso.

Anderson, B. 1993 *Die Erfindung der Nation: zur Karriere eines erfolgreichen Konzepts.* Frankfurt a.M: Campus Verlag.

Antier, E. 2011. Formation à l'éthique professionnelle des enseignants de langue-culture: constats et perspectives. *Recherche et pratiques pédagogiques en langues de spécialité – Cahiers de l'APLIUT,* vol. 30, no. 3: 13–29.

Bertschi-Kaufmann, A. & Rosebrock, C. 2013. Literalität erfassen: bildungspolitisch, kulturell, individuell. In C. Rosebrock & A. Bertschi-Kaufmann (Eds.), *Literalität erfassen: bildungspolitisch, kulturell, individuell* (pp.7–12). Weinheim & Basel: Beltz Juventa.

Bhabha, H. 1994/2004. *The location of culture.* London: Routledge.

Block, D. 2003. *The social turn in second language acquisition.* Edinburgh: Edinburgh U. Press.

Bourdieu, P. 1991. *Language and symbolic power.* Cambridge, UK: Cambridge U. Press.

Byram, M. 1997. *Teaching and assessing intercultural communicative competence.* Clevedon, UK: Multilingual Matters.

Byram, M. 2008. *From foreign language education to education for intercultural citizenship.* Clevedon, UK: Multilingual Matters.

Canagarajah, S. 2005. Accommodating tensions in language-in-education policies: An afterword. In A. M. Y. Lin & P. W. Martin (Eds.), *Decolonisation, globalization. Language-in-Education policy and practice* (pp. 194–201). Clevedon, UK: Multilingual Matters.

Canagarajah, S. 2013. *Translingual practice.* London: Routledge.

Cenoz & Gorter, D (Eds.) 2015. *Multilingual education. Between language learning and translanguaging.* Cambridge: Cambridge U. Press.

Dirksmeier, P. 2009. Die Theorie der Praxis von Pierre Bourdieu. In *Urbanität als Habitus,* p. 208. Bielefeld: Transcript Verlag.

Douglas Fir Group. 2016. A transdisciplinary framework for SLA in a multilingual world. *Modern Language Journal* 100, Supplement 19–47.

Ellis, L. 2015. Challenges within the ecology of multilingual interactions in Aboriginal cultural tourism in Central Australia. In U. Jessner & C. Kramsch, *The multilingual challenge* (pp.323–346). Berlin: Mouton de Gruyter.

García, O. 2009. *Bilingual education in the 21st century: A global perspective.* Chichester, UK: Wiley Blackwell.

García, O. & Leiva, C. 2014. Theorizing and enacting translanguaging for social justice. In A. Blackledge & A. Creese (Eds.), *Heteroglossia as practice and pedagogy* (pp. 199–216). Dordrecht, NL: Springer.

García, O. & Li Wei. 2014. *Translanguaging: Language, bilingualism and education.* London: Palgrave Macmillan.

Heller M. & Duchêne, A. 2012. *Language in late capitalism: Pride and profit.* London: Routledge.

Hellmich, E. 2017. *Language learning and technology in and for a global world.* Unpubl. Ph.D. dissertation. UC Berkeley.

Hinton, L. 1994. *Flutes of Fire. Essays on California Indian languages.* Berkeley, CA: Heyday Books.

Holquist, M. 2007. The humanities at work in the world. *MLA Newsletter,* Winter issue (pp. 3–4). New York: Modern Language Association.

Horn, S. 2016. ExxonMobil CEO Rex Tillerson has deep ties to Russia as well. *Reader Supported News* 11 Dec. 2016.

Kern, R. 2000. *Literacy and language teaching.* Oxford: Oxford U. Press.

Kramsch, C. 2000. Second language acquisition, applied linguistics, and the teaching of foreign languages. *The Modern Language Journal* 84, iii (2000), 311–326.

Kramsch, C. 2005. Post 9/11: Foreign languages between knowledge and power. *Applied Linguistics* 26:4, 545–567.

Kramsch, C. 2013. Afterword. In B. Norton, *Identity and Language Learning. Extending the conversation* (2nd edition) (pp.192–201). Clevedon, UK: Multilingual Matters.

Kramsch, C. 2014. Teaching foreign languages in an era of globalization. *Modern Language Journal* 98:1, 296–311.

Kramsch, C. & Huffmaster, M. 2015. Multilingual practices in foreign language study. In J. Cenoz. & D. Gorter (Eds.), *Multilingual Education. Between language learning and translanguaging.* (pp.114–136). Cambridge: Cambridge U. Press.

Kramsch, C. & Narcy-Combes, J. P. 2017. From social tasks to language development: Coping with historicity and subjectivity. In M. J. Ahmadian & M. Del Pilar García Mayo (Eds.), *Recent perspectives on task-based language learning and teaching.* Berlin: De Gruyter Mouton.

Lantolf, J. & Thorne, S. 2006. *Sociocultural theory and the genesis of second language development.* Oxford: Oxford U. Press.

Luke, A. 2005. Foreword: On the possibilities of a post-postcolonial language education. In A. M. Y. Lin & P. W. Martin (Eds.), *Decolonisation, globalization. Language-in-Education policy and practice* (pp.xiv–xix). Clevedon, UK: Multilingual Matters.

Magnan, S. S., Murphy, D. & Sahakyan, N. 2014. Goals of collegiate learners and the Standards of Foreign Language Learning. *Modern Language Journal* 98, Supplement.

Makoni, S. & Pennycook, A. 2007. *Disinventing and reconstituting languages.* Clevedon, UK: Multilingual Matters.

May, S. (Ed.) 2011. *The multilingual turn. Implications for SLA, TESOL and Bilingual Education.* London: Routledge.

Mignolo, W. D. 2002. The geopolitics of knowledge and the colonial difference. *South Atlantic Quarterly* 101:1, Winter issue, 57–96.

MLA AdHoc Committee on Foreign Languages 2007. Foreign language and higher education: New structures for a changed world. *Profession 2007,* 234–45.

National Commission on Excellence in Education. 1983. *A Nation at Risk: The Imperative for Educational Reform.* Washington, DC: U.S. Dept. of Education.

National Standards in Foreign Language Education Project. 2006. *Standards for Foreign Language Learning. Preparing for the 21st century*. Yonkers, NY: American Council for the Teaching of Foreign Languages.

Norton, B. 2013a. *Identity and language learning. Extending the conversation* (2nd edition). Clevedon, UK: Multilingual Matters.

Norton, B. 2013b. Literalität und Mehrsprachigkeit im Unterricht. In C. Rosebrock & A. Bertschi-Kaufmann (Hrsg.) *Literalität erfassen: bildungspolitisch, kulturell, individuell* (pp.123–134). Weinheim und Basel: Beltz Juventa.

Ohm, U. In press. Literater Sprachausbau im Uebergang Schule-Beruf. In A. Daase, U. Ohm & M. Mertens (Eds.), *Interkulturelle und sprachliche Bildung im mehrsprachigen Ubergangsbereich*. Muenster: Waxmann.

Pavlenko, A. & Lantolf, J. 2000. Second language learning as participation and the (re) construction of selves. In J. Lantolf (Ed.), *Sociocultural Theory and Second Language learning*. Oxford: Oxford U. Press.

Pavlenko, A. & Norton, B. 2007. Imagined communities, identity, and English language teaching. In J. Cummins & C. Davison (Eds.), *International handbook of English language teaching* (pp.669–680). New York: Springer.

President's Commission on Foreign Languages and International Studies. 1980. Strength through wisdom: A critique of U.S. capability: A report to the President, Nov. 1979. *Modern Language Journal* 64:1, 9–57.

Pym, A. 2010. *Exploring translation theories*. Chapter 8. Cultural translation (pp.143–164). London: Routledge.

Ricento, T. (Ed.) 2000. *Ideology, politics, and language policies: Focus on English*. Amsterdam: John Benjamins.

Rosebrock, C. & Bertschi-Kaufmann, A. (Eds.) 2013. *Literalität erfassen: bildungspolitisch, kulturell, individuell*. Weinheim & Basel: Beltz Juventa.

Said, E. 1993. *Culture and imperialism*. New York: Vintage.

Scollon, R. 2004 Teaching language and culture as hegemonic practice. *Modern Language Journal* 88:2, 271–274.

Street, B. 2009. "Hidden" Features of Academic Paper Writing. *Working Papers in Educational Linguistics (WPEL)*, 24:1, 1.

Suskind, R. 2016. Faith, certainty and the presidency of George W. Bush. *New York Times Magazine*. Oct. 17.

Trim, J. 2012. "The Common European Framework of Reference: Learning, Teaching, Assessment." In M. Byram & L. Parmenter (Eds.), *The Common European Framework of Reference – The Globalisation of Language Education Policy* (pp. 13–34). Bristol, UK: Multilingual Matters, Languages for Intercultural Communication and Education series.

Vinall, K. 2012. "Un legado historico?" Symbolic competence and the construction of multiple histories. *L2 Journal* 4, 102–123.

Weedon, C. 1987. *Feminist practice and poststructuralist theory*. Oxford, UK: Blackwell.

3

TIME FOR A PARADIGM SHIFT IN U.S. FOREIGN LANGUAGE EDUCATION?

Revisiting Rationales, Evidence, and Outcomes

Timothy Reagan and Terry A. Osborn***

*UNIVERSITY OF MAINE; **UNIVERSITY OF SOUTH FLORIDA

The learning and teaching of foreign languages[1] in the United States in the contemporary 'age of globalization' is a fascinating, as well as frustrating, phenomenon. The fascination comes from the development of thoughtful and reflective national standards tied to curricula, teaching methodologies, and teaching and learning materials, not to mention the calls for the inclusion of constructivist approaches to learning and teaching in foreign language education, while the frustration emerges from the challenges and barriers that make the undertaking so unsuccessful so much of the time, as Jacques Barzun noted more than half a century ago. In addition, the growing concern with and commitment to critical pedagogical approaches in foreign language education, that have their origins in comparable work in TESOL[2] and other disciplinary areas,[3] have led to calls for radical rethinking of the nature and purpose of foreign language education in the United States (see Byram, 2008; Guilherme, 2002; Kumaravadivelu, 1994; Reagan, 2002, 2005, 2009, 2012, 2016; Reagan & Osborn, 1998, 2002; Osborn, 2000, 2006; Osborn & Reagan, 1998). In short, we are witnessing a period of potentially dramatic change in our field.

In this chapter we will begin by presenting what we take to be the traditional and dominant perspectives on the strengths and weaknesses of contemporary foreign language education, and then indicate why we believe these perspectives are inadequate. We will then explore the related concepts of globalization, neocolonialism, and 'McCommunication' with particular focus on how they impact foreign language teaching and learning in the U.S. context, before moving on to discuss the case, in Thomas Kuhn's (1962) words, for a 'paradigm shift' in foreign language education in the United States. Finally we will attempt to outline the conceptual framework of a new paradigm for the learning and teaching of foreign languages, and how this conceptual framework could be implemented in practice both at the classroom level and in university programs engaged in the preparation of future foreign language educators.

The Traditional Perspective

Foreign language education programs in the United States present us with something of a paradox. On the one hand, we would argue that the need for more individuals who are able to function fluently in languages other than English – for reasons of business, diplomacy, national security, cultural understanding, and so on – is greater than it has even been. The national standards for foreign language learning produced by the American Council on the Teaching of Foreign Languages (the *Standards for Foreign Language Learning: Preparing for the 21st century* and the *World-Readiness Standards for Language Learning*) are among the best of the various disciplinary standards documents produced in recent years (National Standards in Foreign Language Education Project, 1996, 1999, 2006).[4] Textbooks and other teaching materials, especially for the more commonly taught languages (especially French and Spanish), are qualitatively superior to any that have existed before, and for the most part create excellent opportunities for the inclusion of appropriate technology in the language learning classroom, as well as being explicitly tied to and integrating the *ACTFL Standards*. And last, if not universally true, for the most part foreign language educators are better prepared as language educators than at any time in our history.

At the same time there is a growing shortage of well-qualified foreign language teachers (U.S. Department of Education, 2016), budgetary limitations increasingly threaten foreign language education programs (especially at the elementary and middle school levels) (Skorton & Altschuler, 2012), student enrollments in foreign languages at all levels are declining, sometimes precipitously (Pufahl & Rhodes, 2011), the percentage of universities that require foreign language study continues to decline (Skorton & Altschuler, 2012), offerings in many less common languages (including, for instance, Arabic, Hebrew, Japanese, and Russian) are being reduced or eliminated altogether (Skorton & Altschuler, 2012), and program articulation remains a major concern (see Pufahl & Rhodes, 2011, p. 267). At the K-12 level, only 18.5 percent of students in the United States study a foreign language – and even in Wisconsin, the state with the highest percentage of students enrolled in a foreign language course, only slightly more than 30 percent of all students study a language other than English (Phillips & Abbott, 2011). Finally, although roughly 18 percent of the U.S. population report speaking a second language (in comparison to 26 percent of Canadians and 54 percent of Europeans), less than 1 percent of American adults are proficient in the language that they studied in a U.S. classroom (Friedman, 2015).

Adding to this paradoxical situation are some of the apparent contradictions in the picture. For example, it is true that a near-record number of students in universities are studying a foreign language, but it is also true that in recent years the number has been declining – by 110,000 places between 2009 and 2013 (Friedman, 2015). Further, although the raw number of students in higher education

State	*Percentage of Students Enrolled in Foreign Language Courses*	*Number of Students Enrolled in Foreign Language Courses*	*Total Student Enrollment*
Alabama	7.38%	54,557	739,327
Alaska	22.46%	29,056	129,350
Arizona	10.76%	121,925	1,132,808
Arkansas	11.58%	53,930	465,631
California	14.63%	917,074	6,268,293
Colorado	15.54%	120,639	776,339
Connecticut	18.41%	102,431	556,370
Delaware	20.16%	24,872	123,364
Florida	17.90%	466,414	2,605,738
Georgia	18.56%	298,795	1,609,681
Hawai'i	13.08%	20,885	159,719
Idaho	11.21%	30,164	269,165
Illinois	15.28%	311,038	2,034,962
Indiana	15.46%	160,123	1,035,442
Iowa	16.67%	78,779	472,625
Kansas	16.01%	77,684	485,161
Kentucky	17.13%	115,031	671,466
Louisiana	15.80%	103,405	654,407
Maine	26.78%	50,200	187,450
Maryland	25.72%	210,539	818,521
Massachusetts	23.73%	222,173	936,328
Michigan	14.80%	243,595	1,645,742
Minnesota	20.17%	166,346	824,783
Mississippi	8.49%	40,917	482,004
Missouri	19.60%	175,103	893,562
Montana	14.06%	20,165	143,405
Nebraska	25.88%	72,637	280,697
Nevada	9.34%	40,166	429,954
New Hampshire	14.70%	29,079	197,856
New Jersey	27.58%	350,622	1,271,481
New Mexico	17.71%	57,313	323,688
New York	29.59%	771,767	2,608,408
North Carolina	22.36%	325,393	1,455,021
North Dakota	26.88%	25,688	95,549
Ohio	17.97%	349,017	1,941,875
Oklahoma	15.94%	96,115	602,995
Oregon	14.62%	82,395	563,392
Pennsylvania	22.61%	404,185	1,787,501
Rhode Island	16.24%	23,824	146,701

FIGURE 3.1 Number and Percentage of K-12 Students Enrolled in Foreign Language Courses

State	*Percentage of Students Enrolled in Foreign Language Courses*	*Number of Students Enrolled in Foreign Language Courses*	*Total Student Enrollment*
South Carolina	24.86%	174,247	700,824
South Dakota	24.23%	29,338	121,089
Tennessee	11.46%	107,931	941,866
Texas	20.48%	912,054	4,453,772
Utah	15.94%	85,711	537,653
Vermont	17.37%	15,540	89,482
Virginia	17.93%	215,651	1,202,933
Washington	18.22%	186,153	1,021,834
West Virginia	21.75%	58,630	269,513
Wisconsin	30.66%	256,593	836,860
Wyoming	17.28%	14,788	85,578
Washington, DC	27.29%	6,524	23,904
National Mean	**18.51%**		
TOTAL		**8,907,201**	**48,112,069**

FIGURE 3.1 Continued

studying a foreign language may appear to be impressive, in fact it represents only 7 percent of all university students (Friedman, 2015). Indeed, according to a 2013 survey conducted by the Modern Language Association, foreign language course enrollments in two- and four-year institutions declined between 2009 and 2015 by some 6.7 percent (Modern Language Association, 2013). Finally, in considering the percentage of Americans proficient in a foreign language, the difference between the 18 percent and the 1 percent largely comes from counting those whose native language is other than English.

In 2002, writing about foreign language education in the K-12 context, we suggested that:

> There are a large number of constraints in the public schools that tend to work against the effectiveness of contemporary foreign language education programs in the United States . . . Among these constraints are the amount of time actually devoted to foreign language teaching and learning, the lack of significant extracurricular institutional support for foreign language learning, institutional and individual biases with respect to which languages are offered and who takes which language, the public justifications for foreign language education, the articulated goals of foreign language education, and finally, what might be termed the social expectation of failure with respect to the learning of languages other than English in the U.S. context.
>
> *(Reagan & Osborn, 2002, pp. 2–3)*

Language	*Change 2009–2015*	*2013 Enrollments*
Spanish	-8.2%	790,756
French	-8.1%	197,757
ASL	+19.1%	109,577
German	-9.3%	86,700
Italian	-11.3%	71,285
Japanese	-7.8%	66,740
Chinese*	+2.0%	61,055
Arabic	-7.5%	32,286
Latin	-16.2%	27,192
Russian	-17.9%	21,962
Ancient Greek	-35.5%	12,917
Biblical Hebrew	-8.7%	12,551
Portuguese	+10.1%	12,415
Korean	+44.7%	12,229
Modern Hebrew	-19.4%	6,698
Other Languages	-2.6%	40,059
TOTAL	-6.7%	1,562,176

**Includes both Cantonese and Mandarin.*

FIGURE 3.2 Percentage Change in Foreign Language Enrollments at the Tertiary Level, 2009-2015

Foreign language educators in higher education faced, and continue to face, comparable challenges. Indeed, not only has the situation not changed in either K-12 or higher education in the United States, but more importantly, we would suggest, the most common proposals and efforts to address the situation have not changed. For instance, in 2013 the American Academy of Arts and Sciences released a report calling on increased foreign language learning in the United States (see Flaherty, 2015). The arguments focused entirely on increasing linguistic proficiency in foreign languages, and offered five major justifications for why such a goal was worth pursuing. The justifications will sound very familiar to any U.S. foreign language educator:

- *National security.* 'The message [is] clear: effective communication is the basis of international cooperation, and a strong national defense depends on our ability to understand our adversaries as well as our friends.'
- *Commercial value.* 'Regarding business, nearly 30 percent of executives say they've missed out on opportunities over a lack of on-staff language skills . . . some 40 percent said they'd failed to reach their international potential due to language barriers.'
- *Vocational value.* 'As an employee of one of the world's largest internet companies, [one person indicated that his] language skills – including proficiency in Mandarin Chinese – are an essential component of my job.'

- *As a 'social imperative.'* 'Growing numbers of American citizens speak languages other than English, and in some major urban areas, as many as half of all residents speak a non-English language at home . . . But all too often, their access to vital services, including health care, and even their ability to exercise simple rights are limited not only by their inability to communicate in English, but also by service providers' inability to speak or secure the help of those who speak other languages.'
- *Cognitive benefits.* 'Foreign language study has numerous cognitive benefits for children and adults, and has been linked to higher academic achievement in other disciplines.'

To this one might of course add such justifications as the enrichment or 'broadening' value of learning a language other than one's own, the personal satisfaction that such an accomplishment might provide, and the doors that proficiency in another language can open with respect to personal relationships, travel, and so on, but these arguments, like those presented in the American Academy of Arts and Sciences report,[5] have thus far failed to inspire more successful language learning in the United States, and are likely to continue to fail to do so. The fundamental problem, as we have argued elsewhere, is that most Anglo-Americans[6] in the United States – students, parents, teachers of other subjects, and even politicians and policy-makers – really do not believe any of these claims, and they do not believe them because they are, in large part, neither true nor compelling. They are also, perhaps as compellingly, very much grounded in a neoliberal agenda, which is deeply problematic as well for anyone concerned with critical pedagogy (see Block, Gray & Holborow, 2012; Holborow, 2015; Reagan & Osborn, in press), a point that we will discuss later in this chapter.

As two individuals who have devoted their lives to the learning and teaching of languages, and who deeply believe in the value of such activities, how can we dismiss such justifications for language learning so easily? The answer is that these rationales have not worked to promote language study in the past, and they are not likely to do so in the future. Let us make this case by examining each of the proposed justifications in turn, pointing out the weaknesses and false assumptions that are embedded in each.

The national security justification, on its face, makes a certain amount of sense. The world is a complex and often dangerous place, and as a nation we *do* need individuals with specific foreign language skills. However, there is a significant mismatch between the languages that are most important for us with respect to national security and those which are most often available for students to study. For instance, we promote some languages through the U.S. State Department's 'Critical Language Scholarship Program', which is part of the National Security Language Initiative. At the present time this program includes some fourteen 'critical languages', including Arabic, Azerbaijani, Bengali, Chinese, Hindi, Indonesian, Japanese, Korean, Persian, Punjabi, Russian, Swahili, Turkish, and Urdu.

Category of Difficulty	*Duration of Instruction Required**	*Class Hours Needed*	*Languages*
I	26 weeks	575–600	French, Italian, Portuguese, Spanish,
II	34 weeks	900	German, Indonesian
III	48 weeks	1,100	Dari/Persian Farsi, Hebrew, Hindi, Russian, Serbian/Croatian, Tagalog, Thai, Turkish, Uzbek, Urdu
IV	64 weeks	2,200	Arabic, Cantonese, Japanese, Korean, Mandarin, Pashto

**To achieve Level 3 General Professional Proficiency in Speaking and Reading for the average native English speaker.*

FIGURE 3.3 The U.S. Defense Language Institute Language Learning Difficulty Scale

These languages are most often far more difficult to acquire than French or Spanish, and the development of real proficiency in them requires far more time and commitment than the vast majority of students are willing to dedicate to the task (see Figure 3.3). There is a serious shortage of qualified teachers for virtually all of these languages, not to mention a dearth of appropriate textbooks and teaching materials. In spite of their importance, these languages are rarely offered in either K-12 or higher education settings, and relatively small numbers of students study them (see Figures 3.4 and 3.5). Further, for all of these languages we already have a native speaker population in our own country, members of which will almost always be both linguistically and culturally more competent than a second language user is likely to become. And last, many of us who are proficient in one of these languages (either as a native speaker or as a fluent second language user) often find ourselves to be the subject of a degree of suspicion, as if our competence in the 'language of the enemy' suggests a lack of patriotism on our part (see Pavlenko, 2010).

The commercial and vocational justifications for language study are closely related and intertwined. Both are basically concerned with the economic value of language competence; the commercial justification focuses on the needs of corporations and businesses to have employees with language skills, while the vocational justification is concerned with the benefits of language proficiency to the individual in the job market. There are several problems with such a rationale for language study in the U.S. context. First, of course, is the fact that the commercial needs for language competence can be met far more easily by utilizing bilingual native speakers of the necessary language as translators and interpreters – employees whose expertise is in language (i.e., 'language brokers'), rather than who have the needed commercial expertise combined with the linguistic competence. Indeed, it

Language	*1997*		
	Elementary	*Middle School*	*Secondary*
Spanish	80	83	99
French	27	50	77
German	7	10	35
Latin	1	6	28
Japanese	2	3	11
Italian	1	2	4
Russian	1	1	5
American Sign Language	3	.4	3
Chinese*	1	.1	2
Greek	–	–	1
Hebrew	–	–	.2
Portuguese	–	–	.2
Tlingit	–	–	.1
Hawai'ian	.3	–	.1
Yagui	.2	–	–
Kutenai	.1	–	–
Arabic	<.1	–	.1
***Languages for Native*Speakers**			
Spanish	13	10	10
Chinese*	1	.2	1
Cherokee	.3	–	–
French	.3	.3	.3
Russian	.3		
Tewa	.1		
Korean	1		
Polish		–	.4
Navajo		.3	–

**Includes both Cantonese and Mandarin.*

FIGURE 3.4 Percentage of Foreign Language Programs in Public Schools, By Language
Based on Rhodes & Branaman (1997)

is rarely the case that it is language skills that are the *primary* requirement for either hiring an employee or for getting a particular job. Rather, one needs other knowledge and skills, and proficiency in a foreign language is, *if* the language is an appropriate one and *if* the individual is truly proficient in a business context, an added benefit in the job market. Relatively few jobs in the United States actually require foreign language competence, unlike the situation in most other parts of the world. The overwhelming majority of foreign language students in the United States do not ever develop either sufficient proficiency in another language or the

Critical Language	*2009 Enrollments*	*2013 Enrollments*
Arabic	34,908	32,286
Azerbaijani	2	-
Bengali	98	64
Chinese*	59,876	61,055
Hindi	2,173	1,800
Indonesian	296	289
Japanese	72,359	66,740
Korean	8,449	12,229
Persian (Dari, Farsi, Uzbek)	2,580	2,704
Punjabi	465	124
Russian	26,753	21,962
Swahili	2,505	2,002
Turkish	648	716
Urdu	330	349

**Includes both Cantonese and Mandarin.*

FIGURE 3.5 Post-Secondary Student Enrollments in Critical Languages
Based on the American Academy of Arts and Sciences (2016)

linguistic and cultural competence needed for the work domain, nor are most foreign language education programs really designed to provide such specialized competence. The challenge, of course, is that most businesspeople who are engaged in international business are much of the time more likely to speak English far better than even the most dedicated English speaker can manage with their language. As for the vocational justification for language study, many years ago Sylvia Porter argued that:

> With a language skill added to your other skills, you might double the chances of getting the job you want. There are openings for an auto mechanic who also speaks Arabic, an electronic radio expert who knows Japanese, a chef . . . who understands French . . . Language is, in fact, your hidden job insurance.
> *(Quoted in Jarvis, 1980, pp. 31–32)*

The basic problem with this argument is quite simply that it is not terribly credible for most Anglo-Americans. The United States is ideologically, if not empirically, profoundly monolingual, and relatively few Anglo-Americans honestly believe that foreign languages are really necessary for the marketplace. Claims about language skills being 'job insurance' are viewed with considerable suspicion in a society in which monolingualism is seen as normative.[7] When coupled with Richard Brecht's observation that most Anglo-Americans do not even believe that foreign language competence is really achievable, it is hardly surprising that the vocational rational for foreign language study has not been particularly successful.

A core element of the attitudes toward both English and foreign languages in the United States can be found in the widespread marginalization of foreign languages. A good place to begin an examination of the marginalization of foreign language education is with what Dell Hymes has identified as the six core assumptions about language generally in the U.S. He suggests that these core, and generally tacit, assumptions include the following:

- Everyone in the United States speaks only English, or should.
- Bilingualism is inherently unstable, probably injurious, and possibly unnatural.
- Foreign literary languages can be respectively studied, but not foreign languages in their domestic varieties (it is one thing to study the French spoken in Paris, another to study the French spoken in Louisiana).
- Most everyone else in the world is learning English anyway, and that, together with American military and economic power, makes it unnecessary to worry about knowing the language of a country in which one has business, bases, or hostages.
- Differences in language are essentially of two kinds, right and wrong.
- Verbal fluency and noticeable style are suspicious, except as entertainment (it's what you mean that counts).

(1996, pp. 84–85)

The argument that foreign language competence is necessary to help us, as a society, meet the needs of non-English speaking citizens (and non-citizens) in the United States is one that suggests a profound ignorance of American society on the part of the authors of the American Academy of Arts and Sciences report. To be sure, some people in our society are moved by such needs, but the more general response of Anglo-Americans to such a suggestion would be to point out that it would make far more sense to find ways to ensure that everyone in the country speaks English. This is a reflection of the ideological monolingualism of the society, as well as the hegemony of English in the United States and the marginalization of other languages, and is reminiscent of the attributed response to the idea of teaching children Spanish in Texas by the first female governor of the state, Miriam 'Ma' Ferguson, who is claimed to have said, while waving her Bible, 'If English was good enough for Jesus Christ, it's good enough for the children of Texas.' There is one interesting exception to the general rejection of learning languages to help others in the society who do not speak English, and that is the case of American Sign Language (ASL). Although not without some degree of controversy,[8] student enrollments in ASL continue to rise both in K-12 programs and in community college and university programs,[9] and while most students do not ever become proficient in ASL, the rationale for such study is, at least in part, the fact that the Deaf [10]face barriers in the learning of English that set them apart from other non-English speaking groups.

There are well-documented cognitive benefits to bilingualism, and especially to bilingualism developed in early childhood (see Adesope, Lavin, Thompson & Ungerleider, 2010; Barac & Bialystok, 2011). The extent to which such benefits accrue to later foreign language study is less clear, however. In addition to questions of the role of age of acquisition of second or additional languages, the benefits of bilingualism are associated with a high degree of bilingualism, so both how we define 'bilingualism' and the degree of fluency students have achieved is a very important factor in determining the cognitive benefits of bilingualism.

However, it should also be noted that while little research has been conducted dealing with the cognitive benefits of foreign language study in adulthood, there is one significant exception to this; as Antoniou, Gunasekera, and Wong have observed with respect to the elderly,

> there is evidence that cognitively stimulating activities protect against the adverse effects of cognitive decline. Similarly, bilingualism is also considered to be a safeguard. We propose that foreign language learning programs aimed at older populations are an optimal solution for building cognitive reserve because language learning engages an extensive brain network that is known to overlap with the regions negatively affected by the aging process.
>
> *(2013, p. 2689)*

To sum up, none of the more common justifications for supporting foreign language study in the United States ultimately passes the 'straight face' test. Given the normative monolingualism of U.S. society, the overwhelming failure of foreign language education programs at all levels to produce meaningful fluency in all but a tiny percentage of students, and the suspicions of individuals who are bilingual (and especially those who are bilingual in many of the 'critical languages') in our society, it seems to us that we have a 'truth in advertising' problem in making the case for the importance of foreign language education in the United States. As Dennis Baron noted, 'Anglo-Americans . . . will continue for the most part to resist learning other languages either in school or after school . . . or they will learn foreign languages imperfectly' (1990, p. 200). At root, the problem here is that we tend, in making the case for foreign language study, to conflate *foreign language study* with *bilingualism* – two radically different things in the U.S. context.

Globalization, Neo-Colonialism, and 'McCommunication'

The end of the colonial era, and of formal colonial relations, did not mean the end of western imperialism. Colonialism was replaced by neo-colonialism and neo-imperialism, which, although no longer formal and somewhat less blatant, nevertheless resulted in the continuing subjugation of peoples around the world. In essence, neo-colonialism refers to the efforts of European powers (including, for the purposes of this discussion, the United States as a 'neo-European' power) to continue to maintain influence in and even domination of former colonial areas (as well as other developing societies) through alternative means (see Altbach, 2014; Blanchard, 1996; Nagesh, 2000). Direct military and political control was replaced with indirect but still powerful economic and cultural control, manifested in capitalist relations and as part of the neoliberal globalization agenda. Key players in making neo-colonialism possible are multinational corporations (see Calvano, 2008), institutions such as the World Bank and the International Monetary Fund (see Broad, 1990; Nguyen, Elliott, Terlouw & Pilot, 2009; Wickens & Sandlin, 2007), and national development agencies such as USAID and the British Council.

In education, neo-colonialism is manifested in several important ways. Philip Altbach (1971), for example, has argued that it can be seen in the following:

- The education systems of most developing countries, on almost all levels, remain rooted in the administrative structures of the former colonial rulers . . . [and] the fact that the structure and organization of the schools reflect a foreign model necessarily has an impact on the nature of the education provided.
- The curriculum of the schools and colleges often reflects orientations of the former colonial rulers or of other advanced countries which provide assistance or are for some other reason powerful in the affairs of the given developing country. Textbooks are imported from advanced countries, and occasionally expatriate teachers can be found in the schools and particularly in the universities. Curriculum and other qualitative aspects of education have sometimes been severely neglected in developing countries because efforts have been concentrated on quantitative expansion.
- The language of the former colonial power remains the medium of instruction in some developing countries. This is important for the nature of the educational system, the values inculcated, and the availability of education to wide sections of the population.
- Foreign aid and technical assistance such as help in designing curriculum, provision of physical facilities and other educational materials have all had an impact on educational systems in developing countries.

One of the clearest manifestations of neo-colonialism is the process of globalization. Globalization is commonly defined as the process of international integration, involving economics, trade, products, culture, and ideas, and when understood in this way is a process that has been taking place for many centuries (see Acocella, 2005; Chaichian, 2014; Osterhammel & Petersson, 2005; Panitch & Gindin, 2012; von Braun & Diaz-Bonilla, 2007). In contemporary practice, though, the idea of globalization is closely tied to a neoliberal economic agenda that favors economic liberalization and encourages policies that support privatization, reductions in government spending and involvement in the economy, various kinds of austerity measures, deregulation, and support for 'free trade' (Huber & Solt, 2004; Nuruzzaman, 2004; Olssen & Peters, 2005; Weyland, 1998). Although many would see such policies as not simply sound but extremely desirable, what is important to note is that they are in no way neutral; rather, they are policies that favor a very specific kind of worldview and set of fundamental political and economic assumptions about the world in which we live. At the same time that we see increased pressures for globalization there has also been a rise in what some have termed a 'global justice movement' that opposes the corporate nature of globalization, instead focusing on issues of social justice, principles of equality, and challenging the growing economic and digital divide (Mander & Goldsmith, 1996; Kohler & José Chaves, 2003). The tension between those advocating globalization and those supporting social justice agendas is a deep one, with important implications for society in the so-called developing world in general, including implications for education (Altbach, 1977).

With respect to language and language study, the most obvious results of globalization and neo-colonialism have been the related dramatic growth in students around the world studying English, the role of linguistic imperialism and the concept of language 'ownership' with respect to English, and the on-going and continuing failure of native speakers of English, in the U.S. and elsewhere, to reciprocate by learning the languages of others. If the numbers of native speakers of English in the United States (and in the U.K., for that matter) who study foreign languages are of serious concern to us, this is definitely not the case with respect to non-English speakers seeking to learn English. According to the British Council, as of 2014 there were roughly 1.5 billion people studying English as a foreign language (Bentley, 2014). The domination and near-hegemony of English in international communication is unmatched in the history of our species. One of the interesting aspects of the growth of English as a global language is that we are now at a point in time when the majority of speakers of English are not native speakers of the language; in fact, native speakers of English are outnumbered by non-native speakers three to one. As Crystal (2012) and others have suggested, the bifurcation of speakers of English into 'native' and 'non-native' is no longer particularly useful much of time. Rather, it has become the norm to employ Kachru's (1992, 2006) 'three circle' model to discuss the English-speaking world. The 'three circle' model divides the English-speaking world into three components: the inner circle, the outer circle, and the expanding circle. The 'inner circle', with a total population of between 320 and 380 million, consists of those countries in which English is the first, and dominant, language of the population: the U.K., the U.S., Anglophone Canada, Australia, Ireland, and New Zealand. The 'outer circle', with a population of English speakers (some native but overwhelmingly non-native) between 300 and 500 million, consists of those post-colonial countries in which

English plays a significant role in many, perhaps most, domains: India, Pakistan, Nigeria, Singapore, and, *inter alia*, South Africa. Finally, the 'expanding circle', which has between 500 million and one billion speakers of English, includes those countries that have no colonial or particular historical link to the inner circle, and in which English has no special legal or constitutional status, but where it is nevertheless widely used and studied as a *lingua franca*: Denmark, Sweden, Japan, Iran, China, etc.

The distinction between the impact of globalization on the relatively successful and certainly popular teaching and learning of English internationally and the increasing challenges faced by programs designed to promote foreign language learning among native speakers of English might at first seem to be counterintuitive, but it makes a great deal of sense when issues of power, neo-colonialism, economics, linguistic dominance, and linguicism are added to the equation. It is these non- and extra-linguistic factors that, at least to a significant extent, help to explain both the popularity (and relative success) of English as a second/additional language in the non-English speaking world, and the lack of interest (and relative *lack* of success) in the 'inner circle'.

The phenomenon of contemporary English raises a number of very important questions, including those of the threat of English linguistic imperialism (see Canagarajah, 1999, 2005; Phillipson, 1992, 1997, 1998, 2007, 2008, 2009), the role of English in the promotion and maintenance of structural inequality around the world and its ties to the neoliberal globalization agenda, the related economic power and influence of English in contrast to most other languages (even other 'languages of wider communication'), and what might be called 'language ownership'. Especially interesting in these regards is that the relative power and position of native speakers of English remains incredibly strong even as the percentage of native speakers among all speakers of the language declines. One interesting aspect of the growth of the English language internationally has been that native speakers of English often see this growth as a compelling argument for not learning a foreign language themselves; after all, if everyone already speaks English then why bother learning another language?

A good place to begin responding to such views is that they are in fact fundamentally untrue. There are somewhere between 320 million and 380 million native speakers of English in the world, and an additional 150 million fluent second language users of English, for a total of about 480 million speakers. If we add to that number the individuals who have some facility in the language, there are probably about one billion speakers of English in the world. Taking into account that there are roughly seven billion people on earth, this means that fewer than 15 percent of the planet's population speak English. We would suggest that a percentage of under 15 percent simply does not make English '*the*' global language, in spite of its importance and dominance in some fields. The issue here, though, is not merely one of numbers. When a person is restricted to using a single language, there are other limitations involved as well. Although it is true that a native speaker of English can usually 'get by' in many parts of the world using only English, this inevitably means that their interpersonal contacts will be only with others who speak English. In non-English speaking settings, such individuals are not representative of the general population: their education, social class, and even values and beliefs are to some extent atypical of other members of their society, and the monolingual English speaker is unable to recognize that, let alone have direct contacts with other members of the population. Further, when two individuals communicate, and do so in the native language of one but the non-native language of the other, there is always a power differential created, and this power differential is virtually never recognized by native speakers of English. There is, then, an issue of social justice and fairness involved in our selection of the language that we use in interactions, and this is as true when speaking to non-native speakers of English in the United States as elsewhere in the world.

Finally, when one relies on interactions only with speakers of English, nuances (often quite important nuances) in the non-English language are lost to the monolingual speaker of English. A simple example of this is the Spanish word *cena*; the dictionary and textbook tell us that *cena* means 'dinner' in English. So it does. But the *mental concept* that is part of the Spanish term is quite different from the English one: *cena* is typically a much smaller meal than its English equivalent and is eaten much later in the evening than is generally true for 'dinner'. Another instance where the dictionary definition of a term is not really adequate is with the names of the days of the week in Hebrew (i.e., יום ראשון, יום שני, יום שלישי, יום רביעי, יום חמישי, יום שישי, and יום שבת). Although these terms *do* correspond to the names for the days that we use in English (Sunday, Monday, Tuesday, Wednesday, Thursday, Friday, and Saturday), in the Jewish tradition – and in modern Hebrew – the day begins at sunset of the preceding day.[11] In short, even as the hegemony of English continues to spread, and as increasing numbers of people around the world study and learn it, native speakers of English generally remain monolingual. Only in the United States, for instance, would a bumper-sticker that asserts that *Monolingualism is Curable* make any sense at all.

The political and educational rhetoric about globalization in the U.S. context is fascinating with respect to its implications for foreign language education. Virtually everyone involved in any manner in public education – parents, other teachers, school board members, business and community leaders, school administrators, politicians, and policy-makers, among others – all agree on the importance of preparing children for the twenty-first century, and all of these groups also agree that a central part of this preparation must be to prepare students to become global citizens capable of functioning in an increasingly globalized world. Surely there is no more powerful argument for the central place of foreign languages in the curriculum; if preparing students to succeed in a globalized world, then they must have language skills that go beyond their first language. Foreign languages, then, must be envisioned not only as an important part of the curriculum, but as a *core* part of the curriculum – and not programs of the sort that we currently have, but rather programs that involve intensive exposure to the languages and cultures we are teaching, coupled with serious content-area study in the target language as well as critical approaches to the study of both language in general and in terms of the study of particular languages (see Byram, 2008; Guilherme, 2002; Kubota & Lin, 2009; Pennycook, 1990; Phipps & Guilherme, 2004; Reagan & Osborn, 2002). Somehow, though, in the alchemy of politics, and filtered through the ideological monolingualism that we have already discussed, this turns out not to be the case at all. In short, in a way perhaps only possible in the context of public education double-speak, we face the idea of monolingual global education. What is even more disturbing is not just that we are seriously talking about global education taking place in a thoroughly monolingual setting, but that no one seems even to notice how absurd this is.

The sociologist George Ritzer first coined the term 'McDonaldization' in the early 1980s (1983, 2008) and it rapidly gained traction as a useful metaphor for the Weberian concept of the rationalization of modern society and culture. Ritzer and others argue that there are four rationalizing aspects of McDonald's that characterize McDonald's as a business: efficiency, calculability, predictability, and control. To some extent the term 'McDonaldization' replaced an earlier term that had first arisen in France in the 1940s, 'Coca-Colonization', which referred to American cultural and economic imperialism (see Wagnleitner, 1991). Although the term 'McDonaldization' is typically used in a pejorative manner, there are a number of positive aspects that can be associated with it: it can be seen to promote egalitarianism, to improve the quality of products, to guarantee a minimum standard of quality, produce goods and services more efficiently and thus more cheaply, utilize new technologies effectively, and so on. At the same time, however, the increased standardization brought about by McDonaldization leads to alienation and, ultimately, a dehumanization of both individuals and institutions (see Alfino, Caputo & Wynyard, 1998). All too often, such McDonaldization – in the linguistic domain sometimes labelled 'McCommunication' – also takes place with respect to language learning and corporate communication (see Block, 2003; Verhoeven, 2015). Whether called 'globalization', 'McCommunication', 'McDonaldization' or 'Coca-Colonization', however, the underlying concept is fundamentally the same: the increasing dominance and hegemony of the United States, its culture and its language, internationally (with respect to language and globalization issues, see Fagyal, Swarup, Escobar, Gasser & Lakkaraju, 2010; Heller, 2010; Heller & Duchêne, 2012; Holborow, 2007, 2015; Park, 2009, 2011; Phillipson, 2008; Piller & Cho, 2013).

'Paradigms' and 'Paradigm Shifts' in Education

The originator of the related concepts of 'paradigms' and 'paradigm shifts', Thomas Kuhn, developed these constructs to describe very specific characteristics and processes in the history of physical science (Kuhn, 1970), but they were quickly appropriated by both scholars and laypeople in a wide variety of areas to discuss far broader matters than Kuhn had intended. In the past few decades, academics in education have written and spoken about 'paradigms' in a variety of contexts, including in terms of the 'bibliographic paradigm', 'constructivist paradigm', the use of gaming and 'gamification' as a new paradigm in education, the 'global-ecocentric paradigm in education', the 'haptic paradigm in education', the 'humanistic paradigm', the 'information-age paradigm of education', the 'learner-centered paradigm', the 'policy paradigm in education', and the 'sustainable education paradigm', among many others. Donmoyer (2006) has critiqued this broad adoption of these concepts, arguing that their use in education, and especially with respect to the acceptance of qualitative research methods, has not been comparable to the kinds of 'paradigmatic revolutions' that Kuhn had in mind.

For Kuhn, a paradigm is far more than merely a model or a theory. Rather, it is best understood as:

> a world view, a general perspective, a way of breaking down the complexity of the real world. As such, paradigms are deeply embedded in the socialization of adherents and practitioners: paradigms tell them what is important, legitimate, and reasonable. Paradigms are also normative, telling the practitioner what to do without the necessity of long existential or epistemological consideration. But it is this aspect of paradigms that constitutes both their strength and their weakness—their strength in that it makes action possible, their weakness in that the very reason for action is hidden in the unquestioned assumptions of the paradigm.
>
> *(Patton, 1978, p. 203)*

Kuhn explained the significance and power of the dominant paradigm in a field of study as follows:

> Scientists work from models acquired through education and through subsequent exposure to the literature often without quite knowing or needing to know what characteristics have given these models the status of community paradigms . . . That scientists do not usually ask or debate what makes a particular problem or solution legitimate tempts us to suppose that, at least intuitively, they know the answer. But it may only indicate that neither the question nor the answer is felt to be relevant to their research. Paradigms may be prior to, more binding, and more complete than any set of rules for research that could be unequivocally abstracted from them.
>
> *(1970, p. 46)*

Paradigms are extremely useful and necessary during periods of 'normal science', but there have been a number of occasions in the history of science when the gradualist methods and ideas of 'normal science' were no longer functioning well and a new 'scientific revolution' in thought and practice occurred. Such changes, on Kuhn's account, are called 'paradigm shifts', and, although rare, they do take place and need to be recognized. Among the clear-cut examples of 'paradigm shifts' are the:

- replacement of Ptolemaic cosmology with the Copernican view of the universe.
- shift from Aristotelean mechanics to classical mechanics.
- replacement of phlogiston theory with Lavoisier's theory of chemical reactions and combustion.
- shift from classical mechanics to quantum mechanics.
- shift from Newtonian physics to Einsteinian relativism.
- discovery of plate tectonics.

In the case of education, however, for the most part the changes that have been identified as 'paradigm shifts' are not really changes of this sort; they are, rather, changes in theories, methods, models, and so on. This does not, of course, mean that a 'paradigm shift' in education is not possible; rather, it simply indicates that the nature of a 'paradigm shift' must be far more fundamental than most changes in education are.

An interesting exception to the general observation that there have not been major 'paradigm shifts' in education, at least in the past century,[12] is provided in the case of foreign language education. The shift from the grammar-translation method to the audiolingual method (ALM) entailed fundamental changes in not only teaching methods, but in the underlying learning theories supporting foreign language learning, the goals and objectives of foreign language study, the requirements and expectations of the classroom foreign language teacher, and the development of whole series of new foreign language textbooks and teaching materials, not the least of which was the emergence of the foreign language laboratory as a central feature of foreign language education programs in the United States (see Larsen-Freeman & Anderson, 2011). More recently, the emergence of communicative language teaching, in a variety of distinct forms, is a comparable shift in many ways, not the least of which is its reliance on constructivist learning theories (Reagan, 1999; Williams & Burden, 1999). Neither the shift from the grammar-translation approach to audiolingualism nor the most recent rise of communication language teaching have achieved the articulated objectives for foreign language education in the U.S., however.[13]

Toward a 'Paradigm Shift' in Foreign Language Education?

Given what we take to be the lack of success in promoting foreign language learning for the overwhelming majority of students at all educational levels in the United States, we believe that it is time for some radical rethinking of the nature, purposes, and goals of foreign language education in our society. We have already suggested here that foreign language education programs in the U.S. do not, in even a very limited sense, achieve the most commonly articulated goals and objectives for foreign language study. Elsewhere we have also argued that, given the way in which foreign language education programs are designed and implemented, this can hardly be a surprise (see Osborn & Reagan, 1998; Reagan & Osborn, 1998). Indeed, in responding to the question as to the causes of the failure of foreign language education in the United States, it is clear to us that:

> The answer is complex, including a variety of structural and institutional constraints, curricular and methodological problems, and a lack of social support. Underlying all of these factors, however, are issues related to power relationships and to the view of foreign languages as just that: foreign and, hence, alien and somewhat suspicious. In short, what we have attempted to demonstrate . . . that to a considerable extent, the real and perceived failures of foreign language education in the United States are, in fact, evidence that such programs are accomplishing specifically what the broader society implicitly expects of them. Foreign language education, in fact, is destined to fail for the vast majority of American students because it is *expected* to fail.
>
> *(Reagan & Osborn, 1998, p. 58)*

We would stress here that the blame for this failure is *not* foreign language classroom teachers, either in K-12 settings or in tertiary institutions. To be sure, not all foreign language educators are as fluent in the target language(s) that they teach as we might like them to be, nor are all foreign language educators as pedagogically sound as they should be. However, we believe that even the most competent foreign language teacher is faced with an almost insurmountable challenge in the U.S. context.

We do not believe that foreign language education in the United States can be turned into a success story without a number of fundamental changes that will affect virtually every part of the field. Essentially, what is needed is a *real* 'paradigm shift' that will create a radically different approach to the way(s) in which foreign languages are taught, our expectations for students in foreign language classes, the scheduling, organization and articulation of foreign language courses and programs, the kinds of teaching and learning materials used with different groups of students, and, perhaps most significantly, our goals for foreign language education.

Perhaps the most basic change that is required, and also the most difficult for many of us, will be the recognition that, in the U.S. context, we will not and cannot be successful in developing second language fluency in all, or even in most, students. There are a number of underlying reasons for this. First, there is a critical shortage of foreign language teachers that is becoming worse rather than better, and this shortage is only in terms of existing needs. Were we to dramatically increase the number of students studying foreign languages, as well as the amount of study required, there would simply be no way to provide well-qualified instructors.

There is, to be sure, something of a 'chicken and egg' problem here – there is a shortage of students studying foreign languages, which leads to a shortage of foreign language educators, which means that fewer students are able to study foreign languages. Hiring more native speakers of the target language(s) is one option here, and there are certainly benefits to this, but there are also a number of problems with doing so, not the least of which is the all too common (and demonstrably false) assumption that if one speaks a language then one is able to teach it. Using distance learning technologies and more effectively utilizing technology in foreign language learning and teaching can also help here, but neither of these can really address the larger problem. Further, the reliance on technology in this context to a significant extent runs the risk of contributing more to the 'digital divide' in society than it does to the effective promotion of foreign language teaching and learning (for discussions of the complexity of the 'digital divide', see Norris, 2001; Servon, 2002; Van Dijk & Hacker, 2003; Warschauer, 2004).

We have already referred to the challenge presented in the U.S. by what we have called 'ideological monolingualism', coupled with the hegemony of English in our society. Of course, U.S. society is by no means really monolingual at all; in fact, it is arguably among the most multilingual society on earth (see Figure 3.6). In a 2015 study, the United States Census Bureau identified some 380 languages other than English spoken as home languages in the country by nearly 62 million people (21 percent of the total population).[14] The United States is the second-largest Spanish speaking country in the world, after Mexico – Spain, for instance, has just under 48 million speakers of Spanish (López Morales, 2009). From an educational perspective, nearly five million children entering the public schools are native speakers of a language other than English (Sanchez, 2016). Regardless of the very real *factual* linguistic diversity in the United States though, for most Anglo-Americans the country is perceived as fundamentally English-speaking, and if English is technically not our 'official language' it certainly should be understood to be so (see Baron, 1990; Crawford, 1992; Tatalovich, 1995; Zentella, 1997). It is the set of beliefs, values and assumptions that underlie this perspective that we have labelled 'ideological monolingualism'. In essence, in any society there are a series of normative assumptions that serve to demarcate and define 'insiders' and 'outsiders' – that is, which define 'Us' and 'the Other', and which allow us to engage in what has been, in post-colonial theory, called 'othering' (see Kapoor, 2004; Monguilod, 2001; Spivak, 1980, 1985; Waggoner, 2005). One of the most powerful ways in which dominance is expressed and maintained in society is through the establishment and maintenance of a 'normative' default position (see Cummins, 1996, 2000; Sleeter & McLaren, 1995; Spring, 2000). In other words, what counts as 'normal' functions also to determine what is 'not normal'. Although this process is by no means deliberate much of the time, it is nevertheless quite real, and the identification and critique of the implicit dominance in such normativization is an important aspect of empowerment. For instance, in

Language	*Number of Native Speakers*	*Percentage of Total U.S. Population*	*Percentage of Most Spoken Non-English Languages*
English	233,780,338	80.38%	–
Spanish[1]	35,437,985	12.19%	62.13%
Chinese[2]	1,685,655	.58%	2.96%
Tagalog	1,542,118	.53%	2.70%
Vietnamese	1,292,448	.44%	2.24%
French	1,288,833	.44%	2.24%
Korean	1,108,408	.38%	1.94%
German	1,107,869	.38%	1.94%
Russian	836,171	.29%	1.48%
Arabic	764,753	.26%	1.33%
Italian	764,326	.26%	1.33%
Portuguese	684,493	.24%	1.22%
French Creole	663,828	.23%	1.17%
Polish	604,234	.21%	
Hindi	586,173	.20%	
Japanese	464,979	.16%	
Urdu	356,621	.12%	
Persian	352,712	.12%	
Gujarati	333,428	.11%	
Greek	321,144	.11%	
Armenian	223,914	.08%	
Panjabi	223,293	.08%	
Hebrew	215,005	.07%	
Bengali	207,596	.07%	
Hmong	202,387	.07%	
Teluglu	202,092	.07%	
Mon-Khmer, Cambodian	199,432	.07%	

[1]Includes Spanish, Spanish Creole, Ladino, and Pachuco.
[2]Includes Cantonese, Mandarin, and other varieties/dialects of Chinese.

FIGURE 3.6 Home Languages Spoken in the U.S. (Population 5 years and older)
Based on the MLA Language Map Data Center (2010)

contemporary U.S. society the dominant perceived 'norm' in racial terms is white; other racial identities are simply 'Other'. Such norms are significant because they in effect legitimize one group over others (see Sleeter, 2001). As McLaren and Muñoz have argued,

> Our attention has been drawn to the fact that the term *ethnic* is rarely applied to populations commonly described as 'white'. If you are white

> you occupy a space that seemingly transcends ethnicity. Whiteness miraculously becomes the 'oneness' without which otherness could not exist – the primogenitor of identity, the marker against which otherness defines itself. Whiteness functions as a frozen state – a dead zone where 'traits' associated with skin color, phenotype, race, class, and gender characteristics historically associated with Anglo-Europeans are held to be perpetually raceless. Whiteness has been positioned as the backdrop against which alternative or unconventional social practices and cultural formations are judged, thus ascribing an unprecedented degree of authority and power to its membership and its ethnocentric cultural, social, and ideological expressions, while at the same time repositioning the 'other' as deviant. Whiteness has become the laboratory which ethnicities are given defining characteristics, assembled, and categorized. Schools are the clinics which 'treat' these ethnic groups, police their behavior, and assimilate them.
>
> *(2000, pp. 32–33)*

This process is especially disempowering when it takes place with groups that have been historically disadvantaged – whether on the basis of race, ethnicity, gender, sexual preference, age, language, disability, or whatever (see Hollins, 2008; Larson & Ovando, 2001; Sleeter & McLaren, 1995).

In the case of language, the common assumption in our society is that monolingualism is both typical and 'normal'. Thus bilingualism or multilingualism are atypical and, in some sense, 'abnormal'. However, the reality, as John Edwards noted, is that:

> To be bilingual or multilingual is not the aberration supposed by many (particularly, perhaps, by people in Europe and North America who speak a 'big' language); it is, rather, a normal and unremarkable necessity for the majority in the world today. A monolingual perspective is often, unfortunately, a consequence of possession of a powerful 'language of wider communication', as English, French, German, Spanish and other such languages are sometimes styled. This linguistic myopia is sometimes accompanied by a narrow cultural awareness and is reinforced by state policies which, in the main, elevate only one language to official status.
>
> *(1994, p. 1)*

The situation of language education in the U.S. is in many ways parallel to the status of the Irish language in contemporary Ireland. The sociolinguist Suzanne Romaine quotes one Irish interviewee as saying that, 'although we are all *for* Irish as we are for cheaper bus fares, heaven and the good life, nobody of the masses is willing to make the effort' to learn and use the language (quoted in Romaine, 2000, p. 43).

Given all of the challenges, limitations and barriers that we face, it is simply not reasonable to believe that we will be able to ensure that most, let alone all, native English speakers in public schools will graduate from high school with a reasonable degree of fluency in a second language. This does not mean, however, that we should cease offering foreign languages in public schools – just that we need to rethink how and why we do so.

Our proposal here is that in the public schools we distinguish between two very different kinds of foreign language education to meet the needs of two different groups of students: the first type of program would be for those students for whom competence in a second language is deemed to be an essential educational outcome, and the second type of program would be for the remaining K-12 student population.[15] The fundamental distinction between these two types of programs is that the former (which we will call 'Language Fluency-Focused Programs', or LFFPs) would have as their articulated outcomes students with a high level of fluency in one or more target languages, in addition to solid content language in other subjects, while the latter (which we will call 'Language for Educated Persons Programs', or LEPPs) would have as their articulated outcomes students with an introduction to and overview of one or more foreign languages as well as a broad understanding of the linguistic, social, political, and historical aspects of human language and language diversity rather than actual fluency in a second language. In other words, LFFPs would be linguacentric programs, while LEPPs would include general education programs, technical/vocational programs, and so on. Such a system is by no means unheard of in other countries,[16] but in the United States we have historically opted for a 'common school' model based on the assumption that all students should receive an education that entails mastery of roughly the same content (see Kaestle, 1983; Reese, 2011; Spring, 2014, pp. 78–105; Urban & Wagoner, 2013, pp. 83–108). In terms of foreign language education, it is clear that this model has been ineffective for all of the reasons already discussed; if we are really concerned as a society with producing individuals who are truly fluent in different foreign languages, a significantly different approach is required.

And yet we are well aware of how the implementation of such a bifurcated approach to foreign language education could easily be seen – not only as a powerful type of tracking, but, even more, as the creation of a foreign language program in which one group of students (those in LEPPs) would learn about the economic and other benefits that those in LFFPs receive because they are actually competent in one or more foreign languages. In other words, the approach that we are advocating could easily be seen as an example of social class reproduction in education, entailing economic, cultural, and linguistic reproduction. This would be true to the extent to which access to such programs favors, either directly or indirectly, children from favored backgrounds – but this need not be the case. For instance, many immersion programs are based on the idea that the students should be mixed between native speakers of the two languages (for example, Spanish and English). In the U.S. setting, non-English native speakers are often (though of course not universally) relatively disadvantaged in comparison to native speakers of English.

Further, it is by no means difficult to build into such a model ways to ensure a fair and appropriate mix of students.

Language Fluency Focused Programs (LFFPs)

LFFPs are in many ways the 'dream programs' for many, perhaps most, foreign language educators. Their goal is to provide a foreign-language rich environment throughout the student's educational experience. These programs would differ radically from those found in most settings in the U.S.; from the earliest years, students would be immersed in the target language(s),[17] and a great deal of content area knowledge throughout the student's educational experience would be taught in the foreign language(s). Teachers would need to be content area specialists, fluent in English as well as the target language(s), and also familiar with both second language acquisition theory and foreign language teaching methods. The goal at the K-12 level would be for graduating students to be fully capable of attending a higher education institution in which the medium of instruction is either English or the target language(s). Students in LFFPs could be native speakers of English, native speakers of the target language(s) of the program, heritage speakers of the target language(s), or students with an altogether different native language for whom multilingualism in the objective. Although a LFFP program could certainly be designed and conducted bilingually in English and one foreign language, such a program could also be fairly easily expanded to include one or more additional foreign languages. Finally, and intriguingly, one of the aspects of a LFFP program would be the likelihood of the use of translanguaging in the classroom as an appropriate and valuable skill (see Canagarajah, 2011; Creese & Blackledge, 2010; García & Kleyne, 2016; Hornberger & Link, 2012; Lewis, Jones & Baker, 2012). Although LFFPs would share certain features with Soviet and post-Soviet specialized schools (*Школа с уклоном*) providing advanced study of foreign languages, they would also differ in significant ways: while the Russian schools are secondary (though all Russian children study foreign languages in primary schools), the LFFPs would be fully integrated K-12 programs, and while admission to the Russian schools is extremely competitive, this would not necessarily be the case with LFFPs (see Cherednichenko, 2000; Sutherland, 1998; Webber, 2000).

Language for Educated Persons Programs (LEPPs)

LEPPs would be fundamentally different from LFFPs. While LFFPs would have as one of their major foci the preparation of individuals who would be expected to achieve a high level of fluency in one or more foreign languages, coupled with a strong academic education, LEPPs would be programs for the vast majority of students for whom competence in a foreign language would not be an expectation of their educational experience. This does not mean, however, that there would be no foreign language component in an LEPP; rather, it would mean that the nature, characteristics, and goals of such programs would be very different from those found in LFFPs. In essence, the key difference is that LFFPs would focus on the benefits that accrue from foreign language *competence* (i.e., bi- or multilingualism), while LEPPs would be concerned with the benefits of language *study* for students. These arguments for the benefits of language *study*, we would argue, are significantly different from those in favor of bilingualism. There can be no doubt that for those who achieve fluency in a foreign language, the benefits of such competence are considerable. But, as we have already suggested, for many – indeed, for the majority – of our students, such competence is an unlikely outcome of foreign language study in the U.S. context. It is for this reason that the arguments in favor of language *study* itself become so important.

It is important to note here that the sort of LEPPs that we are envisioning are *not* merely the *status quo* with different foreign language programs. Rather, we are arguing for a radically reconceptualized approach to curriculum, assessment, teaching methods, and educational ends than currently exist, and into which a quite different approach to foreign language study can be integrated. At the heart of our vision is the concept of the 'educated person', and its relationship to that of 'liberal education'. These concepts have been a key concern of philosophers throughout most of western history; in the decades since the 1960s several different approaches have been taken to understanding and articulating what an 'educated person' should know and be able to do. Even in the more developed discussions of this topic, however, the role of the study of foreign languages has been minimized or ignored altogether. At this point we want to offer an argument for the necessity of such study on both theoretical and practical grounds, offering what is essentially an epistemological justification for the study of foreign languages in liberal education.

The historical tradition of a liberal education, as it emerged in the west, was centered in large part on language. As Leo van Lier has noted, 'There was a time, from the ancient Greeks to the late Middle Ages, when language was central in educational practices, in the form of the three branches of the *trivium:* grammar, logic, and rhetoric. Then, increasingly, language study became separated from other subjects . . . and became merely one other subject . . . As a result, language lost its centrality and relevance as an educational focal point, and it became difficult to see how it connected to other parts of the curriculum' (1995, pp. 7–8). There were a number of different reasons for the centrality of language in the curriculum: the Classical languages (Greek, Latin, and, to a lesser extent, Hebrew) were the languages in which the great literature of antiquity was written, and Latin remained the language not only of the Church but also of diplomacy, science, and scholarship in general. Latin was the mark of the educated person throughout western Europe, and functioned as the unifying *lingua franca* for the social, economic, and political elite. By the nineteenth century, French and German had increasingly come to play these roles, but the study of the Classics was still deemed essential for an 'educated person', in part because of the view, grounded in faculty psychology, that more difficult subjects would strengthen the mind in general (thus making the study of Latin, and even more of Greek, invaluable).

The twentieth century, and especially the second half of the century, saw the rise of the dominance of English as a global language. Concomitantly with the rise of the status and popularity of English in the non-English-speaking world came an increasing decline in the study of foreign languages in the English-speaking world. Native speakers of English are increasingly monolingual, and efforts to teach foreign languages at all levels of the educational systems of English-speaking countries are under threat. With respect to the conceptualization of the 'educated person', the role of foreign language study has been largely missing from the discussion. In the 1960s and 1970s the work of R. S. Peters, Paul Hirst and others (see Barrow, 1981; Barrow & Woods, 1988; Brent, 1978; Chambers, 1983; Dearden, Hirst & Peters, 1972a, b, c; Doyle, 1973; Elvin, 1977; Hamlyn, 1978; Hirst & Peters, 1970; Lloyd, 1976; Peters, 1973a, b; Schofield, 1972; Straughan & Wilson, 1983) focused on articulating the nature and characteristics of the 'educated man' (a term that was supposed to be understood to be gender-neutral, but which was anything but). The Peters-Hirst ideal of the 'educated man' was based on the idea that the student should be exposed to the various 'forms of knowledge', which included pure mathematics and logic, physical (empirical) sciences, history and human sciences, aesthetics, morals, philosophy, and religion (see Hamm, 1989, pp. 67–71). This approach emphasized theoretical rather than practical knowledge, as a number of critics noted (see Pring, 1976), and led Hirst himself to later reevaluate the 'forms of knowledge'. What is important for our purposes here is that language (both native and foreign) is excluded entirely.

The Peters-Hirst ideal was critiqued on a number of grounds; many argued correctly that it was based in and derived from a class-based set of principles and an educational tradition that was grounded firmly in a particular social class system, while the most powerful critique was that brought by feminist philosophers, who cogently argued that the 'educated man' of the Peters-Hirst ideal was just that: an ideal that presupposed certain gender-specific assumptions and which excluded many of the historical and contemporary characteristics of women's contributions to society (Martin, 1984, 1985, 1986, 1994, 2000; Mulcahy, 2002). Jane Roland Martin's emphasis on the reproductive elements of education and the 'educated person', although important, still left language out of the equation altogether. More recent efforts to address the complexities of identifying a justifiable concept of the 'educated person' and 'liberal education' – for example, by thinking about 'liberal education as preparation for life' (see Mulcahy, 2008) – while constituting significant improvements on earlier discussions, remain incomplete, especially with respect to the place of foreign language study.

In our view there remains an extremely compelling argument for some sort of study of foreign languages. One of the reasons for studying a variety of disciplines, as in the tradition of liberal education, is that each discipline approaches problems in its own unique manner. Thus, by studying history, students learn something about the ways in which historians think, just as by studying biology they learn how biologists think. To be sure, initial and limited study in a particular discipline does not mean that students master the epistemological approaches used in the discipline – that comes only with in-depth, long-term study – but the basic idea in a liberal education is that the student should come away from the experience with at least a clearer understanding of how each discipline organizes the world. Study of language can contribute to this understanding on two levels. First, the formal study of a language provides students with a meta-language for discussing the characteristics and components of any language, including their native language. Second, and more important, the study of language can be more fundamental epistemologically than the study of any other discipline, since different languages do indeed construct reality in somewhat different ways (see Han & Cadierno, 2010; Niemeier & Dirven, 2000). Although linguistic relativism remains a somewhat controversial topic,[18] there is growing acceptance among linguists that, at least in a weak form, the idea that 'human perceptions of reality are structured and constrained – not controlled, but structured and constrained – by human languages, in interesting and significant ways' (Elgin, 2000, p. 52) is absolutely correct. Further, as the philosopher Michel Foucault has argued, even the effort to 'name' things is, ultimately, about issues of power, control, and, ultimately, violence (Foucault, 2010). In other words, language can and does play an important role in how we perceive and understand reality, and recognition of this role of human language can be an important outcome of the study of *any* language.

Conclusion

In this chapter we have attempted to offer a critique of the traditional justifications for the study of foreign languages in the United States, and especially in the K-12 context. We have suggested that the justifications and rationales typically used to support foreign language education programs conflate two very different things: foreign language *study*, and *bilingualism* in a second language. The articulated rationales for foreign language study generally presuppose that the outcome of such study will be bilingualism, while in point of fact that is simply untrue for the overwhelming majority of Anglo-American students in the United States. Given this situation, we have argued that in the neoliberal world in which we live it is time for a paradigm shift in foreign language education to reconceptualize the rationale for foreign language study. We have further argued that there are nevertheless some fundamental benefits to foreign language study for all students – benefits related not necessarily to bilingualism, but rather to the general enlightenment goals of education. At the same time we have also suggested it is essential that serious and effective foreign language study, leading to meaningful bi- and multilingualism, be offered as an option to some students who are so inclined.

Notes

1 We are deliberately rejecting the common use of 'world languages' as the more politically correct way of describing foreign languages in the U.S. context. Although we accept the point that, for many students in the United States, languages such as Spanish are obviously not 'foreign' – for large numbers of students they are the individual's first language – we nevertheless believe that the term 'foreign' remains the most accurate one. In the U.S. setting, the label 'foreign' represents the clear identification of the target language of the classroom as 'Other' in contrast with English (see Osborn, 1998). Recent efforts to change nomenclature, utilizing the term 'world languages' in place of 'foreign languages', to some extent addresses such concerns, but only at the level of what might be termed articulated bias. Regardless of what they are called, in U.S. schools languages other than English are in fact perceived, by both adults and students, as 'foreign'. This perception is in fact only strengthened, we believe, by encouraging the use of what is seen as a politically correct label (i.e., 'world languages'). The risk with such word games, as Michael Apple has noted, is that 'historically outmoded, and socially and politically conservative (and often educationally disastrous) practices are not only continued, but are made to sound as if they were actually more enlightened and ethnically responsive ways of dealing with children' (1979, p. 144).

2 There is a growing body of literature about critical pedagogy and applied critical linguistics in the TESOL context. See, for instance, Benesch (2001), Brutt-Griffler and Samimy (1999), Canagarajah (1999, 2005), and Pennycook (1994, 1998, 2000).

3 Critical pedagogy is difficult to define, in part because it does not, in the words of one of its leading proponents, Peter McLaren, 'constitute a homogenous set of ideas' (2003, pp. 185–186). Rather, critical pedagogy is defined and manifested in a wide variety of ways by many different scholars and educators who, while sharing certain common assumptions and objectives, differ in many other important ways (see Darder, Torres & Baltodano, 2009; Denzin, 2003; Freire, 2002a, 2002b, 2002c, 2002d; Gay, 1995; Giroux, 1983, 1988, 1991, 1997; 2001a, 2001b, 2003a, 2003b, 2005, 2008; Gruenewald, 2003; Kanpol, 1999; Kincheloe, 2008; McLaren, 2003, 2005a, 2005b; McLaren & Kincheloe, 2007; Morrow, 2002; Wink, 2000; Young, 1993). At its heart, critical pedagogy seeks 'to empower the powerless and transform existing social inequalities and injustices' (McLaren, 2003, p. 186). It is, as Joan Wink suggests, 'a process that enables teachers and learners to join together in asking fundamental questions about knowledge, justice, and equity in their own classroom, school, family, and community' (2000, p. 71).

4 See Phillips and Abbott (2011). More critical perspectives on the ACTFL Standards can be found in both Fox and Diaz-Greenberg (2006) and Magnan (2008).

5 Such criticisms are by no means new or novel, of course. Similar concerns were raised in the discourse surrounding the National Defense Education Act (NDEA) in the late 1950s, and more recently in National Commission on Excellence in Education's *A nation at risk: The imperative for educational reform* in 1983 (see Watzke, 2003).

6 Although originally used to describe Americans and Canadians of English ancestry, the term 'Anglo-American' is now generally used more broadly to refer to all native English-speaking people in the United States and Canada. In contemporary usage, 'Anglo-American' denotes more of a cultural and linguistic identity than an ethnic one.

7 In every society there are assumptions that are deemed to be normative – that is, beliefs about what is 'normal' or 'typical', and, concomitantly, what is in some way 'abnormal' or 'atypical'. Regardless of our very real diversity, examples of normative assumptions in

the United States include race (where the norm is white), religion (where the norm is Christian, and most often Protestant), and, of course, language (where the norm is native English-speaking). These norms are important not only because they marginalize others, but also because they encourage fears that 'real' Americans are somehow threatened. We see this in fears about people of color becoming the majority in our population, in growing fears of Islam and our Muslim population, and, of course, in xenophobic fears of both immigrants and minority languages.

8 The controversies surrounding the teaching and learning of ASL in both K-12 and university settings are largely based on serious misunderstandings of the nature of sign languages in general. See Miller (2008) and Reagan (2011) for discussions of the resistance to the acceptance of ASL.

9 See Rosen (2008).

10 A common distinction made in writing about deafness is between 'deaf' and 'Deaf': the former refers to deafness solely as an audiological condition, the latter to deafness as a cultural condition. The basic idea underlying this distinction is that, when writing about cultural groups in general, upper case letters are employed ('African American', 'Hispanic', 'Native American', etc.). Thus a person can be 'deaf' without being 'Deaf' (as in the case of an older person who gradually loses his/her hearing).

11 The rationale for this is found in *Genesis* (*Bereishit*) 1:5: 'And it was evening and it was morning, one day.'

12 The impact of John Dewey and Progressive Education in the early years of the twentieth century may constitute a noteworthy exception to this general claim. See Garrison (2009) and Soltis (1988).

13 This does not mean that the quality of foreign language education in the U.S. has not improved, however. The issue is not, though, whether such programs have improved, but rather with whether they are actually achieving their articulated goals and objectives for most (or even many) students, and we believe it is clear they are not.

14 Prior to 2015, U.S. Census data with regard to languages other than English spoken at home was available only for 39 languages. See https://www.census.gov/newsroom/press- releases/2015/cb15-185.html, retrieved on April 3, 2017.

15 Although this proposal has important implications for tertiary education, our focus in this chapter is solely on K-12 schooling.

16 The challenge created by such systems is often that distinctions among different types of educational institutions reflect and reproduce social class divisions in a society. Although strictly functionalist theories of the role of educational institutions in social class reproduction have been strongly critiqued in the past three decades, it is nevertheless true that 'social class is the strongest determinant of the opportunity to learn what is required to gain educational qualifications, because that opportunity is structured by arrangements that lie outside the school as well as inside' (Demaine, 2003, p. 136).

17 There is an immense body of excellent empirical research documenting the effectiveness of immersion bilingual programs in various contexts around the world (see Fortune & Tedick, 2008; Hermanto, Moreno & Bialystok, 2012; Jong & Howard, 2009; Tedick, Christian & Fortune, 2011).

18 For instance, see January and Kako (2007) and Wolff and Holmes (2011).

References

Acocella, N. (2005). *Economic policy in the age of globalization*. Cambridge, UK: Cambridge University Press.

Adesope, O., Lavin, T., Thompson, T. & Ungerleider, C. (2010). A systematic review and meta-analysis of the cognitive correlates of bilingualism. *Review of Educational Research, 80*(2), 207– 245.

Alfino, M., Caputo, J. & Wynyard, R. (Eds.) (1998). *McDonaldization revisited: Critical essays on consumer culture.* Westport, CT: Praeger.

Altbach, P. (1971). Education and neocolonialism. *Teachers College Record, 72*(4), 543–558.

Altbach, P. (1977). Servitude of the mind? Education, dependency, and neocolonialism. *Teachers College Record, 79*(2), 187–204.

Altbach, P. (2014). MOOCs as neocolonialism: Who controls knowledge? *International Higher Education, 75,* 5–7.

American Academy of Arts and Sciences. (2016). *The state of languages in the U.S.: A statistical portrait.* Cambridge, MA: Author.

Antoniou, M., Gunasekera, G. & Wong, P. (2013). Foreign language training as cognitive therapy for age-related cognitive decline: A hypothesis for future research. *Neuroscience and Biobehavioral Reviews, 37*(10), 2689–2698.

Apple, M. (1979). *Ideology and curriculum.* Boston: Routledge and Kegan Paul.

Barac, R. & Bialystok, E. (2011). Cognitive development of bilingual children. *Language Teaching, 44*(1), 36–54.

Baron, D. (1990). *The English-only question: An official language for Americans?* New Haven, CT: Yale University Press.

Barrow, R. (1981). *The philosophy of schooling.* Brighton, UK: Harvester Press.

Barrow, R. & Woods, R. (1988). *An introduction to the philosophy of education* (3rd edition). London: Routledge.

Barzun, J. (1954). *Teacher in America.* Garden City, NY: Doubleday Anchor Books. Benesch, S. (2001). *Critical English for academic purposes.* London: Blackwell.

Bentley, J. (2014). Report for TESOL 2014: 1.5 billion English learners worldwide. International TEFL Academy. Retrieved from https://www.internationalteflacademy.com/blog/bid/205659/Report-from-TESOL-2014-1-5-Billion-English-Learners-Worldwide on March 16, 2017.

Blanchard, W. H. (1996). *Neocolonialism American style, 1960–2000.* Westport, CT: Greenwood.

Block, D. (2003). 'McCommunication': A problem in the frame for SLA. In D. Block and D. Cameron (Eds.), *Globalization and language teaching* (pp. 117-133). London: Routledge.

Block, D., Gray, J. & Holborow, M. (2012). *Neoliberalism and applied linguistics.* London: Routledge.

Brent, A. (1978). *Philosophical foundations for the curriculum.* London: George Allen & Unwin.

Broad, R. (1990). *Unequal alliance: The World Bank, the International Monetary Fund, and the Philippines.* Berkeley, CA: University of California Press.

Brutt-Griffler, J. & Samimy, K. (1999). Revisiting the colonial in the postcolonial: Critical praxis for nonnative English-speaking teachers in a TESOL program. *TESOL Quarterly, 33,* 413–431.

Byram, M. (2008). *From foreign language education to education for intercultural citizenship: Essays and reflections.* Clevedon, UK: Multilingual Matters.

Calvano, L. (2008). Multinational corporations and local communities: A critical analysis of conflict. *Journal of Business Ethics, 82*(4), 793–805.

Canagarajah, A. S. (1999). *Resisting linguistic imperialism in English teaching.* Oxford, UK: Oxford University Press.

Canagarajah, A. S. (Ed.) (2005). *Reclaiming the local in language policy and practice.* Mahwah, NJ: Lawrence Erlbaum Associates.

Canagarajah, A. S. (2011). Translanguaging in the classroom: Emerging issues for research and pedagogy. *Applied Linguistics Review, 2*(1), 1–28.

Chaichian, M. (2014). *Empires and walls: Globalization, migration, and colonial control.* Leiden, NL: Brill.

Chambers, J. (1983). *The achievement of education: An examination of key concepts in educational practice.* New York: Harper & Row.

Cherednichenko, G. (2000). School reform in the 1990s: Innovations and social selection. *Russian Education and Society, 42*(11), 6–32.

Crawford, J. (1992). *Language loyalties: A source book on the official English controversy.* Chicago, IL: University of Chicago Press.

Creese, A. & Blackledge, A. (2010). Translanguaging in the bilingual classroom: A pedagogy for learning and teaching? *The Modern Language Journal, 94*(1), 103–115.

Crystal, D. (2012). *English as a global language* (2nd edition). Cambridge, UK: Cambridge University Press.

Cummins, J. (1996). *Negotiating identities: Education for empowerment in a diverse society.*
Ontario, CA: California Association for Bilingual Education.

Cummins, J. (2000). *Language, power and pedagogy: Bilingual children in the crossfire.*
Clevedon, UK: Multilingual Matters.

Darder, A., Torres, R. & Baltodano, M. (2009). *The critical pedagogy reader.* New York: Routledge/Falmer.

Dearden, R., Hirst, P. & Peters, R. S. (Eds.) (1972a). *Education and the development of reason, Part 1: A critique of current educational aims.* London: Routledge & Kegan Paul.

Dearden, R., Hirst, P. & Peters, R. S. (Eds.) (1972b). *Education and the development of reason, Part 2: Reason.* London: Routledge & Kegan Paul.

Dearden, R., Hirst, P. & Peters, R. S. (Eds.) (1972c). *Education and the development of reason, Part 3: Education and reason.* London: Routledge & Kegan Paul.

Demaine, J. (2003). Social reproduction and educational policy. *International Studies in Sociology of Education, 13*(2), 125–140.

Denzin, N. (2003). *Performance ethnography: Critical pedagogy and the politics of culture.* Thousand Oaks, CA: Sage.

Donmoyer, R. (2006). Take my paradigm . . . please! The legacy of Kuhn's construct in educational research. *International Journal of Qualitative Studies in Education, 19*(1), 11–34.

Doyle, J. (Ed.) (1973). *Educational judgments: Papers in the philosophy of education.* London: Routledge & Kegan Paul.

Edwards, J. (1994). *Multilingualism.* New York: Routledge.

Elgin, S. (2000). *The language imperative.* Cambridge, MA: Perseus Books.

Elvin, L. (1977). *The place of commonsense in educational thought.* London: George Allen & Unwin.

Fagyal, Z., Swarup, S., Escobar, A. M., Gasser, L. & Lakkaraju, K. (2010). Centers and peripheries: Network roles in language change. *Lingua, 120*(8), 2061–2079.

Flaherty, C. (2015, February 11). Not a small world after all. Retrieved from https://www.insidehighered.com/news/2015/02/11/mla-report-shows-declines-enrollment-most-foreign-languages on March 13, 2017.

Fortune, T. & Tedick, D. (Eds.) (2008). *Pathways to multilingualism: Evolving perspectives on immersion education.* Clevedon, UK: Multilingual Matters.

Foucault, M. (2010). *The archaeology of knowledge and the discourse on language.* New York: Vintage.

Fox, R. & Diaz-Greenberg, R. (2006). Culture, multiculturalism, and foreign/world language standards in US teacher preparation programs: Toward a discourse of dissonance. *European Journal of Teacher Education, 29*(3), 401–422.

Freire, P. (2002a). *Cartas a quien pretende enseñar.* Buenos Aires: Siglo XXI Editores Argentina S.A.

Freire, P. (2002b). *Pedagogía de la autonomía.* Buenos Aires: Siglo XXI Editores Argentina S.A.

Freire, P. (2002c). *Pedagogía de la esperanza.* Buenos Aires: Siglo XXI Editores Argentina S.A.

Freire, P. (2002d). *Pedagogía del oprimido.* Buenos Aires: Siglo XXI Editores Argentina S.A.

Friedman, A. (2015, May 10). America's lacking language skills. *The Atlantic.* Retrieved from https://www.theatlantic.com/education/archive/2015/05/filling-americas-language-education-potholes/392876/ on March 13, 2017.

García, O. & Kleyn, T. (Eds.) (2016). *Translanguaging with multilingual students: Learning from classroom moments.* London: Routledge.

Garrison, J. (2001). An introduction to Dewey's theory of functional 'trans-action': An alternative paradigm for activity theory. *Mind, Culture, and Activity, 8*(4), 275–296.

Gay, G. (1995). Mirror images on common issues: Parallels between multicultural education and critical pedagogy. In C. Sleeter and P. McLaren (Eds.), *Multicultural education, critical pedagogy, and the politics of difference* (pp. 155-189). Albany, NY: State University of New York Press.

Giroux, H. (1983). *Theory and resistance in education: A pedagogy for the opposition.* South Hadley, MA: Bergin & Garvey.

Giroux, H. (1988). *Escola crítica e política cultural* (2nd edition). São Paulo: Cortez Editora.

Giroux, H. (Ed.) (1991). *Postmodernism, feminism, and cultural politics: Redrawing educational boundaries.* Albany, NY: State University of New York Press.

Giroux, H. (1997). *Pedagogy and the politics of hope: Theory, culture, and schooling.* Boulder, CO: Westview Press.

Giroux, H. (2001a). *Public spaces, private lives: Beyond the culture of cynicism.* Lanham, MD: Rowman & Littlefield.

Giroux, H. (2001b). *Stealing innocence: Corporate culture's war on children.* New York: Palgrave.

Giroux, H. (2003a). *Democracy beyond the culture of fear.* New York: Palgrave Macmillan.

Giroux, H. (2003b). *La escuela y la lucha por la ciudadanía.* Buenos Aires: Siglo XXI Editores Argentina S.A.

Giroux, H. (2005). *Estudios culturales, pedagogía crítica y democracia radical.* Madrid: Editorial Popular.

Giroux, H. (2008). *La universidad secuestrada: El reto de confrontar a la alianza military-académica.* Caracas: Centro Internacional Miranda.

Gruenewald, D. (2003). The best of both worlds: A critical pedagogy of place. *Educational Researcher, 32,* 3–12.

Guilherme, M. (2002). *Critical citizens for an intercultural world: Foreign language education as cultural politics.* Clevedon, UK: Multilingual Matters.

Hamlyn, D. (1978). *Experience and the growth of understanding.* London: Routledge & Kegan Paul.

Hamm, C. (1989). *Philosophical issues in education: An introduction.* New York: The Falmer Press.

Han, Zhaohong & Cadierno, T. (Eds.) (2010). *Linguistic relativity in SLA: Thinking for speaking.* Clevedon, UK: Multilingual Matters.

Heller, M. (2010). The commodification of language. *Annual Review of Anthropology, 39,* 101–114.

Heller, M. & Duchêne, A. (2012). Pride and profit: Changing discourses on language, capital and nation-state. In A. Duchêne and M. Heller (Eds.), *Language in late capitalism: Pride and profit* (pp. 1–21). New York: Routledge.

Hermanto, N., Moreno, S. & Bialystok, E. (2012). Linguistic and metalinguistic outcomes of intense immersion education: how bilingual? *International Journal of Bilingual Education and Bilingualism, 15*(2), 131–145.

Hirst, P. & Peters, R. S. (1970). *The logic of education*. London: Routledge & Kegan Paul.

Holborow, M. (2007). Language, ideology and neoliberalism. *Journal of Language and Politics, 6*(1), 51–73.

Holborow, M. (2015). *Language and neoliberalism*. London: Routledge.

Hollins, E. (2008). *Culture in school learning: Revealing the deep meaning* (2nd edition). New York: Routledge.

Hornberger, N. & Link, H. (2012). Translanguaging and transnational literacies in multilingual classrooms: A biliteracy lens. *International Journal of Bilingual Education and Bilingualism, 15*(3), 261–278.

Huber, E. & Solt, F. (2004). Successes and failures of neoliberalism. *Latin American Research Review, 39*(3), 150–164.

Hymes, D. (1996). *Ethnography, linguistics, narrative inequality: Toward an understanding of voice.* London: Taylor and Francis.

January, D. & Kako. E. (2007). Re-evaluating evidence for linguistic relativity: Reply to Boroditsky. *Cognition, 104*(2), 417–426.

Jarvis, G. (1980). The value of second-language learning. In F. Grittner (Ed.), *Learning a second language: Seventy-Ninth Yearbook of the National Society for the Study of Education* (pp. 26– 43). Chicago, IL: University of Chicago Press.

Jong, E. & Howard, E. (2009). Integration in two-way immersion education: Equalising linguistic benefits for all students. *International Journal of Bilingual Education and Bilingualism,* 12(1), 81–99.

Kachru, B. (1992). *The other tongue: English across cultures.* Urbana, IL: University of Illinois Press.

Kachru, B. (2006). The English language in the outer circle. In K. Bolton and B. Kachru (Eds.), *World Englishes: Critical concepts in linguistics, vol. 3* (pp. 241–255). New York: Taylor and Francis.

Kaestle, C. (1983). *Pillars of the republic: Common schools and American society, 1780–1860.* New York: Farrar, Straus and Giroux.

Kanpol, B. (1999). *Critical pedagogy: An introduction* (2nd edition). Westport, CT: Bergin & Garvey.

Kapoor, I. (2004). Hyper-self-reflexive development? Spivak on representing the Third World 'Other'. *Third World Quarterly, 25*(4), 627–647.

Kincheloe, J. (2008). *Critical pedagogy* (2nd edition). New York: Peter Lang.

Kohler, G. & José Chaves, E. (Eds.) (2003). *Globalization: Critical perspectives.* Hauppauge, NY: Nova Science Publishers.

Kubota, R., & Lin, R. (Eds.) (2009). *Race, culture, and identities in second language education: Exploring critically engaged practice.* London: Routledge.

Kuhn, T. (1970). *The structure of scientific revolutions* (2nd enlarged edition). Chicago, IL: University of Chicago Press. (Original publication, 1962)

Kumaravadivelu, B. (1994). The postmethod condition: (E)merging strategies for second/foreign language teaching. *TESOL Quarterly, 28*(1), 27–48.

Larsen-Freeman, D. & Anderson, M. (2011). *Techniques and principles in language teaching* (3rd edition). Oxford, UK: Oxford University Press.

Larson, C. & Ovando, C. (2001). *The color of bureaucracy: The politics of equity in multicultural school communities.* Belmont, CA: Wadsworth.

Lewis, G., Jones, B. & Baker, C. (2012). Translanguaging: Developing its conceptualisation and contextualisation. *Educational Research and Evaluation, 18*(7), 655–670.

Lloyd, D. (Ed.) (1976). *Philosophy and the teacher.* London: Routledge & Kegan Paul.

López Morales, H. (Ed.) (2009). *Enciclopedia del español en los estados unidos.* Madrid: Instituto Cervantes.

Magnan, S. (2008). Reexamining the priorities of the national standards for foreign language education. *Language Teaching, 41*(3), 349–366.

Mander, J. & Goldsmith, E. (1996). *The case against the global economy: And for a turn toward the local.* San Francisco, CA: Sierra Club Books.

Martin, J. R. (1984). Bringing women into educational thought. *Educational Theory, 27,* 85–95.

Martin, J. R. (1985). *Reclaiming a conversation: The ideal of the educated woman.* New Haven, CT: Yale University Press.

Martin, J. R. (1986). Redefining the educated person: Rethinking the significance of gender. *Educational Researcher, 15,* 6–10.

Martin, J. R. (1994). *Changing the educational landscape: Philosophy, women, and curriculum.* New York: Routledge.

Martin, J. R (2000). *Coming of age in academe: Rekindling women's hopes and reforming the academy.* New York: Routledge.

McLaren, P. (2003). *Life in schools: An introduction to critical pedagogy in the foundations of education* (4th edition). Boston, MA: Allyn and Bacon.

McLaren, P. (2005a). *Capitalists and conquerors: A critical pedagogy against empire.* Lanham, MD: Rowman & Littlefield.

McLaren, P. (2005b). *Teaching against global capitalism and the new imperialism: A critical pedagogy.* Lanham, MD: Rowman & Littlefield.

McLaren, P. & Kincheloe, J. (Eds.) (2007). *Critical pedagogy: Where are we now?* New York: Peter Lang.

McLaren, P. & Muñoz, J. (2000). Contesting whiteness: Critical perspectives on the struggle for social justice. In C. Ovando and P. McLaren (Eds.), *The politics of multiculturalism in bilingual education: Students and teachers in the cross fire* (pp. 22–49). Boston, MA: McGraw-Hill.

Miller, K. (2008). American Sign Language: Acceptance at the university level. *Language, Culture and Curriculum, 21,* 226–234.

Modern Language Association. (2013). Enrollments in languages other than English in United States Institutions of Higher Education. Retrieved from https://www.mla.org/Resources/Research/Surveys-Reports-and-Other-Documents/Teaching-Enrollments-and-Programs/Enrollments-in-Languages-Other-Than-English-in-United-States-Institutions-of-Higher-Education on March 13, 2017.

Monguilod, C. (2001). Ordering others and othering orders: The consumption and disposal of otherness. *The Sociological Review, 49*(S2), 189–204.

Morrow, R. (2002). *Reading Freire and Habermas: Critical pedagogy and transformative social change.* New York: Teachers College Press.

Mulcahy, D. (2002). *Knowledge, gender, and schooling: The feminist educational thought of Jane Roland Martin.* Westport, CT: Bergin & Garvey.

Mulcahy, D. (2008). *The educated person: Toward a new paradigm for liberal education.* Lanham, MD: Rowman & Littlefield.

Nagesh, R. (2000). 'Neocolonialism' or 'globalization'?: Postcolonial theory and the demands of political economy. *Interdisciplinary Literary Studies, 1*(2), 165–184.

National Commission on Excellence in Education. (1983). *A nation at risk: The imperative for educational reform.* Washington, DC: Government Printing Office.
National Standards in Foreign Language Education Project (1996). *Standards for Foreign Language Learning: Preparing for the 21st Century.* Lawrence, KS: Allen Press.
National Standards in Foreign Language Education Project (1999, 2006). *Standards for Foreign Language Learning in the 21st Century* (2nd and 3rd editions). Lawrence, KS: Allen Press.
Nguyen, P., Elliott, J., Terlouw, C. & Pilot, A. (2009). Neocolonialism in education: Cooperative learning in an Asian context. *Comparative Education, 45*(1), 109–130.
Niemeier, S. & Dirven, R. (Eds.) (2000). *Evidence for linguistic relativity.* Amsterdam, NL: John Benjamins.
Norris, P. (2001). *Digital divide: Civic engagement, information poverty, and the Internet worldwide.* Cambridge, UK: Cambridge University Press.
Nuruzzaman, M. (2004). Neoliberal economic reforms, the rich and the poor in Bangladesh. *Journal of Contemporary Asia, 34*(1), 33–54.
Olssen, M. & Peters, M. (2005). Neoliberalism, higher education and the knowledge economy: From the free market to knowledge capitalism. *Journal of Education Policy, 20*(3), 313–345.
Osborn, T. A. (1998). *The concept of 'foreignness' in U.S. secondary language curricula: A critical philosophical analysis.* Ph.D. dissertation, University of Connecticut.
Osborn, T. A. (2000). *Critical reflection and the foreign language classroom.* Greenwich, CT: Information Age.
Osborn, T. A. (2006). *Teaching world languages for social justice: A sourcebook of principles and practices.* Mahwah, NJ: Lawrence Erlbaum Associates.
Osborn, T. A. & Reagan, T. (1998). Why Johnny can't *hablar, parler,* or *sprechen:* Foreign language education and multicultural education. *Multicultural Education, 6*(2), 2–9.
Osterhammel, J. & Petersson, N. (2005). *Globalization: A short history.* Princeton, NJ: Princeton University Press.
Panitch, L. & Gindin, S. (2012). *The making of global capitalism: The political economy of American empire.* London: Verso.
Park, J. Sung-Yul. (2009). *The local construction of a global language: Ideologies of English in South Korea.* Berlin: Mouton de Gruyter.
Park, J. Sung-Yul. (2011). The promise of English: Linguistic capital and the neoliberal worker in the South Korean job market. *International Journal of Bilingual Education and Bilingualism, 14*(4), 443–455.
Patton, M. (1978). *Utilization-focused evaluations.* Beverly Hills, CA: Sage.
Pavlenko, A. (2010). 'Language of the enemy': Foreign language and national identity. *International Journal of Bilingual Education and Bilingualism, 6*(5), 313–331.
Pennycook, A. (1990). Critical pedagogy and second language education. *System, 18*(3), 303–314.
Pennycook, A. (1994). *The cultural politics of English as an international language.* London: Longman.
Pennycook, A. (1998). *English and the discourses of colonialism.* London: Routledge.
Peters, R. S. (Ed.) (1973a). *The concept of education.* London: Routledge & Kegan Paul.
Peters, R. S. (Ed.) (1973b). *The philosophy of education.* Oxford, UK: Oxford University Press.
Phillips, J. & Abbott, M. (2011, October). *A decade of foreign language standards: Impact, influence, and future directions.* Report of Grant Project # P017A080037, Title VII,

International Research Studies, U.S. Department of Education to the American Council on the Teaching of Foreign Languages.

Phillipson, R. (1992). *Linguistic imperialism*. Oxford, UK: Oxford University Press.

Phillipson, R. (1997). Realities and myths of linguistic imperialism. *Journal of Multilingual and Multicultural Development, 18*(3), 238–248.

Phillipson, R. (1998). Globalizing English: Are linguistic human rights an alternative to linguistic imperialism? *Language Sciences, 20*(1), 101–112.

Phillipson, R. (2007). Linguistic imperialism: a conspiracy, or a conspiracy of silence? *Language Policy, 6*(3), 377–383.

Phillipson, R. (2008). The linguistic imperialism of neoliberal empire. *Critical Inquiry in Language Studies, 5*(1), 1–43.

Phillipson, R. (2009). *Linguistic imperialism continued*. London: Routledge.

Phipps, A. & Guilherme, M. (Eds) (2004). *Critical pedagogy: Political approaches to language and intercultural communication*. Clevedon, UK: Multilingual Matters.

Piller, I. & Cho, Jinhyun. (2013). Neoliberalism as language policy. *Language in Society, 42*, 23–44.

Pring, R. (1976). *Knowledge and schooling*. London: Open Books.

Pufahl, I. & Rhodes, N. (2011). Foreign language instruction in U.S. schools: Results of a national survey of elementary and secondary schools. *Foreign Language Annals, 44*(2), 258–288.

Reagan, T. (1999). Constructivist epistemology and second/foreign language pedagogy. *Foreign Language Annals, 32*(4), 413–425.

Reagan, T. (2002). *Language, education and ideology: Mapping the linguistic landscape of U.S. schools*. Westport, CT: Praeger.

Reagan, T. (2005). *Critical questions, critical perspectives: Language and the second language educator*. Greenwich, CT: Information Age Publishing.

Reagan, T. (2009). *Language matters: Reflections on educational linguistics*. Charlotte, NC: Information Age Publishing.

Reagan, T. (2011). Ideological barriers to American Sign Language: Unpacking linguistic resistance. *Sign Language Studies, 11*(4), 594–624.

Reagan, T. (2012). Should there be a sixth 'C'? Critical pedagogy in the foreign language teaching and learning context. In P. Miller, J. Watzke and M. Mantero (Eds.), *Readings in language studies, Volume 3: Language and identity* (pp. 541–564). Lakewood Ranch, FL: International Society for Language Studies.

Reagan, T. (2016). Language teachers in foreign territory: A call for a critical pedagogy-infused curriculum. In L. Cammarata, T. Osborn and D. Tedick (Eds,), *Content-based foreign language teaching: Curriculum and pedagogy for developing advanced thinking and literacy skills* (pp. 173–191). London: Routledge.

Reagan, T. & Osborn, T. A. (In press). Reification of the English language and the hegemonic turn. In M. Djuraeva and F. Touchon (Eds.), *Language policy or the politics of language: Reimagining the role of language in a neoliberal society*. Blue Mounds, WI: Deep University Press.

Reagan, T. & Osborn, T. A. (1998). Power, authority and domination in foreign language education: Toward an analysis of educational failure. *Educational Foundations, 12*(2), 45–62.

Reagan, T. & Osborn, T. A. (2002). *The foreign language educator in society: Toward a critical pedagogy*. Mahwah, NJ: Lawrence Erlbaum Associates.

Reese, W. (2011). *America's public schools: From the Common School to 'No Child Left Behind'.* Baltimore, MD: The John Hopkins University Press.

Ritzer, G. (1983). The 'McDonaldization' of society. *The Journal of American Culture, 6*(1), 100–107.

Ritzer, G. (2008). *The McDonaldization of society.* Los Angeles, CA: Pine Forge Crest.

Romaine, S. (2000). *Language in society: An introduction to sociolinguistics* (2nd edition). Oxford, UK: Oxford University Press.

Rosen, R. (2008). American Sign Language as a foreign language in U.S. high schools: State of the art. *The Modern Language Journal, 92,* 10–38.

Sanchez, C. (2016, May 13). Survey raises concern about non-English speaking students. Retrieved from http://www.npr.org/2016/05/13/477974455/survey-raises-concerns-about-non-english-speaking-students on March 21, 2017.

Schofield, H. (1972). *The philosophy of education: An introduction.* London: George Allen & Unwin.

Servon, L. (2002). *Bridging the digital divide: Technology, community and public policy.* Oxford, UK: Blackwell.

Skorton, D. & Altschuler, G. (2012, August 27). America's foreign language deficit. *Forbes.* Retrieved from http://www.forbes.com/sites/collegeprose/2012/08/27/americas-foreign-language-deficit/ on March 13, 2017.

Sleeter, C. (2001). Epistemological diversity in research on preservice teacher preparation for historically underserved children. In W. Secada (Ed.), *Review of research in education: 25* (pp. 209–250). Washington, DC: American Educational Research Association.

Sleeter, C. & McLaren, P. (Eds.) (1995). *Multicultural education, critical pedagogy, and the politics of difference.* Albany, NY: State University of New York Press.

Soltis, J. (1988). Dewey and Thorndike: The persistence of paradigms in educational scholarship. *Canadian Journal of Education/Revue canadienne de l'education, 13*(1), 39–51.

Spivak, G. C. (1985). The Rani of Sirmur: An essay in reading the archives. *History and Theory, 24*(3), 247–272.

Spivak, G. C. (1980). Revolutions that yet have no model: Derrida's Limited Inc. *Diacritics, 10*(4), 29–49.

Spring, J. (2014). *The American school, A global context: From the Puritans to the Obama administration* (9th edition). New York: McGraw Hill.

Spring, J. (2000). *The intersection of cultures: Multicultural education in the United States and the global economy* (2nd edition). Boston, MA: McGraw-Hill.

Straughan, R. & Wilson, J. (1983). *Philosophizing about education.* London: Cassell.

Sutherland, J. (1998). *Schooling in new Russia: Innovation and change, 1984–1995.* London: Springer.

Tatalovich, R. (1995). *Nativism reborn? The official English language movement and the American states.* Lexington, KY: University Press of Kentucky.

Tedick, D., Christian, D. & Fortune, T. (Eds.) (2011). *Immersion education: Practices, policies, possibilities.* Clevedon, UK: Multilingual Matters.

U. S. Census Bureau. (2015, November 3). Census Bureau reports at least 350 languages spoken in U.S. home. Release Number: CB15-185. Retrieved fromhttps://www.census.gov/newsroom/press-releases/2015/cb15-185.htmlon March 21, 2017.

U.S. Department of Education. (2016, August). *Teacher shortage areas: Nationwide listing, 1990–91 through 2016–2017.* Washington, DC: U.S. Department of Education, Office of Postsecondary Education.

Urban, W. & Wagoner, J. (2013). *American education: A history* (5th edition). New York: Routledge. Van Dijk, J. & Hacker, K. (2003). The digital divide as a complex and dynamic phenomenon. *The Information Society, 19*(4), 315–326.

van Lier, L. (1995). *Introducing language awareness.* London: Penguin.

Verhoeven, P. (2015). Corporate communication or McCommunication? Considering a McDonaldization of corporate communication hypothesis. *Journal of Promotion Management, 21*(2), 288–298.

von Braun, J. & Diaz-Bonilla, E. (2007). *Globalization of food and agriculture and the poor.* Oxford: Oxford University Press.

Waggoner, M. (2005). Death of a discipline. *Journal for Cultural and Religious Theory, 6,* 130–141.

Wagnleitner, R. (1991). *Coca-Colonisation und Kalter Krieg: Die Kulturmission de USA in Österreich nach dem Zweiten Weltkrieg.* Wien: Verlag für Gesellschaftskritik.

Warschauer, M. (2004). *Technology and social inclusion: Rethinking the digital divide.* Cambridge, MA: MIT Press.

Watke, J. (2003). *Lasting change in foreign language education: A historical case for change in national policy.* Westport, CT: Praeger.

Webber, S. (2000). *School, reform and society in the new Russia.* London. Springer.

Weyland, K. (1998). Swallowing the bitter pill: Sources of popular support for neoliberal reform in Latin America. *Comparative Political Studies, 31*(5), 539–568.

Wickens, C. & Sandlin, J. (2007). Literacy for what? Literacy for whom? The politics of literacy education and neocolonialism in UNESCO- and World Bank-sponsored literacy programs. *Adult Education Quarterly, 57*(4): 275–292.

Williams, M. & Burden, R. (1999). *Psicología para profesores de idiomas: Enfoque del constructivismo social.* Cambridge, UK: Cambridge University Press.

Wink, J. (2000). *Critical pedagogy: Notes from the real world* (2nd edition). New York: Longman. Wolff, P. & Holmes, K. (2011). Linguistic relativity. *Cognitive Science, 2*(3), 253–265.

Young, R. (1993). *Teoría crítica de la educación y discurso en el aula.* Barcelona: Ediciones Paidós.

Zentella, A. C. (1997). The hispanophobia of the Official English movement in the U.S. *International Journal of the Sociology of Language, 127*(1), 71–86.

4

SLA FOR THE 21ST CENTURY

Disciplinary Progress, Transdisciplinary Relevance, and the Bi/multilingual Turn*

Lourdes Ortega

GEORGETOWN UNIVERSITY

Introduction

In the 50th jubilee special issue of *Language Learning*, Wolfgang Klein (1998) offered a pessimistic appraisal of the place of the field of second language acquisition (SLA) among other fields in the language sciences. He recognized many achievements in 25 years of disciplinary existence and considered that SLA had reached maturity by most practical, theoretical, methodological, and disciplinary indicators—all in baffling opposition to the limited influence that it had thus far had on neighboring fields. According to him, the accumulated research was sufficiently relevant neither to offer guidelines for optimal language teaching nor to provide a knowledge base toward a general theory of second language (L2) acquisition. Furthermore, SLA researchers had imported theories from other fields one-way only, producing nonreciprocal insights which had had great internal but limited external value. His overall conclusion was that "among the various disciplines investigating the manifold manifestations of human language capacity, SLA research does not rank very high" and he described SLA researchers as "bottom dwellers in the language sciences" (p. 530). Klein blamed this bleak state of affairs on SLA researchers' fixation with what he termed *a target deviation perspective*, or the tendency to consider L2 systems as failed approximations to the yardstick of native language systems. This perspective, he argued in 1998, hindered the field's ability to study how second languages are acquired in their own right, and it ultimately hampered the generation of genuinely relevant knowledge about the human capacity for language.

In the present article, I will agree with Klein (1998) on the main culprit he singles out for his negative appraisal of SLA. But I am also interested in revisiting his wider observation that the large amounts of rigorous and interesting research generated by SLA research communities are not commensurable with the considerably lesser reach this knowledge exerts among the other language sciences. It seems befitting to engage in this exercise of critical disciplinary self-examination particularly now, not only because it has been long enough— about 15 years—since Klein's (1998) indictment, but also because at the time of this writing SLA celebrates its 40-year anniversary, taking Selinker's (1972) field-defining publication as a convenient official marker of its disciplinary beginnings. The notion of transdisciplinarity will be important in my arguments. Trandisciplinarity draws from a movement in the sciences (Pohl & Hirsch Hadorn, 2008) and humanities (Osborne, 2011) that offers the concept as a response to increasing academia's capacity to solve problems in what applied linguists would call the real world and transdisciplinarity scientists call the life-world. Transdisciplinarity ensues when scholarly communities attempt to solve complex knowledge problems with social impact by working across multiple disciplinary boundaries as well as with social actors outside academia, willing to integrate diverse and often discipline-internal perspectives into more than the sum of each discipline-specific fund of knowledge. The goal of transdisciplinarity, therefore, is to generate a theoretical unity of knowledge beyond any one of the disciplines or perspectives involved. Broadening knowledge bases in this way increases experts' capacities to meet complex contemporary demands for socially useful knowledge. Given the complexities of human language acquisition, as well as the serious consequences that such complexities carry for the lives of individuals and communities who learn to live with several languages, a transdisciplinary approach offers a valuable lens through which to evaluate disciplinary progress in SLA.

Currents, Tides, and Flows in SLA Research at Age Forty

Let me first appraise recent disciplinary progress. Many interesting developments have taken place in SLA over the last 15 years. Taking a bird's eye view, a few recent trends seem particularly noteworthy as SLA moves forward into the 21st century at age 40.

The most noticeable of recent trends is the remarkable epistemological diversity of the contemporary SLA landscape. This is an achievement fueled by a social turn initiated in SLA in the mid 1990s (Block, 2003; Firth & Wagner, 1997). What was different about this development was not just the call to place social dimensions at the center of research on L2 learning. After all, social factors have always figured in SLA explanations, all the way from the early foundational years (Beebe, 1988; Klein & Dittmar, 1979), through the identification of interaction as a key site for language development (Long, 1981; Pica, 1987; see Gass, 1997), up to a most recent revival of interest in studying the L2 acquisition of variational rules (e.g., Gudmestad, 2012). Unprecedented in the social turn was the convergence of, on the one hand, efforts to dissociate from the quantitative, cognitive, positivist epistemologies dominant in SLA until the mid 1990s and, on the other hand, to refocus empirically on variation rather than universals and on individuals as much as on groups, with the allowance and even privileging of nontraditional explanations involving noncausal and probabilistic perspectives (e.g., as in Bayesian statistics). These efforts have brought about social respecifications of many central SLA constructs (Ortega, 2011b). Thus, *cognition* has been respecified in at least two ways, as a sociocultural phenomenon in Vygotskian theory, and as an embodied sociocognitive adaptation in the usage-based family of SLA approaches; *grammar* has been reconstrued as social meaning making in Hallidayan systemic functional linguistics and as meaning construal in cognitive linguistics; *interaction* has been redefined as a socially distributed accomplishment in conversation analysis; *learning* has been investigated as social apprenticing in language socialization theory; and *sense of self* has been reconceptualized in identity theory as socially constructed and contested positionings for being in the world. The social turn seems completed by now. It has boosted the field's capability to study social dimensions of additional language learning by adding at least six new theoretical frameworks to eight existing ones (compare Atkinson, 2011, and VanPatten & Williams, 2007). The resulting epistemological diversity constitutes something of a disciplinary tidal change in SLA that has been watched by some as a worrisome theoretical proliferation, greeted by others as salutary intellectual ethos, and celebrated by yet others as a needed reconceptualization of the field.

A twin theoretical development has been the consolidation of usage-based thinking about second language learning, as reflected in the importation into SLA of an extended family of theories including emergentism, connectionism, construction grammar, cognitive linguistics, and dynamic systems and complexity theories. I like to think of this development (admittedly with a positive bias) as a sea current akin to the California Current, which makes the climate of the Hawaiian Islands pleasantly cool despite their tropical latitude. Functionalist linguistic theories have always been welcomed in SLA, as shown, for example, in work by Sato (1990), Klein and Perdue (1992), and Bardovi-Harlig (2000). New, however, is the application to SLA problems of novel functional approaches that are closely associated with the fields of psychology of language and cognitive science (e.g., Elman et al., 1996; Thelen & Smith, 1994; Tomasello, 1998). The beginning of the trend was marked in the mid 1990s by the publication of seminal papers by N. Ellis (1996), Gasser (1990), Larsen-Freeman (1997), MacWhinney (1997), and O'Grady (1996). A more recent period was spent in the task of adapting the theory to SLA concerns (e.g., Larsen-Freeman & Cameron, 2008; Robinson & Ellis, 2008), occasionally marked by critical comparisons of usage-based linguistic versus generative linguistic approaches to SLA (e.g., a special issue in *Lingua* edited by Hawkins in 2008). A further development of this trend that can be forecast for the 21st century is that empirical accumulation of usage-based SLA research is imminent now, as a critical mass number of data-based studies are entering the published record (e.g., Collins & Ellis, 2009; Ellis & Cadierno, 2009; Eskildsen, 2012; Nelson, 2013; Tyler, 2012; Schmid & Lowie, 2011).

A third, noticeable trend in SLA looks more like a natural river flow. It pertains to research methodological prowess, reflected among many other indicators in the impressive variety of books devoted to covering research methods for the study of SLA data and topics. A far from exhaustive list includes the following: Blom and Unsworth (2010), Jiang (2011), Mackey and Gass (2012), McDonough and Trofimovich (2008), Norris and Ortega (2006), and Verspoor, de Bot, and Lowie (2011). The methodological advancement has occurred partly thanks to the first two theoretical developments already discussed. Namely, as part of the social turn, diverse empirical qualitative and interpretive methodologies were needed that would be appropriate for the study of not just language development but also social dimensions of L2 learning, including conversation analytical, ethnographic, and microgenetic methods, as well as combinations of them. Likewise, the recent wave of empirical usage-based studies has contributed new methods for the analysis of L2 data, with particular innovation in the three areas of developmental corpus analysis, dynamical systems techniques for formally gauging variation-centered changes, and computational simulations. Formal-linguistic (generative) SLA researchers have also expanded their experimental methods greatly and now regularly employ cutting-edge psycholinguistic and neurolinguistic methodologies (e.g., Marinis, 2003; Sabourin, 2009). This trend has been in response to the realization that knowledge of the L2 must be studied vis-à-vis processing effects (Bley-Vroman, 2009), a theoretical necessity also recognized by Chomsky (e.g., 2011) in the wider field of generative linguistics.

The fourth and final trend I would like to note is a steady broadening of the contexts and populations that contemporary SLA researchers investigate, together with the consolidation of instructed SLA as a burgeoning subdomain in the field. Over its 40-year history, a view of contexts and populations has prevailed in SLA that is essentially dichotomous, along a four-way distinction of naturalistic vs. instructed and, within the latter, foreign vs. second language acquisition. These dichotomies are too simplistic for many (Cook, 2009; Siegel, 2003). As of recent years, by contrast, variegated contexts for L2 learning involving distinct learner populations have begun to attract keen attention from theoretically diverse quarters. They include heritage language learners (Montrul, 2008; Valdés, 2005), preschool-age child L2 learners (Schwartz, 2004), international adoptees (Fogle, 2012; Hyltenstam, Bylund, Abrahamsson, & Park, 2009), school-age minority language learners (Ardasheva, Tretter, & Kinny, 2012; Schleppegrell, 2004), low-literacy and/or limited-education L2 learners (Ramírez-Esparza et al., 2012; Tarone & Bigelow, 2005; Schöneberger, van de Craats, & Kurvers, 2011), L2 learners with special learning needs (Kormos & Smith, 2012; Sparks, Humbach, & Javorsky, 2008), college students studying abroad (Kinginger, 2009), missionaries serving abroad (Hansen, 2012), or healthy aging L2 learners (Lenet, Sanz, Lado, Howard, & Howard, 2011; van der Hoeven & de Bot, 2012). The affirmation of interest by SLA researchers to contribute knowledge about language education and language teaching (e.g., R. Ellis, 2008; Long & Doughty, 2009; Spada, 2011) is likely related to this very increase in attention to diverse learner populations, because across contexts acquisition of a new language later in life often occurs in conjunction with formal instruction. In the long run, attention to some of the recently added contexts and populations may prove to be ephemeral, similar to surface ocean currents that are driven by seasonal winds. Other context- and population-specific interests, however, may be more sustainable and become deep sea currents that, given favorable upwelling conditions, can at times bring up deeper, nutrient-rich insights to the rest of the field. The conduct of SLA research across a broad spectrum of populations and contexts is likely to foster reconsideration of taken-for-granted knowledge and germination of new ideas; it may also challenge researchers to search for ever innovative methods, and it will hopefully increase the willingness to think ethically, engaging with the societal impact and educational consequences of the knowledge generated within SLA. The continued coverage of language education issues by the instructed SLA community is crucial to meet the potential for the field to be a central source of knowledge in support of language education in the 21st century that fosters bilingualism as a societal asset not only to elites but also to linguistic minority populations (see Dixon et al., 2012).

Transdisciplinary Relevance

The four trends reviewed above suggest impressive disciplinary vibrancy and strong interdisciplinary predispositions. SLA is moving forward into the 21st century with a glowing record of disciplinary progress. As Klein (1998) noted, however, disciplinary achievements may result in high internal worth for the knowledge generated by a field while nevertheless buying only limited outside influence. That is, in addition to disciplinary progress, it is worth considering transdisciplinarity, or the proclivity to pursue and generate knowledge that can be seen as relevant across many disciplinary boundaries and can contribute to overall knowledge about a given object of inquiry and its associated real-world or life-world problems (Pohl & Hirsch Hadorn, 2008). Thus, I would like to pose the question of whether SLA's remarkable disciplinary progress has been accompanied by commensurate transdisciplinary relevance. To what extent do the positive trends observed help make the field's contributions useful and relevant to the other language sciences?

There is strong indication that the perceived outside value of SLA has considerably improved in the last 15 years. For example, all major international publishers seem to be eager to include SLA in their offerings, which has led to a wealth of textbooks and handbooks (in both cases too many to cite here), together with at least one encyclopedia (Robinson, 2012), one anthology (Ortega, 2011a), and a dictionary of key terms (VanPatten & Benati, 2010). In addition, increasing communication between SLA researchers and researchers in fields such as psycholinguistics and bilingualism is seen, as reflected in the number of SLA-influenced publications in journals like *Applied Psycholinguistics* and *Bilingualism: Language and Cognition*, coupled with a mirror rise in publications influenced by cognitive science in journals that are home to SLA research, such as *Language Learning*, *Second Language Research*, and *Studies in Second Language Acquisition*. The vibrancy and sophistication that has been reached inside the field of SLA speaks well for even greater outside relevance of SLA knowledge in the future, and we will hopefully see two-way flow of theories from SLA to other fields and vice versa, with SLA generating rich reciprocal insights that enjoy great internal as well as external value in the future. But how is the steady increase in transdisciplinary relevance to be supported and maximized?

In part, transdisciplinary relevance is about SLA research communities being able to ask themselves what SLA can do for the other language sciences. Other things being equal, it is those contemporary SLA programs that are able to attune themselves to wider interests among the language sciences which are more likely to command attention and relevance outside SLA. Thus, I would argue one way in which the ethos of transdisciplinarity can be supported is by understanding the place of one's discipline in a wider landscape of fields that share an overarching common goal. In addition, transdisciplinary relevance is also about developing critical awareness of one's disciplinary framings of the objects of inquiry and the goals for the field and others' likely reception of them. This other way to support transdisciplinary relevance is more akin to the corresponding research communities being able to ask themselves whether the chosen insider justifications for demonstrating the value of disciplinary knowledge are effective in convincing neighboring research communities of that same value. This second strategy, therefore, requires cultivating an awareness of how SLA's object of inquiry, the goals of the field, or the value of knowledge generated, are explained and justified by insiders within SLA and whether, by comparison, these may be—for good or for bad, rightly or wrongly—recognized by neighboring fields as central to the wider goal of understanding the ontogeny of the human language capacity. In the remainder of this article, I explore these two ways in which the transdisciplinary relevance of SLA can be cultivated and taken to new, unprecedented levels in the 21st century.

The Place of SLA in the Study of Language Ontogeny

The scope of SLA is well known to *Language Learning* readers: SLA investigates L2 acquisition, or how humans can learn additional languages later in life, subsequent to having acquired a language or languages from birth. The object of inquiry in SLA must thus be understood as *late learned*, that is, a type of acquisition that begins late enough to qualify as coming after the first language(s) (L1), namely at a wide variety of ages other than from birth, and *bi/multilingual*, that is, a type of acquisition that involves more than one language. But L2 acquisition is only one of many types of language acquisition, and SLA is only one of several fields devoted to the study of language ontogeny. Figure 4.1 shows eight different types of nonpathological, individual acquisition/loss of language. As it turns out, all eight can be said to vary along the two parameters already observed to be relevant for describing L2 acquisition: whether language learning happens from birth or later in life, and whether it involves one or more than one language.

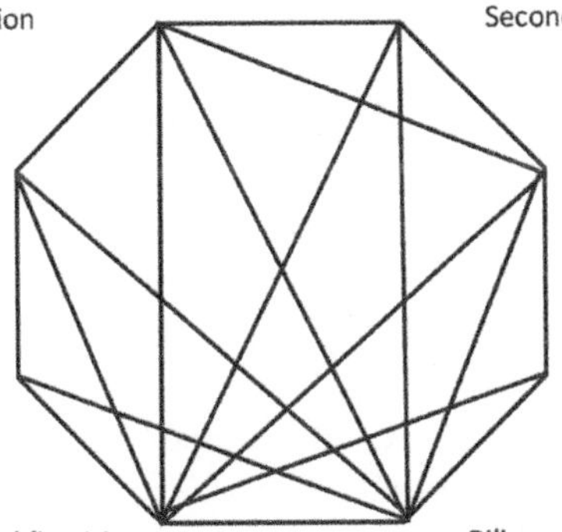

FIGURE 4.1 Types of nonpathological language acquisition (LA) and attrition in the study of language ontogeny. Each line joining two types represents present or potential inter-section of research interests.

This two-parameter variation along the timing of learning and the number of languages involved is reflected in the arrangement seen in Figure 4.1. Monolingual and bilingual child language acquisition are located at the bottom of the octagon and share the definitional feature of early (from birth) learning. To the left are listed other types of acquisition that involve one language only and can be later learned, while to the right are types of acquisition that involve two or more languages under conditions of later learning. When the study of L2 acquisition is situated in this larger context, a complicated place arises for SLA, but one that is full with opportunities for cultivating transdisciplinary relevance.

A first observation to be made is that child language acquisition from birth can involve one or more than one language (see accounts in Saxton, 2010, and De Houwer, 2009, respectively). Nonetheless, it is often only monolingual L1 acquisition that appears to be taken as the default against which the study of L2 acquisition (and all other kinds of acquisition, for that matter) might be justified. This tendency is true of discussions by lay people as much as by acquisition researchers. It is possible, however, to reject the privileged juxtaposition of adult L2 acquisition with child L1 acquisition, on the grounds that they are not directly comparable because the former is bi/multilingual and the latter is monolingual in nature. Furthermore, I would argue, as have others (e.g., Singleton 2003), that L2 acquisition should be contrasted not only to monolingual L1 acquisition from birth, but also and foremost to bilingual L1 acquisition from birth. Attunement by SLA researchers to the goals of the field of bilingual L1 acquisition is desirable in the future.

A second observation can be made by moving up to the right of the octagon in Figure 4.1: The parameter of timing of learning seems more open to ambiguity than the parameter of number of languages involved in the learning task. Namely, children can be extremely young when an additional language enters their lives (e.g., see Pfaff, 1992, for a study of children starting their L2 at age 2 and Paradis,

2011, for a study of children starting their L2 between 4 and 7 years of age). The nature of this successive but very early learning of two languages eludes an easy definition of what should count as L1 or L2 for a given young speaker. It also makes the juxtaposition of first bilingual acquisition versus very early second language acquisition look like a continuum. This complexity may explain the terminological indeterminacy seen across relevant fields, with researchers alternating among "early sequential bilingual acquisition," "early second language acquisition," and "child L2 acquisition" when they describe what may be the same object of inquiry. Thus, both SLA and bilingual L1 acquisition may share (and at times compete for) disciplinary claims of relevance upon the study of multiple language acquisition with onset at very early childhood ages.

Third, yet another complication is that late-learned languages are not always L2s, but they can also be L1s (see left side of Figure 4.1). In fact, L1 acquisition regularly occurs later in life for a population such as deaf signers: L1 sign language is late learned for 90% of deaf children who are born to hearing parents (Ramírez, Lieberman, & Mayberry, 2012). Furthermore, any acquired language (whether learned late, early, or from birth and whether L1 or L2) can be forgotten (and relearned again) on a variety of time scales over the life span. Evidence about the loss of language (see upper left side in Figure 4.1) thus offers another unique window into language ontogeny. Appreciation of this perspective can illuminate bi/multilingual processes in the reverse, as shown in the burgeoning field of language attrition (Köpke, Schmid, Keijzer, & Dostert, 2007; Murtagh, 2011), which offers many reciprocal connections with SLA (Bylund, 2009). Both fields study acquisition versus loss under situations of late learning and bi/multilingualism. Evidence of language loss also sheds light on monolingual learning processes in extreme cases of abrupt attrition due to language replacement at young ages, as in the recent interest in the study of so-called successive monolingual language acquisition by international adoptees (Hyltenstam et al., 2009; Snedeker, Geren, & Shafto, 2012). (The latter situation is such a unique case of language attrition that I have included it as its own type in Figure 4.1.) There appear to be intriguing empirical parallelisms across types of acquisition that begin later in life, regardless of whether one or more than one languages are involved. For instance, a reported advantage in rate of learning has surfaced as a consistent finding in studies across the various acquisition types characterized by late learning: delayed L1 acquisition of sign language (Ramírez et al., 2012), successive monolingual acquisition by international adoptees (Snedeker et al., 2012), and early successive bilingual acquisition (Paradis, 2009, 2011). A faster rate of learning, of course, has also been well established in studies of SLA as an initial advantage that adolescents and adults enjoy over children (Krashen, Long, & Scarcella, 1979; Muñoz, 2006). In sum, there are important insights to be had from comparing empirical evidence from late language learning, specifically, across situations that are monolingual and bi/multilingual.

Finally, for many people, the additional language learning task that must be undertaken later in life is not exactly that of learning a new L2, but a new dialect

(D2), that is, a new variety of a language they already know (shown in the upper right of Figure 4.1). This object of inquiry has given way to the new field of second dialect acquisition or SDA (Siegel, 2010). In studying L2 versus D2 acquisition, SLA and SDA exhibit many shared disciplinary interests. First, what counts as an "L2" vs. a "D2" can be blurry, as notions of language and dialect are social constructions by linguists and laymen rather than linguistically bounded objective entities (Klein, 1998, was outspoken on this). Heritage language teaching in the USA constitutes a good example of this complexity. For instance, Mandarin is taught in classrooms to many heritage language students whose home exposure is not to Mandarin but to a so-called (mutually intelligible or unintelligible) Chinese dialect (Wang & Xiao, 2010); likewise, the school varieties of Spanish that are taught in classrooms to most heritage language students likely differ from the national and/or regional varieties these students experience in the home (Lacorte & Leeman, 2009). Who then among Chinese or Spanish heritage learners offers evidence for SLA and who for SDA? Further, many L2 learners may be in a context where they need to become bidialectal in their L2. Such is the case of many immigrant children who are schooled in the official or majority variety within a bidialectal society (Ender & Straßl, 2009) and of young people who may choose as their target a stigmatized variety of the L2 with high covert prestige in the peer communities they wish to affiliate with, rather than the standard variety of the majority (Schleef, Meyerhoff, & Clark, 2011). Acquiring socially meaningful L2 variation is something that SLA researchers have shown to be possible (e.g., Hansen Edwards, 2011). But becoming bidialectal in an L2 also requires learning to differentiate between two varieties of the same language, something that SDA research shows to be difficult even in an L1 (Siegel, 2010). Two additional socioeducational intersections between SDA and SLA are also striking. Both L2 and D2 learning may position learners as linguistic minorities who learn a socially more powerful language/variety spoken by the surrounding majority speech community. And the onset of both L2 and D2 learning can often coincide with the onset of formal schooling, introducing self-regulation of learning, explicit and metalinguistic awareness, formal instruction, and literacy as factors to be considered in both types of acquisition. All these shared interests bring to the fore fruitful areas for mutual disciplinary relevance, creating opportunities for transdisciplinary, bidirectional flows of knowledge between SLA and SDA that may be seized in the future.

The present discussion has offered but a glimpse of a global view of the study of language ontogeny, against which SLA can place itself transdisciplinarily. Nevertheless, the points to be made are that acquisition types vary along the two parameters of timing of learning and number of languages involved in the learning and that this two-fold variation creates fruitful areas of convergence and divergence across disciplinary interests. The common goals in the study of language ontogeny should be to clarify the nature of constraints (i.e., biological, cognitive, linguistic, environmental, social, and educational) that are operative in developing human language, and to show when and how the relative contribution of constraints and forces may differ in different types of acquisition and their evolving contexts. Imagining SLA as a piece of this larger global view unveils opportunities for future bidirectional flow of ideas and fine attunement toward differences and similarities in the objects of inquiry and in disciplinary goals. This flow and this attunement, in turn, make it more likely that the knowledge one field generates will reach new levels of outside relevance among neighboring disciplines in the future.

The Importance of Disciplinary Framings

Having argued that SLA's transdisciplinary relevance can be greatly enhanced in the future by understanding the place of SLA in the wider landscape of fields that study language ontogeny, let me now turn to the second strategy for cultivating the ethos of transdisciplinarity in the 21st century, namely, the evaluation of chosen and available disciplinary framings. I understand framings as recurrent explanations and justifications of the value of the discipline's object of study, goals, and overall raison d'être, which come to be recognized, expected, and anticipated inferential models by others exposed to them; this definition is related to the uses of the concept in cognitive linguistics (Lakoff & Johnson, 1980) and critical discourse analysis (van Dijk, 1998).

Different framings of the goals and scope of a given research program are likely to command attention from different disciplinary neighbors, thereby resulting in different loci for inside and outside value and thus different kinds of potential transdisciplinary relevance. For example, researchers studying laterlearned types of acquisition involving only one language frame their contribution as distinctly valuable to the overall study of language ontogeny by arguing that evidence from late learning of language affords the opportunity to disentangle linguistic development from development in cognitive and social domains. To use an illustration from Snedeker et al. (2012), nouns have been found to be easiest to learn in child monolingual and bilingual acquisition, whereas the corresponding inventory of verbs and adjectives is initially smaller and slow-growing by comparison. Is the initial predominance of nouns in firstword inventories a reflection of some human-language specific property of this word category vis-à-vis verbs and adjectives, or an artifact of infants being unable to conceptually process relations, states, and processes until a later age? Snedeker et al. argued that evidence from later acquisition of one language by international adoptees allows for the investigation of this question, given that in such evidence linguistic development is independent from cognitive maturation. The question, they argued, is by comparison essentially unanswerable on the basis of traditional child L1 evidence. The disentangling argument has had broad applicability as a positive framing that adds value to the study of late learning of various kinds, including the value of studying delayed first sign language acquisition (Ramírez et al., 2012) and adult literacy (see Carreiras et al.'s 2009 interesting framing of the value of recruiting former Colombian guerrilla members who become literate after their 20s and comparing them to age-matched adult illiterates as well as early literates).

It begs pondering why the same positive framing has been unavailable in SLA, even when studying young L2 acquirers—as Paradis (2009) has also noted—whose timing of learning is similar to that of international adoptees and delayed first sign language acquisition. In fact, SLA researchers more often than not choose instead a negative framing in which cognitive and social maturity are portrayed as confounds that on the one hand complicate the study of SLA and on the other hand hinder any linguistic development that may happen later in life. Thus, for example, SLA models and theories abound that link adults' neural and physiological maturity to a posited irreparable atrophy of the human capability for new language learning, that identify linguistic maturity of the already acquired language as a road block to learning the L2, and that connect cognitive maturity to an overreliance on explicit cognition that is deemed inefficient for the task of language learning. There are also abundant SLA theoretical accounts volunteering social maturity as the culprit for affective, motivational, and attitudinal forces that negatively impact on adult learners' willingness or ability to learn from the input and from others.

Available and chosen (positive and negative) disciplinary framings can be evaluated so as to achieve self-awareness of how SLA's object of inquiry, the goals of the field, or the value of knowledge generated are explained and justified by insiders within SLA and whether, by comparison, each framing may be— for good or for bad, rightly or wrongly—read by neighboring fields as making SLA knowledge central to the wider goal of understanding the ontogeny of the human language capacity. If so, SLA's transdisciplinary relevance in the 21st century would be greatly aided by asking: What is the relative outside appeal or exportability of knowledge that obtains from available framings of the goals, scope, and overall raison d'être of a given research program? Further, if framings of the value of disciplinary knowledge are all-important for supporting and cultivating transdisciplinarity and outside relevance, it follows that the research collective of a field may from time to time agree that a rather large reframing of some disciplinary issue may be desirable.

My final argument in this article is that a reframing of SLA is needed, one that helps the field embrace the late-learned, bi/multilingual nature of L2 acquisition. For 40 years now, SLA has engaged in the pursuit of explaining the vexing question of how different L2 adult acquisition is by comparison to the acquisition of an L1 by monolingual children. This is a narrow approach to defining the purview and goals for the field. It contents itself with asking a self-directed question: What is L2 acquisition? It also limits itself to a comparative dialogue between two fields, one investigating the monolingual acquisition of an L1 in the first years of life and the other investigating the bi/multilingual acquisition of a new language later in life. In this dialogue, SLA runs the constant danger of accepting a subordinating role that hampers any hopes for transdisciplinary relevance. The narrow approach also gives short shrift to other fields that investigate other equally relevant types of acquisition exhibiting important connections with L2 acquisition in the focus on late learning, bi/multilingual learning, or both. In sum, the narrow view fails to connect with an all-encompassing vision of the study of human language ontogeny to which SLA contributes.

I believe it is the ability for SLA researchers to invest in future positive reframings of the late-learned, bi/multilingual nature of L2 acquisition that will most radically impact on the field's continued and growing transdisciplinary relevance in the 21st century. Moreover, I predict it will take a bi/multilingual turn in SLA, one of similar depth and magnitude as the earlier social turn SLA experienced (Block, 2003), for these reframings to flourish. The argument comes full circle back to Klein (1998) and engages with his charge 15 years ago against the target deviation perspective in SLA.

Three Reframings of L2 Acquisition

Indeed, the disciplinary reorientation I am calling for has several illustrious precedents within SLA. That some kind of reconsideration of disciplinary goals is needed has been suggested in at least three SLA guises: Bley-Vroman's (1983) comparative fallacy, Cook's (1992 and passim) multicompetence, and Klein's (1998) target deviation perspective. (Remarkably, all three articles were published in *Language Learning*.) However, these powerful calls, based on markedly different arguments by seminal scholars, have left most of the field's framings and practices untouched.

Bley-Vroman (1983) brought attention to the fact that "work on the linguistic description of learners' languages can be seriously hindered or sidetracked by a concern with the target language" (p. 2). However, he did not offer a concrete solution except for recommending that SLA researchers analyze learner language in its own right and concentrate "on the construction of linguistic descriptions of learners' languages which can illuminate their specific properties and their own logic" (p. 16). Furthermore, the criticism of the comparative fallacy is of a limited scope; it is just (although importantly enough) about the need to find new ways of analyzing L2 evidence that are not enslaved and distorted by a constant subordinating comparison to the competence assumed of monolingual native speakers.

Klein's (1998) criticism was more ambitious in that he identified negative framings explicitly as part of the problem, including the fallacy of believing there is "real" language and that learner language is a deficient version of it. He summoned SLA researchers not to produce so much knowledge about "where and why our species-specific capacity to learn and to process languages does not work under particular circumstances" (p. 537) and instead to use L2 evidence as revealing of the utmost principles that can be taken to govern the human capacity for language. Klein also opened up the following positive framing of SLA's object of study. Just as in biology the study of elementary forms of life like bacteria and molluscs are of equal importance as the study of advanced forms of life, he reasoned, so should SLA researchers be able to see that learner varieties—although perhaps not enjoying the same social and normative reputation as early-acquired languages—reflect the normal manifestation of human language, stripped from the additional but not essential adornments of other language varieties. Learner varieties, Klein argued, are in fact important because, like elementary forms of life in biology, they "do not show everything possible in the evolution of living organisms, but they are more transparent in their structural properties and processes" (p. 543). This comparison of L2 learner language with elementary forms of life—the point being that both are uniquely informative about the phenomena in need of scientific explanation—is helpful in suggesting positive framings that can undo existing deficit framings.

Cook's (1992, 2008) proposal offered an even more encompassing reframing that engages with not only the nature of the object of inquiry but also the goals of the field, thus calling for a reconceptualization of the very raison d'être for SLA. In terms of SLA's object of study, he argued that monolinguals and bilinguals are different, and hence the nature of the linguistic competence they possess is qualitatively different. This led Cook to coin a distinct term for a needed new construct: multicompetence. In terms of disciplinary goals, he contended SLA should pursue knowledge about what is unique in learning a new language later in life. This new goal Cook framed as superior to the present disciplinary goal of seeking knowledge that explains the differences and similarities between nonnative and native speaker, an approach that, he argued, asks why nonnative speakers are what they cannot be and thus is doomed to focus on deficiencies in addition to being tautologically circular.

A Bi/multilingual Turn for SLA

With such distinguished SLA advocates, and with such powerful and increasingly comprehensively articulated arguments, why has SLA had such difficulty breaking away from the straightjacket of the comparative fallacy, the target deviation perspective, and the monolingual native speaker bias? As in any field, time may be needed for changes in SLA to take effect. One might also wonder if Cook's (1992) strategic move to cast a light of uniqueness on nonnative speakers (e.g., as multicompetent L2 users), despite the obvious benefit of redressing the deficit portrayal of nonnativeness, might not entail some counterproductive dangers of disciplinary isolationism. Framings that capitalize on disciplinary uniqueness rather than on transdisciplinarity inspired by common goals, in other words, may be less likely to connect with outside fields that also study language ontogeny. Perhaps a more profound and complete reframing for SLA in the 21st century is needed, one that targets a deeper renewal of disciplinary goals and harnesses the unique benefits of studying bi/multilingualism and late learning, all while making transdisciplinary connections of relevance. I have come to think of this encompassing reframing as a bi/multilingual turn in SLA (Ortega, 2010, in press).

The vantage point that is earned by placing SLA in the wider landscape of fields which share the overarching common goal of studying language ontogeny (cf. Figure 4.1) affords the certainty that SLA is not alone in investigating the late learning of languages or the learning of more than one language. It also makes it possible to insist that, because "the human mind is as prepared to acquire two L1s as it is to acquire one" (Werker & Byers-Heinlein, 2008, p. 144), bi/multilingualism is the quintessential phenomenon that all disciplines studying the ontogeny of language should seek to explain. Cook (e.g., 2002, 2003) himself has also touched on this available framing of disciplinary goals:

> Any theory about the acquisition of languages by ordinary human beings has to account for the fact that many of them acquire two languages simultaneously from the beginning, and that many others acquire one or more other language consecutively at a later time.
>
> *(Cook, 2002, p. 24)*

Under this view, it would behoove all fields that study types of acquisition involving more than one language to empirically and exhaustively investigate the working hypothesis that the human language faculty is potentially by default bi/multilingual. SLA researchers should add the stipulation that the possibility of bi/multilingualism remains true all along the life span, from birth and across all ages, and thus is also true of late learned bilingualism. In this light, L2 acquisition becomes as worthy of study as any other type of acquisition—neither more unique nor less interesting or less pure—and full with opportunities for reciprocal flows of knowledge and transdisciplinarity. Explaining how late bilingualism is possible and even normal, not impossible or exceptional, would be part of this overarching research program.

In forging a disciplinary alliance with the study of bi/multilingual acquisition in all its manifestations, other new positive framings and greater transdisciplinary relevance would ensue for SLA in the future. Harnessing and embracing the study of L2 acquisition as the study of late bi/multilingualism would help SLA research communities to generate knowledge that contributes to overarching research goals in the study of language ontogeny. But SLA researchers will first need to convince themselves of the value of generating knowledge about the pathways to developing late bilingualism before they are able to sway others.

Conclusion

I began my review of recent trends in SLA with optimism, and I noted that at age 40 the field looks to have expanded and be healthy in at least four ways. Studies of SLA are epistemologically more theoretically diverse and interdisciplinary than ever; within this diversity has appeared a thriving line of empirical activity into usage-based views of language and acquisition; unprecedented sophistication in research methods has been reached; and the research community is gradually embracing the task of investigating L2 development in a complex constellation of diverse contexts inhabited by distinct populations of learners, many of whom resort to formal instruction for much-needed support to achieve their learning goals. A field engaged in such vigorous disciplinary progress must also aspire to ever higher levels of transdisciplinary relevance. Fifteen years ago, Klein (1998) identified the target deviation perspective as the main culprit for SLA's lack of disciplinary impact on the other language sciences that he perceived at the time. While great strides have been made since then, I agree with Klein (as many others outside SLA do too, e.g., May, 2011) that a deficit approach to studying late bilingualism is a liability that limits the field's full potential for generating knowledge that is internally valid as well as valued and valuable beyond its disciplinary bounds (Ortega, 2010).

SLA researchers have been very good at asking what the other language sciences can do for SLA. As the field enters the 21st century, it is time now to ask what SLA can do for the other language sciences. Knowledge about the nature of bi/multilingual and late learning of languages has maximal potential for shaping answers to fundamental questions that are of central interest to the overarching study of language ontogeny. Both disciplinary progress and transdisciplinary relevance will continue to rise in SLA in the future. But progress and relevance will be maximal if, instead of always (only) asking how adult L2 acquisition is different from monolingual child L1 acquisition, and instead of invoking negative framings surrounding the daunting complexity of factors that allegedly explain the lack of success in L2 acquisition, SLA invests in a range of broader-looking, more positive framings of disciplinary goals for the field in the 21st century. It is not the accomplishments over SLA's disciplinary history, as impressive as they are, but the rethinking of goals for the field, with awareness of how different framings of those goals impact on outside research communities, that will be helpful in fulfilling SLA's contributions in the 21st century to the study of language ontogeny and the support of language education across contexts. If such a disciplinary investment is made and a bi/multilingual turn is embraced, I predict the returns will be worthwhile.

Note

* This work was supported in part by an External Senior Research Fellowship at the Freiburg Institute for Advanced Studies at the University of Freiburg, Germany. For feedback and conversations that have led to much needed refinements and even reframings in my arguments, I am deeply grateful to my *Language Learning* colleagues, and particularly Alister Cumming, Nick Ellis, Scott Jarvis, Diane Larsen-Freeman, John Schumann, and Richard Young. I also thank Casey Keck and several audiences in recent years at the annual meetings of the American Association for Applied Linguistics and the Second Language Research Forum. I gladly accept responsibility for the shortcomings that remain.

Correspondence concerning this article should be sent to Lourdes Ortega, Department of Linguistics, Georgetown University, 1437 37th Street NW, Box 571051, Washington, DC 20057-1051. E-mail: lo3@georgetown.edu

References

Ardasheva, Y., Tretter, T. R., & Kinny, M. (2012). English language learners and academic achievement: Revisiting the Threshold Hypothesis. *Language Learning*, *62*, 769–812. doi:10.1111/j.1467–9922.2011.00652.x

Atkinson, D. (Ed.). (2011). *Alternative approaches in second language acquisition.* New York: Routledge.
Bardovi-Harlig, K. (2000). *Tense and aspect in second language acquisition: Form, meaning, and use. Language Learning* Monograph Series, *50,* supplement 1. Malden, MA: Blackwell.
Beebe, L. M. (1988). Five sociolinguistic approaches to second language acquisition. In L. M. Beebe (Ed.), *Issues in second language acquisition* (pp. 43–75). New York: Newbury House.
Bley-Vroman, R. (1983). The comparative fallacy in interlanguage studies: The case of systematicity. *Language Learning, 33,* 1–17.
Bley-Vroman, R. (2009). The evolving context of the Fundamental Difference Hypothesis. *Studies in Second Language Acquisition, 31,* 175–198.
Block, D. (2003). *The social turn in second language acquisition.* Washington, DC: Georgetown University Press.
Blom, E., & Unsworth, S. (Eds.). (2010). *Experimental methods in language acquisition research.* Amsterdam: John Benjamins.
Bylund, E. (2009). Maturational constraints and first language attrition. *Language Learning, 59,* 687–715. doi:10.1038/nature08461
Carreiras, M., Seghier, M. L., Baquero, S., Estévez, A., Lozano, A., Devlin, J. T., et al. (2009). An anatomical signature for literacy. *Nature, 461,* 983–986.
Chomsky, N. (2011). Language and other cognitive systems: What is special about language? *Language Learning and Development,* 7, 263–278.
Collins, L., & Ellis, N. C. (Eds.). (2009). *Input and second language construction learning: Frequency, form, and function* [Special issue]. *Modern Language Journal, 93,* 329–429.
Cook, V. (1992). Evidence for multicompetence. *Language Learning, 42,* 557–591.
Cook, V. (2002). Background of the L2 user. In V. Cook (Ed.), *Portraits of the L2 user* (pp. 1–28). Clevedon, UK: Multilingual Matters.
Cook, V. (2003). Introduction: The changing L1 in the L2 user's mind. In V. Cook (Ed.), *Effects of the second language on the first* (pp. 1–18). Clevedon, UK: Multilingual Matters.
Cook, V. (2008). Multi-competence: Black hole or wormhole for second language acquisition research? In Z. Han (Ed.), *Understanding second language process* (pp. 16–26). Clevedon, UK: Multilingual Matters.
Cook, V. (2009). Language user groups and language teaching. In V. Cook & Li Wei (Eds.), *Contemporary applied linguistics* (Vol. 1, pp. 54–74). London: Continuum.
De Houwer, A. (2009). *Bilingual first language acquisition.* Bristol, UK: Multilingual Matters.
Dixon, Q., Zhao, J., Shin, J.-Y., Wu, S., Su, J.-H., Burgess-Brigham, R., et al. (2012). What we know about second language acquisition: A synthesis from four perspectives. *Review of Educational Research, 82,* 5–60. doi:10.3102/0034654311433587
Ellis, N. C. (1996). Sequencing in SLA: Phonological memory, chunking, and points of order. *Studies in Second Language Acquisition, 18,* 91–126.
Ellis, N. C., & Cadierno, T. (Eds.). (2009). Constructing a second language [Special section]. *Annual Review of Cognitive Linguistics,* 7, 111–290.
Ellis, R. (2008). *The study of second language acquisition* (2nd ed.). Oxford, UK: Oxford University Press.
Elman, J. L., Bates, E. A., Johnsons, M. H., Karmiloff-Smith, A., Parisi, D., & Plunkett, K. (1996). *Rethinking innateness: A connectionist perspective on development.* Cambridge, MA: Bradford Books/MIT Press.
Ender, A., & Straßl, K. (2009). The acquisition and use of German in a dialect-speaking environment: Facets of inclusion and exclusion of immigrant children in Switzerland. *International Journal of Applied Linguistics, 19,* 173–187.

Eskildsen, S. (2012). L2 negation constructions at work. *Language Learning, 62*, 335–372.

Firth, A., & Wagner, J. (1997). On discourse, communication, and (some) fundamental concepts in SLA research. *The Modern Language Journal, 81*, 285–300.

Fogle, L. W. (2012). *Second language socialization and learner agency: Adoptive family talk.* Tonawanda, NY: Multilingual Matters.

Gass, S. M. (1997). *Input, interaction, and the second language learner.* Mahwah, NJ: Lawrence Erlbaum.

Gasser, M. (1990). Connectionism and universals of second language acquisition. *Studies in Second Language Acquisition, 12*, 179–199.

Gudmestad, A. (2012). Acquiring a variable structure: An interlanguage analysis of second language mood use in Spanish. *Language Learning, 62*, 373–402.

Hansen, L. (Ed.). (2012). *Second language acquisition abroad: The LDS missionary experience.* Amsterdam: John Benjamins.

Hansen Edwards, J. G. (2011). Deletion of /t, d/ and the acquisition of linguistic variation by second language learners of English. *Language Learning, 61*, 1256–1301.

Hawkins, R. (Ed.). (2008). Current emergentist and nativist perspectives on second language acquisition [Special Issue]. *Lingua, 118*, 445–642.

Hyltenstam, K., Bylund, E., Abrahamsson, N., & Park, H.-S. (2009). Dominant-language replacement: The case of international adoptees. *Bilingualism: Language and Cognition, 12*, 121–140.

Jiang, N. (2011). *Conducting reaction time research in second language studies.* New York: Routledge.

Kinginger, C. (2009). *Language learning and study abroad: A critical reading of research.* Basingstoke, UK: Palgrave Macmillan.

Klein, W. (1998). The contribution of second language acquisition research. *Language Learning, 48*, 527–550.

Klein, W., & Dittmar, N. (1979). *Developing grammars: The acquisition of German syntax by foreign workers.* Berlin, Germany: Springer-Verlag.

Klein, W., & Perdue, C. (1992). *Utterance structure: Developing grammars again.* Amsterdam: John Benjamins.

Kormos, J., & Smith, A. M. (2012). *Teaching languages to students with specific learning differences.* Clevedon, UK: Multilingual Matters.

Köpke, B., Schmid, M. S., Keijzer, M., & Dostert, S. (Eds.). (2007). *Language attrition: Theoretical perspectives.* Amsterdam: John Benjamins.

Krashen, S., Long, M. H., & Scarcella, R. (1979). Accounting for child-adult differences in second language rate and attainment. *TESOL Quarterly, 13*, 573–582.

Lacorte, M., & Leeman, J. (Eds.). (2009). *Español en Estados Unidos y en otros contextos de contacto: Sociolingüística, ideología y pedagogía / Spanish in the US and other contact environments: Sociolinguistics, ideology and pedagogy.* Madrid, Spain: Iberoamericana.

Lakoff, G., & Johnson, M. (1980). *Metaphors we live by.* Chicago: University of Chicago Press.

Larsen-Freeman, D. (1997). Chaos/complexity and second language acquisition. *Applied Linguistics, 18*, 141–165.

Larsen-Freeman, D., & Cameron, L. (2008). *Complex systems and applied linguistics.* New York: Oxford University Press.

Lenet, A. E., Sanz, C., Lado, B., Howard, J. H. J., & Howard, D. V. (2011). Aging, pedagogical conditions, and differential success in SLA: An empirical study. In C. Sanz & R. P. Leow (Eds.), *Implicit and explicit language learning: Conditions, processes, and knowledge in SLA and bilingualism* (pp. 73–84). Washington, DC: Georgetown University Press.

Long, M. H. (1981). Input, interaction, and second language acquisition. *Annals of the New York Academy of Sciences, 379*, 259–278.
Long, M. H., & Doughty, C. J. (Eds.). (2009). *Handbook of language teaching*. Malden, MA: Wiley-Blackwell.
Mackey, A., & Gass, S. M. (Eds.). (2012). *Research methods in second language acquisition: A practical guide*. Malden, MA: Wiley-Blackwell.
MacWhinney, B. (1997). Second language acquisition and the competition model. In A. M. B. d. Groot & J. F. Kroll (Eds.), *Tutorials in bilingualism: Psycholinguistic perspectives* (pp. 113–144). Hillsdale, NJ: Lawrence Erlbaum.
Marinis, T. (2003). Psycholinguistic techniques in second language acquisition research. *Second Language Research, 19*, 144–161.
May, S. (2011). The disciplinary constraints of SLA and TESOL: Additive bilingualism and second language acquisition, teaching and learning. *Linguistics and Education, 22*, 233–247. doi:10.1016/j.linged.2011.02.001
McDonough, K., & Trofimovich, P. (2008). *Using priming methods in second language research*. New York: Routledge.
Montrul, S. A. (2008). Review article: Second language acquisition welcomes the heritage language learner: Opportunities of a new field. *Second Language Research, 24*, 487–506.
Muñoz, C. (Ed.). (2006). *Age and the rate of foreign language learning*. Clevedon, UK: Multilingual Matters.
Murtagh, L. (2011). Second language attrition: Theory, research and challenges. In M. S. Schmid & W. Lowie (Eds.), *Modeling bilingualism: From structure to chaos* (pp. 135–154). Amsterdam: John Benjamins.
Nelson, R. (2013). Expanding the role of connectionism in SLA theory. *Language Learning, 63*(1).
Norris, J. M., & Ortega, L. (Eds.). (2006). *Synthesizing research on language learning and teaching*. Amsterdam: John Benjamins.
O'Grady, W. (1996). Language acquisition without Universal Grammar: A proposal for L2 learning. *Second Language Research, 12*, 374–397.
Ortega, L. (2010). *The bilingual turn in SLA*. Plenary speech delivered at the American Association for Applied Linguistics Conference, Atlanta, GA, March 6–9.
Ortega, L. (Ed.). (2011a). *Second language acquisition. 6-volume set [Critical Concepts in Linguistics Series]*. London: Routledge.
Ortega, L. (2011b). SLA after the social turn: Where cognitivism and its alternatives stand. In D. Atkinson (Ed.), *Alternative approaches in second language acquisition* (pp. 167–180). New York: Routledge.
Ortega, L. (in press). Ways forward for a bi/multilingual turn in SLA. In S. May (Ed.), *The multilingual turn: Implications for SLA, TESOL and bilingual education*. New York: Routledge.
Osborne, P. (2011). Philosophy after theory: Transdisciplinarity and the new. In D. Attridge & J. Elliott (Eds.), *Theory after "theory"* (pp. 19–33). London: Routledge.
Paradis, J. (2009). Maturation: For better of for worse? Peer commentary on Meisel, J. (2009), Second language acquisition in early childhood. *Zeitschrift für Sprachwissenschaft, 28*, 41–45.
Paradis, J. (2011). Individual differences in child English second language acquisition: Comparing child-internal and child-external factors. *Linguistic Approaches to Bilingualism, 1*, 213–237.
Pfaff, C. W. (1992). The issue of grammaticalization in early German second language. *Studies in Second Language Acquisition, 14*, 273–296.

Pica, T. (1987). Second language acquisition, social interaction, and the classroom. *Applied Linguistics, 8*, 1–25.

Pohl, C., & Hirsch Hadorn, G. (2008). Methodological challenges of transdisciplinary research. *Natures Sciences Sociétés, 16*(2), 111–121.

Ramírez, N. F., Lieberman, A. M., & Mayberry, R. I. (2012). The initial stages of first-language acquisition begun in adolescence: When late looks early. *Journal of Child Language.* doi:10.1017/S0305000911000535

Ramírez-Esparza, N., Harris, K., Hellermann, J., Richard, C., Kuhl, P. K., & Reder, S. (2012). Socio-interactive practices and personality in adult learners of English with little formal education. *Language Learning, 62*, 541–570. doi:10.1111/j.1467–9922.2011.00631.x

Robinson, P. (Ed.). (2012). *Routledge encyclopedia of second language acquisition.* New York: Routledge.

Robinson, P., & Ellis, N. C. (Eds.). (2008). *Handbook of cognitive linguistics and second language acquisition.* London: Routledge.

Sabourin, L. (Ed.). (2009). Neuroimaging and research into second language acquisition [Special Issue]. *Second Language Research, 25*(1). doi:10.1177/0267658308098994

Sato, C. (1990). *The syntax of conversation in interlanguage development.* Tübingen, Germany: Gunter Narr.

Saxton, M. (2010). *Child language: Acquisition and development.* London: Sage.

Schleef, E., Meyerhoff, M., & Clark, L. (2011). Teenagers' acquisition of variation: A comparison of locally-born and migrant teens' realisation of English (ing) in Edinburgh and London. *English World-Wide, 32*, 206–236.

Schleppegrell, M. J. (2004). *The language of schooling: A functional linguistics perspective.* Mahwah, NJ: Lawrence Erlbaum.

Schmid, M. S., & Lowie, W. (Eds.). (2011). *Modeling bilingualism: From structure to chaos. In honor of Kees de Bot.* Amsterdam: John Benjamins.

Schöneberger, C., van de Craats, I., & Kurvers, J. (Eds.). (2011). *Low educated adult second language and literacy acquisition: Proceedings of the 6th Symposium, Cologne 2010.* Nijmegen, Netherlands: Centre for Language Studies.

Schwartz, B. D. (2004). Why child L2 acquisition? In J. v. Kampen & S. Baauw (Eds.), *Proceedings of GALA 2003* (Vol. 1, pp. 47–66). Utrecht, Netherlands: Netherlands Graduate School of Linguistics (LOT).

Selinker, L. (1972). Interlanguage. *International Review of Applied Linguistics, 10*, 219–231.

Siegel, J. (2003). Social context. In C. Doughty & M. H. Long (Eds.), *Handbook of second language acquisition* (pp. 178–223). Malden, MA: Blackwell.

Siegel, J. (2010). *Second dialect acquisition.* New York: Cambridge University Press.

Singleton, D. (2003). Critical period or general age factor(s)? In M. P. García Mayo & M. L. García Lecumberri (Eds.), *Age and the acquisition of English as a foreign language* (pp. 3–22). Clevedon, UK: Multilingual Matters.

Snedeker, J., Geren, J., & Shafto, C. L. (2012). Disentangling the effects of cognitive development and linguistic expertise: A longitudinal study of the acquisition of English in internationally-adopted infants and preschoolers. *Cognitive Psychology, 65*, 39–76.

Spada, N. (2011). Beyond form-focused instruction: Reflections on past, present and future research. *Language Teaching, 44*, 225–236. doi:10.1017/S0261444810000224

Sparks, R., Humbach, N., & Javorsky, J. (2008). Comparing high and low achievement, LD, and ADHD foreign language learners: Individual and longitudinal differences. *Learning and Individual Differences, 18*, 29–43.

Tarone, E., & Bigelow, M. (2005). Impact of literacy on oral language processing: Implications for second language acquisition research. *Annual Review of Applied Linguistics, 25,* 77–97.

Thelen, E., & Smith, L. B. (Eds.). (1994). *A dynamic systems approach to the development of cognition and action.* Cambridge, MA: Bradford Books/MIT Press.

Tomasello, M. (Ed.). (1998). *The new psychology of language: Cognitive and functional approaches to language structure.* Mahwah, NJ: Lawrence Erlbaum.

Tyler, A. (2012). *Cognitive linguistics and second language learning.* New York: Routledge.

Valdés, G. (2005). Bilingualism, heritage language learners, and SLA research: Opportunities lost or seized? *Modern Language Journal, 89,* 410–426.

van der Hoeven, N., & de Bot, K. (2012). Relearning in the elderly: Age-related effects on the size of savings. *Language Learning, 62,* 42–67. doi:10.1111/j.1467–9922.2011.00689.x

van Dijk, T. (1998). *Ideology: A multidisciplinary approach.* London: Sage.

VanPatten, B., & Benati, A. G. (2010). *Key terms in second language acquisition.* New York: Continuum.

VanPatten, B., & Williams, J. (Eds.). (2007). *Theories in second language acquisition: An introduction.* Mahwah, NJ: Lawrence Erlbaum.

Verspoor, M. H., de Bot, K., & Lowie, W. (Eds.). (2011). *A dynamic approach to second language development: Methods and techniques.* Amsterdam: John Benjamins.

Wang, K. F., & Xiao, Y. (2010). Diversity and difference: Identity issues of Chinese heritage language learners from dialect backgrounds. *Heritage Language Journal,* 7(2), 153–187.

Werker, J. F., & Byers-Heinlein, K. (2008). The youngest bilinguals: First steps in perception and comprehension of language. *Trends in Cognitive Sciences, 12*(4), 144–151.

5

TOWARDS DECOLONIZING HERITAGE LANGUAGE TEACHER EDUCATION

Theresa Austin

UNIVERSITY OF MASSACHUSETTS AMHERST

> La descolonización implica un compromiso con los asuntos cotidianos de nuestras propias vidas para que podamos darle sentido al mundo en relación al poder hegemónico, y también un compromiso con los colectivos que se basan en ideas de autonomía y autodeterminación, es decir, en la práctica democrática.
>
> *(Chandra Talpade Mohanty, 2003, as cited by Antonia Darder & Zeus Yiamouyiannis, 2009)*

This chapter begins with the premise that we can define heritage language and teacher education despite the discrepancies that exist in defining heritage language (Leeman, 2016), and is based on the recognition of teacher education as education rather than training (Darder, Baltodano & Torres, 2002). Furthermore, I locate these two areas of examination within local, regional, and national social relations and practices, which include consideration of economic, social, and power relations within society. In doing so I recognize heritage teacher education as a field that is far from homogeneous and stable across time. However, I argue that decolonization efforts are significant to envisioning a field that engages with the complex realities of educating heritage teacher/learners and of learning from their experiences. Thus a decolonizing heritage teacher education could further problematize the economic violence of colonization, which manifests itself both symbolically and materially in language instruction and assessment through policy and planning efforts. Moreover, decolonizing efforts can offer feasible ways to work to end the ethical insensitivity towards the legitimate moral and political claims by those who are colonized.

I situate myself as a second language researcher in teacher education who is a multiracial heritage language learner and educator. My perspective on decolonization draws on the personal experiences gained from working with multilingual populations in monolingual preferred/privileged educational contexts over 25 years. Intertwined in my discussion is the scholarship that examines decolonization in language teacher education and a testimonio of a heritage language educator whose life experiences remind us to be ever vigilant in our efforts to end the impact of colonization.

Undoubtedly making a distinction between multilingual and monolingual can become a reductive attempt to make stable a privileging social condition that offers prestige to those who skillfully manage the current dominant variety of language. While not stable, characterizing this enduring situation as a monolingual context temporarily allows me to both challenge the current state of affairs by offering an alternative viewpoint and to create space to envision possibilities without negating the social nature of language to be durable over time. At the same time this definition remains interactionally malleable, diverse, and yet transcends nation-state boundaries (Makoni & Pennycook, 2007; Rampton, 2011; Sharma & Sankaran, 2011).

This chapter thus provides an examination of decolonizing efforts in the personal, professional, and social worlds of teacher education. Using testimonio as an inquiry approach, I braid my lived experience learning a heritage language with the national history of heritage language education and teacher education. Testimonios, founded in Latinx feminist scholarship, are narratives that privilege lived experiences that challenge the traditional apartheid of knowledge that devalues and marginalizes forms of knowledge that exist outside of the academy (Delgado Bernal & Villalpando, 2002). In a sense, testimonios acknowledge and value this knowledge to gain insight into how the impact of systems of oppression intersect to operate within educational institutions.

To complete the third strand of this braided narrative I conducted a series of four semi-structured interviews over several weeks in the spring of 2017 with Yvonne, a heritage language educator and leader in the field of heritage language education, who herself is a heritage language learner. Yvonne provided her testimonio about growing up in Massachusetts in the 1980s after her arrival from Ecuador. I have known Yvonne for 15 years, including the time she spent completing her doctoral degree. She was eager to discuss her own education and how these experiences first made her a reluctant learner of Spanish, a "native speaker" in some contexts of learning, a "not-native enough speaker," and later a committed heritage language teacher. Because Yvonne's testimonio reflects a familiar history to Latinos becoming bilingual teachers (Galindo, 2007; Guerrero, 2003) I have selected her testimonio as one of my three strands in discussing heritage language teacher and decolonizing efforts.

Through this effort I bring together sense-making over our lifetime to advocate for decolonizing heritage language teacher education. In particular, this chapter will address several of the challenges involved in moving teacher education, in particular heritage language teacher education, towards a process of decolonization. In addition, it will provide evidence of several cases of mobilization of local efforts to leverage resources that build resistance and resilience towards decolonization within an adverse and hostile national context.

This chapter addresses these questions: what is heritage language education and why is this area significant for decolonization?; who are heritage language teachers?; what are the significant struggles that heritage language teachers face?; and what practices can help teachers build towards decolonizing education for heritage language learners?

What is Heritage Language Education and Why is Decolonizing Effort Needed?

Let me explain how I became a heritage language educator/ researcher. Across my early family experiences of learning my mother's languages, Okinawan and Japanese, the lines were blurred between these languages as they were used minimally in my daily life. Distant from any maternal relatives and in touch with few communities of Okinawan- or Japanese-using communities, this heritage was cultivated primarily at home. In contrast with my father's African-American English variety from Louisiana, my frequent contact with paternal family and friends from this location fortified my familiarity and identification with and use of this variety. However, the absence of learning opportunities of either Okinawan or Japanese language in my formal elementary and secondary education spurred me to seek to learn Japanese as an undergraduate minor in college, and our family's previous sojourn in Panama gave me confidence to major in Spanish.

The informal and blurred relationships between the Okinawan and Japanese languages were intensified as I learned the informal and formal registers of Japanese in my university language courses. What I quickly understood was that what I had learned prior to these classes was not "Japanese". Thus the initial feeling of familiarity in learning syntax and morphology dissipated quickly into feelings of estrangement from the emphasized classroom practices of translation exercises with lexical items, and the written mode in use of kanji (Chinese characters) and syllabaries. However, my daily reality in the late 1970s was that I was learning in class a type of Japanese that did not serve me well in my outside social encounters with family members from Okinawa, exchange students, or even visitors from Japan. The worlds of lived experiences with language use and classroom practice with language coincided rarely to build my identity as a fledgling user of Japanese. The heritage language appeal appeared to be a fictive kinship that I would have to struggle to not only maintain but to cultivate in formal schooling and lived experiences across many years.

Aside from my vignette, the reality of heritage language education in the US as both an enticing and off-putting experience also results from the sociopolitical context of language education for learners and their teachers. Assumptions held by each about the very nature of language and language learning produce moments of connection as well as clashes. In 2017 the majority of heritage learners came from two major language groups: Chinese and Spanish users. Even examining the diversity within these two can give us a perspective on approaching "heritage language" that can also be used when discussing any language variety. For example, within the Chinese varieties of Mandarin, Cantonese, Hainanese, and so forth, differences exist primarily in phonology, lexicon, and similarities in written texts, whether with simplified or complex characters. Within Spanish, varieties from the US, the Americas, and peninsular Spain produce differences and similarities across discourse, phonology, lexicon, and, to a lesser extent, morphology and syntax. Socioeconomically dominant groups in each language have colonized institutions such as education to view the other varieties as unimportant or less significant to warrant their exclusion from use, relegating them to contexts of the home or popular culture. Nonetheless, many of these varieties continue to be used within classrooms, hospitals, and businesses because of their vitality in these regions. Educating everyone about the nature and value of these varieties is an important area to consider when preparing teachers.

Yvonne was the youngest of three children who immigrated from Ecuador in 1980 to join their mother, a single-woman head of household. In another testimonio Yvonne recalled her first experiences in the 6th grade Massachusetts class into which she was placed. Of her two siblings that immigrated with her, Yvonne was the only one placed at grade level. The continuity of education for her older brother and sister was disrupted when each was placed a grade lower than their previous studies, a common practice for public schools that saw this as a remedy for the need to develop English.

> "They could not figure out what to do with me because I was literate in Spanish. We had gym classes for two periods, ESL and reading instruction. Later in high school where Spanish was offered, at that time Spanish classes followed a grammatical syllabus and it was not geared to developing further literacy in Spanish. I was not learning in the Spanish classes. In fact, though I was increasingly submersed in English, even as I struggled to understand it, I also started wanting to avoid using Spanish."

In the end, although Yvonne was not in advanced placement courses, she opted to sit for exams to gain six college credits prior to graduating from high school.

Yvonne's and my story of alienation from our heritage languages happens even in a class that is conducted in "our" language. This context is exacerbated by the dominant ideology of "English only" instruction for immigrant children. In fact, Seals & Kreeft-Peyton (2017: 89) report that "students often come to English-dominant schools uncomfortable with and unwilling to speak their language (Duff, 2001), and parents often discourage them from speaking it at all (King & Mackey, 2007). New immigrants and refugees who come to English-dominant countries such as the US and who are proficient in one, and often many, languages other than English may strive to stop speaking that language or those languages in the effort to learn English, thinking they must choose between these languages, and parents may do little to promote use and learning of the language by their children." It is critical to point out how colonizers in the global South use similar tactics with the language of the colonized in their contexts by constructing certain negative discourses about the Other, colonizers also implicitly or explicitly assigned positive representations to themselves (Pennycook, 1998; Migge & Léglise, 2007). The procedures for placement (Ziegler, 1981), the content of courses, as well as instructional programs (Beaudrie & Ducar, 2005) constitute sites of struggle for a large number of heritage learners, particularly those who are minoritized and who are being socialized by peers, teachers, and the institution in general to loathe using the strengths afforded by a heritage language.

As Yvonne steadily learned to overcome each academic content areas' difficulty in her high school, she gained advanced placement college credit in Spanish and later admission to university. In six short years Yvonne claims she "lost her ability to use Spanish" and still did not see her heritage language as a resource to be actively utilized and cultivated. Yvonne claimed that:

> "I couldn't speak Spanish . . . until I met my Puerto Rican friend who helped me regain Spanish. I came to understand how quickly we forget and how fragile maintaining one's language is; so I made an effort to never forget it. She made me realize the advantages I had and resources by being bilingual, especially after visiting her family on the island and seeing how similar we were in language and culture. She never treated me as an inferior because I had lost fluency; instead, she would say 'Ok, nena. Vamos a practicar todos los días. Yo te ayudo.'"

In fact Yvonne initially resisted taking up a major in Spanish until her sophomore year, when she met her friend. While most undergraduates were delighting in their life as young adults far from parental surveillance, Yvonne reported:

> "I did not have time for that. I spent most of my time studying for my general education courses leading to my major in accounting. After recognizing that this wasn't sufficient, I learned of the academic support available from a bilingual collegiate program designed to bolster the success rate of students from diverse backgrounds. In my next years of study I not only received support but took on employment in that very program."

Through her courses, friendships with Puerto Rican classmates, and work experiences she also realized that her wealth of knowledge of the Spanish language could be a resource in a Spanish major.

> "As a major and undergraduate I was judged to have advanced levels of Spanish. This allowed me to enroll in the master's graduate-level literature

> classes, while others who did not have this level of literacy in Spanish were required to enroll in advanced language courses.
>
> I also was able to take a course in multicultural education in the School of Education. In that course I saw a video about the same school district that I had attended. In it a district spokesperson claimed how the students in her district became fluent because they didn't delay the learning of English by using the students' language, but rather immersed them into the English language and culture. Obviously that was so wrong . . . and of course she was a monolingual."

Moreover, Yvonne came to see herself as preparing to become a future teacher. In a sense she was developing "political clarity," a deepening consciousness of sociopolitical and economic realities that were shaping her life and her capacity to transform these material and symbolic conditions (Bartolomé, 2004).

In community language schools/programs, many of which have existed for more than 300 years since the founding of the US (Fishman & Nahirny, 1966), this private education of heritage language learners has been supported by immigrant communities who draw on resources supplied not only by grassroots organizations and their economically well-situated sponsors, but also by their respective corporate and government sponsors who provide education to sojourners in the US (Fishman, 1980, 2001; McGinnis, 2008; Schmidt, 2001). These include heritage programs that receive governmental support from, among others, Greece, Japan, Italy, Taiwan, the People's Republic of China, and Spain.

These teachers in K-12 may work in all-day schools or weekday afternoon and weekend schools. In addition, special summer programs, evening classes, and classes in community centers are offered (Fishman & Nahirny, 1966). However, the term "heritage" has been adopted since the 1990s (Polinsky & Kagan, 2007; Valdes, 2005).

Together universities and community schools have provided education in heritage languages in formal courses and in after-school and weekend courses to cultivate language and literacy learning, and, most importantly, affirming a strong identification with culture and community building (Shibata, 2000).

Who Are Heritage Language Teachers?

It is not clear how many teachers are gainfully employed or how many volunteer in heritage language education. While some formal programs limit their offerings by enrollment figures that fluctuate, other informal programs emerge as leaders in community schools to establish programs for families. Nor is it clear to what extent the teachers have educational backgrounds in their home countries and professional education. Some have become heritage language teachers because of their commitment to their communities, while others come from the ranks of foreign language teachers. While some of these teachers in formal community schools are credentialed by sponsoring governments, many are not necessarily language professionals in terms of formal teacher preparation and, for this reason, requests often emerge for such support.

Teachers of heritage languages who themselves are heritage language learners are survivors of the US educational system. Similarly, Yvonne's history of being underserved by public education is still a quite common experience in the US even for members of the two largest groups of heritage learners, Chinese and Spanish language users, let alone those from less commonly taught language groups that are smaller in number. Washington State has embarked on a consortium of interests (heritage, dual, and 2nd language teacher educators) funded by STARTALK to seek alternative teacher certification and World Language Endorsement.

Yvonne succeeded in graduating from university with a Spanish major. She later became gainfully employed as a Spanish teacher in a public school located in an economically privileged neighborhood, but faced micro-aggression from teachers who had learned Spanish as a foreign language. Yvonne recounts her experience as increasingly "tension-filled" as she was positioned as inferior through the day-to-day interactions of her school. As a "native speaker of Spanish" she faced challenges from her senior White colleagues, who had learned a peninsular variety (from Spain) and who perceived their variety to be more prestigious than hers. On one occasion Yvonne recalled that they questioned any native speaker's ability to teach Spanish to US learners. This ideology was also a concern raised by some parents, whom Yvonne had to reassure that their children would not miss out by being taught her variety of Spanish.

Yvonne also recognized herself as a heritage Spanish teacher, as she identified with the students who faced similar immigrant experiences. Accordingly, she demonstrated her commitment to overcome the institutional barriers that worked to prevent these students from being enrolled in and identified as capable of advanced placement course work. This work is even more significant in light of the limited instruction these minoritized students were receiving as English language learners. Yvonne sought to enrich her Spanish courses with study skills, project-based learning, and support in developing critical literacies for success in academic and community settings.

> "I knew that some of my students would not have opportunities that the dominant group's students were receiving. And I wanted them to compete and not get behind these others who had the opportunity to develop these skills through support from schooling and their wealthy parents. So I did all kinds of enrichment activities in my classes long before the term 'project-based inquiry' was a widespread concept. I even worked outside of school with them, taking them on field trips and informing their parents so that both learned about how they could take advantage of college opportunities."

Yvonne's hard work paid off as larger numbers of parents to the high school's open house found their way to her and as she gained recognition from administrators as a school leader.

Despite her success with students, Yvonne began to doubt that she was prepared enough to be successful without a higher degree. Her fluid identity trajectory—from native speaker to Spanish teacher to heritage language teacher to heritage educational leader—demonstrates the sociopolitical influences and actions she has taken to shape her professional life.

As a heritage language learner herself, Yvonne's history in becoming a Spanish teacher epitomizes the critical consciousness-raising that is essential to understand Audre Lorde's words ". . . survival is not an academic skill. It is learning how to stand alone, unpopular and sometimes reviled, and how to make common cause with those others identified as outside the structures in order to define and seek a world in which we can all flourish. It is learning how to take our differences and make them strengths. For the master's tools will never dismantle the master's house. They may allow us temporarily to beat him at his own game, but they will never enable us to bring about genuine change" (Lorde, 1979).

After realizing her ability to thrive in graduate courses while an undergraduate, Yvonne decided to seek admission into the master's program. There she faced the colonial gaze of "native speakers" enrolled in graduate programs who were recent sojourners from Spanish-speaking countries.

> "They made me feel as if I did not know Spanish, correcting me by saying 'we don't say it that way in my country.'"

Whether or not these Spanish users were from Spain or the Americas, their dialectal varieties were held in high regard while Yvonne's was not. Yvonne's variety was a product of Ecuadorian elementary education, her classroom language learning experiences in US high school and undergraduate education, and her own travel and study abroad in Spain. What made her variety less legitimate? After two degrees majoring in Spanish at a prestigious university in the US, how did her linguistic variety not become legitimate?

In many heritage language programs, in addition to perpetuating the dominant language variety, power relations are reproduced from those existing in the countries of origin. Doerr and Lee (2016) document how power relationships between resident Koreans and Japanese in Japan are reproduced in the Japanese heritage language classroom. In particular, Doerr and Lee (2016) show how structural racism is evidenced in schools' erasure of non-Japanese heritage even when their student populations have more than one heritage, being both Japanese and European American. All too often heritage language programs may reproduce hegemonic power relations in promoting a dominant heritage without regard to the actual cultural diversity of its students.

History of Heritage Language Teacher Education: Class and Linguistic Entanglements

In what context did this come about? As heritage language programs in the US did not exist until the late 1990s, Polinsky & Kagan (2007) attribute the term "heritage language" to the influential body of multilingual research in Canada. However, in the US context the heritage language education movement has emerged without the public contentiousness or the anti-bilingualism and biliteracy that bilingual and native-speaker oriented courses produced in K-12 public education. After all, who could be against heritage? Perhaps because this field initially focused on college-level foreign language education and included a range of learners whose prior learning of English goes unquestioned at the college level, the heritage discourse may have allowed for persuading dominant groups to positively value this type of public education.

Within the long contentious history of public education for bilingual learners in K-12, there was also a consequence for foreign language education. Pufahl & Rhodes (2011) provide further evidence of neglect in educating those with another language other than English. They report the case that ". . . in K-12 public and private schools, where language programs have experienced a decline in numbers in the past decade, only a small percentage of 'foreign' language programs are designed for speakers of those languages" (Seals & Kreeft-Peyton, 2017: 89).

While some foreign language or native-speaker courses were initiated in high schools and colleges, where courses for native speakers of Spanish or Chinese were provided, public education faced a growing demographic that challenged assumptions about who the learners actually were. Faculty members who recognized the lack of appropriate placement of "native" users of a language, and a concentration of this population in certain circumstances, began advocating separate courses for "native speakers" (McGinnis, 1996; Teschner, 1983; Valdés, 2005). A subset of this population was also known as "receptive bilingual" learners, those with receptive skills or incomplete acquisition in the heritage language, and were also counted among "false beginners," those with prior knowledge or study of a language yet still enrolled in lower level or beginning language classes. Not coincidentally, in general these alternative terms tended to attribute deficits in the education of these heritage students, who in general had a range of skills yet were provided little formal instruction in the academic study of "their heritage" language (Valdés, 2005).

Other long-term heritage groups have endured a rocky reception in the US, depending on the US's economic and political history with other nations of the world. Ironically, support for these resources has experienced the strongest educational push during times of war and economic competition.

Since 1990 the creation of National Foreign Language Resource Centers in the US has raised the nation's level of world language education through research, professional development, and dissemination of materials. Today several of the 16 centers have directed their attention to heritage language research and pedagogy. Seven of these—located at the University of Hawaii at Manoa; George Washington University in Washington, DC; Pennsylvania State University; University of California Los Angeles; California State University, Fullerton; Duke University; and City University of New York's Graduate Center—have carved a niche for providing teachers' professional development through institutes, conferences, and workshops.

Wiley & Bhalla (2017) suggest that there are only crude measures of the number of heritage language educators. This under-representation of heritage teachers occurs because in "national" surveys this area has not been addressed.

At the University of California Los Angeles' National Heritage Language Resource Center (NHLRC) the majority of these professional development opportunities are offered for teaching at the university level and, until recently, have focused almost exclusively on building a research base for language education to achieve higher proficiency/competence through university language programs that address linguistic and identity needs. As such, formal linguistic theory has been used to address acquisition of features of the learner's heritage language needing correction or to conduct a broader sociolinguistic survey on issues such as linguistic diversity and the learner's formal features of language use and intercultural competence, areas that could be discretely defined and researched through positivist methodologies. A few examples of early exceptions of researchers addressing the social context of learners' academic progress can be found in Bhatt, 2009 (Hindi heritage learners in the US) and Lykke Nielsen, 2009 (Arabic heritage learners in Denmark). One of the characteristic features of the early professional development carried out by the NHLRC was the building of a research agenda that could distinguish at the university level between the instructional needs of heritage language learners (HLLs) and foreign language learners (FLLs) or second language learners.

In 2017 the NHLRC, in a noteworthy collaboration with the Center for Advanced Research on Language Acquisition, focused their annual conference on language teacher development and teaching practices across contexts of inservice/preservice preparation, collegiate instruction, in foreign language, ESL, and EFL. Seventy-six of the non-plenary scheduled presentations ranged from technical issues on skills and knowledge in proficiency-oriented second language acquisition, assessment, native/non-native teacher issues, intercultural competence, technology-assisted teaching and language program coordination, community engagement, mentoring, reflective practice, to presentations addressing issues that ideologically challenge the field, such as teachers' language ideologies, pluri/translingualism, critical pedagogy and critical literacy, social justice, intercultural and cultural diversity, and global citizenship.

Among these sessions, only a fraction focused directly on heritage language teacher education (Aoki & Yaden; Brown, Amahedian & Aziz; Duder & Cowell;

Erlam; Ellis; Elliott; Mitchell; Muhonen; Seo; and Tigret). Of these, several re-inscribed versions of native/non-native teacher issues from the ESL and foreign language field emerged in the sessions that focused on the cultural knowledge contrasting American-born versus foreign-born educators (Brown, Amahedian & Aziz), an acceptance of globalizing learner-centered pedagogy, authentic language practice, and multiple perspectives on cultural learning (Duder & Cowell; Mitchell) and technical issues (language teaching principles and pedagogical knowledge, etc).

However, the two most progressive linguistic challenges to the technicist orientation in teacher education were presentations by Tigret and Muhonen, whose research on Finnish and Swedish bilingualism informed a heritage language program to re-conceptualize pedagogical practices as multilingual, as distinct from the monolingual model which continues to undergird much of heritage language instruction and teacher education.

Only five presentations addressed the issue of identity and relationship of teacher educators to teachers, albeit foreign language educators (Angus & Fikes; Gallego; Glynn, Wesley & Wassell; Halvorsen Malone; and O'Donald). If we are to examine heritage teacher education critically, research is needed on the nature of the relationship between teacher educators and the teachers they mentor.

What Are the Significant Struggles That Heritage Language Teachers and Teacher Educators Face?

Currently, in order to engage with a process of decolonization, heritage language teachers and the teacher education programs that educate them must face institutional traditions, legacies from popular ideologies about language education and learning, and material challenges.

Institutional obstacles at the Pre-K to 12 level include certification/licensure pathways and continuing professional education. Heritage language educators are vulnerable in the accreditation area as no national acknowledgement of requirements for heritage language teachers has been established. While there are promising movements in the Dual Language Field to identify entry-level requirements for teachers in dual language programs (MABE, 2012), there remain expectations that heritage language teachers adhere to what is known thus far from applied linguistics' second language teacher education, chief among them the English as a second language and foreign language teacher professions. Critically viewing these expectations is that there is a noticeable absence of expectations about receiving the contributions from a field that has a long history of research for many of the same populations. Often left out is the more than 80 years of research from the bilingual teacher education field and the expectations for educating multilingual communities, often from immigrant and diasporic communities that are under-served by public education. Therefore, within the programs that prepare language teachers, often-valuable contributions from the bilingual field are not drawn upon when they could promote further student engagement with successful academic upward mobility.

Furthermore, we acknowledge that language teacher education programs are not given high priority as compared to teacher education in elementary and secondary science, math, technology, and literacy fields. Since institutions allocate resources based on these priorities, even English as a second language and foreign language teacher educators may be under-resourced. For example, courses for preparing language teachers in university courses for Pre-K or for college level language instruction are often relegated to the status of institutional service courses that are staffed by non-tenure track faculty. Thus in the specialized area of heritage language teaching, particularly for those without a professional home in a bilingual teacher education program, participants are often educated by those with credentials from the foreign language teacher or ESL teacher field. Moreover, those teachers without the support of these credentialing programs will face even greater difficulty in finding pathways to licensure or a degree. While there are certainly overlaps in terms of content and pedagogy with the foreign language teacher or ESL teacher field, there are also issues specific to heritage language that are not being addressed by these programs or periodic professional conferences and workshops. Chief among these issues is the need to synergistically contribute to the maintenance and continued vitality of communities using heritage languages, a goal that has not been a part of foreign language teacher education or assimilative ESL teacher education programs that are technically acquisition-oriented.

Another major area of decolonization is a struggle that requires critically examining the practices in the foreign language teacher or ESL teacher field that are taken for granted. Communities using heritage languages are increasingly diverse, with varieties that are not merely standardized. Thus, while there is a growing push for language educators to have an understanding of language variation (i.e., the varieties of languages that their students use), an underlying assimilative monolingual model—the educated person standard—is often the main goal for heritage language learners. Heritage teacher educators and teachers may even accept this normative ideology though it reifies the status of one dialect over the others. Heritage educators then must question how a plurilingual identity can be cultivated with instruction geared to a monolingual goal. Consequently, teachers must struggle to imagine how a plurilingual goal can revitalize the heritage language-using community.

Finally, heritage language educators face material struggles not only in the tangible sense of scarcity of accessible curricular materials and texts, but in the sense of an embodied presence of licensed/credentialed heritage language teachers. Having a community of heritage language educators to resist the colonizing effects of the English as a second language and foreign language teacher professions could address critically questioning areas of knowledge that de Oliveira & Burke (2015) identify as important to teachers: "(a) knowledge of teachers as learners of language teaching, (b) teacher practice and knowledge of self, (c) knowledge and understanding of language learning and assessment, and (d) procedural and declarative knowledge about language." Is this sufficient to stem the tide of losing heritage language resources in a community? How could the field of heritage language education be effective in undoing the colonizing effects of our context? We need new understandings that could guide the designing of new futures for heritage learners and for constructing useful knowledge for the field—principles of non-hierarchy for language studies, and democratic participation of all heritage learners in contributing to their communities.

What Practices Can Help Teachers Build Towards Decolonizing Education for Heritage Language Learners?

In the battleground of education world-wide, political stakes are high for those who depend on free public universal education. Among those who count on public education are families from the full spectrum of social economic classes, but the most vulnerable are those whose neighborhoods can mobilize the fewest resources because of, in part, differential levels of institutional knowledge and skills and lower incomes; in essence, the working class and immigrants/refugees. The stakes are high for heritage language learners who come from these populations. In the US, heritage language learners who become graduates with a four-year college degree would acquire a median weekly salary of $1,137, whereas those with a high-school degree would average $678. This difference is even greater when comparing workers with doctoral degrees, where the median weekly salary is $1,623 compared with $738 for those with some or no college degree (US Bureau of Labor Statistics, 2017). One way for heritage language learners to increase their chances of financial stability is to invest in school.

Yvonne saw schooling as her way to do just that. While her older siblings did not have this opportunity, Yvonne's academic investments paid off. Drawing from her experiences in college, when she became a teacher Yvonne was able to incorporate what she felt her high-school students needed in order to be better prepared than she had been. She recalled:

> In my school I saw that my heritage language students were not getting the same opportunities to develop research skills and literacies that were going to be needed later in college. So I turned my lessons in the Spanish classes into inquiries and project-based activities to involve them in the types of thinking, reading, and writing that would get them ready for college. I organized field trips to different sites for their projects—libraries, museums, and places they could gather information and conduct interviews. I conducted fundraisers with their families to get the funds to help pay for our activities.

Yvonne recognized that her students' futures were being jeopardized. Not all populations of heritage language teachers will necessarily see it their responsibility to take measures to build pathways to college. Not all have to, as some of their students may already possess the social capital and financing needed, as well as the necessary conditions to do this, with help from their parents or expert others. In assessing her responsibility, Yvonne resisted the standard curriculum and engaged her students in critical literate activities, building the potential to contribute to decolonizing heritage language education.

My first vivid memory of an encounter with the concept of decolonization came from the experiences of a Chamorro scholar who was denied a university teaching assistantship unless she would submit to an official test of her ability to use English. At that time, 1981, Guam had been a free-associated state of the US for more than 83 years and all her education from elementary school to college had been conducted through the medium of English. Her success in school and college was only rivaled by her activism in her community as a community leader. Both arenas of work allowed her to claim success, and yet now she was seen as a questionable English speaker. Her anger led her to protest the policy but this was met by professorial indifference from those whose middle-class varieties of English hailed from Britain, South Africa, and various US regions. She chose not to sit the exam and years later chose not to complete her doctoral program but to assume a primary role in researching and teaching Chamorro linguistics at an institute of higher education in Guam. Could she have been considered a bilingual language learner, if not a heritage language learner of English? I was acutely aware of the loss of a great scholar, in part due to the native-speaker ideology that reigned in applied linguistics and ESL education during the 1980s and continues being challenged to this day.

Ironically, at that time, when I was a student in the Spanish and Portuguese Department's master's program, I was selected as teaching assistant at the same institution partially because of the central peninsular accent I had learned to emulate from my year of study abroad in Spain. At the time there wasn't even an option to study abroad within other countries of the Americas. The professors in charge of undergraduate language instruction were Spaniards who favored those who used their variety, and not the varieties found in the Americas. While there were graduate students who came from the Caribbean, Mexico, and Central and South America, there were only a handful of students who were learners of Spanish as a second language and even fewer than a handful of heritage language learners. Thus at the same time, in the foreign language field, as a non-native speaker of Spanish, privileges of those in power were bestowed upon those using their variety. Undoubtedly using the prestige variety in that department gave me access to funding that I would not otherwise have had to complete my master's program.

While I was not aware of the workings of colonial relations or formal theories of decolonization, despite being located in the US I experienced the impact and became aware of the privilege of a dominant group (Castillian Spanish). Hence in thinking about decolonizing heritage language, the field must address complex issues globally that have ignored the diversity that is integral to any heritage language group and exerted hegemonic influence beyond borders. In seeking to decolonize heritage language education, structures of dominance emerge from accepting power relations created through the very nature of defining language, literacies, and culture.

Language

In the literature, heritage language is described as a product of those who claim it; "individuals with familial or ancestral ties to a language other than [the dominant language] who exert their agency in determining if they are HLLs of that language" (Hornberger & Wang, 2008: 6). Thus a heritage language speaker's identity is indexed by the use of a language other than English. A heritage language speaker is defined as an individual "who is raised in a home where a non-English language is spoken, who speaks or at least understands the language, and who is to some degree bilingual in that language and in English" (Valdés, 2001: 38). This distinction operates to create a boundary between foreign language learners who cannot claim any contact with the heritage language to serve them as a resource in the classroom. Still other scholars see heritage language as "a process of human action and agency (thus proposing the verb *heritaging*)" (Harvey, 2001).

Kramsch (this volume) states, "Decolonizing foreign language education research would require a collective effort to question notions taken from one language into another, reconstruct their historical meanings, engage with other theories produced elsewhere without judging them less progressive, less relevant, or less important than those produced in the Anglo-American center." Aligned with this notion, one direction that is readily viable would be to challenge the hierarchical language ideology underlying heritage language education by taking a decolonizing orientation to question heritage languages programs' maintenance of instruction limitation to only a prestige variety. Ironically, heritage languages are taught often without much attention to the varieties actually used by the learners (Valdés, González, García & Márquez, 2008). In contrast, by legitimizing the multiple varieties in a heritage language education, those engaged in decolonizing efforts can take leadership in critically ending the nation/state linkage that subjugates certain varieties of language. Students could then learn about how their home repertoires can be used to accomplish social goals in a variety of communities. Such a step towards a broader notion of language as shaped by human agents and used agentively to enact social goals accomplishes at least three aims. First, it creates critical awareness of these language varieties. Second, it cultivates the value of these varieties and their use. Third, it potentially empowers learners to engage in transforming their heritage communities to ensure growth and sustenance.

Yvonne's teaching has long challenged the privileging of one variety by building more than just linguistic knowledge. In her classroom she taps the heritage learners' "funds of knowledge," that is the skilled ways of culturally and economically sustaining their family. Moll, Amanti, Neff and Gonzalez (2001) defined this type of knowledge "to refer to the historically accumulated and culturally developed bodies of knowledge and skills essential for household or individual functioning and well-being" (p. 133).Yvonne contacted her students' families and was able to utilize what she learned to relate not only to them but also connect what they already knew to what they would be learning. One example that Yvonne found was particularly effective for working with her high-school students' knowledge of various categories of music and their preferences and linking these to learning about literature, both poetry and prose, as well as art. Yvonne remembered that her students were often pressured to fit in, to assimilate even when they were not accepted. Creating opportunities where their projects displayed their creativity and quality of thinking not only shifted public perceptions of them but also their own recognition of their achievements and contributions.

Bateman & Wilkinson (2010) found that successful heritage language teachers tap the resources of their heritage language students, particularly with regard to lexical and cultural issues. But to operate on a social political scale, heritage teacher education needs to extend language lessons beyond the lexical levels. This means preparing teachers to explore popular texts; for example, genres that circulate in their students' lives as well as the social life in their communities. In this way, critical literacies figure into teacher preparation to enable them to "read the word and read the world" (Freire & Macedo, 1987)

Literacies

Also with regard to heritage languages, significant developmental work is needed in those communities who languages are not yet codified in written forms. When a community maintains a heritage language through mainly oral traditions, the community's day-to-day existence may easily be dominated by another language community's pervasive written modality and literate practices. In fact it may lead to hybridization of the heritage variety, colonized by the dominant group's literate ways of usage. This is the case of indigenous languages whose oral literate practices may be undermined by Disneyfication, a process of turning culturally particular oral practices into popular mainstream genres; for example, Pocahontas versus Matoaka (Shilling, 2017.) Understanding contradictions inherent in the location of heritage language education within various social structures can help clarify which political challenges can be made and what effective directions can be taken.

Cultural–Scales of Community Extinction or Revitalization

In contrast with the ways that culture in foreign language education is approached in the US as consisting of building intercultural competence, heritage language learning has a greater social role in community building. Seals & Kreeft-Peyton (2017: 88) advocate that heritage language education can play an important role in staving off intergenerational language loss. In families we see patterns of intergenerational language loss, where a language other than English is generally not spoken after two or three generations of arrival in the US (Alba, Logan, Lutz & Stults, 2002; Lam, 2008; Veltman, 2000).

Though Fishman doubts the ability of educational institutions alone to accomplish this, if this were a more emphasized requirement in the preparation of heritage language teachers there would be possibilities of working with diasporic communities locally or virtually that held the promise of helping sustain these communities. The cultural area in heritage language teacher education could be a significant space for critical efforts in decolonization. One step would be to help teachers challenge the ideologies that homogenize heritage language communities. One blindness exists in the failure to recognize the diversity within; how are teachers prepared to examine differences within their communities' diverse multiracial and ethnic members and how these affect social mobility.

All teachers would benefit from recognizing ideologies at play in education, but foremost would be heritage language educators who must resist those that denigrate resources that are useful to sustaining and revitalizing heritage language communities. Teacher educators have a responsibility to continuously review their legitimizing practices in recognizing how state, national, and international policies are shaping the education of teachers and, when necessary, resist and reframe these. A prime example has been to use the lure and attractiveness of "heritage language" to position students in a positive light rather than identifying them as lacking in language proficiency, as English language learners in the US context.

Conclusion

In 2017 the stakes for public education became even more precariously high as the nation gradually grasped the impact of Donald Trump's appointment of Betsy DeVos as Secretary of Education in his administration. What hope can heritage language teachers have of decolonizing education when the very nature of public education is threatened by the neoliberal orientations of the nation's leaders and current tides of anti-immigrant sentiment?

Through arguments presented and embodied by testimonios and the current scholarship, teacher education for the heritage language field has enormous promise for contributing to both the teaching profession and to a decolonization of language education in the US. While not all teachers may identify with Yvonne's experience, the hegemony of a privileged groups is recognizable in all language varieties, with minoritizing effects for all those who use a different linguistic variety. Similarly, heritage teacher educators may choose to stop perpetuating colonial hegemonies by recognizing their negative influence on the lives of teachers, students, and their communities. Support for the academic success, not just language competency, of heritage learners and teachers is needed. By building the health of a profession and the lofty goals to counter intergenerational linguistic and cultural heritage loss, cancerous ideologies can be faced and addressed, thereby undoing the effects of colonized thinking about linguistic and cultural difference. This is both a health and moral imperative. Seizing this opportunity leverages our current work towards a hope-filled future of a transformed educational system for heritage communities and the wider society's socially just cultural and multilingual development.

References

Alba, R., Logan, J., Lutz, A. & Stults, B. (2002). Only English by the third generation? Loss and prevention of the mother tongue among the grandchildren of contemporary immigrants. *Demography, 39(3),*467–484.

Bartolomé, L. (2004). Critical pedagogy and teacher education: Radicalizing prospective teachers. *Teacher Education Quarterly,* 97–122.

Bateman, B. E. & Wilkinson, S. L. (2010). Spanish for heritage speakers: A statewide survey of secondary school teachers. *Foreign Language Annals, 43,* 324–353.

Beaudrie, S. & Ducar, C. (2005). Beginning-level university heritage programs: Creating space for all heritage language learners. *Heritage Language Journal, 3,* 1–26.

Bhatt, R. (2009, June). Sociolinguistic inquiries into heritage language learning: The Indian diaspora. Paper presented at the Third Heritage Language Summer Institute, Urbana, IL. Retrieved [November 2017] from http://www.international.ucla.edu/languages/nhlrc/2009summer/presentations/Bhatt.pptGoogle Scholar.

Blackmer Reyes, K. & Curry Rodríguez, J. E. (2012). Chicana/Latina testimonios: Methodologies, pedagogies, and political urgency. *Equity & Excellence in Education 45(3),* 525–538.

Cummins, J. (2005). A proposal for action: strategies for recognizing heritage language competence as a learning resource within the mainstream classroom. *The Modern Language Journal 89,* 585–592.

Darder, A., Baltodano, M. & Torres, R. D. (2002). *The critical Pedagogy reader.* London: Routledge.

Darder, A. (2012). *Culture and power in the classroom.* New York: Paradigm.

Darder, A. & Yiamouyiannis, Z. (2009). Valentía política y la lucha por descolonizar el trabajo en las comunidades. *Rhizoma Freireano, 4.* www.rizoma-freireano.org/valentia-politica-y-la-lucha-por-descolonizar-el-trabajo-en-las-comunidades--antonia-darder-y-zeus-yiamouyiannis.

Delgado Bernal, D. & Villalpando, O. (2002). An apartheid of knowledge in academia: The struggle over the "legitimate" knowledge of faculty of color. *Equity & Excellence in Education, 35(2),* 169–180.

Delgado Bernal, D., Burciaga, R. & Flores Carmona, J. (2012). Chicana/Latina testimonios: Mapping the methodological, pedagogical, and political. *Equity & Excellence in Education, 45(3),* 363–372.

Duff, P. (2001). Language, literacy, content and (pop) culture: Challenges for ESL students in mainstream courses. *Canadian Modern Language Review, 58,* 103–132.

Clandinin, D. J. & Connelly, F. M. (2000). *Narrative inquiry: Experience and story in Qualitative research.* San Francisco, CA: Jossey-Bass.

de Oliveira, L. C. & Burke, A. M. (2015). Mainstream elementary teachers' perspectives about teaching English Language Learners. In *Preparing Teachers to work with English*

Language Learners in mainstream classrooms (pp. 3–15). Charlotte, NC: Information Age Publishing.

Doerr, N. M. & Lee, K. (2016) Heritage language education without inheriting hegemonic ideologies: Shifting perspectives on "Korea" in a weekend Japanese-language school in the United States. Diaspora, indigenous, and minority education. *Studies of Migration, Integration, Equity, and Cultural Survival, 10(2)*, 112–126.

Fishman, J. A. (1980). Ethnic community mother tongue schools in the U.S.A.: Dynamics and distributions. *International Migration Review, 14,* 235–247.

Fishman, J. (2001). 300-plus years of heritage language education. In J. K. Peyton, D. A. Ranard and S. McGinnis (Eds.), *Heritage languages in America: Preserving a national resource language in education: Theory and practice* (pp. 87–97). Washington, DC: Center for Applied Linguistics.

Fishman, J. A. & Nahirny, V. C. (1966). The ethnic group school and mother tongue maintenance. In J. A. Fishman (Ed.), *Language loyalty in the United States: The maintenance and perpetuation of Non-English mother tongues by American ethnic and religious groups* (pp. 92–126). London: Mouton & Co.

Freire, P. & Macedo, D. (1987). *Literacy: Reading the word and the world.* Boston, MA: Taylor & Francis.

Galindo, R. (2007). Voices of identity in a Chicana teacher. Occupational narratives of the self. *The Urban Review, 39(3),* 251–280.

Guerrero, M. (2003). Acquiring and participating in the use of academic Spanish: Four novice Latina bilingual education teachers' stories. *Journal of Latinos and Education, 2,* 159–181.

Harvey, D. C. (2001). Heritage Pasts and Heritage Presents: Temporality, Meaning and the Scope of Heritage Studies. *International Journal of Heritage Studies, 7:4*, 319–338.

Hinton, L. (2001). Involuntary language loss among immigrants. Asian American linguistic autobiographies. Georgetown University Round Table on Languages and Linguistics 1999, 203–252.

Hornberger, N. H. & Wang, S. C. (2008). Who are our heritage language learners? Identity and biliteracy in heritage language education in the United States. In D. Brinton, O. Kagan and S. Bauckus (Eds.), *Heritage language education: A new field emerging* (pp. 3–35). New York: Routledge.

King, K. & Mackey, A. (2007). *The bilingual edge: How, when and why to teach your child a second language.* New York: HarperCollins.

Lam, H. (2008). Language shift and language loss. In J. Gonzalez (Ed.), *Encyclopedia of bilingual education* (pp. 476–479). Los Angeles, CA: Sage.

Liu, N. (2010). The role of heritage language schools in building a multilingual society. *The heritage brief,* Alliance for the Advancement of Heritage Languages, Center for Applied Linguistics (CAL): Washington, DC.

Lorde, A. (1979). The master's tools will never dismantle the master's house. www.historyisaweapon.com/defcon1/lordedismantle.html 4/7.

Lykke Nielsen, H. (2009, June). The hidden barriers: Heritage learners of Arabic in a Danish university. Paper presented at Third Heritage Language Summer Institute. Developing a Research Base for the Heritage Field. University of Illinois Urbana-Champaign.

MABE—Massachusetts Association for Bilingual Education (2012). Dual language educator license: Highlights of competencies, knowledge and skills. www.massmabe.org/resources/What%20We%20Do/MABE%20Dual%20Language%20Educator%20License%20Organized%20by%20TESOL%20Teacher%20Standards%20copy.pdf.

Makoni, S. & Pennycook, A.(Eds.) (2007). *Disinventing and reconstituting languages*. Bristol, UK: Multilingual Matters.

McGinnis, S.(1996).Teaching Chinese to the Chinese: The development of an assessment and instructional model. In. J. E. Liskin Gasparro (Ed.), *Patterns and policies: The changing demographics of foreign language instruction* (pp. 107–121). Boston, MA: Heinle & Heinle.

McGinnis, S. (2008). From mirror to compass: The Chinese heritage language education sector in the United States. In D. Brinton, O. Kagan and S. Bauckus (Eds.), *Heritage language education: A new field emerging* (pp. 229–242). New York: Routledge.

Migge, B. & Léglise, I.(2007). Language and colonialism. Applied linguistics in the context of creole communities. In M. Hellinger and A. Pauwels (Eds.), *Language and communication: diversity and change. Handbook of applied linguistics* (pp. 297–338). Berlin: Mouton de Gruyter.

Moll, L., Amanti,C., Neff, D. & Gonzalez, N.(2001). *Funds of knowledge for teaching: Using a qualitative approach to connect homes and classrooms.* Mahwah, NJ: Lawrence Erlbaum Associates.

Pennycook, A.(1998).*English and the discourses of colonialism: The politics of language.* London: Routledge.

Polinsky, M. & Kagan, O.(2007).Heritage languages: In the 'wild' and in the classroom. *Language and Linguistics Compass 1/5,* 368–395.

Pufahl, I. & Rhodes, N.(2011).Foreign language instruction in U.S. schools: Results of a national survey of elementary and secondary schools. *Foreign Language Annals, 44(2),* 258–288.

Rampton, B.(2011).From 'multi-ethnic adolescent heteroglossia' to 'contemporary urban vernaculars.' *Language & Communication, 31,* 276–294.

Schmidt, C.(2001).*The politics of language: Conflict, identity and cultural pluralism in comparative perspective.* Oxford, UK: Oxford University Press.

Seals, C.(2014).*Making Heritage Language Speakers Visible in the Mainstream Classroom.* Alliance for the Advancement of Heritage Languages, Washington, DC: Center for Applied Linguistics. Available from: www.researchgate.net/publication/273444277_Making_Heritage_Language_Speakers_Visible_in_the_Mainstream_Classroom.

Seals, C. A. & Kreeft-Peyton, J.(2017).Heritage language education: Valuing the languages, literacies, and cultural competencies of immigrant youth, *Current Issues in Language Planning, 18(1),* 87–101.

Sharma, D. & Sankaran, L.(2011).Cognitive and social forces in dialect shift: Gradual change in London Asian speech. *Language Variation and Change, 23(3),* 399–428.

Shibata, S.(2000).Opening a Japanese Saturday school in a small town in the United States: Community collaboration to teach Japanese as a heritage language. *Bilingual Research Journal 24(4),* 465–474.

Shilling, V.(2017).The true story of Pocahontas: Historical myths versus sad reality https://indiancountrymedianetwork.com/history/genealogy/true-story-pocahontas-historical-myths-versus-sad-reality/.

Showstack, R. E.(2012).Symbolic power in the heritage language classroom: How Spanish heritage speakers sustain and resist hegemonic discourses on language and cultural diversity. *Spanish in Context, 9,* 1–26.

Suarez, D. (2007). Second and third generation heritage language speakers: HL scholarship's relevance to the research needs and future directions of TESOL. *Heritage Language Journal, 5(1),* 27–49.

Teschner, R. V.(1983).Spanish placement for native speakers, nonnative speakers and others. *ADFL Bulletin, 13*, 37–42.

US Department of Labor. Bureau of Labor Statistic (2017) Employment projections April 17. www.bls.gov/emp/ep_chart_001.htm.

Valdés, G. (2001). Heritage language students: Profiles and possibilities. In J. K. Peyton, D. A. Ranard and S. McGinnis (Eds.), *Heritage languages in America: Preserving a national resource* (pp. 37–77). Washington, DC & McHenry, IL: Center for Applied Linguistics & Delta Systems.

Valdés, G. (2005). Bilingualism, Heritage Language Learners, and SLA Research: Opportunities Lost or Seized? *The Modern Language Journal, 89(3)*, 410–426.

Valdés, G., González, S. V., García, D. L. & Márquez, P. (2008). Heritage languages and ideologies of language: Unexamined challenges. In D. M. Brinton, O. Kagan and S. Bauckus (Eds.), *Heritage language education: A new field emerging* (pp. 107–130). New York: Routledge

Veltman, C. J. (2000). The American linguistic mosaic: Understanding language shift in the US. In S. L. McKay and S. C. Wong (Eds.), *New immigrants in the United States: Readings for second language educators* (pp. 58–94). Cambridge, UK: Cambridge University Press.

Wiley, T. & Bhalla, S. (2017). The demographics of heritage and community languages in the United States. In O. E. Kagan, M. M. Carreira and C. H. Chik (Eds.), *The Routledge handbook of heritage language education* (pp. 33–47). New York: Routledge.

Wong Fillmore, L. (1991). When learning a second language means losing the first. *Early Childhood Research Quarterly, 6*, 323–346.

Ziegler, J. D. (1981). Guidelines for the construction of a Spanish placement examination for the Spanish-dominant Spanish-English bilingual. In G. Valdés, A. G. Lozano and R. Garcia-Moya (Eds.), *Teaching Spanish to the Hispanic bilingual: Issues, aims and methods* (pp 211–214). New York: Teachers College Columbia.

6

DECOLONIZING FOREIGN, SECOND, HERITAGE, AND FIRST LANGUAGES

Implications for Education

Ofelia García

THE GRADUATE CENTER, CITY UNIVERSITY OF NEW YORK

Introduction

Language has been used as a tool of domination, conquest and colonization throughout history. This paper argues that the divisions of language into those that are said to be "foreign," "second," "heritage," and even "first" are constructions of western powers, and especially their schools, to consolidate power and create governable subjects. If language was seen not as an autonomous whole, where one whole can be added to another whole, but as a system of complex and dynamic language practices in which speakers engage to make meaning, then named languages, as we know them today, would lose their power.

This paper explores the reasons why in the past, as well as in the present, the dynamic language practices of most people in the world have been viewed with suspicion, as powerful elites have imposed a way of using language that is constrained by artificial conventions and that reflects their own language practices. Nation-states have co-opted the human potential of language as a meaning-making semiotic tool, relegating many speakers to a position of speechlessness.

The conception of autonomous languages constructed by nation-states and their schools has also co-created the concepts of bilingualism, multilingualism and plurilingualism prevalent in the world today. The expectation continues to be that languages could be "added" as separate wholes, without taking into account the notion that true multilingual speakers never behave in this way.

Because named languages are constructions of nation-states, they are identified, especially by schools and in education, as *first* (having been born into it in one land) or *foreign* (belonging to another land). And as many nation-states are lured by the supposed economic benefits of acquiring especially English, and as some minoritized groups gain recognition in the 21st century, new nomenclatures have emerged—*second, third, heritage language*. This chapter reviews the types of language education programs that fit those categories and suggests that they fail to leverage the actual language practices of learners, called here *translanguaging*.

Taking up the example of Latinx in the U.S., this paper argues that these language divisions are artificial and take up an external nation-state point of view. Seen from the individual speakers' perspective, the language practices in which speakers engage are simply theirs—not first, second, third, heritage or foreign. But language education programs are implemented as being foreign language, second language, heritage language, bilingual education or multilingual education programs. Taking the perspective of speakers, and not of these constructions, we describe how different Latinx students in U.S. classrooms experience language education programs in ways that leave out their own language practices. We describe how these different programs are inadequate for these minoritized bilingual learners, for their language practices go beyond what is billed as "Spanish" or "English." The result is the production of an inferior subjectivity that justifies their academic failure as their inability to use language "correctly."

Named Languages: Historical Origins

That the named languages of nation-states were constructed is a well-known fact. Makoni and Pennycook (2007) insist that we refer to this construction as "inventions," so as to recognize that the process was not innocent, but that, in the naming, categorizations of exclusion were created. The naming of Spanish, English, Portuguese etc. as the only legitimate language practice of nation-states has always been purposeful, a way of excluding those who were conquered and colonized. Language standardization has been accompanied by military victories and successful colonial and imperialistic ventures. A brief history of the historical construction of Spanish and English, the named languages assigned to US Latinx, helps contextualize the process.

Construction of Castilian Spanish

What was named Castilian Spanish started to become the standard in the Iberian Peninsula concomitantly with the Reconquista against the Moors (718–1492) (Hall, 1974). Its orthography was codified, following the speech of the upper classes of Toledo, in the compilation of Castile's legal tradition of Alfonso X the Wise (1221–1284), known as his *Siete Partidas* (1265). But it wasn't until the marriage of the Catholic monarchs, Isabella I of Castile and Ferdinand of Aragon, in 1469 that Castilian Spanish gained more power and authority. In 1492, as the last Moors were expelled from Granada, Antonio de Nebrija published his *Gramática de la Lengua Castellana*, the first grammar of any Romance language. Nebrija dedicates the grammar to Queen Isabella by saying: "*Siempre la lengua fue compañera del imperio*" [Language always was the companion of empire]. Speaking about Nebrija's purpose in writing this grammar, Walter Mignolo (1995) argues: "He knew that the power of a unified language, via its grammar, lay in teaching it to barbarians, as well as controlling barbarian languages by writing their grammars" (p. 39).

This Castilian Spanish was then used in the *catequización* of the Indigenous population to Catholicism (Briceño Perozo, 1987) throughout the 16th century. In 1596 King Phillip issued an edict that authorized some indigenous languages to be used in evangelization—*lenguas generales* studied and named by Jesuit missionaries as Náhuatl, Quechua, Chicha, and Tupí-Guaraní. The linguistic practices of many white Europeans who accompanied the missionaries and conquistadores, as well as those of the indigenous people, were ignored.

In 1713 the Real Academia Española was founded on the instructions of Philip V, the first Bourbon ruler of Spain, to guarantee a Spanish norm and to "*velar por que los cambios que experimente [. . .] no quiebren la esencial unidad que mantiene en todo el ámbito hispánico.*" ["to watch that the changes that it undergoes [. . .] do not disrupt the essential unity that it maintains in the entire Hispanic context"] (http://noticias.juridicas.com/base_datos/Admin/rd1109-1993.html#a1). That is, the Academy's principal task was to ensure the unity of Spanish throughout what was constructed as being a "Spanish-speaking world," although many different ways of using language were prevalent. Thus the motto of the Academy was "*limpia, fija y da esplendor*" ["cleans, fixes and gives splendor"]. A year later, in 1714, Castilian was declared the language of the state. Castilian Spanish served as the way to suppress the rights and laws of people who were not in power, both in the Old and in the New World. In 1768 King Charles III of Spain decreed that there should be one language and one currency in his kingdom, including its colonies, and engaged in a mission to eradicate all other ways of speaking. Today the struggle to control the language practices of those who speak differently both in Spain and in the Americas continues (for more on this history, see Del Valle, 2013; García, 2008, 2011; García & Otheguy, 2015).

Construction of English

The economic and military might of the Kingdom of England did not require the language named English to be protected by a prescriptive grammar or a language academy. It was the ways of speaking of the Germanic invaders to the British Isles that originally gained ground, pushing the ways of speaking of the Celts north and west. The multilingual origins of modern English have been well documented (Baugh & Cable, 2002); especially important was the influence of the speech of the Norman kings that ruled the Kingdom of England after William the Conqueror defeated King Harold at Hastings in 1066. But as the Kingdom of England started to project itself as a powerful state within the British Isles and then beyond its borders, the construction of English as an entity (Park & Wee, 2012) became paramount. Publishers started preferring the dialect of the dominant class in London, where the king resided.

In 1588 England defeated the Spanish armada, consolidating the might of British maritime power. The plan of the growing power was to acquire the many people and their riches in a territory over which the sun never set. To do so, English as constituted by the ruling class was seen as the only legitimate way of speaking.

The British Empire grew in the next three centuries, and the constructed English language was used to categorize people so as to produce the "governable subjects" (Foucault, 2008; Flores, 2013) that the empire needed. Only white people of means, born in England, were considered native English-speakers. Other whites were said to speak "dialects." The Welsh, Scots and Irish were branded as "bilingual," and therefore their speech was delegitimized. When the British Empire expanded to the New World, enslaved blacks and Native Americans were not given access to the language named English, thus they were rendered "speechless." This was the same treatment offered to the brown and black people of Asia, Africa, and the Pacific. Only those who were at the top of the colonial social class were given the privilege of learning English and participating as second-class citizens in the life of the colony. The others were not recognized as legitimate speakers. The imposition of the language named and recognized as English was an important tool for the colonization and oppression of many (for more on this history, see García & Lin, forthcoming).

More constructions

As the powerful class of both the Spanish and British empires came into contact with Others who spoke differently, they legitimated only their own language practices, which were named Spanish in one case and English in the other, and these were carefully restricted. The powerless Others, most often brown and black, were rendered without language, and their linguistic practices described as "jumbled." The ideologies about the superiority of named languages were used as racist tools to exclude and oppress.

But named languages were not sufficient to exert the racist policies that were needed to continue colonizing people as the colonies gained independence. Also involved in this process was the construction of bilingualism and multilingualism. As we will see in the next section, the "parallel monolingualism" (Heller, 1999) that was expected had little to do with the multilingual practices of the colonized populations, delegitimizing once again the practices of minoritized multilingual speakers.

Bilingualism and Multilingualism: Other Constructions

It was precisely around the time that many Asian, African and Pacific countries were achieving their independence that the scholarly pursuit of what we call today bilingualism/multilingualism became prevalent. Multilingual learning had always been a sign of enrichment for the wealthy. For example, from the second century onwards Greek-Latin bilingual education was the way to educate boys from Roman aristocratic homes (Lewis, 1977). Bilingualism and multilingualism were understood as simply the learning of an additional named language that was standardized, written, and that was the language of another "foreign" power. Through most of the 20th century "foreign language education" provided the impetus for this type of bilingualism. This was the understanding of bilingualism/multilingualism with which scholars faced the growing voices and sounds of multilingual people in many of the newly formed nation-states.

In the 1950s Uriel Weinreich (1953), a Yiddish-English speaker, and Einar Haugen (1956), a Norwegian-English speaker, published their now famous monographs on bilingualism, comparing the bilingual speech to the monolingual constructed norm. Despite their interest in bilingualism, both Weinreich and Haugen identified what they termed "interferences" in the speech of bilinguals, and spoke about borrowings, loan shifts and code-switching, phenomena in the speech of bilinguals that differentiated them from the monolinguals who were considered the norm.

Also around this time, the study of sociolinguistics was formalized. What became known as the field of *language planning and language policy* came into being, proposing ways of solving what was seen as the linguistic problems of the newly constituted multilingual states. The thinking was that the ways people spoke in these new states could also be controlled; their corpus and status planned (Fishman, 1972; Rubin & Jernudd, 1971). Monolingualism in one named language was not going to work in the new social order, and so another system of governmentality had to emerge. An elite version of bilingualism/multilingualism, a simple addition of western languages always used separately, was seen as the answer. This ensured that this type of multilingualism would continue to expand among white elites, whereas the multilingual practices of black and brown people would be further stigmatized.

Working in Canada, Wallace Lambert (1974) called for schools to develop what he termed "additive bilingualism"—an addition of a second language (L2) to the first language of the child (L1). In the U.S., Joshua Fishman (1967) reformulated Charles Ferguson's definition of diglossia, claiming that, for bilingualism to be maintained, speakers had to use the two languages for different functions or in different territories. The focus on nation-states and social groups prevented Fishman from describing what was common knowledge in the eastern world—that the linguistic practices of multilingual speakers are not constrained by the boundaries of named languages and that these had existed for centuries (Canagarajah & Liyanage, 2012; Khubchandani, 1997).

As the 20th century came to a close, the world was experiencing the hold of a neoliberal economy that supported privatization and the free flow of capitalism in ways that benefited transnational corporations and economic elites (Flores, 2013). One named language was no longer sufficient in this globalized world, and so our understandings of multilingualism took yet another turn in order to establish itself as a linguistic regime that consolidated power among white Europeans of means.

One obvious product of the push toward a globalized neoliberal economy was the formation of the European Union. In a united Europe one European language was not going to be sufficient, so the Council of Europe coined the concept of "plurilingualism." Plurilingualism was defined as the ability of European citizens to "use several languages to varying degrees and for distinct purposes" (2000). The term multilingualism was reserved for social groups; for example, classrooms were said to be multilingual. The concept of plurilingualism extended the conventional vision of multilingual individuals as being those who are "two monolinguals in one," a notion that had been debunked by Grosjean (1982). But as a concept coined to assure the unity of the countries of the European Union, plurilingualism does not question the construction of named European languages, reifying them even when "partial competence" in a second or third language is promoted.

It is these named languages and these visions of bilingualism/multilingualism that schools, the instruments of nation-states, have promoted. Languages are branded as "first," "foreign," "second or third," "heritage." Language education programs build bilingualism/multilingualism as additive with a goal of bilingual/multilingual development, meaning two or more western named languages, and usually including English. For minoritized people, language education programs, even those that use two languages as medium of instruction, often cultivate what Lambert (1974) called "subtractive bilingualism;" that is, transition to a dominant named language(s) other than what is considered the learner's "first" language. And even when the schools' expectation for minoritized multilingual speakers is that of "additive bilingualism," the enforcement of named languages as wholes to be used separately stigmatizes even further their more dynamic and fluid multilingual practices. The linguistic reality of most learners is a lot more complex than all of these categories suggest.

In the next section we suggest that language education programs often fail because they're operating in concert with the category assigned to the named language, instead of adjusting their practices to the linguistic reality of students. We first review different types of language education programs as we reflect on why these boundaries between programs do not work.

The Construction of Language Education Programs

Language education programs in schools today respond to the nomenclature that we have created for named languages, languages that are seen as belonging to nation-states or social groups, and not to people. We briefly describe the most prevalent language education programs today, focusing only on mainstream education financed by nation-states. These programs all have a monoglossic ideology even when they promote bilingualism; that is, they protect the named dominant language of the nation-state, and they "add" other languages that are also standardized and named.

Native Language Arts

Native language arts refers to the teaching of reading, writing and composition, speaking and the analysis of literature. It is assumed that all students are "native-speakers" of the language that is the subject of instruction, and thus only the standardized version of that language is validated.

Foreign Language Education

These programs, common throughout the world, focus on the learning of a language that is not in any way associated to the nation-state in which the subject is taught, usually at secondary and tertiary levels. All students are considered to have the same "first" language of the dominant society and to engage in the learning of this "foreign" language as speakers of that dominant language. The focus is on the "foreign" language as a subject—its structure, as well as how it can be used either in the "native" land or when traveling or during sojourns in another land.

Heritage Language Education

The realization that increasingly students who are required to take a "foreign language" as a subject are either speakers of that language, live in homes where that language is spoken, or have an ancestral relationship to that language has led to the development of "heritage language programs." Students who are categorized as "heritage-language speakers" are grouped for instruction in the language, usually taught as a subject. The focus is on the development of that language for academic purposes.

Bilingual/Multilingual Education

Bilingual/multilingual education programs have proliferated in the last half-century. The difference with first, core, foreign and heritage language education programs is that the additional language is used as a medium of instruction, instead of being taught as a subject. These programs are of different types. Regardless of the type of students in the programs, or the linguistic goal of a program, languages in these programs are also taught as natural entities, their construction or invention never questioned (for more on these programs, see García, 2009):

- *Immersion bilingual education*, where speakers of a named majority language are taught *initially* only through the medium of what is considered a "second" language, although there is also "first" language instruction. This type of program originated in Québec in the 1960s. Some minoritized groups, who want to revitalize what are seen as their "heritage languages" after achieving some measure of power, have modeled their educational programs after immersion. This is the case, for example, in the language nest programs among the Māoris and other indigenous groups.

- *Developmental bilingual/multilingual education,* where two or more named languages—one considered "first," the other(s) considered "second" or "third"—are used as medium of instruction, generally in a 50/50 allocation, although the proportions of language used may vary and the languages may be introduced simultaneously or sequentially. Both majority and minority groups who want their children to be bilingual have developed programs of this type. Recently in the United States, because of the push back against the term "bilingual," developmental bilingual programs are known as "dual language." Most often these programs are "two-way," meaning that half of the students are speakers of the majority language, whereas the other half is not.
- *Content and Language Integrated Learning (CLIL)* has increasingly taken the place of core "foreign language" programs deemed insufficient to make students bilingual, especially in Europe. In CLIL programs the learner's "second" language is used as a medium of instruction, generally for one to two periods of instruction.
- *Transitional bilingual education,* used with minoritized populations, where the students' "first language" or "mother-tongue" is used only initially and where students are expected to transition to the dominant language of society.
- *Mother-tongue-based multilingual education,* used with minoritized populations, especially in Asia and Africa, where the students' "mother-tongue" is used only initially, with the goal of developing two dominant named languages in society.

It is clear from the description of the language education programs given above that different types of languages have been assigned to school learners in an effort to control access to opportunities. And it is also evident that both elite and minoritized populations have participated in legitimizing these constructions. The reason for the acquiescence of minoritized people in this educational pretense has to do with what Quijano (2007) has called the "coloniality of power" (see also Mignolo, 2007). The only system of knowledge accepted today continues to be a Eurocentric one, circulated precisely through standardized named languages, and thus even minoritized speakers desire to "have" the powerful codes of society. Named languages are not in any way revealed as a most important tool in the racialization of those whose labor had to continue to be exploited for the economic profit of the elite after political "independence." Minoritized black and brown speakers had to be created in order to protect the hierarchical structure of white European superiority. Standardized named western European languages, and especially English, have been the key to the continuation of this "coloniality of power."

Bilingualism/multilingualism have certainly entered the scholarly discourse today, identified as a multilingual turn (May, 2013). And yet multilingualism continues to be interpreted through a European lens that ignores the multilingual practices of the many black and brown people of the world. Today the commodification of multilingualism has become a fundamental ingredient in a neoliberal economy with deregulated markets. But this multilingualism excludes the fluid multilingual practices of brown and black bodies, especially in language education programs that purport to develop multilingualism. To show how this categorization of languages and language education programs works against minoritized students, we describe some of the practices we have observed in schools serving Latinx populations.

Latinx and Language Education: Decolonizing Understandings

Latinx students are a very complex group—some are new to what schools call English, some are new to what schools call Spanish, others have had lots of experience with what schools call English and/or Spanish, others have less, and this varies according to whether they are listening, speaking, reading or writing. Some Latinx students are born in Latin American countries, although Spanish may, or may not be, their "first" acquired language. Some are born in the U.S. and, again, English may or may not be their "first" acquired language. To describe the great diversity that there is among Latinx students, we introduce four Latinx students in a middle school.

Alexis, Yahaira, Alejandra and Kabil are categorized as "English language learners" and are in the same "English as a *second* language classroom," although they are extremely different. Even though Alejandra and Kabil have recently arrived from Argentina and Mexico respectively, Alejandra had gone to a private school in Argentina where she studied English, whereas Kabil, from an indigenous Tsotsil-speaking family in Chiapas, had never had any contact with English and spoke Spanish only when he accompanied his mother outside of the community. Although Alejandra and Kabil are considered "newcomer English language learners," they are differently situated in the same "English as a second language" class. The other two students, Alexix and Yahaira, were born in the United States. There is nothing "second" about English for Alexis and Yahaira. Both grew up in homes where English was spoken from birth, and it is English that they most frequently use in their communities and homes. The four very different students sit in the same English as a second language classroom. The teacher, Ms. Heston, is a white, middle-class monolingual-speaker of English, and views these four students through the lens of the "English language subject" she is teaching. She follows the official "ESL curriculum," ignoring the actual varied language experiences and practices of the students and the ways in which they "do" language.

These four students also sit in the same "Spanish as a heritage language" class taught by a bilingual Spanish-English teacher, Ms. Medina. But Spanish is not Kabil's "heritage" language—Tsotsil is. Ms. Medina is baffled by what she considers Kabil's "poor" "native-language" abilities. She recommends him for evaluation, believing that he has a learning disability. Ms. Medina also knows that Alexis and Yahaira have been born in the United States, so she expects and looks for "English influences and interferences." She constantly compares their use of "Spanish" with that of Alejandra, who has been schooled in Spanish in Argentina. Knowing that Alexis and Yahaira are categorized as English language learners, she complains that they do not have language, for, compared to Alejandra, they cannot use Spanish either. Ms. Medina is particularly worried about Alexis. She notices that Alexis' use of Spanish in oral argumentation is much weaker than that of Yahaira's. But Ms. Medina fails to take into consideration that, whereas Yahaira is the oldest sibling in the family and her mother doesn't speak English, Alexis is the youngest sibling and is growing up in a bilingual family. Ms. Medina assumes that because both Alexis and Yahaira are "English language learners," their "first language," spoken at home, must be Spanish. However, Alexis understands Spanish but he almost always uses English at home. Ms. Medina decides to send Alexis to the "Spanish as a foreign language" classroom because he is getting lost in her class.

After a week the teacher of the "Spanish as a foreign language" classroom, Ms. Maconi, objects strenuously to this placement for Alexis. She claims Alexis gets bored in this classroom because he understands Spanish, whereas the other white, Asian or African American students in the class do not. But there is more going on to fuel Ms. Maconi's objection. Ms. Maconi, who learned Spanish in college, doesn't understand anything when Alexis rambles on and speaks! Alexis uses Spanish not according to some textbook norm, but to the ways of using language in his community. This puts Ms. Maconi in an uncomfortable position, for she is threatened as a speaker of Spanish. To maintain the superiority of the structural forms of Spanish she has learned in books over the "Spanish" as done in a bilingual community, Ms. Maconi excludes Alexis from her classroom.

Alexis' mother becomes fed up with the treatment that Alexis is getting in school, for she has been told that he is not making progress in standardized tests in English and she has become aware that her son doesn't fit the Spanish language program either. She has heard that there is a good developmental bilingual education program in the school, so she insists that they transfer Alexis there. In the "dual language" bilingual program, Alexis also becomes a "problem." The program is two-way, meaning that half of the students are monolingual English speakers and have started learning Spanish that year, whereas the other half are categorized as English language learners, which Alexis is. The teacher, Ms. Gutiérrez, has been taught to insist that the two languages be always used separately. After all, the program is "dual language" and requires "dual" proficiency in two separate languages. But Alexis' language practices in what is said to be "Spanish" are very different from those of the Spanish-speaking newcomers in the program. And although Alexis speaks English, his English literacy, as measured in standardized tests and performed in school, is very different from that of the mostly white, monolingual students. Alexis is between two worlds—an English world and a Spanish one—that do not represent his life in the borderlands, in the interstices and spaces in which language practices are fluid and always available, and in which all bilingual minoritized students live. The school's insistence that Alexis "have" English and use it exclusively in the English part of the "dual language" program, and "have" Spanish and use it only in the Spanish part of the program, violates his bilingualism, his fluid language practices that are the norm in bilingual communities. Only "dual languages" are used and expected, as if these were entities that could be "had," instead of promoting bilingual children's ability to "do" language for the learning of math, science, social studies, art, music, theater, etc. Success in academic tasks should not require standardized language conventions; they should instead require thinking, criticality and creativity. Alexis and his mother are left helpless. There are no educational programs that recognize her son's fluid multilingualism.

Latinx students' language practices go beyond those of named English and named Spanish, and thus, no matter who they are, whether immigrant newcomer or native-born in the United States, their language practices do not fit the artificial boundaries created by different educational programs. Because their language practices are not in any way recognized and legitimized, Latinx students are made to fail in schools, whether in foreign language, heritage language, second language or bilingual education programs. The knowledge-power (Foucault, 2008) of invented named languages and elite bilingualism continues to marginalize many multilingual communities of brown and black bodies. To disrupt this cycle of failure, the ways in which named languages have been used in society and schools, and their relationship to racism and governmentality, need to be unmasked. If we were truly interested in the academic success of Latinx students we would be accepting of what we call here their *translanguaging*, and not insist on monolingual performances, especially in English, in order to give them access to educational and economic opportunities. In the next section we explore translanguaging, one of many terms used today that have the potential to decolonize our conception of language and, especially, language education.

Translanguaging

It is a well-known fact that linguists have never been able to make decisions *on structural or lexical grounds* about the boundaries of named languages. Decisions on what constitutes a language, a dialect, a creole, etc. are always social and political, having to do with power and will. Once the boundaries of a named language have been set, then linguists can, of course, describe its structure, phonology, morphology, syntax, etc. (Otheguy, García & Reid, 2015), but not before. The dictum of Max Weinreich about language being a dialect with an army and a navy is instructive in this regard. For example, Afrikaans could be identified as a creole, or as a dialect of Dutch, but the authoritative demands of a racist apartheid regime required that it be named as one of two official languages of South Africa in 1961. And Luxembourgish, formerly considered a dialect of German, was named the national language of Luxembourg in 1984, in part a reaction against the occupation of the country by Germany from 1940 to 1944. So if named languages are indeed social and political constructions, what is left? What is it that people engage in as they communicate?

In the recent past the fluid language practices of speakers have been increasingly recognized in western sociolinguistic scholarship, stimulated especially by the heteroglossic conceptualizations of language that the translation of Bakhtin's work (1981) brought to our attention. Multilingual speakers are today said to have mobile resources (Blommaert, 2010) or flexible bilingual practices (Blackledge & Creese, 2010). And many terms have been coined to refer to speakers' fluid multilingual practices—polylanguaging/polylingual languaging (Jørgensen, 2008), metrolingualism (Otsuji & Pennycook, 2010; Pennycook & Otsuji, 2015), translingual practices (Canagarajah, 2013) and translanguaging (Blackledge & Creese, 2010; García, 2009; García and Li Wei, 2014; Otheguy, García & Reid, 2015).

I prefer the term *translanguaging* for two reasons. One, translanguaging has been used both to refer to the fluid language practices of multilingual communities, *and* to the pedagogical practices that leverage those practices (Flores & Schissel, 2014; García, 2009; García & Li Wei, 2014). Without education, the more heteroglossic scholarly conceptions of language will have little impact in the lives of people. Two, and even more important, translanguaging was coined in bilingual borderlands, in Welsh (see Baker, 2011), and its use has been extended in work with other language-minoritized groups (García & Li Wei, 2014). Thus the use of the term translanguaging is political, disrupting the hierarchies of named languages that were installed by colonial expansion and nation-building (see Mignolo, 2000). The goal of translanguaging pedagogical practices is to liberate sign systems that have been constrained by socio-political domination, attempting to give voice to all and redress power differentials among speakers.

If named languages are external societal constructions, translanguaging refers to the internal mental grammar of speakers shaped in social interaction, and the ways in which features in their complex linguistic repertoire are deployed. As Otheguy, García and Reid (2015) have said, translanguaging refers to "the deployment of a speaker's *full linguistic repertoire* without regard for watchful adherence to the socially and politically defined boundaries of named (and usually national and state) languages" (p. 283). Rather than possessing two or multiple autonomous language systems, speakers viewed as bilingual/multilingual select and deploy particular features to make meaning and to negotiate particular communicative contexts from a *unitary linguistic repertoire*. For example, just earlier as I wrote this I heard my daughter say: "Dónde está el tray? If we don't hurry up, vamos a eat frío, frío." And I replied: "Está somewhere. Mira en el drawer." Now, my daughter would have known to say "Where is the tray?" if she had been in her monolingual friend's house, and "¿Dónde está la bandeja?" if she had been in her grandmother's house in Puerto Rico. Likewise, I certainly would have known how to say "It's somewhere," or "Está en algún lugar." But there is no need to adhere to the boundaries of standardized English and standardized Spanish in my bilingual home. My daughter and I are simply communicating, and these are *our* words, our own words, and not those of a nation-state or of a school. They are simply ours, used effectively to communicate in our bilingual context. Seen from an internal perspective, my daughter and I are not code-switching, as the external viewpoint would have us say. Instead, we are simply deploying all the features of our repertoire; we are translanguaging.

When speakers said to be bilingual or multilingual are *not* exhibiting what are interpreted as "fluid" language practices (that is, emitting features that are said to be from one language or another because the receptor of the message is monolingual), they are suppressing some linguistic features and selecting others. Speakers said to be bilingual/multilingual learn to do this *suppression and selection* very early in life, but they do not do it always. In unmonitored or less monitored settings, the unsuppressed flow of the bilingual's entire unpartioned linguistic inventory will often be unleashed because all of it is "their" language, not one named and legitimized by a political state.

As agents of political states, schools are the *monitored* settings par excellence. In them, children whom the society calls bilingual or multilingual are asked to engage in severe acts of suppression of about half the contents of their linguistic repertoire, whereas white, monolingual students are asked to suppress just a little. Bilingual and multilingual students are then assessed with instruments that forbid the use of the full content of their linguistic system, whereas monolingual students are allowed to enlist almost its full content. Not only is the instruction and assessment of students said to be bilingual or multilingual deeply *biased,* it is then given as the reason for their academic failure, their achievement gap, and even their poverty!

Rather than starting with students to whom a named language is assigned, a *translanguaging pedagogy* starts with the language practices of multilingual learners. By leveraging the multilingual learners' entire language repertoire, translanguaging returns the power of language to speakers and engages their communicative potential, rather than authorizing only the conventions of named languages that have been codified by the nation-state to develop governable subjects. Teachers who engage with translanguaging pedagogical practices see students who have been linguistically minoritized for their *language potential*, that is, their ability "to do" language—to make arguments orally and in writing, to find text-based evidence, to explain a theorem, to describe the rain forest, to historicize facts, to create art and music, to imagine myths and fictions, to conceptualize problems and solutions for today, to express compassion and tolerance, to have deep understandings of scientific, mathematic, historical, artistic and social phenomena. This is the language potential that we will need in the future, shared by all and not just by white, powerful speakers who have the "appropriate" features of language. Human language gives us the capacity to imagine abstractions and to be critical and creative human beings, and we are wasting that capacity in schools by insisting that language can only be used, and students can only be successful, if they can express their knowledge with conventions of standard named languages, whether one or the other.

García, Johnson and Seltzer (2017) have identified three components of a translanguaging pedagogy—stance, design and shifts. Teachers who leverage students' translanguaging have a *stance*, a deep belief that their students' language practices are a resource that transcends the standardized named language(s) of schools and can be used to make meaning of academic tasks and learn. Besides a stance, these teachers also *design* units, lessons, instructions and assessments that integrate home and school languaging practices. But beyond the translanguaging design, a translanguaging pedagogy also relies on *shifts*, the appropriate moment-by-moment decisions teachers make to respond to learners' languaging.

If the four teachers mentioned above—Ms. Heston, the "ESL" teacher; Ms. Medina, the "Spanish as a Heritage Language" teacher; Ms. Maconi, the "Spanish as a Foreign Language" teacher; and Ms. Gutiérrez, the bilingual teacher—had taken up translanguaging pedagogical practices, Alexis, Yahaira, Alejandra and Kabil would have been taught as human beings with linguistic potential, and not simply as speakers or not of English, and as speakers or not of Spanish. For example, Alexis would be recognized for his engineering potential, for he is great at applying science and math to solve problems; and Kabil would be celebrated for his ability to imagine fictional stories and create poetic images. Instead of not giving Alexis and Kabil access to rich instruction because they do not fit the language education paradigm installed in schools, they would be educated for success as scientists, mathematicians, writers, poets, etc. It would then be their meaningful participation and engagement in these real and interesting pursuits that would drive the extension of their language practices, as they engaged with others in activities significant for them.

Translanguaging pedagogy is a tool for social justice, disrupting the linguistic hierarchizations of named languages and people that nation-states and their schools have created. Only by leveraging the real language practices that make up the linguistic repertoire of students who are linguistically minoritized, and building their critical understandings of how the invention of named languages has worked to produce governable subjects, will multilingual youth be able to engage in their education and become agentive learners.

Conclusion

We have described the construction of named languages by the powerful elite of nation-states. We have also analyzed how the construction of a version of bilingualism and multilingualism ensures that only the use of two or more named languages separately is legitimated. This has also contributed to consolidated power among white majorities while stigmatizing the practices of multilingual speakers. We have also seen that it is these conceptions of named languages and bilingualism/multilingualism that are used in the many language education programs that exist in society today.

Using the example of Latinx students, we have shown how categories of language and educational programs based on those categories do not fit their needs. Attempting to fit them into these categories then excludes them from successful schooling experiences. We have proposed that taking up translanguaging, an epistemology that takes the point of view that language is what speakers do, rather than what nation-states legitimate and schools teach, could transform the present reality of language and education.

The road ahead is difficult, for the transformation of language education programs will not happen without a political struggle for structural change that has the potential to push white, monolingual speakers from their present position of power. As I write this it seems unlikely that the neoliberal climate in which we educate would be transformed. For Latinx students, the election of Donald Trump in the United States has unleashed a racism that may, more than ever, divide us, even without building a physical wall. The walls of named languages and categories of students are more solid today than ever. The raciolinguistic ideologies (Flores & Rosa, 2015) that have been at play since language was made a proxy for race and oppression are very much present.

And yet we must continue to denounce the coloniality of power that keeps named languages as walls and barriers to opportunities. We must poke at the cracks that are evident in the walls. Decolonizing languages might not be feasible in the present climate, but decolonizing our knowledge about languages and the language education programs that exist might destabilize the support that many language education programs enjoy today, exposing them for their role in restricting opportunity for minoritized learners instead of expanding it.

References

Baker, C. (2011). *Foundations of bilingual education and bilingualism* (5th edition). Bristol, UK: Multilingual Matters.

Bakhtin, M. (1981). *Dialogic Imagination: Four Essays*. Austin, TX: University of Texas Press.

Baugh, A. and Cable. T. (2002). *The History of the English Language*. Upper Saddle River, NJ: Prentice-Hall.

Blackledge, A. and Creese, A. (2010). *Multilingualism: A Critical Perspective*. London: Continuum.

Blommaert, J. (2010). *The sociolinguistics of globalization*. Cambridge, UK: Cambridge University Press.

Briceño Perozo, M. (1987). *La obligación de enseñar el castellano a los aborígenes de América*, Colección Logos, Caracas.

Canagarajah, S. (2013). *Translingual practice: Global Englishes and cosmopolitan relations*. London: Routledge.

Canagarajah, S. and Liyanage, I. (2012). Lessons from pre-colonial multilingualism. In M. Martin-Jones, A. Blackledge & A. Creese (Eds.), *The Routledge Handbook of Multilingualism*. London & New York: Routledge.

Council of Europe. (2000). Common European framework of reference for languages: Learning, teaching, assessment. Language Policy Division. Strasbourg. Retrieved from http://www.coe.int/t/dg4/linguistic/source/framework_en.pdf.

del Valle, J. (Ed.) (2013). *A Political History of Spanish*. Cambridge, UK: Cambridge University Press.

Fishman, J. A. (1967). Bilingualism with and without diglossia; Diglossia with and without bilingualism. *Journal of Social Science* 23(2): 29–38.

Fishman, J. A. (1972). *Language and Nationalism. Two integrative essays*. Rowley, MA: Newbury House.

Flores, N. (2013). The unexamined relationship between neoliberalism and plurilingualism: A cautionary tale. *TESOL Quarterly, 47,* 500–520.

Flores, N. and Schissel, J. L. (2014). Dynamic bilingualism as the norm: Envisioning a heteroglossic approach to standards-based reform. *TESOL Quarterly* 48(3): 454– 479. Doi:10.1002/tesq.182.

Flores, N. and Rosa, J. (2015). Undoing appropriateness: Raciolinguistic ideologies and language diversity in education. *Harvard Educational Review* 85 (2): 149–171.

Foucault, M. (2008). The birth of biopolitics: Lectures at the College de France, 1978–1979. New York: Picador.

García, O. (Ed.) (2008). Spanish as a global language. *The International Multilingual Research Journal 2, Issue 1*. Routledge.

García, O. (2009). *Bilingual education in the 21st century: A global perspective*. Malden, MA/Oxford, UK: Wiley/Blackwell.

García, O. (2011). Planning Spanish: Nationalizing, minoritizing and globalizing performances. In M. Díaz-Campos (Ed.), *The Handbook of Hispanic Sociolinguistics* (pp. 665–685). Malden, MA/Oxford, UK: Wiley/Blackwell.

García, O. and Kleyn, T. (Eds.) (2016). *Translanguaging with multilingual students: Learning from classroom moments*. New York and London: Routledge.

García, O. and Lin, A. (2018). English and Multilingualism. In P. Seargeant, A. Hewings & S. Pihlaja (Eds.), *Routledge Handbook of English Language Studies* (pp. 77–92). New York: Routledge.

García, O. and Li Wei. (2014). *Translanguaging: Language, bilingualism and education*. London/New York: Palgrave Macmillan.

García, O. and Otheguy, R. (2015). Spanish and Hispanic bilingualism. In M. Lacorte (Ed.), *The Routledge Handbook of Hispanic Applied Linguistics* (pp. 639–658). New York: Routledge.

García, O., Johnson, S. and Seltzer, K. (2017). *The translanguaging classroom. Leveraging student bilingualism for learning*. Philadelphia, PA : Caslon.

Grosjean, F. (1982). *Life with two languages*. Cambridge, MA: Harvard University Press. Hall, R. (1974). External history of the Romance languages. New York: Elsevier.

Haugen, E. (1956). *Bilingualism in the Americas: A bibliography and research guide*. New York: American Dialect Society.

Heller, M. (1999). *Linguistic Minorities and Modernity: A sociolinguistic ethnography*. London: Longman.

Jørgensen, J. N. (2008). Polylingual languaging around and among children and adolescents. *International Journal of Multilingualism, 5*(3), 161–176.

Khubchandani, L. M. (1997). *Revisualizing boundaries: A plurilingual ethos.* New Delhi: Sage.

Lambert, W. E. (1974). Culture and language as factors in learning and education. In F. E. Aboud & R. D. Meade (Eds.), *Cultural Factors in Learning and Education* (pp. 91–122). Bellingham, WA: 5th Western Washington Symposium on Learning.

Lewis, E. G. (1977). Bilingualism and bilingual education – The ancient world to the Renaissance. In B. Spolsky & R. L. Cooper (Eds.), *Frontiers of Bilingual Education* (pp.22–93). Rowley, MA: Newbury House.

Makoni, S. and Pennycook, A. (2007). *Disinventing and Reconstituting Language.* Clevedon, UK: Multilingual Matters.

May, S. (Ed.) (2013). *The Multilingual Turn: Implications for SLA, TESOL and Bilingual Education.* New York: Routledge.

Mignolo, W. D. (1995). *The Darker Side of the Renaissance: Literacy, Territoriality and Colonization.* Ann Arbor, MI: The University of Michigan Press.

Mignolo, W. (2000). *Local Histories/Global Designs. Coloniality, Subaltern Knowledges, and Border Thinking.* Princeton, NJ: Princeton University Press.

Mignolo, W. (2007). Delinking: The rhetoric of modernity, the logic of coloniality and the grammar of de-coloniality,' *Cultural Studies*, 21 (2): 449–514.

Otheguy, R., García, O. and Reid, W. (2015). Clarifying translanguaging and deconstructing named languages: A perspective from linguistics. *Applied Linguistics Review* 6(3): 281–307.

Otsuji, E. and Pennycook, A. (2010). Metrolingualism: Fixity, fluidity and language in flux. *International Journal of Multilingualism*, 7(3), 240–254.

Park, J. S-Y and Wee, L. (2012). *Markets of English. Linguistic capital and language policy in a globalizing world.* New York and Oxford: Routledge.

Pennycook, A. and Otsjui, E. (2015). *Metrolingualism. Language in the city.* Oxford and New York: Routledge.

Quijano, A. (2007) Coloniality and Modernity/Rationality, *Cultural Studies*, 21 (2):168–178.

Rubin, J. and Jernudd, B. (Eds.) (1971). *Can Language be Planned? Sociolinguistic theory and practice for developing nations.* Honolulu, HI: University Press of Hawaii.

Weinreich, U. (1953/1974). *Languages in Contact, Findings and Problems.* The Hague: Mouton.

7

FROM TRANSLANGUAGING TO TRANSLINGUAL ACTIVISM

Alastair Pennycook

UNIVERSITY OF TECHNOLOGY SYDNEY

Recent work on translanguaging has opened up a range of insights into contemporary language use, helping us rethink the ways we talk about languages, bilingualism, and language mixing. As García and Li Wei (2014: 2) explain, translanguaging is an approach to bilingual language use and education that "considers the language practices of bilinguals not as two autonomous language systems as has been traditionally the case, but as one linguistic repertoire with features that have been societally constructed as belonging to two separate languages." This move toward translanguaging is part of a wider shift exploring new terminology beyond bilingualism, multilingualism, code-mixing, and the like, since these appear to suggest a rigidity of languages, a set of fixed codes that people choose between. Canagarajah (2013: 6) has argued along similar lines for a need to look at *translingual practices* where communication transcends both individual languages as well as more traditional accounts of what is considered to be a language, thus involving "diverse semiotic resources and ecological affordances."

The recent growth in studies of translanguaging in education has created several important avenues for research and pedagogy. It has opened up, for example, more useful ways of thinking about why using varied linguistic resources matters beyond the reductive discourses of the "bilingual advantage." While studies of bilingualism based on word and sentence manipulation in cognitive isolation, or positing increased executive control functions in order to manage two or more languages (Bialystok, 2007), have enabled well-intentioned attempts to persuade parents, educators, and institutions that bilingualism is an inherently good thing (King & Mackey, 2007), they tend to operate as if languages are easily identifiable objects operating in a social vacuum. If we view bilingualism only in additive and cognitive terms (speaking more than one language brings benefits), we miss the point that bilingualism is more usefully understood in terms of "resources which circulate in unequal ways in social networks and discursive spaces" (Heller, 2007: 2).

Bilingualism is concerned with social practices, language in real life, discrimination, access to resources, and inequality (Piller, 2016). We cannot deal with "bilingualism" as an abstract ideal of linguistic manipulation outside the contexts of language practices. The different resources students bring to their learning contexts are better understood not so much in terms of an assumed bilingual advantage—where languages are considered to confer a cumulative cognitive benefit on their users—but rather in terms of what we might call the *translingual advantage* (Otsuji & Pennycook, 2018), whereby translingual resources become part of a set of distributed linguistic and learning practices. We cannot assume that such advantages accrue to someone deemed bilingual without taking into account the social, cultural, economic, and educational context of their use. A translingual advantage may occur when a student is able to use a variety of linguistic and other resources in their learning but will not do so when these resources are denied or denigrated.

Translanguaging thus also urges us to avoid the demolinguistic labels that characterize our students as bilingual, second language learners, or speakers of named languages (García, this volume); rather, we need to appreciate the diversity of linguistic resources and cultural practices with which they may be engaged. These resources are not only linguistic but multimodal: students may employ a complex array of resources in their learning and, as educators, we need to be wary of that trap that links learning only to forms of language and literacy with which we may be familiar. The translingual advantage is a multimodal affair, so as educators we need ways to appreciate and facilitate what learners may be bringing to the table. Students are online in our classes, and their offline lives are part of their online activities. They are sitting in our classes, watching us (now and then), checking their mobile devices (more often), and living in multiple linguistic, cultural, and spatial worlds. Varied modes of popular culture form not just a backdrop to their daily lives, not just a pastime when they are not doing something else, but a fabric around which parts of their lives are built (Dovchin, Pennycook & Sultana, 2018).

There is a danger, however, that the critical agenda that underpins work on translanguaging may be consumed by the apolitical focus of the liberal academy (Jaspers, 2018). Both Canagarajah (2013) and García (2014; and see this volume) see translanguaging in political terms, as part of a challenge to the restrictive labels and practices of language education. García (2014) suggests that *transglossia* (Dovchin, Pennycook & Sultana, 2018) can be understood in Mignolo's (2010) decolonial terms as a challenge to the identities and structures of the modern/colonial world system. It is important, therefore, that the politics that motivate work on translanguaging or transglossia are not reinscribed into the ortholinguistic labels and practices of educational normativity (Pennycook, 2016). In many instances it has become little more than a term to describe code-mixing and bilingualism in ways that differ little from what went before (Lee, 2018). Critical educational projects may therefore need to add a more activist dimension—*translingual activism* (Pennycook, 2008)—to ensure that the decolonization of foreign language education includes transformational practices. A central goal of language education is surely the development of critical and resourceful language users who have good access to a range of linguistic resources, are good at shifting between styles, discourses, registers and genres, and whose developing language practices aim not just at personal but also social change.

In the rest of this chapter I make a case for a form of translingual activism (Pennycook, 2008), with a particular focus on English language teaching (ELT). It is worth reminding ourselves that although "foreign language teaching" is a term often used to refer to languages other than English (as if English were not foreign to the majority world), ELT is in fact the world's biggest foreign language teaching project. And if any language teaching project is in need of decolonization, it is ELT. The following sections set forth three aspects of this translingual activism in relation to English: (1) a need to decolonize and provincialize English; (2) an expanded notion of resourcefulness and resourceful speakers; and (3) the need for a politics that can engage with the Commons. First, however, I discuss the importance of appreciating how English needs to be understood in terms of unequal access and style and its local embeddedness in relation to class, culture, and politics.

The Local Embeddedness of English

To grasp the extent and consequences of the vast ELT enterprise is a task of near impossible complexity. Rather than the bland terms in which English is often understood—as a neutral medium of international communication, as a language that holds out the promise of social and economic development to all those who learn it, as a language of equal opportunity, as a language that the world needs in order to be able to communicate—it is clear that it is also an exclusionary class dialect, favoring particular people, countries, cultures, forms of knowledge, and possibilities of development. It is a language that creates barriers as much as it presents possibilities. Tollefson (2000: 8) warns that "at a time when English is widely seen as a key to the economic success of nations and the economic well-being of individuals, the spread of English also contributes to significant social, political, and economic inequalities." Bruthiaux (2002: 292–93) argues convincingly that English language education is "an outlandish irrelevance" for many of the world's poor, and "talk of a role for English language education in facilitating the process of poverty reduction and a major allocation of public resources to that end is likely to prove misguided and wasteful."

For those "who do not have access to high-quality English language education, the spread of English presents a formidable obstacle to education, employment, and other activities requiring English proficiency" (Tollefson, 2000: 9), so ELT may have as much to do with the creation as the alleviation of inequality. Ramanathan's (2005: 112) study of English and vernacular medium education in India shows, for example, how English is a deeply divisive language, tied on the one hand to the denigration of vernacular languages, cultures, and ways of learning and teaching, and, on the other, dovetailing "with the values and aspirations of the elite Indian middle class." While English opens doors to some, it is simultaneously a barrier to learning, development, and employment for others.

As Ferguson (2013: 35) points out, alongside the not unreasonable belief that "without English-language skills, one's labour mobility and employment prospects are restricted" in the current global economy, at the same time English language education has many deleterious effects, including distorting already weak primary education sectors, advantaging urban elites over rural poor, constraining the use of other languages, and diverting resources from other areas. When we observe the growth and increasing global role of South East Asian economies, we can also see the constant pressure to teach English at an earlier stage in a region with wide linguistic diversity. There are real causes for concern that current language education policies favoring only the national language plus English will lead to the reduction of Asian multilingualism to bilingualism only in the national language and English (Kirkpatrick, 2011), a concern also being expressed in South America (Fortes, 2015).

And yet, as Gray suggests, "ideologies associated with English which take it as self-evident that it is perforce the language of economic prosperity and individual wealth are also those of the ELT industry itself" (2012: 98). However daunting it may seem to deal with such concerns, it is also clear that for those of us involved in English language education it is not adequate either to ignore them or to adopt individually-oriented access arguments on the basis that any improvement in a learner's English will likely bring them benefits. There is much more at stake here, but we have been poorly served by dominant discourses on ELT that offer either a monologically dystopian approach to language and culture in the shape of linguistic imperialism (Phillipson, 1992: 2009) or pluralistic utopian visions of diversity in the form of World Englishes (Kachru, 2005) or English as a lingua franca (ELF) (Jenkins, 2009; Mackenzie, 2014).

As Kubota (2015: 33) points out, while pluralist approaches to English have opened up an understanding of post-colonial diversity, there has also been a tendency to "romanticize the multiplicity of local language use without sufficiently interrogating inequalities and injustices involving race, gender, class and so on." The "unspoken acquiescence to and default acceptance of the neoliberal (and therefore capitalist) status quo" (O'Regan, 2014: 5) in English as a lingua franca research does not serve a critical educational project well. All varieties of English are in complex relations of power with other varieties. As Martin (2014) observes, for example, the sociolinguistics of English in the Philippines is far more complex than merely placing it in the "outer circle" as if that explained the many Englishes used there. There are circles within circles in the Philippines amid questions of access, education, style, disparity, and difference (Tupas, 2010).

The issue, therefore, is not centrally about how Philippine English differs from American English but how English resources are spread and used and become available or inaccessible to people of different classes and ethnicities across these islands. "Can all English users regardless of their racial, gender, socioeconomic, and other background equally transgress linguistic boundaries and engage in hybrid and fluid linguistic practices?" (Kubota, 2015: 33). Any claim to a variety of English, while at one level a defiance of inner-circle norms, is also always a political claim in relation to other varieties, and a claim amid competing social, economic, and political values, a question of *unequal Englishes*, "the unequal ways and situations in which Englishes are arranged, configured, and contested" (Tupas & Rubdy, 2015: 3).

Neither a dystopian approach to monolithic English nor a utopian focus on varieties of English can account for the complex relations between English and its users. More useful are close and detailed understandings of how English is embedded in local economies of desire, how demand for English is part of a larger set of images of change, modernization, access, and longing. It is tied to the languages, cultures, styles, and aesthetics of popular culture, with its particular attractions for youth, rebellion, and conformity; it is enmeshed within local economies, and all the inclusions, exclusions, and inequalities this may entail; it is bound up with changing modes of communication, from shifting internet uses to its role in text-messaging; it is increasingly entrenched in educational systems, bringing to the fore many concerns about knowledge, pedagogy, and the curriculum. We need to understand the diversity of what English is and what it means in all these contexts, and we need to do so not with prior assumptions about globalization and its effects but with critical studies of the local embeddedness of English.

Decolonizing and Provincializing English

Whether we see English as a monster, juggernaut, bully, or governess (Rapatahana & Bunce, 2012), we clearly need to do something about this pedagogically. While we might, like ostriches (Pennycook, 2001), be tempted to bury our heads in the classroom and refuse to engage with these issues, we surely owe more to the educational needs of our students than to ignore the many dimensions of power and politics in ELT. Let's first focus on projects of provincialization and decolonization. Arguing in an Indian context that it is impossible to think of *political modernity*—modern state institutions, bureaucracy, and the capitalist enterprise—without invoking a range of concepts that have their roots in Western modernity, Chakrabarty (2000: 6) maintains that European thought is "both indispensable and inadequate in helping us to think through the various life practices that constitute the political and the historical in India." It is not possible to think of political modernity without invoking concepts such as citizenship, civil society, human rights, equality before the law, relations between public and private, the subject, democracy, social justice, and so on, concepts that "found a climactic form in the course of the European Enlightenment and the nineteenth century" (2000: 4). These were the ideas of enlightenment humanism preached by the European colonizer but denied in practice.

The dilemma is how to acknowledge the debt owed to this tradition—the critical analytic approach of Marx and the hermeneutic project of Heidegger, for example—while also provincializing it in relation to Indian history, institutions, and cultures. How to dislodge or decenter European thought in the world, a provincializing project that does not seek to reject European thought but rather to find its rightful, provincial place? Following this line of thinking, Motha (2014: 129) argues for an understanding of *provincialized English* so that "inherent in the learning of English would be an intense awareness of the effects of English's colonial and racial history on current-day language, economic, political and social practices" (129). Such a project likewise seeks to acknowledge the role English has played in the world: its possible indispensability within current conditions of globalization, but also its inadequacy for communication, difference, and equality. This is to appreciate both its usefulness in universalizing, liberating, making certain things possible, but also its insufficiency for global communication, its role in the perpetuation of inequalities, its destructiveness in relation to other languages and cultures. English and English teaching cannot be rejected but need to be understood in their specific localities. English needs to be rendered provincial.

Important in such a project are the *decolonial politics* of Mignolo (2011) that seek to undermine the assumptions that can allow for a belief in the "zero point" of English articulation. The "hubris of the zero point" for Mignolo (2009: 162) is the assumption that one can speak from an anonymous, generalizable, universal position. This is also arguably an assumption behind the global role of English: it is a neutral language, a language of the world, a language in which anyone can articulate what they wish. This is the hubris of the zero point of English articulation, the idea that English is disconnected from culture, politics, and its colonial history. Mignolo's decolonial struggle aims to "change the terms and not just the content of the conversation" (2010: 313) and to *delink* language, culture, and thought from the Eurocentric categories that have defined them. The question pedagogically is how to open up English as part of the decolonial project. So let us next consider how translingual activism can change the meanings of English.

Toward Resourceful Speakers

We would do well to question the linguistic and educational ideologies behind "the one-classroom-one-language pedagogical straitjacket" (Lin, 2013: 540) that many current ELT approaches continue to endorse, and embrace instead a broader, multilingual approach to our classrooms. Approaches such as communicative language teaching are far from neutral pedagogical technologies (Pennycook, 1989). They are "intimately linked to the production of a certain kind of student and worker subjectivity suitable for participating in a certain kind of political economy" (Lin, 2013: 540). Instead of focusing so intently on English as the sole objective of our teaching, we can start to reimagine classes as part of a broader multilingual context. Such multilingualism needs to be understood not so much in terms of separate monolingualisms (adding English to one or more other languages) but rather in more fluid terms.

If we acknowledge both the problem of the dominance of English as well as the need to think about bi- and multilingualism differently, we are left with the question: how else in the face of English can we pursue diversity? A focus on heritage languages, multilingualism, or foreign language learning is important but does not in itself answer the question of diversity. As Kramsch (2006; and see this volume) warns, we need to ask what meanings are being borne by languages, what cultural politics underlie the learning and use of different languages. It is not enough to assume that more is better—multilingualism, multilingual language policies, more foreign language education—in numerical terms (Makoni & Pennycook, 2007). For Kramsch (2006), monolingualism is the name not only for a linguistic handicap but also for a dangerously monolithic traffic in meaning.

Here, then, is an argument, following Halliday (2002), that we need to take *semiodiversity* as seriously as *glossodiversity*, the possibility of a multiplicity of meanings within a language as seriously as a multiplicity of languages (Pennycook, 2004). This argument is important for several reasons: it urges us to question the epistemologies or linguistic ideologies on which support for diversity may be based. Thus a rights-based approach to support for linguistic diversity as a counterpoint to a dystopian view of linguistic imperialism, as Sonntag (2003: 25) points out, does not fundamentally challenge the politics it needs to engage with "because a rights-based approach to promoting linguistic diversity reinforces the dominant liberal democratic project rather than dismantling it." If oppositional strategies are conducted from within the same framework as that which they oppose, they run the danger of reproducing those same positions. Hence the need, as Hoy (2004) argues, for a more complex form of *critical resistance.*

This argument opens up the potential to see our work as contributing to diversity not only in terms of increasing the number of people using languages or the number of languages being used, but also in terms of the breadth of meanings available within a language. It is one of the great crimes of the global hegemony of communicative language teaching over the last few decades that not only did it promote a monolingual, native-speaker-norm-based, and educationally shallow version of English (or other languages), but it eschewed the complexity and depth of understanding language education as a translingual project. Translation, argues Cronin (2003: 133), plays a crucial role within globalization, since one of its primary functions is "to replenish the intertextual resources of a culture."

Like Venuti's (1998: 10) approach to translation that aims to "shake the regime of English," Cronin (2003) argues that "textual scrupulousness" only addresses part of the contemporary responsibility of the translator, since there must also be "an *activist dimension* to translation which involves an engagement with the cultural politics of society at national and international levels" (134, italics added). Here we might start to think in terms of what Clifford (1997: 39) calls "translation terms," the strategic use of particular terms to shed light on their role across languages. *Travel*, for example, "has an inextinguishable taint of location by class, gender, race, and a certain literariness." And *travel*, as critical work on global ELT textbooks has shown (Gray, 2010), is one of the staple diets of the ELT industry, with its focus away from class, gender, race, discrimination, conflict, and inequality, and its emphasis instead on a bland vision of consumerism, lifestyle choices, and global privilege.

If we connect this understanding of the traffic of meaning to recent work on translanguaging (García & Li Wei, 2014), metrolingualism (Pennycook & Otsuji, 2015) and transglossia (Dovchin, Pennycook & Sultana, 2018), the question becomes how the diverse linguistic resources that are constantly at play can be drawn on to increase the semiotic diversity available to students. From this point of view we can start to think of ELT classrooms in terms of *principled polycentrism* (Pennycook, 2014). When we explore how communication happens in contexts of both past and contemporary diversity, it is clear that it is not so much enabled by the use of a pre-existing language but rather in terms of complex chains of communication and emergent commonalities. It is on these grounds that Canagarajah (2007: 925) opts for the idea of Lingua Franca English (LFE) rather than English as a Lingua Franca (ELF), since from this position LFE is emergent from its contexts of use: it is "intersubjectively constructed in each specific context of interaction. The form of this English is negotiated by each set of speakers for their purposes" and thus "it is difficult to describe this language a priori" (Canagarajah, 2007: 925). This "translingual perspective" takes "diversity as the norm" and "challenges the assumption of other models of global Englishes that sharedness and uniformity of norms at different levels of generality are required for communicative success" (Canagarajah, 2013: 75).

This suggests the need for a more flexible model for learning English. Far removed from the notion that intelligibility might be guaranteed by everyone speaking the same variety of English, or by the codification of either English varieties or a lingua franca, a more polycentric model presents different possibilities. When we talk of being intelligible, we have to ask for whom? As Rajagopalan (2010) notes, much of the discussion of intelligibility in the context of the global spread of English still posits some undisclosed central norm as the hidden standard by which we judge intelligibility. We have to ask, instead, for whom is something intelligible? The specter of mutual unintelligibility that is raised when confronted by divergent ways of speaking needs to take into account for whom such unintelligibility is presupposed.

As studies of emergent communication in English in South East Asia have started to show, the norms for such intelligibility are locally formed and negotiated rather than being predefined exonormative standards (Deterding & Kirkpatrick, 2006). A polycentric approach suggests that, rather than seeking a model of English that assumes we can accommodate the diversity of English within a single framework, we need to turn our focus instead on how people manage to communicate in contexts of diversity. This is not so much a model, therefore, but a form of principled polycentrism, more akin to Canagarajah's LFE than ELF. These different strands of work have all started to question our assumptions about pre-existing, nameable things called languages: "What would language education look like," asks García (2007: xiii), "if we no longer posited the existence of separate languages?" This allows us to think in terms of resources, alignment, and a diversity of meanings.

We use a range of things to communicate and do not therefore need to assume that two speakers "must both know the same language in order to engage in verbal communication" (Harris, 2009: 74). Rather, they need to know "how to integrate their own semiological activities with those of their interlocutor" (75). Languages start to be seen not so much in terms of systems as in terms of practices, as something we do, not as an object in the curriculum but as an activity. We need, therefore, to ask ourselves what language myths we perpetuate through the language ideologies we reproduce in our language classes, with our bounded entities, such as French, German, Japanese, Chinese, Korean, Indonesian, Italian, and so on. These language labels are very different from the ways languages work. We need to ask ourselves what we mean when we say we're trying to teach this or that language, between 3 o'clock and 4 o'clock on Wednesday afternoon, and we'll be getting back to it the following week again because it's a thing you learn on that afternoon in that way: what myths are we perpetuating about languages?

We do not actually "speak languages"; we are not, in fact, "native speakers" of things called "languages." Rather, we engage in language practices (Pennycook, 2010), we draw on linguistic repertoires, we take up styles, we partake in discourse, we do genres. Indeed, languages can be seen not as pregiven entities but as sets of possibilities that emerge from practices, registers, discourses, and genres. From this point of view we can start to see language education in terms of multimodal semiotics, principled polycentrism, and the need to develop resourceful speakers. This principled polycentrism points to the relativity of locality. This is not the polycentrism of a World Englishes focus, with its established norms of regional varieties of English, but a more dynamic concept, based on the idea that peoples' linguistic repertoires "reflect the polycentricity of the learning environments in which the speaker dwells" (Blommaert & Backus, 2013: 20). It does not mean "anything goes": a *principled* polycentrism suggests we should acknowledge commonalities and shared resources.

From the point of view of translingual activism, therefore, this is not only a question of methodology (challenging monolingual pedagogies), of more efficient language use in the classroom (the argument that using rather than banning other languages in the classroom is helpful for learners), of reveling in difference and the fascinations of cultural comparison (introducing elements of critical multiculturalism into the class); rather, this is a question of unsettling common relations, not only of entering the traffic but of disrupting the traffic. ELT as translingual activism is about increasing the possible meanings available to those we teach. Yet we have to take this a step further, since this is not only about an expansion of any meanings but also part of a broader politics that aims to provincialize and decolonize English. We also, therefore, need to reconnect the development of resourceful speakers to forms of critical pedagogy.

A Critical ELT Pedagogy of the Commons

The activist part of translingual activism brings the notion of resourceful speakers into conversation with a longer history of critical practice, with a perspective that acknowledges the politics of language and education and seeks to address and transform social, cultural, and economic inequalities. From the diversity of approaches to critical literacy and language education we can see a number of commonalities (Chun, 2015): drawing on the lived experience of students and teachers, forming shared and common goals, using an approach to language that focuses broadly on social semiotics, making questions of power at both local and global levels central to an understanding of language and education, engaging with students' and teachers' understanding of the everyday, incorporating a form of critical self-reflexive practice, and creating and renewing a sense of community. The challenge here is how to develop forms of critical ELT pedagogy that aim to bring about social change or, as Crookes (2013) puts it, a form of critical ELT that focuses on social change, social justice, and the development of active, engaged citizens through learning English.

Such goals are arguably even more pressing in these difficult times in which we now live, a time of historical disjuncture, with millions of refugees struggling to find alternative places to survive among increasingly reluctant and hostile hosts, while walls and fences become the new response to mobile populations; with the rise of trenchant forms of xenophobic and isolationist populism in Europe, the United States, and elsewhere driving deep divides between people of different backgrounds and faiths; with the redistribution of income away from labor and toward profit bringing greater inequality as capital is concentrated in the hands of the very rich while huge economic disparities are ideologically normalized; with a new emergent class of mobile, impoverished, and insecure workers supporting growing extravagances by the wealthy while the very idea of welfare and the public good is increasingly on the retreat; with the world scrambling to avoid further ecological devastation while access to water, food, and basic resources comes under even greater threat through climate change and inequitable distribution.

Rather than a focus on social justice and citizenship, therefore, which arguably maintain current political norms and institutions, a critical agenda appropriate to the role of ELT can more usefully be based on the idea of the Commons. The current era is one in which the enclosure of the commons (an idea that links back to the enclosure of public land in eighteenth-century England) is conducted through increased privatization and commodification of public goods determined by market values. Central to our understanding of these processes has been Harvey's (2005) work on the expansive logic of capitalism and its need for continual enclosure through the incorporation of resources, people, activities, and land via a process of *accumulation by dispossession*. Standard political economy—whether liberal or Marxist—and common approaches to critical pedagogy do not have much of an answer to this, and yet we need ways of thinking and acting in terms other than the maximization of performance, incessant production, and neoliberal governmentality.

The way forward, Dardot and Laval (2009) suggest, is to think in terms of the commons: shared knowledge, mutual help, cooperative work, common property. Once we grasp that neoliberalism is not merely a glorification of the market and an expansion of the commodity sphere but also a form of governmentality, we can start to see how modes of opposition can operate beyond the twin poles of *transformative recognition* (challenges at the superstructural level to social categories such as gay vs. straight, male vs. female, black vs. white) and *transformative redistribution* (challenges at the infrastructural level to the political economy of the state) (Block, 2014). Understanding neoliberalism as governmentality enables us to see, on the one hand, how it enjoins us all, from wage earners to professionals, to operate in competition with each other, aligning the social world with the logic of the market, promoting and validating increased inequality, and pushing the individual to operate as an entrepreneur. It draws attention to the constant taking over of the commons, new modes of *instrumentation* (Berson, 2015), the enclosure of public space, the encroachment on public life of the new technologies, the new discourses of compliance that insist on new practices of obedience, and the commodification of languages.

On the other hand, this understanding of new forms of governmentality—on our wrists, in our workplaces, in our cities—also suggests a need to push back in different ways. It enables us to see how the idea of the commons can become an alternative to neoliberalism, a form of resistance to capital, and a rallying point for alternative politics and discourses (Dardot & Laval, 2014). The challenge from the perspective of the commons is to focus on "spatio-temporal and ethical formations that are concerned with ways of living together that resist the privatisation and individualisation of life" (Dawney, Kirwan & Brigstocke, 2016: 12–13). This rethinking can escape the battle lines between use value and exchange value, common use and commodification, communities and corporations—dividing lines that are defined by the old political economy and materialism and are now weighted so heavily in favor of the final enclosure—and instead embrace new platforms of cooperation and collective action, from solidarity networks to digital commons, from commonalities to local affiliations.

Rather than focusing on more traditional questions of citizenship or social justice, there is a return here to alternative anarchist roots, drawing on a range of thinkers from Mikhail Bakunin or Ivan Illich to the "postanarchist" thought of Michel Foucault and Judith Butler (Day, 2005; Kuhn, 2009). Seeking redress is not best pursued by recourse to the failing structures of the twentieth-century state: most democracies on the one hand currently offer no real alternative while at the same time encouraging the rise of new forms of populist nationalism. We have to reconsider our politics, epistemologies, and pedagogies while making a reclamation of the commons a common goal. In relation to language, the focus needs to be not so much on languages as entities that are enclosed or on people who are dispossessed of their languages while others accumulate them, but rather through much more grounded analyses of local language practices and assemblages (Pennycook, 2017; 2018), of the ways in which people, politics, place, economics, policy, practices, and things come together.

For a critical ELT pedagogy of the commons, therefore, the question becomes how to connect forms of resistance to English teaching. The point here, as Judith Butler notes (Heckert, 2011), is by no means to battle all forms of power indiscriminately but rather to appreciate the importance of taking the struggle to the streets, of maintaining a critical attitude to law and the state. And so, "as we reconsider our pedagogical practices and spaces," Armaline (2009: 145) suggests, let us "do so in light of the needs and desires of an anarchist society." The question is how to resist the new forms of enclosure (privatization, incarceration, commodification) demanded by capital through a new focus on the commons, as space, community, and possibility. Moving beyond the rally, union, or ballot box to explore new modes of politics, new modes of resistance have focused on more anarchist traditions of social media-connected occupation (Martín Rojo, 2016). It is this kind of critical ELT for the commons that we need to engage in.

Conclusion: Speaking Otherwise

Translingual activism asks questions of the normative assumptions that define languages along statist and institutional lines and connects this translingual focus to an activist pedagogy that does not seek to bring students into conformity with central norms, but rather aims to destabilize the normative meanings of society. If language education can be seen not so much as a functionalist enterprise always in the service of other agendas (specific purposes) but rather as *a practice of translingual activism*, the traffic of meanings would be far better served. There are several dimensions to this view of ELT as translingual activism. First is the need to understand the embeddedness of English in local and global relations of desire, discrimination, disparity, and difference. Not only do we need to appreciate the collusionary, delusionary, and exclusionary effects of English (the ways that English colludes with many of the pernicious processes of globalization, deludes many learners through the false promises it holds out for social and material gain, and excludes many people by operating as a segregational class dialect), but we also need to explore the ways its exclusionary focus—eschewing translation and an engagement with the traffic of meaning—has served to bolster English as a monolithic and monolingual enterprise and to deny the ethical imperative for students to be able to *speak otherwise*.

Second is the need to provincialize and decolonize English, to question the zero point of English articulation, and to *delink* language, culture, and thought from the Eurocentric categories that have defined them. For those of us involved in ELT we need to consider how all that we do in the name of English teaching is ineluctably connected to power and politics, coloniality, and modernity. What are the wider implications of promoting an English-only policy in a classroom, of choosing a textbook with glossy images of international travel, of deciding that "furnitures" is acceptable or unacceptable, of choosing between a private language school and a community college, of knowing or not knowing the first language(s) of our students, of choosing to hire "native" or "non-native" speakers at a school? We cannot, at least at this historical juncture, turn our back on English, but we can seek to provincialize it, to place it where it belongs, to decolonize its words.

Third, in order to unsettle the role that English plays in the world, as language educators we need to bring translingualism as a broad cultural practice fully into the center of our educational practice. To take the two terms—translingual and activism—as central to the English language teaching enterprise is to contest current pedagogical discourses in a number of ways. It is to disregard the long history whereby translation has been eschewed, where the use of languages other than English is denigrated as old-fashioned, as causing interlingual interference, as the strategy of the non-native teacher who knows no better, as indelibly tied to the chalk-and-talk methodologies that focus on grammar. It is to oppose the many interests and complicities that have supported the use of English and only English in classrooms, where English has been seen as *a language that operates only in its own presence*, much to the benefit of textbook sales and native speakers of English. It is to reintroduce translanguaging in all its complexity into English language teaching, to open up and explore the many possible meanings that can start to flow in and out of languages in relation to English. This is not about teaching translanguaging, or even redesigning a curriculum along translingual principles, but rather about rethinking politics and pedagogy along translingual lines (Lee, 2018). In its focus on activism, it is to see this as political action, as a way of confronting the possible threats to diversity posed by English. It is to do so not through the defense of other languages, or a focus on a new core of English or a plurality of Englishes, but rather through a focus on the traffic of meaning. Translingual activism opens up possibilities of a diversity of meaning for both teachers and students.

This means not only reincorporating translation into ELT practices and recognizing that English is always a language in translation (Pennycook, 2008) but also working toward a more flexible understanding of resourceful speakers. Important here is the focus on resources and positioning: it is not so much that we need a shared code to communicate but rather that we are able to bring our different resources into sufficient alignment. So an emerging goal of education may be less toward proficient native-speaker-like speakers (which has always been a confused and misguided goal) but to think instead in polycentric terms of *critical activist resourceful speakers* who can draw on multiple linguistic and semiotic resources, who can accommodate, negotiate, and understand such language use in activist terms. This is about changing the monolingual straitjackets of our language classes as part of a wider political engagement with the politics of diversity, the traffic of meaning, the availability of resources, and the capacity to rethink the social, economic, and political structures that do so much damage to people and their possibilities. This is about enabling our students to speak otherwise.

So, finally, in order to reconnect this agenda to a wider politics that seeks to delink English from the tentacles of neoliberalism, a *critical pedagogy of the commons* needs to focus on resistance to modes of enclosure, and the development of alternative modes of expression. If our critical activist resourceful speakers are to speak otherwise, they need not merely a form of principled polycentrism that enables a diversity of resources and meanings in educational contexts, not only a challenge to the zero point of English articulation, but also a translingual activism that seeks to connect these resources to political action aimed at decolonizing both public spaces (such as schools) and languages (such as English).

References

Armaline, W. (2009). Thoughts on anarchist pedagogy and epistemology. In R. Amster, A. DeLeon, L. Fernandez, A. Nocella II, & D. Shannon (Eds.), *Contemporary anarchist studies: An introductory anthology of anarchy in the academy* (pp 136–146). New York: Routledge.

Berson, J. (2015). *Computable bodies: instrumented life and the human somatic niche.* London: Bloomsbury.

Bialystok, E. (2007). Cognitive effects of bilingualism: How linguistic experience leads to cognitive change. *International Journal of Bilingual Education and Bilingualism*, 10:3, 210–223

Block, D. (2014). *Social class in applied linguistics.* London: Routledge.

Blommaert, J. and Backus, A. (2013). Super diverse repertoires and the individual. In I. de Saint-Georges & J. J. Weber (Eds.), *Multilingualism and multimodality: Current challenges for educational studies* (pp. 11–32). Rotterdam: Sense Publishers.

Bruthiaux, P. (2002). Hold your courses: Language education, language choice, and economic development. *TESOL Quarterly,* 36/3. 275–296.

Canagarajah, S. (2007). Lingua Franca English, multilingual communities, and language acquisition. *Modern Language Journal,* 91, 923–939.

Canagarajah, S. (2013). *Translingual practice: Global Englishes and cosmopolitan relations.* London: Routledge.

Chakrabarty, D. (2000). *Provincializing Europe: Postcolonial thought and historical difference.* Princeton, NJ: Princeton University Press.

Chun, C. (2015). *Power and meaning making in an EAP classroom: Engaging with the everyday.* Bristol, UK: Multilingual Matters.

Clifford, J. (1997). *Routes: Travel and translation in the late twentieth century.* Cambridge, MA: Harvard University Press.

Cronin, M. (2003). *Translation and globalization.* London: Routledge.

Crookes, G. (2013). *Critical ELT in action: Foundations, promises, praxis.* New York: Routledge.

Dardot, P. and Laval, C. (2009). *La nouvelle raison du monde: Essai sur la société néolibérale.* Paris: Éditions La Découverte.

Dardot, P. and Laval, C. (2014). *Commun: Essai sur la révolution au XXIe siècle.* Paris: Éditions La Découverte

Dawney, L., Kirwan, S. and Brigstocke, J. (2016). Introduction: The promise of the commons. In J. Brigstocke, L. Dawney & S. Kirwan (Eds.), *Space, power and the commons: The struggle for alternative futures* (pp. 12–31). London: Routledge.

Day, R. (2005). *Gramsci is Dead: Anarchist currents in the newest social movements.* London: Pluto Press.

Deterding, D. and Kirkpatrick, A. (2006). Emerging South-East Asian Englishes and intelligibility. *World Englishes* 25 3/4, 391–409.

Dovchin, S., Pennycook, A. and Sultana, S. (2018). *Popular culture, voice and linguistic diversity: Young adults on- and offline.* London: Palgrave-Macmillan.

Ferguson, G. (2013). English, development and education: Charting the tensions. In E. Erling & P. Seargeant (Eds.), *English and development: Policy, pedagogy and globalization* (pp. 21–44). Bristol, UK: Multilingual Matters.

Fortes, L. (2015). The emergence of bilingual education discourse in Brazil: Bilingualisms, language policies, and globalizing circumstances. *International Journal of Bilingual Education and Bilingualism.* http://dx.doi.org/10.1080/13670050.2015.1103207.

García, O. (2007). Foreword. In S. Makoni and A. Pennycook (Eds.), *Disinventing and reconstituting languages* (pp. xi–xv). Clevedon, UK: Multilingual Matters.

García, O. (2014). Countering the dual: Transglossia, dynamic bilingualism and translanguaging in education. In R. Rubdy & L. Alsagoff (Eds.), *The global-local interface and hybridity: Exploring language and identity* (pp. 100–120). Bristol, UK: Multilingual Matters.

García, O. & Li Wei. (2014). *Translanguaging: Language, bilingualism and education.* Basingstoke, UK: Palgrave Macmillan.

Gray, J. (2010). *The construction of English: Culture, consumerism and promotion in the ELT global coursebook.* Basingstoke, UK: Palgrave Macmillan.

Gray, J. (2012). "Neoliberalism, celebrity and 'aspirational content' in English language teaching textbooks for the global market." In D. Block, J. Gray & M. Holborow (Eds.), *Neoliberalism and applied linguistics* (pp. 86–113). London: Routledge.

Halliday, M. A. K. (2002). Applied linguistics as an evolving theme. *Plenary address to the International Association of Applied Linguistics.* December, 2002, Singapore.

Harris, R. (2009). *After Epistemology.* Sandy: Authors Online.

Harvey, D. (2005). *A brief history of neoliberalism.* Oxford, UK: Oxford University Press.

Heckert, J. (2011). On Anarchism: An Interview with Judith Butler. In J. Heckert & R. Cleminson (Eds.), *Anarchism & sexuality: Ethics, relationships and power.* New York: Routledge.

Heller, M. (2007). Bilingualism as ideology and practice. In M. Heller (Ed.), *Bilingualism: A social approach* (pp. 1–22). Hampshire, NY: Palgrave.

Hoy, D. C. (2004). *Critical Resistance: From poststructuralism to post-critique.* Cambridge, MA: The MIT Press.

Jaspers, J. (2018). The transformative limits of translanguaging. *Language and Communication,* 58, 1–10.

Jenkins, J. (2009). Exploring attitudes towards English as a Lingua Franca in the East Asian context. In K. Murata & J. Jenkins (Eds.), *Global Englishes in Asian contexts: Current and future debates* (pp. 40–56). Basingstoke, UK: Palgrave Macmillan.

Kachru, B. (2005). *Asian Englishes: Beyond the canon.* Hong Kong: Hong Kong University Press.

King, K. and Mackey, A. (2007). *The bilingual edge: why, when, and how to teach your child a second language*. New York: HarperCollins.

Kirkpatrick, A. (2011). English as an Asian lingua franca and the multilingual model of ELT. *Language Teaching,* 44, 212–224.

Kramsch, C. (2006). The traffic in meaning. *Asia Pacific Journal of Education,* 26(1), 99–104.

Kubota, R. (2015). Inequalities of Englishes, English speakers, and languages: A critical perspective on pluralist approaches to English. In R. Tupas & R. Rubdy (Eds.), *Unequal Englishes: The politics of Englishes today* (pp. 21–42). Basingstoke, UK: Palgrave Macmillan.

Kuhn, G. (2009). Anarchism, postmodernity, and poststructuralism. In R. Amster, A. DeLeon, L. Fernandez, A. Nocella II and D. Shannon (Eds.), *Contemporary anarchist studies: An introductory anthology of anarchy in the academy* (pp. 18–25). New York: Routledge.

Lee, J. W. (2018). *The politics of translingualism: After Englishes.* New York: Routledge.

Lin, A. (2013). Toward paradigmatic change in TESOL methodologies: Building plurilingual pedagogies from the ground up. *TESOL Quarterly,* 47/3. 521–545.

Mackenzie, I. (2014). *English as a lingua franca.* London: Routledge.

Makoni, S. and Pennycook, A. (2007). Disinventing and reconstituting languages. In S. Makoni & A. Pennycook (Eds.), *Disinventing and reconstituting languages* (pp. 1–41). Clevedon, UK: Multilingual Matters.

Martin, I. (2014). Philippine English revisited. *World Englishes* 33(1) 50–59.

Martín Rojo, L. (2016). Occupy: The spatial dynamics of discourse in global protest movements. In L. Martín Rojo (Ed.), *Occupy: The spatial dynamics of discourse in global protest movements* (pp. 1–22). Amsterdam: John Benjamins.

May, T. (2009) Anarchism from Foucault to Rancière. In R. Amster, A. DeLeon, L. Fernandez, A. Nocella II & D. Shannon (Eds.), *Contemporary anarchist studies: An introductory anthology of anarchy in the academy* (pp. 11–17). New York: Routledge.

Mignolo, W. (2009). Epistemic disobedience, independent thought and decolonial freedom. *Theory, culture, society* 26(7–8): 159–181.

Mignolo, W. (2010). Delinking: The rhetoric of modernity, the logic of coloniality and the grammar of de-coloniality. In W. Mignolo & A. Escobar (Eds.), *Globalization and the decolonial option* (pp. 303–368). New York: Routledge.

Mignolo, W. (2011). *The darker side of western modernity: Global futures, decolonial options.* Durham, NC: Duke University Press.

Motha, S. (2014). *Race, empire, and English language teaching: Creating responsible and ethical anti-racist practice.* New York: Teachers College Press, Columbia University.

O'Regan, J. (2014). English as a lingua franca: An Immanent critique. *Applied Linguistics,* 35(5): 533–552.

Otsuji, E. and Pennycook, A. (2018). The translingual advantage: Metrolingual student repertoires. In J. Choi & S. Ollerhead (Eds.), *Plurilingualism in teaching and learning: Complexities across contexts* (pp.71–88). New York: Routledge.

Pennycook, A. (1989). "The concept of Method, interested knowledge, and the politics of language teaching". *TESOL Quarterly,* 23/4, 589–618.

Pennycook, A. (2001). *Critical applied linguistics: A critical introduction.* Mahwah, NJ: Lawrence Erlbaum.

Pennycook, A. (2004). Language policy and the ecological turn. *Language Policy,* 3, 213–239.

Pennycook, A. (2008). English as a language always in translation, *European Journal of English Studies,* 12:1, 33–47.

Pennycook, A. (2010). *Language as a local practice.* London: Longman.

Pennycook, A. (2014). Principled polycentrism and resourceful speakers. *Journal of Asia TEFL*, 11/4, 1–19.

Pennycook, A. (2016). Mobile times, mobile terms: The trans-super-poly-metro movement. In N. Coupland (Ed.), *Sociolinguistics theoretical debates* (pp. 201–206). Cambridge, UK: Cambridge University Press.

Pennycook, A. (2017). Translanguaging and semiotic assemblages. *International Journal of Multilingualism*, 14(3), 269–282.

Pennycook, A. (2018). *Posthumanist applied linguistics*. New York: Routledge.

Pennycook, A. and Otsuji, E. (2015). *Metrolingualism: Language in the city*. London: Routledge.

Phillipson, R. (1992). *Linguistic imperialism*. Oxford, UK: Oxford University Press.

Phillipson, R. (2009). *Linguistic imperialism continued*. New York: Routledge.

Piller, I. (2016). *Linguistic diversity and social justice: An introduction to applied sociolinguistics*. Oxford, UK: Oxford University Press.

Rajagopalan, K. (2010). The soft ideological underbelly of the notion of intelligibility in discussions about "world Englishes". *Applied Linguistics*, 31(3), 465–470.

Ramanathan, V. (2005). *The English-Vernacular divide: Postcolonial language politics and practice*. Clevedon, UK: Multilingual Matters.

Rapatahana, V. and Bunce, P. (Eds.) (2012). *English language as hydra: Its impacts on non-English language cultures*. Bristol, UK: Multilingual Matters.

Sonntag, S. (2003). *The local politics of global English: Case studies in linguistic globalization*. Lanham, MD: Lexington Books.

Tollefson, J. (2000). Policy and ideology in the spread of English. In J. K. Hall & W. Eggington (Eds.), *The sociopolitics of English language teaching* (pp. 7–21). Clevedon, UK: Multilingual Matters.

Tupas, T. R. (2010). Which norms in everyday practice and why? In Andy Kirkpatrick (Ed.), *The Routledge handbook of world Englishes* (pp. 567–79). London: Routledge.

Tupas, T. R. and Rubdy, R. (2015). Introduction: From World Englishes to Unequal Englishes. In R. Tupas & R. Rubdy (Eds.), *Unequal Englishes: The politics of Englishes today* (pp. 1–21). Basingstoke, UK: Palgrave Macmillan.

Venuti, L. (1998). *The scandals of translation: Towards an ethics of difference*. London: Routledge.

8

A MULTILINGUAL PERSPECTIVE ON TRANSLANGUAGING

*Jeff MacSwan**

UNIVERSITY OF MARYLAND

Translanguaging has emerged as a new term within bilingual education and has given voice to a heteroglossic language ideology (Bailey, 2007; Bakhtin, 1975; García, 2009) that values bilingualism as a sustainable community resource in its own right rather than a merely tolerated transition to majority language monolingualism (a monoglossic ideology). However, some translanguaging scholars have recently called the existence of discrete languages into question, arguing that multilingualism[1] itself does not exist (compare Blommaert, 2010; Davidson, 1986; Harris, 1981; Heller, 2007; Heller & Duchêne, 2007; Kemp, 2009; Kravchenko, 2007; Makoni & Makoni, 2010; Makoni & Pennycook, 2007; Pennycook, 2006). For instance, Makoni and Pennycook (2007) argue that "languages do not exist as real entities in the world and neither do they emerge from or represent real environments; they are, by contrast, the inventions of social, cultural and political movements" (p. 2). These conclusions are motivated by a consideration of the colonial history of language names and their boundaries viewed through a postmodernist lens on language planning and policy:

> A postmodern (or postcolonial) approach to language policy ... suggests we no longer need to maintain the pernicious myth that languages exist. Thus we can start to develop an anti-foundationalist view of language as an emergent property of social interaction and not of prior system tied to ethnicity, territory, birth, or nation. The very notion that ... we can decide to have one, two, three, five or eleven languages in a language policy becomes highly questionable ... Yet the questions I have raised here suggest that languages cannot in fact be planned ... since there is ultimately no good reason to continue to posit their existence.
>
> *(Pennycook, 2006, p. 67)*

Pennycook (2006) sees languages as "not so much ontological systems" but rather as "products of language use sedimented through acts of identity" (p. 71).

Makoni and Pennycook (2007) note that if discrete languages do not exist, neither do "many of the treasured icons of liberal-linguistic thought ... such as language rights, mother tongues, multilingualism or code-switching" (p. 22). Building on this basic idea, García and colleagues (García & Otheguy, 2014; Otheguy, García, & Reid, 2015) offer a clarification of translanguaging theory in which they similarly reject (individual) multilingualism, insisting that a bilingual individual has an internally undifferentiated, unitary linguistic system uniquely configured as an *idiolect*, or individual language. Consistent with this point of view, codeswitching[2] must also be rejected for García and colleagues as it "constitutes a theoretical endorsement of the idea that what the bilingual manipulates, however masterfully, are two separate linguistic systems" (Otheguy et al., 2015, p. 282).

Codeswitching is a speech style in which bilinguals alternate languages between or within sentences. For instance, Spanish-English bilinguals might say, *This morning mi hermano y yo fuimos a comprar some milk* ("This morning my brother and I went to buy some milk"), where the sentence begins in English, switches to Spanish, and then moves back to English again. The practice is very common throughout the world, especially among members of bilingual families and communities.

The consequences of denying the existence of multilingualism and therefore of codeswitching are far reaching. If codeswitching does not exist, then neither does the empirical basis for the repudiation of a deficit perspective on language mixing, a critically important and frequently cited (e.g., Cook, 2001; Durán & Palmer, 2013; Fuller, 2009; García, 2009; García, Flores, & Woodley, 2015; Gort, 2012; Grosjean, 1982, 2010; Martínez, 2010; Valdes-Fallis, 1978) body of basic scientific research. In other words, we cannot both rely on codeswitching scholarship to support a positive view of bilingualism and simultaneously deny that multilingualism and codeswitching exist, and by choosing to do the latter over the former, we lose the empirical case against a deficit perspective on bilingualism and are left only with an ideological one.

In the present review, I offer a critical assessment of the theory of bilingualism proposed by García and colleagues (García & Otheguy, 2014; Otheguy et al., 2015), showing that it is at odds with what we know empirically and theoretically about bilingualism and that it seriously weakens the associated conceptual framework, which I will call *holistic bilingualism*, following Grosjean (1982). I suggest an alternative point of view, called a *multilingual perspective on translanguaging*, which acknowledges the existence of discrete languages and multilingualism (in a sense I will clarify) along with other "treasured icons" of the field, including language rights, mother tongues, and codeswitching. My intention is not to disparage translanguaging or discourage researchers from using it as a lens; rather, I offer a clarification of the linguistic theory underlying translanguaging, hoping to reconcile educational and linguistic research.

As a field of research, codeswitching emerged in the middle of the last century, energized by the pioneering work of Weinreich (1953), Haugen (1956), and Mackey (1967), just as social and educational policy began to keenly focus on marginalized and economically disadvantaged groups in the context of the Civil Rights Movement and Johnson's War on Poverty (Benson, 2001; Riegelhaupt, 2000). Language and its relation to educational achievement dominated conversations about African American students and similarly moved to the forefront of conversations about achievement of Latino students in the wake of the Mexican American student walkouts in East Los Angeles in 1968 (Crawford, 2004). Scholars concerned with academic underachievement among bilingual students began to address important questions about the language these children bring to school and how language may relate to our understanding of school failure. Much as Labov (1965, 1970), Wolfram (1969), Fasold (1972), and others had shown through painstaking analysis that stigmatized language varieties spoken by African Americans were just as rich and complex as the language of the privileged classes, codeswitching researchers undertook to show that language mixing was not "haphazard" or a reflection of language confusion but was rule governed and systematic, like other ways of speaking (Riegelhaupt, 2000). Among the earliest to observe that language alternation revealed systematic, rule-governed behavior were Gumperz (1967, 1970), Gumperz and Hernández-Chávez (1970), Hasselmo (1972), Timm (1975), Wentz (1977), Wentz and McClure (1977), and Poplack (1978). By now, an extensive body of research has shown conclusively through rigorous empirical and theoretical analysis that bilinguals are exquisitely sensitive to tacit rules that govern codeswitching itself, leading to the conclusion that language alternation is sophisticated, rule-governed behavior that in no way reflects a linguistic deficit (for summaries, see MacSwan, 2013, 2014, 2016a; Ritchie & Bhatia, 2013).

As Lipski (2014) recalled,

> Seeking to dispel popular notions that equate code-switching with confusion, "alingualism," imperfect acquisition, and just plain laziness, linguists have since the early 1970s devoted considerable effort to demonstrating grammatical and pragmatic conditions favoring or constraining code-switching. Bilingual code-switching so analyzed is not regarded … as a deficiency or anomaly.
>
> *(p. 24)*

Rampton (2007) similarly remarked, "research on code-switching has waged a war on deficit models of bilingualism and on pejorative views of syncretic language use by insisting on the integrity of language mixing and by examining it for its grammatical systematicity and pragmatic coherence" (p. 306).

Codeswitching research usefully informs bilingual education theory and practice, especially with regard to views about the linguistic resources that bilingual children bring with them to school (Faltis, 1989; Jacobson, 1978; Paulston, 1983; Ramirez & Milk, 1986; Valdés-Fallis, 1978; Zentella, 1981, 1997). The way teachers, researchers, and others view children's language ability is important because it affects their views of what children know and of their families and communities, and influences the treatment children are likely to receive in school. Indeed, the beliefs teachers hold about parents and communities may become tacit tracking mechanisms, serving to restrict the educational opportunities of bilingual students. Oakes's (1985) classic work on tracking noted that ability grouping for children correlated highly with children's self-perceptions of ability and career promise. More specifically with regard to bilingual children, if teachers believe that codeswitching relates to an inherent disability in children that might be remedied by instruction, then children's perceptions of the funds of knowledge (Moll, Soto-Santiago, & Schwartz, 2013) they bring to school, as conveyed by classroom teachers, will likely have a negative impact on their success in school. Conversely, if teachers recognize that codeswitching is richly structured and evidence of linguistic talent, as research has shown, then children's bilingual ability is more likely to be viewed as a resource rather than a deficit in educational settings.

Translanguaging was originally used by Williams (1994) to refer to "the planned and systematic use of two languages inside the same lesson" at school (Baker, 2011, p. 288), as also noted by García (2009) and Lewis, Jones, and Baker (2012). Similar proposed terms, each used a bit differently, include *heteroglossia* (Bakhtin, 1975), *polylanguaging* and *polylingual languaging* (Jørgensen, 2008; Jørgensen, Karrebæk, Madsen, & Møller, 2011), *metrolingualism* (Otsuji & Pennycook, 2011), *codemeshing* (Canagarajah, 2011), *translingual practice* (Canagarajah, 2013), and *multilanguaging* (Nguyen, 2012). In recent studies of language alternation in classrooms, researchers have examined the way students use their two languages in combination to support bilingual acquisition in small group activities (Martin-Beltrán, 2014), teachers' dynamic and interactive use of two languages in classroom instructional settings (Palmer, Martínez, Henderson, & Mateus, 2014), and the effects of using two languages concurrently in the teaching of reading (Soltero-González & Butvilofsky, 2015; Soltero-González, Sparrow, Butvilofsky, Escamilla, & Hopewell, 2016), among many others. In education-focused research, a variety of nomenclature have been used to describe language alternation, including *translanguaging* (Durán & Palmer, 2013; García, 2009; Gort, 2015; Gort & Sembiante, 2015; Henderson & Palmer, 2015; Hornberger & Link, 2012; Martin-Beltrán, 2014; Martínez, Hikida, & Durán, 2015; Martínez-Roldán, 2015; Palmer et al., 2014; Sayer, 2013; Smith & Murillo, 2015), *hybrid language practices* (Gutiérrez, Baquedano-López, & Tejeda, 1999; Gutiérrez, Bien, Selland, & Pierce, 2011; Palmer & Martínez, 2013), *holistic bilingualism* (Soltero-González, Escamilla, & Hopewell, 2011; Soltero-González, 2009; Soltero-González & Butvilofsky, 2015; Soltero-González et al., 2016), and *codeswitching* (Cook, 2001; Fuller, 2009, 2010; Gort, 2012; Martínez, 2010; Moschkovich, 2007; Nava, 2009; Palmer, 2009; Reyes, 2004; Shin, 2005), following the foundational work of Jacobson (1978, 1981, 1990), Milk (1986,

1990), and Faltis (1989, 1990, 1996). Some have used a variety of terms within the same publication to capture nuanced differences or used different terms in different publications depending on their research purpose. While these terminological contrasts reflect subtle differences, they also share many common attributes.

As a conceptual framework, translanguaging and related ideas promote a positive view of bilingualism, permitting bilinguals to act naturally, using language as they do at home and in their communities. Indeed, Cenoz and Gorter (2011) situate translanguaging and related proposals as instances of *holistic bilingualism*, that is, Grosjean's (1982) important observation that a bilingual is not two monolinguals in one but a linguistically unique language user whose languages reflect the differential experience a bilingual may have with each language. Grosjean (1982, 2010) contrasts the holistic view with the fractional or monolingual view of bilingualism, which looks to native speakers of each language as "monolingual norms" against which the bilingual's two languages are each compared. Grosjean used a sports analogy to illustrate the holistic perspective: Hurdlers blend two separate athletic competencies, high jumping and sprinting, as an integrated whole. Compared individually to high jumpers or sprinters, hurdlers meet neither set of expectations, but by blending both, hurdlers compete athletically in their own right, excelling in their sport in ways that neither high jumpers nor sprinters could. Grosjean's perspective draws extensively on linguistic and sociolinguistic research on bilingual codeswitching as an illustration of the special ways in which bilinguals exhibit their linguistic talents.

The article is organized in three parts. First, I discuss the idea of discrete languages, arguing that Chomsky's (1980, 1986) useful distinction between *E-language* (language in the external sense) and *I-language* (language in the internal sense) allows us to accept linguistic diversity while rejecting language as an instrument of hegemony, and to recognize speech communities as useful idealizations. This leads to a discussion in the second part of the question of whether bilingual *individuals* have internally differentiated linguistic systems. I show that the study of language alternation and mixing compels us to acknowledge that they do have internally differentiated systems, but in a specific sense not considered by García and colleagues: Multilingual grammars include both shared and internally differentiated, language-particular components. In this context, I distinguish three views of multilingualism—a unitary model, a dual competence model, and an integrated multilingual model—arguing that evidence supports the integrated perspective, which I situate in the context of *universal multilingualism*, the view that everybody, even so-called monolinguals, are in fact multilinguals in important respects. In a final section, I distinguish *mental grammars* from *linguistic repertoires*, agreeing with García and colleagues that bilinguals, like monolinguals, have "*one linguistic repertoire* from which they select features *strategically* to communicate effectively" (García, 2012, p. 1) but not an internally undifferentiated unitary *grammar*. This allows us to recognize the oneness of a bilingual's language use without the many undesirable consequences of denying the existence of community or individual multilingualism. I end with a brief conclusions section advocating a multilingual perspective on translanguaging, one that affirms the value and multiplicity of linguistic diversity for children, families, and communities.

Language(s)

People generally associate languages with nations and states: Japanese with Japan, French with France, and Urdu with Pakistan. Language is often used to consolidate political power and marginalize minorities who speak a language or language variety that differs from the one those in power use. States sanction as legitimate not a specific language but one or more language varieties—privileging some ways of talking and stigmatizing others. Such concerns motivated Makoni and Pennycook (2007) to describe languages as social and political "inventions," not as discoveries. Linguistic stigma, whether it is associated with a marginalized language or language variety, is reinforced through traditional prescriptivism, the view that one language or language variety has an inherently higher value than others and that it ought to be imposed on an entire nation-state to maintain standards of communication (Crystal, 1986; MacSwan, 2000b; Pinker, 1994). Prescriptivists have often characterized minority languages (or dialects) as "inexpressive," "primitive," or lacking complexity in comparison to their own language, for example, as with the language academies committed to the task of "purifying" the regional linguistic descendants of Latin established as early as 1582 in Italy, 1635 in France, and 1713 in Spain.

Traditional U.S. school curricula generally include familiar prohibitions against using double negatives, *ain't*, or among the very strict, ending a sentence with a preposition, and many more. These prohibitions turn on Latinate analyses advanced in the late 19th and early 20th centuries and are used to validate varieties of speech associated with the privileged classes in England and the United States (Baugh & Cable, 1978). In contrast to this prescriptivist tradition, structuralist linguists undertook an empirical project, following Bloomfield's (1928, 1933) lead, in which all languages were analyzed *descriptively*, using the same taxonomy, leading to the conclusion that all languages, even those that many people had thought of as "primitive languages," were equally complex. This research agenda ultimately had serious consequences that threatened sacred distinctions that kept linguistic and social prestige in the hands of the privileged classes. As Newmeyer (1986) put it,

> As long as American structuralists confined their campaign to the languages of remote tribes, they did little to upset their colleagues in departments of modern and classical languages—in which almost all linguists were situated in the interwar years. But such was certainly not the case when they began crusading for the linguistic equality of *all* dialects of English and

> other literary languages, no matter how "substandard" they were regarded. This egalitarian view came in direct conflict with the long-seated tradition in the humanities that values a language variety in direct proportion to its literary output.
>
> *(p. 42)*

While 17th-century Europe was preoccupied with the "special languages" of elites, the *Port Royale Grammar* of 1660 advanced a very different view of language and of the human condition. Written in French, the *Port Royale Grammar* formed part of the movement to displace Latin as an outdated mode of academic discourse. However, what marked the *Port Royale Grammar* as deeply distinct from contemporaneous approaches was its devotion to philosophical and universal properties of human language in descriptive terms (Chomsky, 1968; Newmeyer, 1988; Robins, 1967). As in modern approaches in the linguistic sciences, the *Port Royale* grammarians worked on the assumption that normal human intelligence is capable of acquiring knowledge through its own internal resources, making use of the data of experience but moving on to construct a cognitive system in terms of concepts and principles that are developed independently.

Hence, language has both a sociopolitical dimension and an individual cognitive dimension. Chomsky (1980, 1986) referred to language in the sociopolitical sense as *E-language*, where *E* denotes *externalized* and *extensional*. Language in this sense is not the product of an individual per se but of a community of speakers, and it is *extensional* in the formal sense: Its expressions can only be listed, not defined by a generative system of rules; it is a collection of overlapping individual languages, or *I-languages*, where *I* denotes *internalized, individual*, and *intensional* (formally, given by a recursive rule system).

Linguistic theories about language structure and acquisition are focused on I-language, not E-language. "What we call 'English,' 'French,' 'Spanish,' and so on, even under idealizations to idiolects in homogeneous speech communities," Chomsky (1995) noted, "reflect the Norman Conquest, proximity to Germanic areas, a Basque substratum, and other factors that cannot seriously be regarded as properties of the language faculty" (p. 11). Chomsky's use of the term *idiolect* derives from Bloch (1948), who used it to denote "the totality of the possible utterances of one speaker at one time" (p. 7), differing from a *dialect*, or community language, which Bloch defined as "a class of idiolects" (p. 8). Bloch's distinction was used by early sociolinguists (Hymes & Fought, 1975; Labov, 1972) to conceptualize the linguistic study of language variation and remains an important concept in linguistics and sociolinguistics today. An I-language is similar to an idiolect in that it denotes an individual's language, and an E-language is similar to a national or community language in that it denotes an externalized collection of I-languages.

Just as Makoni and Pennycook (2007) recently contended that languages are social and historical "inventions," Chomsky (1980) similarly regarded languages in the E-language sense as fictional. The realization that speech communities are idealizations, in this respect, is also evident in the work of early structuralist linguists like Leonard Bloomfield (1928), who defined a language as "the totality of utterances that can be made in a speech community" (p. 26). For Bloomfield and those who followed, it was understood, as Chomsky (1986) further noted, that speech communities, or "collections of individuals with the same speech behavior," actually "do not exist in the real world." Rather,

> Each individual has acquired a language in the course of complex social interactions with people who vary in the ways in which they speak and interpret what they hear and in the internal representations that underlie their use of language.
>
> *(p. 16)*

While I-languages reflect the individual internalized grammatical system each of us has and are likely to each vary one from the other in some respect, it is important to recognize that I-languages do not vary at random. Our divergent experiences result in individual linguistic differences, but the mechanisms and circumstances of language acquisition are such that we expect learners exposed to similar linguistic input to converge on similar I-languages. For instance, a learner exposed to a community of "English speakers" will come to place subjects before verbs (e.g., *Sam ate lunch*), but a learner exposed to a community of "Irish speakers" will place them after verbs (e.g., *Cheannaigh Máire carr* [bought Maíre car, Maíre bought a car]; Stenson, 2007). A child raised in South Carolina might use double modal constructions like *I thought you might could help me* (Mishoe & Montgomery, 1994), and a language learner in London might acquire a phonological rule that changes *t* to the *d*-like sound (flapped *t*) in *water* ([wɑːɾɚ]) and *writer* ([raɪɾɚ]) because somewhere in her diverse language experience she spent significant time with somebody who learned English in the United States, Canada, Australia, or New Zealand. Thus, while I-languages each vary one from the other, language learning experience generally confines variation to narrow limits. We each speak individual languages, but our individual languages are remarkably similar to the individual languages used by members of our linguistic community (or communities).

Despite the recognition that language is individually represented, linguists refer to languages and even classes of languages by name in order to capture generalizations that hold across languages. Scientists in other fields use idealizations in a similar way. As Weisberg (2007) noted, idealization plays an important epistemic role across a wide range of disciplines (e.g., biology, physics, economics, mathematics), defined in the philosophy of science as "the intentional introduction of distortion into scientific theories" (p. 639). "Frictionless planes, point masses, infinite velocities, isolated systems, omniscient agents, and markets in perfect equilibrium are but some well-known examples" of scientific idealization (Frigg & Hartmann, 2012; see also Cartwright, 1989; Nowak, 1972, 1992). In linguistics, researchers interested in the range of structural variation associated with *wh*-constructions (questions that use words like *who, what,* and *why*, among others) might refer to "Chinese" or "English" to capture structural generalizations about these languages despite the presence of other language-internal variation, noting that English moves *wh*-question words to the front of an utterance (e.g., *What does Steve like?*, where *what*, as the object of *like*, has been moved from its position after the verb to the front of the sentence), while Chinese leaves these words in place (e.g., *Zhangsan xihuan shenme?*, with word order *Zhangsan like what* to mean "What does Zhangsan like?"). Or researchers may even find it useful to refer to broad classes of languages with similar typologies, using terms like *wh*-movement languages (e.g., English, French, Hungarian) and *wh*-in situ languages (e.g., Chinese, Korean, Swahili), or even English-type languages and Chinese-type languages. Sociolinguists interested in studying language use among African Americans might refer to African American Vernacular English (AAVE), another idealization across individual-level variation, seeking to understand any number of language-related behaviors specific to one or another community of speakers.

Idealizations like these treat members of a speech community as though they are homogeneous, purposely ignoring irrelevant variation as a tool of focused inquiry. Linguists interested in studying language diversity refer to E-languages (named languages or other speech communities) or even collections of E-languages (linguistic typology) by name as a convenience; this permits them to idealize across cases of individual variation to focus on relevant aspects of language that appear to be common to a community of speakers. These methods are used by linguists interested in language structure as well as those specializing in sociolinguistics, who study both structural characteristics of discrete speech communities and the social practices surrounding their language use.

Unpacking the ambiguity in the term *language* in this way helps us recognize the inherent sociopolitical nature of named languages, or E-languages, while still recognizing the linguistic reality of language diversity in the form of I-languages, or individual languages. Indeed, the linguistic study of language diversity is an important tool in our efforts to expose the political uses of language to justify meritocracy. For example, in studying AAVE, linguists have shown that AAVE consonant cluster reduction occurs when a consonant pair in word-final position shares the same place of articulation within the vocal tract and the same voicing (vibration of the vocal folds). Thus, *test* is pronounced like *Tess*, and *passed* like *pass* in AAVE. This pronunciation is sociopolitically stigmatized, but from a linguistic point of view, it is understood as a simple case of language variation, not different in principle from, say, the deletion of *r* in postvocalic position in words like *hard* and *butter* (pronounced [hɑːd] and [bʌtə]) in some parts of the eastern United States (Labov, Ash, & Boberg, 2006). Thus, by acknowledging and studying language diversity, we can uncover the sociopolitical nature of language prejudice.

For linguists interested in the theory of grammar—or the nature of *mental grammars*, the focus of García and Otheguy (2014) and Otheguy et al. (2015)—individual grammars form the object of study, and speech communities are idealizations. For linguists who study the social variables of language variation, however, speech communities, while still idealizations, are themselves the objects of study, guided by questions about how language structure and use vary by geography, social class, age, sex, sexual orientation, and other factors (see Chambers & Schilling, 2013). Groups use language differently within varied and overlapping speech communities (Gumperz, 1964; Labov, 1972) to engage in different language practices (e.g., Eckert, 2000) or discourses (e.g., Gee, 2016b; Resnik, Asterhan, & Clarke, 2015). In large part, our linguistic uniqueness (I-language) is defined by our participation in multiple overlapping speech communities, resulting from the effects that each of these has had on the individual cognitive representation of language. Makoni and Pennycook's (2007) central concern is that "named languages," which are typically identified with nation-states, form part of the colonial agenda and should be understood as social and political constructs, a widely held view in mainstream linguistics (e.g., Bloch, 1948; Chomsky, 1965, 1986, 1995; Gee, 2016a; Labov, 1972; Lyons, 1981; MacSwan, 2000a). However, if we dispense with *any* conception of speakers as members of idealized speech communities, then sociolinguistic research becomes wholly incongruous.

Indeed, some of the earliest work on codeswitching concerned switching between community and sanctioned languages, such as Ranamal, used in a Norwegian fishing village, and Bokmål, a legally sanctioned variety of Norwegian (Blom & Gumperz, 1972; Gumperz, 1964). Ranamal and Bokmål represent discrete communities insofar as speakers within each group understand one another by virtue of the great structural similarity across individual linguistic knowledge. Some individuals participate in both communities, some in just one or the other. Researchers have also studied codeswitching between AAVE and "standard" English, a politically sanctioned variety (DeBose, 1992).

Makoni and Pennycook's (2007) novel contribution is not the observation that named languages are sociopolitical and arbitrary with respect to their boundaries but is rather their contention that this observation invalidates linguistic phenomena predicated on the existence of discrete speech communities—"such as language rights, mother tongues, multilingualism or code-switching" (p. 22). However, the existence of these phenomena depends not on whether named languages are political constructs but on whether we may reasonably speak of discrete speech communities by *any* name or for *any* purpose. Language names are used for potentially distinct but frequently overlapping *political, social*, or *structural* purposes. Sometimes the political distinctions are farcical from a structural point of view (e.g., Romanian vs. Moldovan), or social registers (e.g., academic English, gamer English) may lack clear political identification or significant structural distinctions. And sometimes structural generalizations pertain to broad (e.g., *wh*-in situ languages) or narrow (e.g., AAVE consonant cluster reduction) distinctions that cannot be neatly sorted politically or socially. The political use of language names can and should be distinguished from the social and structural idealizations used to study linguistic diversity. Whether we can reasonably speak of discrete languages or speech communities depends on the analytic utility of these constructs, not their political associations.

For García and colleagues (García & Otheguy, 2014; Otheguy et al., 2015), the implications of the sociopolitical nature of named languages relate specifically to *individuals* rather than *groups*. They distinguish their view from Makoni and Pennycook (2007) in this regard; rather than "simply abandoning the distinction or scuttling the concepts of language and bilingualism," Otheguy et al. (2015) see discrete languages as restricted to the political sphere; as such, named languages

> have nothing to do with individuals when seen from their own internal linguistic perspective, categories that have nothing to do, that is, with the billions of the world's idiolects, which exist in a separate, linguistically unnamed and socially undifferentiated mental realm.
>
> (p. 293)

Here the question becomes not whether we may reasonably speak of discrete speech communities, but whether we may speak of an individual as having discretely represented linguistic systems that correspond to different speech communities (say, "Spanish" and "English"), that is, whether such a bilingual person has a single underlying grammar (in precisely the same way a "monolingual" does) or two discrete grammars, each corresponding to a different community. Of course, this is a question about I-language, and it is informed by a consideration of the nature of individual multilingualism. Fundamentally, the relevant question is whether bilingualism is *psychologically real*, that is, actually represented in the mind/brain of bilingual individuals. I turn to this question next.

Individual Multilingualism

Individual multilingualism concerns the nature of language in a multilingual or bilingual individual; it asks about the makeup of I-language, or what García and colleagues prefer to call *idiolect*, for such a person.

García and Otheguy (2014) present an approach to bilingualism that is "skeptical of the discreteness of named languages" and views "linguistic resources as disaggregated in the sense that features are separable and not integrated into linguistic systems" (p. 645). More specifically, they believe that bilingual mental grammars "consist of large and complex arrays of disaggregated structural features (phonetic, phonological, morphological, and semantic) that do not belong to or reside inside of the speaker's two or more languages by virtue of inherently differentiated linguistic membership" (p. 644). Thus, codeswitching and related areas of research in bilingualism "labor under serious limitations"—stemming specifically from "the uncritical adoption of the external perspective that trades on the sociocultural separateness of languages and on the monoglossic ideology that privileges the monolingual speaker and the monolingual setting as the natural and unmarked condition of languaging" (p. 649).

Otheguy et al. (2015) observe, like others, that language in the sociopolitical sense is "a social construct, not a mental or psychological one" (p. 283). Because each individual's language, and hence grammar, is unique, García and colleagues see each as an idiolect, conceptualized as unitary and lacking of any internal structural differentiation that might correspond to named languages like Mohawk, Farsi, Spanish, or English. By contrast, according to García and colleagues, codeswitching researchers see bilingualism as "dual competence," a view they say codeswitching scholars take for granted rather than derive empirically: "The duality is assumed a priori, and it is established in a manner that mirrors directly the bifurcation of the socially named language categories" (p. 298). Unfortunately, in both García and Otheguy (2014) and Otheguy et al. (2015), these characterizations of codeswitching research are merely asserted and not tied to an actual analysis of theoretical proposals in the literature, nor are any actual relevant citations provided.

The distinction in García and colleagues between named languages and idiolects has a long history in sociolinguistics and is uncontroversial, as noted, and likewise generally reflects the E-language/I-language distinction accepted in theoretical linguistics. The controversial thesis in the work of García and colleagues, with consequences for how we think about codeswitching, multilingualism, and related concepts, is the idea that individual bilinguals, like monolinguals, have unitary systems that lack any internal differentiation corresponding to the structural descriptions of named languages.

We may isolate three distinct perspectives on the nature of individual multilingualism, illustrated in Figure 8.1. The unitary model, advocated by García and colleagues (García & Otheguy, 2014; Otheguy et al., 2015), insists that bilinguals are the same as monolinguals in that in both instances, structural knowledge associated with what appear sociopolitically as two discrete languages actually reflects a single, internally undifferentiated system. García and colleagues attribute the dual competence model to codeswitching scholars, which they understand as the view that bilinguals have "two separate languages," which are "switched" or "manipulated" according to their context of use (p. 298). A third perspective, which I will call the *integrated multilingual model*, posits that bilinguals have a single system with many shared grammatical resources but with some internal language-specific differentiation as well; I will show that this perspective is the view that has emerged from codeswitching research, not the dual competence model, as García and colleagues assert. Extending the integrated view further, I will argue that multilingualism, not monolingualism, is universal, and that each of us, even so called monolinguals, has multiple overlapping rule systems acquired through our participation in divergent speech communities.

Cummins (1981) correctly observed that the dual competence model, which is akin to the separate underlying proficiency (SUP) model he discussed, is a folk theory of multilingualism that "is not seriously proposed by any researcher" (p. 23). The idea suggests that the two linguistic systems have no point of contact, which would make routine translation impossible (see MacSwan & Rolstad, 2005, for discussion). Since García and colleagues also reject the dual competence model, we are only concerned with the question of whether an individual bilingual grammar might reflect organized internal differentiation of some kind (favoring the integrated multilingual model) or not (favoring the unitary model).

It is not plausible that the grammars of bilinguals lack internal language-particular differentiation, as one expects within the unitary model, because such a system could not represent the contradictory requirements that bilinguals effortlessly manage and sustain. To illustrate this point, consider a child who grows up hearing Farsi, an object-verb (OV) language, and English, a verb-object (VO) language. The child comes to know that in Farsi, objects come before verbs, as in *Ye morqabi did-ænd* (one duck saw I, "I saw a duck," Mahootian, 1997), while in English, objects come after verbs (*I saw a duck*). This bilingual expertly navigates the integration of these systems in separate contexts despite the contradictory evidence observed regarding the basic word order of verbs and objects. Moreover, as Mahootian (1993) shows for codeswitching contexts, a Farsi-English bilingual will use Farsi word order with a Farsi verb, even if the object is English (*Ten dollars dad-e*, ten dollars give-PERF, "She gave ten dollars"), and English word order with an English verb, even if the object is Farsi (*Tell them you'll buy xune-ye jaedid when you sell your own house*, Tell them you'll buy house-POSS new when you sell your own house, "Tell them you'll buy a new house when you sell your own house"). How does the linguistic system of a Farsi-English bilingual reliably generate OV word order for Farsi, VO word order for English, OV word order for English-Farsi codeswitching when the verb is Farsi, and VO word order for English-Farsi codeswitching when the verb is English? Any appropriately detailed answer to this question will entail that the Farsi-English bilingual grammar has some level of internal differentiation, implying that bilingualism is psychologically real—that is, an actual part of our linguistic knowledge.

In addition to word order facts such as these, codeswitching research also reveals interesting grammaticality effects. Grammaticality effects serve in large part as the basis for linguists' theories about the structure of our tacit knowledge of language. For example, English speakers regard *John saw the red barn* and *John painted the barn red* as well formed (or grammatical) but regard *John saw the barn red* as ill formed (or ungrammatical). *John put the book back on the coffee table* is well formed, but *Table coffee the on back book the put John* is not. Data such as these allow linguists to posit theories about grammatical structure; such theories (or grammars) must define all the well-formed expressions of a language to the exclusion of all the ill-formed expressions, both of which are infinite sets.

With this in mind, consider another illustration, this one from Spanish-English codeswitching. A Spanish determiner like *los* may precede an English noun like *teachers*, giving us *los teachers* ("the teachers"), but if we reverse the direction of the

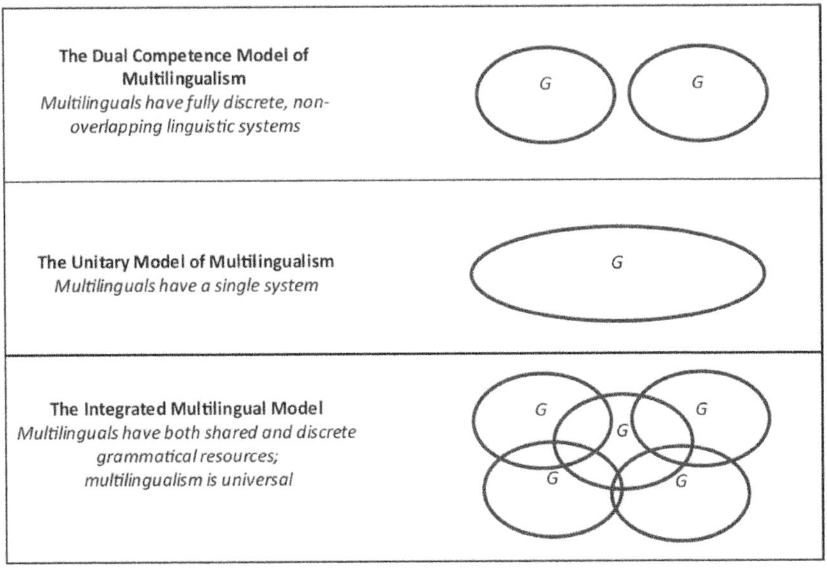

FIGURE 8.1 Three views of multilingualism.

codeswitch, a different pattern emerges: An English determiner before a Spanish noun is ill formed, so that examples like *the casa* ("the house") are unattested in corpora and judged to be ill formed by Spanish-English bilinguals (Jake, Myers-Scotton, & Gross, 2003; Liceras, Spradlin, & Fernández Fuertes, 2005; Lipski, 1978; Moro, 2014; Moyer, 1993). This is a surprising fact and presents intriguing challenges for a theory of bilingual grammar. What property of determiners or nouns results in these different patterns of intuitions for Spanish-English bilinguals? A sufficiently precise theory will need to posit an underlying system that attributes different properties to "Spanish" and "English" to explain such data, again implying language-specific internal differentiation.

Consider a final illustration. A Spanish-English bilingual knows two contradictory things about adjective/noun word order in the abstract: Adjectives follow nouns (e.g., *casa blanca*), and nouns follow adjectives (e.g., *white house*). She consistently applies the Spanish rule to Spanish words and the English rule to English words, never uttering expressions like *house white* or *blanca casa* (unless engaged in poetic license or marked language play). Furthermore, she will codeswitch in a structured way, strongly preferring *the white casa* over *the casa white* (Belazi, Rubin, & Toribio, 1994; Gumperz, 1967; Lipski, 1978; Poplack, 1981; Sankoff & Poplack, 1981). So the underlying linguistic system of a Spanish-English bilingual will generate *the white house, la casa blanca,* and *the white casa,* but not *the house white, la blanca casa,* or *the casa white.* What is the nature of the internal rule system such that these patterns emerge? Again, any sufficiently detailed response will entail that the bilingual grammar makes use of structured and internally organized differentiation of some kind.

Otheguy et al. (2015) believe that "from the inception of research in code switching," researchers have begged the question of language differentiation, embedding the truth of their conclusions within the basic premises of their research:

> It is an assumption, and this is the point, that makes the conclusion of internal duality of competence to a large extent pre-ordained by the dual tagging of the data, a tagging performed on the basis of the external named language categories.
>
> *(p. 298)*

In actuality, codeswitching researchers have guarded carefully against this fallacy, the potential for which is real, and have taken care to conceptualize language differences according to the structural patterns evidenced by speakers, not according to the political identifications of languages. At an individual cognitive level, whether a system is internally differentiated or not relates to the nature of the linguistic rule system and whether the hypothesized system of grammar could capture the observed facts without internal differentiation.

One sees this care even "from the inception" of codeswitching research, evident in Sankoff and Poplack (1981), who noted the existence of "some debate over whether discourse containing code-switches is generated by the alternate use of the two monolingual grammars or whether a single code-switching grammar exists, combining elements of the monolingual grammars" (p. 10). To address this question, codeswitching scholars use standard methods of linguistic analysis to draw conclusions about what specific properties bilingual grammars actually have in light of relevant data. As in other scientific enterprises, this approach takes the simplest solution to be preferred as it likely captures the broadest generalization, moving on to more complex solutions only as the facts require.

To evaluate the simplest assumption, that monolinguals have a single undifferentiated system, Sankoff and Poplack (1981) began by considering a grammar that consisted of the logical union of two phrase structure grammars, one for English and another for Spanish. A phrase structure grammar, which was a component of a generative-transformational grammar as developed in Chomsky (1957, 1965), is a system of rules that "recursively enumerates structural descriptions of sentences" (Chomsky, 1968, p. 165) to capture the creative aspect of language use. The rule system generates a tree structure, with internal branching capturing the relatedness among nodes in the tree. A phrase structure rule such as *S* → *NP VP*, for instance, defines a structure in which *S* (a sentence) immediately dominates two branches, *NP* (noun phrase) and *VP* (verb phrase). Another rule, *NP* → *Det N Adj*, further expands *NP* within the structure with an additional layer, this time a determiner

(*Det*), noun (*N*), and adjective (*Adj*) sequence. Lexical insertion rules (e.g., *Det la, N casa, Adj →blanca*) apply in this simple system to fill in the terminal nodes of the tree, with a final result such as *la casa blanca.* An English version of this simplified grammar differs in (at least) two key respects: The phrase structure rule for *NP* is *NP →Det Adj N,* placing the adjective before the noun, and examples of lexical insertion rules include *Det → the, Adj→ white*, and *N → house*, with results such as *the white house.*

Sankoff and Poplack (1981) observed that an internally undifferentiated system (their "free union grammar") would generate many ill-formed results, giving us not only ill-formed codeswitches like *the casa white* instead of *the white casa*, but it would even permit Spanish expressions with English word order and English expressions with Spanish word order, as illustrated in Figure 8.2. Sankoff and Poplack engaged in this exercise to illustrate that a free union grammar, or unitary system, could not succeed as it generates ill-formed sentences. Having shown that the simplest solution is inadequate, they restricted this system in a way that tied the lexical insertion rules to language-particular phrase structure rules to the extent required by the facts. They accomplished this by introducing a superscripting mechanism, known as a *language tag*. In effect, this convention introduced internal differentiation within the system as it associated Spanish lexical items with phrase structure rules specific to Spanish, and English lexical items with English rules, but allowed rules common to both to be lexically filled by either language. In Figure 8.2, using this system, the subject *NP* would be tagged as an English phrase structure rule, eligible for lexical insertion from English, and the object *NP* would be tagged as a Spanish phrase structure rule, eligible for lexical insertion from Spanish. Rules common to both English and Spanish are not so tagged and represent shared resources. Lipski (1978), Pfaff (1979), and Woolford (1983) similarly proposed that an equivalence condition governed the ways in which languages could be mixed.

As linguistics evolved in the 1980s and 1990s, driven by new discoveries, approaches to handling internal diversity of the linguistic system took advantage of new theories. The grammatical theories underlying Sankoff and Poplack's work built structure top-down, first generating a tree structure, which represented word order, then inserting lexical items after the word order had been set. This limitation of the linguistic theory under which Sankoff and Poplack labored required them to tinker with the system, introducing a language tag as an ad hoc stipulation to tie structure-building rules to lexical insertion rules. Similarly, Di Sciullo, Muysken, and Singh (1986) made use of a *language index*, and Belazi et al. (1994) used a *language feature* to derive their results. While these approaches shared limitations with Sankoff and Poplack (1981), they used a common methodological approach: Committed to theoretical parsimony, they assumed minimal internal differentiation within the bilingual grammar, aligning lexical items and syntactic rules only to the extent the facts compelled them to do so. The resulting system could be understood, as Sankoff and Poplack intended, as "a single grammar based on the two monolingual ones"—an *integrated* system.

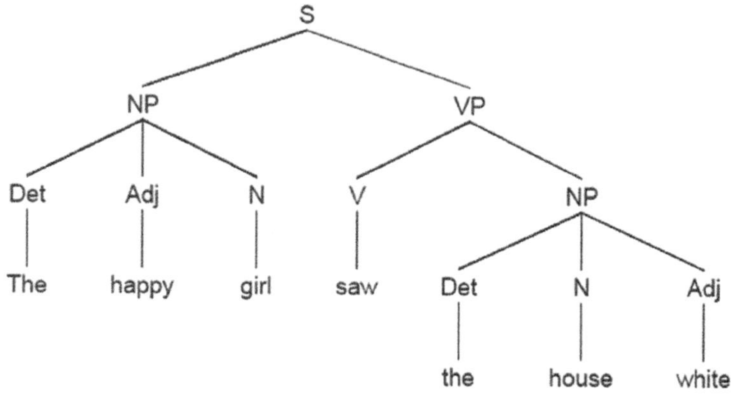

FIGURE 8.2 A syntactic tree generated by Sankoff and Poplack's (1981) Spanish-English free union grammar, showing an ill-formed result.

Current theories of codeswitching take advantage of a different syntactic architecture that builds structure from the bottom up (Chomsky, 1995, 2007; Uriagereka, 2012). In this system, known as the minimalist program, trees such as the one exemplified in Figure 8.2 are not generated by phrase structure grammars but by an operation called *Merge*, which uses lexical information (encoded in each lexical item, or word) to combine elements into (binary branching) trees. Other functions operate on branching points such as *V, VP, NP* to create derivative structures.

A basic intuition underlying the minimalist program is that language-specific differences are encoded in the lexicon, with the rest of the underlying linguistic system held to be invariant across different languages. As Chomsky (1991) explained,

> If there were only one human language, the story would essentially end there. But we know that this is false, a rather surprising fact. The general principles of the initial state evidently allow a range of variation. Associated with many principles there are parameters with a few—perhaps just two—values. Possibly, as proposed by Hagit Borer [1984], the parameters are actually restricted to the lexicon, which would mean that the rest of the I-language is fixed and invariant, a far-reaching idea that has proven quite productive.
>
> *(p. 23)*

The lexicon stores information other than just the phonetic shape and meaning of words in this framework. Each item within the lexicon also encodes morphological, syntactic, and phonological features of various kinds; these feature arrays and their possible values vary for different languages.

This core idea, that parameters of linguistic variation are "restricted to the lexicon" and "the rest of the I-language is fixed and invariant," suggests an integrated view of bilingualism in which the fixed and invariant aspects of language are shared linguistic resources while those that include aspects of language variation are encoded in the lexicon. This idea is fleshed out in detail in MacSwan (1999, 2000a, 2005a, 2005b, 2014) and further developed in Bandi-Rao and den Dikken (2014); Cantone and MacSwan (2009); Cantone and Müller (2005, 2008); Di Sciullo (2014); Finer (2014); Giancaspro (2015); González-Vilbazo and López (2011, 2012); Grimstad, Lohndal, and Åfarli (2014); Lillo-Martin, Müller, and Chen Pichler (2016); MacSwan and Colina (2014); Milian (2014); Moro (2014); Sánchez (2012); Toribio and González-Vilbazo (2014); Van Dulm (2007, 2009); and van Gelderen and MacSwan (2008), among others. Specifically, this codeswitching model uses discrete lexicons and morphophonological systems to represent language-particular features, with invariant syntactic and semantic features serving as shared resources.[3] As such, it presents an integrated model of individual multilingualism. Thus, the field does not take language differentiation for granted, based on naïve assumptions that ignore the well known history of linguistic colonization; rather, it posits the existence of an internally differentiated system based on an analysis of the bilingual data themselves and the nature of the representations that generate them.

For precisely these reasons, some have proposed that all linguistic systems, even those of so-called monolinguals, are internally richly diverse, leading many to view *monolingualism*, not *multilingualism*, as a social construction. For instance, Roeper (1999, 2003, 2011, 2016) has argued that the sort of system-internal differentiation typically associated with multilinguals is universal and that even monolinguals have an integrated system of internally differentiated subcomponents developed to manage the contradictory structural requirements of their grammars. I have incorporated Roeper's idea in the representation of the integrated multilingual model in Figure 8.1. (Also see Adger, 2006, and references cited there.)

Roeper observed that English speakers (for instance) have stylistic variations, or social registers, that exhibit structural characteristics typical of many Germanic languages but not typical of English, such as *A single salad does not a dinner make* and *One captured fish does not a fisherman make.* Other stylistic alternatives include *Say you so?* and *It matters not what you do.* Here, as in many other Germanic languages, the main verb occurs in sentence-final position. However, this structure is not generalizable to all contexts, as Roeper illustrates with examples like *A tiny orange does not someone peel*, generally regarded as ill formed. Roeper's multiple grammars theory, then, posits that all speakers have internally differentiated grammars, each containing multiple "mini-grammars," which represent the underlying system of the several linguistic registers we know.

In codeswitching research, as in any robust field, specific theories and proposals develop over time, and researchers will disagree as to the best way to capture a phenomenon theoretically. However, regardless of one's preferred codeswitching framework, the data lead to a similar conclusion with regard to the organization of bilingual grammars. Farsi-English bilinguals consistently use VO word order with English verbs and OV word order with Farsi verbs in monolingual and bilingual contexts alike. Spanish-English bilinguals place adjectives after nouns when speaking Spanish, place nouns after adjectives when speaking English, and use English adjectives before Spanish nouns when codeswitching but not vice versa; they also will use English determiners before Spanish nouns but not vice versa. There seems to be no conception of *grammar* in the usual sense of the word in which such data could be explained in the absence of system-internal, language particular differentiation of some kind.

In addition, it is worth noting that the unitary perspective is at odds not only with codeswitching research but also with scholarship on bilingual first language acquisition, where researchers have found that children's syntactic and phonological development in two languages proceeds essentially independently of one another, respecting the developmental timetable specific to each language as documented in monolingual acquisition research (Genesee & Nicoladis, 2006; Lindholm & Padilla, 1978; Müller & Cantone, 2009). For example, Paradis and Genesee (1996) found that developing French-English simultaneous bilingual children used finite verb forms earlier in French than in English, used subject pronouns in French exclusively with finite verbs but subject pronouns in English with both finite and nonfinite verbs, and placed verbal negatives after lexical verbs in French (e.g., *n'aime pas* "do not like," where *pas* is negation) but before lexical verbs in English (e.g., *do not like*). An alternative view, known as the *unitary language system hypothesis*, was advanced by Volterra and Taeschner (1978) but quickly fell into disfavor based on considerable empirical evidence. For further discussion, see Genesee (2001) and Silva-Corvalán (2014). The neurolinguistics literature has also confirmed the early differentiation perspective in bilingual first language acquisition (Kovelman, Baker, & Petitto, 2008).

In linguistics, explicit theories of phenomena are critically important (Chomsky, 1957; Gee, 2016b). An explicit linguistic theory is one that does not rely on tacit assumptions about how language works but rather overtly states all relevant details. In this way, we protect ourselves from allowing our unexamined assumptions to guide our perceptions or analysis of language, language differences, or bilingualism. The unitary view of bilingual competence of García and colleagues (García & Otheguy, 2014; Otheguy et al., 2015) offers a general perspective on a key postulate that might underlie an eventual explicit theory of bilingualism, but their ideas about mental architecture are not sufficiently detailed to permit empirical investigation. Specifically, we do not know how they imagine features to be both organized and disaggregated or what these features actually are. We expect linguistic analyses that show us, for instance, that Spanish agreement features (called φ-features) specifying person, number, and gender can be preserved alongside English φ-features specifying just person and number, with consequences for feature theory that are consistent with the bilingual data (e.g., Moro, 2014). An explicit theory so developed would allow us to see how these features are organized in a unitary system such that these distinctions could be maintained, and consider in concrete terms whether the hypothesized system is unitary or integrated in nature. We would furthermore expect analyses that show us what specific property of Farsi and English is responsible for the OV/VO word order distinction and how that property is represented in a disaggregated system of features like the one suggested, such that it has the consequences for word order observed in the linguistic data (e.g., MacSwan, 2004), or what properties of adjective noun word order might account for the grammaticality effects observed for Spanish-English and other language pairs (e.g., Cantone & MacSwan, 2009). In a unitary system, how do we explain these language differences such that we could still regard the grammar as a single, disaggregated system, and how does the new analysis differ from explicit proposals put forward in the codeswitching literature?

Because details of this nature are not provided, García and colleagues' basic idea is not sufficiently clear to be directly evaluated. My strategy here has been to show that the unitary model is inconsistent with what we know empirically from the data of language alternation and theoretically from the codeswitching literature and that the facts are such that a theoretically rigorous solution promoting a unitary model is unlikely to succeed, just as generations of codeswitching researchers have found.

Based on an examination of the evidence, I-languages are clearly linguistically diverse, in the sense that a single I-language will exhibit sometimes contradictory patterns (e.g., OV and VO word order), supporting the integrated model of multilingualism illustrated in Figure 8.1. I have made the point, too, following Roeper (1999, 2016), that so-called monolinguals are also linguistically diverse, each possessing knowledge of different social languages and speech registers appropriate to different contexts of use. This evidence is sufficient to make the case that individual multilingualism is psychologically real, contrary to the view expressed by García and colleagues as the basis for their critique of codeswitching.

Linguistic Repertoires and Mental Grammars

Linguists who study language variation in social contexts often use the metaphor of a *repertoire* to refer to the broad stock of speech styles, registers, varieties, and languages people know (Coulmas, 2005; Spolsky, 1998). The term was classically introduced by John Gumperz, who defined a "verbal repertoire" as "the totality of linguistic forms regularly employed in the course of socially significant interaction" (1964, p. 137). One way to conceptualize a verbal or linguistic repertoire is as a collection of what Gee (2016a) calls *social languages*.

> Languages the size of "English" or "Russian" are composed of a myriad of what I will call "social languages" (Gee, 2014). Social languages (some of which might be called dialects, registers, varieties, or styles or by other names) are styles of using words, grammar, and discourse to enact a socially significant identity.
>
> *(p. 69)*

These social languages are enacted in different contexts to create one or more social identities in interaction with others.

Everybody has a diverse linguistic repertoire consisting of multiple social languages. These social languages are each appropriate to one or more social contexts but may feel out of place in some settings. Gee (2016a) gives an example:

> Imagine I park my motorcycle, enter my neighborhood "biker bar," and say to my leather-jacketed and tattooed drinking buddy, as I sit down: "May I have a match for my cigarette, please?" What I have said is perfectly grammatical English, but it is "wrong" nonetheless, unless I have used a heavily ironic tone of voice. It is not just the content of what you say that is important, but how you say it. And in this bar, I haven't said it in the "right" way. I should have said something like "Gotta match?" or "Give me a light, wouldya?"
>
> *(p. 3)*

The formal register inappropriately used in this context would be contextually appropriate in other settings, such as school. School language, on this view, is just one (set) of many social languages used to create a particular persona in specific contexts and for specific tasks (Gee, 2016b).

We are all multilinguals in the sense that we each use different ways of talking in different social contexts. But for some, these social languages are enacted through more dramatic structural differences, broadly described with labels like *English* and *Spanish.* A bilingual in this sense selects different social languages according to social and situational contexts, like any of us—sometimes making use of both languages simultaneously (codeswitching) and sometimes making use of just one. A bilingual may exclusively use a heritage language with a monolingual grandparent, use English with an interlocutor whom she believes not to speak her community language, and switch between her languages with siblings, parents, and other members of her community. Or matters may be much more complex, involving the active use of multiple varieties of both, used to navigate families, local communities, and schools (Sayer, 2013).

Importantly, for present purposes, a *repertoire* is not a *grammar* but a catalog of the ways we each can talk in different social contexts. It includes our richly diverse internalized mental grammars as well as the diverse vocabulary and systems of knowledge pertaining to discourse, pragmatics, and other social conventions that we recruit in verbal interactions with others. In Gumperz's (1964) terms, it reflects "contextual and social differences in speech ... subject both to grammatical and social restraints" (pp. 137–138). Mental grammars are thus but a small part of our overall knowledge of how to use language in social contexts, defining the narrow structural mapping from sound to meaning.

For monolinguals and bilinguals alike, a *grammar* is a set of interrelated components that are defined by the nature of the representations they generate and transform. Even in the context of typical theories of monolingual language, theories of structure posit that speakers have discrete subsystems corresponding to syntax and phonology as well as other dimensions of linguistic knowledge. Phonology uses processes very different from syntax; it modifies word structures and introduces prosodic features, proceeding in a linear derivation, whereas syntax is hierarchically represented, as illustrated in Figure 8.2, and modifies word order (Bermúdez-Otero & Honeybone, 2006; Bromberger & Halle, 1989; Chomsky, 1995). Grammatical features responsible for cross-linguistic differences, such as OV/VO word order and noun/adjective word order, are discretely represented for bilinguals in a way that permits them to manage contradictory requirements of the two languages they know. Human beings effortlessly navigate these and other discrete subsystems of linguistic knowledge without a hint of distraction, just as they effortlessly process visual images, recognize familiar faces, and engage in other ordinary cognitive tasks. We are not compelled to refer to these subsystems as undifferentiated and unitary and should likewise be unconcerned about theories of grammar that posit subsystems to manage language-particular (e.g., English, Spanish) structural differences.

Although García and colleagues focus their discussion on the nature of an individual bilingual's *mental grammar*, the definition of translanguaging itself is usually offered in terms of *linguistic repertoire*. For instance, García (2012) argued that "bilinguals have *one linguistic repertoire* from which they select features *strategically* to communicate effectively" (p. 1), and in the more recently refined definition presented in Otheguy et al. (2015) translanguaging is "the deployment of a speaker's full linguistic repertoire without regard for watchful adherence to the socially and politically defined boundaries of named (and usually national and state) languages" (p. 283).

There is broad agreement on this point of view, which is also consistent with program effectiveness research showing that inclusion of children's home language in classroom settings is positively associated with conventional measures of school success (Reljić, Ferring, & Martin, 2015; Rolstad, Mahoney, & Glass, 2005). It is widely believed that inclusion of children's home language in school not only makes instruction comprehensible but also affirms the language and cultural identities children bring from their homes and communities (Moll et al., 2013; Paris, 2012; Ruiz, 1984). However, our shared view that multilingual children should have access to their "full linguistic repertoire without regard for watchful adherence to the socially and politically defined boundaries of named (and usually national and state) languages" in no way implies that our linguistic knowledge is not internally diverse. The multilingual perspective on translanguaging offered here is wholly consistent with this point of view and indeed may be seen as adding important support: We are not all individually *monolingual* but rather *multilingual*, with rich internal diversity; as with any person in any community, the richness of the linguistic diversity of multilingual students should be viewed as a critically important resource promoting their educational success.

Conclusions

Translanguaging invites children to use language in school as they do in their community, a crucial component of a culturally sustaining pedagogy (Paris, 2012) and one that permits children and families to develop forms of human capital (Smith & Murillo, 2015). Ideologically, translanguaging views bilingualism holistically, a perspective Grosjean (1982) has advocated. But for Grosjean and others, bilingualism is not just social and political; it is also psychologically real. A bilingual is a uniquely situated language user who functions bilingually, drawing on whatever language resources are appropriate, and is not the sum of two monolinguals. Translanguaging theory has made important and promising contributions to language ideology, policy, pedagogy, and the way educators think about language use in classroom settings. It extends the metaphor of holism to the linguistic repertoire of bilingual children, noting that schools should make use of the full range of diverse linguistic talents that bilinguals bring with them to the classroom.

However, it is mistaken and ultimately counterproductive to claim that the colonial history of language differentiation implies that talk of (idealized) named languages and other identifiable speech communities is incongruous and that individual bilingual grammars are internally unitary and undifferentiated. It erroneously ascribes to codeswitching researchers a dual competence perspective on bilingual mental grammar, attributing to them a "monoglossic ideology that privileges the monolingual speaker and the monolingual setting as the natural and unmarked condition of languaging" (García & Otheguy, 2014, p. 649). This attribution is not only factually incorrect, but taken seriously, it would undermine critical research support for a view of bilingualism as a linguistic talent rather than a worrisome deficit. Like research on AAVE, codeswitching research has shown through detailed analysis that bilinguals are exquisitely sensitive to an incredibly rich and intricate underlying system of rules for both languages in their repertoires.

A significant consequence of dispensing with conceptions of multilingualism is that doing so would put familiar and important topics of study out of reach, along with the theoretical and conceptual utility they bring. It not only renders such topics as language rights, mother tongues, and codeswitching incongruous (Makoni & Pennycook, 2007) but also removes from discussion any notion of community-level variation, second language acquisition, and much of the field of sociolinguistics. For researchers concerned with multilingualism in schools, these are critically important areas of inquiry, and many of them (not just codeswitching) are commonly used as an empirical defense of a view of bilingualism as a rich resource reflective of linguistic talent, not confusion or "semilingualism."

I have proposed an alternative view of the underlying theory of translanguaging, which I call a *multilingual perspective*. This perspective accepts individual multilingualism as not only psychologically real, in the integrated sense, but also universal. Here, codeswitching may be seen as an instance of translanguaging, alongside other bilingual phenomena such as translation, borrowing, and additional processes, in a range of modalities, as in earlier treatments (García, 2009, p. 45; García, 2011, p. 147). Translanguaging research has made important contributions to our conception of bilingual language policy and practice and has sparked new research on language distribution in multilingual classrooms. Most importantly, it problematizes conventional assumptions regarding language mixing in classroom settings, where new research has contributed to our understanding of the ways in which codeswitching may be instrumental in teaching and learning. As a pedagogical approach, translanguaging emphasizes the dynamic use of multiple languages to enhance learning and make schools more welcoming environments for multilingual children, families, and communities. It can and should affirm the value and multiplicity of linguistic diversity—across and within communities and individuals.

Notes

I am grateful to colleagues for helpful feedback on a version of this paper presented at the 2016 AERA Bilingual Education Research SIG business meeting, and to students for fruitful discussion in my Language and Education doctoral seminar in spring 2016 at the University of Maryland. Donna Christian, Natalia Guzman, John Petrovic, Kellie Rolstad, Terrence G. Wiley, and three anonymous reviewers of the *American Educational Research Journal* also provided helpful comments on an earlier draft. Of course, I alone am responsible for the final content and views expressed. This paper was originally published in 2017 in the *American Educational Research Journal,* 54(1), pages 167–201.

★ JEFF MACSWAN is professor of applied linguistics and language education in the College of Education at the University of Maryland (UMD), 2311 Benjamin Building, College Park, MD 20742; e-mail: *macswan@umd.edu.* He is also professor of neuroscience and cognitive science at UMD and affiliate professor in the UMD Linguistics Department and Center for the Advanced Study of Language. He is a Fellow of the American Educational Research Association and the National Education Policy Center.

1 I use the term *multilingualism* to refer to knowledge of at least two languages and the term *bilingualism* to specifically denote a multilingual who knows just two languages. The alternation reflects slightly different contexts of use that will not be of issue in the present discussion. See Edwards (2013) for discussion.

2 Codeswitching is variously spelled *code-switching, codeswitching*, and *code switching*. Quoted texts retain their original preferred spelling in this review.

3 The approach in Bandi-Rao and den Dikken (2014); Grimstad, Lohndal, and Åfarli (2014); and Lillo-Martin, Müller, and Chen Pichler (2016) explores a slightly different architecture based on research in distributed morphology in which vocabulary insertion is guided by a rich feature array postsyntactically. See MacSwan (2016b) for discussion.

References

Adger, D. (2006). Combinatorial variability. *Journal of Linguistics, 42*(3), 503–530.

Bailey, B. (2007). Heteroglossia and boundaries. In M. Heller (Ed.), *Bilingualism: A social approach* (pp. 257–274). New York, NY: Palgrave Macmillan.

Baker, C. (2011). *Foundations of bilingual education and bilingualism* (5th ed.). Bristol, UK: Multilingual Matters.

Bakhtin, M. (1975). *Bakhtinian thought: An introductory reader.* New York, NY: Routledge.
Bandi-Rao, S., & den Dikken, M. (2014). Light switches: On v as a pivot in codeswitching, and the nature of the ban on word-internal switches. In J. MacSwan (Ed.), *Grammatical theory and bilingual codeswitching* (pp. 161–184). Cambridge, MA: MIT Press.
Baugh, A. C., & Cable, T. (1978). *A history of the English language* (3rd ed.) Englewood Cliffs, NJ: Prentice-Hall, Inc.
Belazi, H. M., Rubin, E. J., & Toribio, A. J. (1994). Code switching and X-bar theory: The functional head constraint. *Linguistic Inquiry, 25*(2), 221–237.
Benson, E. J. (2001). The neglected early history of codeswitching research in the United States. *Language & Communication, 21*(1), 23–36. doi:10.1016/s0271-5309(00)00012-4
Bermúdez-Otero, R., & Honeybone, P. (2006). Phonology and syntax: A shifting relationship. *Lingua, 116*, 543–561.
Bloch, B. (1948). A set of postulates for phonetic analysis. *Language, 24*, 3–46.
Blom, J. P., & Gumperz, J. J. (1972). Social meaning and structure: Code-switching in Norway. In J. Gumperz & D. Hymes (Eds.), *Directions in sociolinguistics* (pp. 407–434). New York, NY: Holt, Reinhart, Winston.
Blommaert, J. (2010). *The sociolinguistics of globalization.* Cambridge, UK: Cambridge University Press.
Bloomfield, L. (1928). A set of postulates for the science of language. *Language, 2*, 153–164.
Bloomfield, L. (1933). *Language.* New York, NY: Holt, Rinehart and Winston.
Borer, H. (1984). *Parametric syntax: Case studies in Semitic and Romance languages.* Dordrecht: Foris.
Bromberger, S., & Halle, M. (1989). Why phonology is different. *Linguistic Inquiry, 20*, 51–70.
Canagarajah, S. (2011). Codemeshing in academic writing: Identifying teachable strategies of translanguaging. *The Modern Language Journal, 95*, 401–417. doi:10.1111/j.1540-4781.2011.01207.x
Canagarajah, S. (2013). *Translingual practice: Global Englishes and cosmopolitan relations.* New York, NY: Routledge.
Cantone, K., & MacSwan, J. (2009). The syntax of DP-internal codeswitching. In L. Isurin, D. Winford, & K. de Bot (Eds.), *Multidisciplinary approaches to codeswitching* (pp. 243–278). Amsterdam: John Benjamins Publishing.
Cantone, K., & Müller, N. (2005). Codeswitching at the interface of language-specific lexicons and the computational system. *International Journal of Bilingualism, 9*(2), 205–225.
Cantone, K., & Müller, N. (2008). Un nase or una nase? What gender marking within switched DPs reveals about the architecture of the bilingual language faculty. *Lingua, 118*(6), 810–826.
Cartwright, N. (1989). *Nature's capacities and their measurement.* Oxford, UK: Oxford University Press.
Cenoz, J., & Gorter, D. (2011). A holistic approach to multilingual education: Introduction. *The Modern Language Journal, 95*, 339–343. doi:10.1111/j.1540-4781.2011.01204.x
Chambers, J. K., & Schilling, N. (Eds.). (2013). *The handbook of language variation and change* (2nd ed.). Oxford, UK: Wiley-Blackwell.
Chomsky, N. (1957). *Syntactic structures.* The Hague: Mouton.
Chomsky, N. (1965). *Aspects of the theory of syntax.* Cambridge, MA: MIT Press.
Chomsky, N. (1968). *Language and mind.* New York, NY: Harcourt Brace Jovanovich.
Chomsky, N. (1980). *Rules and representations.* New York, NY: Columbia University Press.

Chomsky, N. (1986). *Knowledge of language: Its nature, origins, and use.* New York, NY: Praeger.

Chomsky, N. (1991). Linguistics and cognitive science: Problems and mysteries. In A. Kasher (Ed.), *The Chomskyan turn* (pp. 26–53). Cambridge, UK: Blackwell.

Chomsky, N. (1995). *The minimalist program.* Cambridge, MA: MIT Press.

Chomsky, N. (2007). Approaching UG from below. In U. Sauerland & H.-M. Gartner (Eds.), *Interfaces 1 recursion = language?: Chomsky's minimalism and the view from syntax-semantics* (pp. 1–29). Berlin: Mouton de Gruyter.

Cook, V. J. (2001). Using the first language in the classroom. *Canadian Modern Language Review, 57*(3), 402–423.

Coulmas, F. (2005). *Sociolinguistics: The study of speakers' choices.* Cambridge, UK: Cambridge University Press.

Crawford, J. (2004). *Educating English learners: Language diversity in the classroom* (5th ed.). Los Angeles, CA: Bilingual Educational Services.

Crystal, D. (1986). The prescriptive tradition. In D. Crystal (Ed.), *The Cambridge encyclopedia of language* (pp. 2–5). Cambridge, UK: Cambridge University Press.

Cummins, J. (1981). The role of primary language development in promoting educational success for language minority students. In California State Department of Education (Ed.), *Schooling and language minority students: A theoretical framework* (pp. 3–49). Los Angeles, CA: California State University, Evaluation, Dissemination and Assessment Center.

Davidson, D. (1986). A nice derangement of epitaphs. In E. Lepore (Ed.), *Truth and interpretation: Perspectives on the philosophy of Donald Davidson* (pp. 433–446). Cambridge, UK: Blackwell.

DeBose, C. E. (1992). Codeswitching: Black English and standard English in the African American linguistic repertoire. *Journal of Multilingual and Multicultural Development, 13,* 157–167.

Di Sciullo, A. M. (2014). On the asymmetric nature of the operations of grammar: Evidence from codeswitching. In J. MacSwan (Ed.), *Grammatical theory and bilingual codeswitching* (pp. 63–87). Cambridge, MA: MIT Press.

Di Sciullo, A-M., Muysken, P., & Singh, R. (1986). Government and code-switching. *Journal of Linguistics, 22,* 1–24.

Durán, L., & Palmer, D. (2013). Pluralist discourses of bilingualism and translanguaging talk in classrooms. *Journal of Early Childhood Literacy, 22,* 367–388. doi:10.1177/1468798413497386

Eckert, P. (2000). *Linguistic variation as social practice.* Oxford, UK: Blackwell.

Edwards, J. (2013). Bilingualism and multilingualism: Some central concepts. In T. Bhatia & W. C. Ritchie (Eds.), *The handbook of bilingualism and multilingualism* (2nd ed., pp. 7–25). Oxford, UK: Wiley-Blackwell.

Faltis, C. (1989). Code-switching and bilingual schooling: An examination of Jacobson's new concurrent approach. *Journal of Multilingual and Multicultural Development, 10*(2), 117–127.

Faltis, C. (1990). New directions in bilingual research design: The study of interactive decision making. In R. Jacobson & C. Faltis (Eds.), *Language distribution issues in bilingual schooling* (pp. 45–59). Clevedon, UK: Multilingual Matters.

Faltis, C. (1996). Learning to teach content bilingually in a middle school bilingual classroom. *Bilingual Research Journal, 20*(1), 29–44.

Fasold, R. (1972). *Tense marking in Black English: A linguistic and social analysis.* Washington, DC: Center for Applied Linguistics.

Finer, D. L. (2014). Movement triggers and reflexivization in Korean-English codeswitching. In J. MacSwan (Ed.), *Grammatical theory and bilingual codeswitching* (pp. 37–62). Cambridge, MA: MIT Press.

Frigg, R., & Hartmann, S. (2012). Models in science. In E. N. Zalta (Ed.), *The Stanford encyclopedia of philosophy* (fall ed.). Retrieved from http://plato.stanford.edu/archives/fall2012/entries/models-science.

Fuller, J. M. (2009). Multilingualism in educational contexts: Ideologies and identities. *Language and Linguistics Compass, 3*, 338–358. doi:10.1111/j.1749-818X.2008.00101.x

Fuller, J. M. (2010). Gendered choices: Codeswitching and collaboration in a bilingual classroom. *Gender and Language, 3*(2), 181–208. doi:10.1558/genl.v3i2.181

García, O. (2009). *Bilingual education in the 21st century: A Global perspective.* Malden, MA: Basil/Blackwell.

García, O. (2011). Educating New York's bilingual children: Constructing a future from the past. *International Journal of Bilingual Education and Bilingualism, 14*(2), 133–153. doi:10.1080/13670050.2010.539670

García, O. (2012). Theorizing translanguaging for educators. In C. Celic & K. Seltzer (Eds.), *Translanguaging: A CUNY-NYSIEB guide for educators* (pp. 1–6). Retrieved from http://www.nysieb.ws.gc.cuny.edu/files/2012/06/FINAL-Translanguaging-Guide-With-Cover-1.pdf

García, O., Flores, N., & Woodley, H. H. (2015). Constructing in-between spaces to "do" bilingualism: A tale of two high schools in one city. In J. Cenoz & D. Gorter (Eds.), *Multilingual education: Between language learning and translanguaging* (pp. 199–224). Cambridge, UK: Cambridge University Press.

García, O., & Otheguy, R. (2014). Spanish and Hispanic bilingualism. In M. Lacorte (Ed.), *The Routledge handbook of Hispanic applied linguistics* (pp. 639–658). New York, NY: Routledge.

Gee, J. P. (2014). *An introduction to discourse analysis: Theory and method* (4th ed.). London: Routledge.

Gee, J. P. (2016a). The vexed nature of language learning and teaching. In R. H. Jones & J. C. Richards (Eds.), *Creativity in language teaching: Perspectives from research and practice* (pp. 63–76). New York, NY: Routledge.

Gee, J. P. (2016b). *Social linguistics and literacies: Ideology in discourses* (5th ed.). New York, NY: Routledge.

Genesee, F. (2001). Bilingual first language acquisition: Exploring the limits of the language faculty. *Annual Review of Applied Linguistics, 21*, 153–170.

Genesee, F., & Nicoladis, E. (2006). Bilingual acquisition. In E. Hoff & M. Shatz (Eds.), *Handbook of language development* (pp. 324–342). Oxford, UK: Blackwell.

Giancaspro, D. (2015). Code-switching at the auxiliary VP boundary: A comparison of heritage speakers and L2 learners. *Linguistic Approaches to Bilingualism, 5*(3), 380–408. doi:10.1075/lab.5.3.04gia

González-Vilbazo, K., & López, L. (2011). Some properties of light verbs in codeswitching. *Lingua, 121*, 832–850.

González-Vilbazo, K., & López, L. (2012). Little v and parametric variation. *Natural Language and Linguistic Theory, 30*(1), 33–77. doi:10.1007/s11049-011-9141-5

Gort, M. (2012). Code-switching patterns in the writing-related talk of young emergent bilinguals. *Journal of Literacy Research, 20*(10), 1–31. doi:10.1177/1086296X11431626

Gort, M. (2015). Transforming literacy learning and teaching through translanguaging and other typical practices associated with "doing being bilingual." *International Multilingual Research Journal, 9*(2), 1–6. doi:10.1080/19313152.2014.988030

Gort, M., & Sembiante, S. F. (2015). Navigating hybridized language learning spaces through translanguaging pedagogy: Dual language preschool teachers' languaging practices in support of emergent bilingual children's performance of academic discourse. *International Multilingual Research Journal*, *9*(1), 7–25.

Grimstad, M., Lohndal, T., & Åfarl, i T. A. (2014). Language mixing and exoskeletal theory: A case study of word-internal mixing in American Norwegian. *Nordlyd*, *41*, 213–237.

Grosjean, F. (1982). *Life with two languages: an introduction to bilingualism*. Cambridge, MA: Harvard University Press.

Grosjean, F. (2010). *Bilingual: Life and reality*. Cambridge, MA: Harvard University Press.

Gumperz, J. (1964). Linguistic and social interaction in two communities. *American Anthropologist*, *66*(6), 137–153.

Gumperz, J. (1967). On the linguistic markers of bilingual communication. *Journal of Social Issues*, *23*(2), 48–57.

Gumperz, J. (1970). Verbal strategies in multilingual communication. In J. Alatis (Ed.), *Report of the Twenty-First Annual Round-Table Meeting on Linguistics and Language Studies* (pp. 129–147). Washington, DC: Georgetown University School on Languages and Linguistics.

Gumperz, J., & Hernández-Chávez, E. (1970). Cognitive aspects of bilingual communication. In W. H. Whitely (Ed.), *Language and social change* (pp. 115–125). Oxford, UK: Oxford University Press.

Gutiérrez, K., Baquedano-López, P., & Tejeda, C. (1999). Rethinking diversity: Hybridity and hybrid language practices in the third space. *Mind, Culture and Activity*, *6*, 286–303. doi:10.1080/10749039909524733

Gutiérrez, K. D., Bien, A. C., Selland, M. K., & Pierce, D. M. (2011). Polylingual and polycultural learning ecologies: Mediating emergent academic literacies for dual language learners. *Journal of Early Childhood Literacy*, *11*(2), 232–261.

Harris, R. (1981). *The language myth*. London: Duckworth.

Hasselmo, N. (1972). Code-switching as ordered selection. In E. S. Firchow (Ed.), *Studies for Einar Haugen* (pp. 261–280). The Hague: Mouton.

Haugen, E. (1956). *Bilingualism in the Americas: A bibliography and research guide*. Jacksonville, IL: American Dialect Society.

Heller, M. (2007). *Bilingualism: A social approach*. New York, NY: Palgrave Macmillan.

Heller, M., & Duchêne, A. (2007). Discourses of endangerment: Sociolinguistics, globalization and social order. In A. Duchêne & M. Heller (Eds.), *Discourses of endangerment: Ideology and interest in defense of languages* (pp. 1–13). London: Continuum.

Henderson, K. I., & Palmer, D. K. (2015). Teacher and student language practices and ideologies in a third-grade two-way dual language program implementation. International Multilingual Research Journal, 9(2), 75–92. doi:10.1080/19313152.2015.1016827

Hornberger, N. H., & Link, H. (2012). Translanguaging in today's classrooms: A biliteracy lens. *Theory Into Practice*, *51*, 239–247.

Hymes, D. H., & Fought, J. G. (1975). *American structuralism*. Berlin: Walter de Gruyter.

Jacobson, R. (1978). Code-switching in south Texas: Sociolinguistic considerations and pedagogical applications. *Journal of the Linguistic Association of the Southwest*, *3*, 20–32.

Jacobson, R. (1981). The implementation of a bilingual instructional model: The new concurrent approach. In R. V. Padilla (Ed.), *Ethnoperspectives in bilingual education research* (Vol. *3*, pp. 14–29). Ypsilanti, MI: Eastern Michigan University.

Jacobson, R. (1990). Allocating two languages as a key feature of bilingual methodology. In R. Jacobson & C. Faltis (Eds.), *Language distribution issues in bilingual schooling* (pp. 3–17). Clevedon, UK: Multilingual Matters.

Jake, J. L., Myers-Scotton, C. M., & Gross, S. (2003). Making a minimalist approach to codeswitching work: Adding the matrix language. *Bilingualism: Language and Cognition, 5*, 69–91.

Jørgensen, J. N. (2008). Polylingual languaging around and among children and adolescents. *International Journal of Multilingualism, 5*(3), 161–176.

Jørgensen, J. N., Karrebæk, M. S., Madsen, L. M., & Møller, J. S. (2011). Polylanguaging in superdiversity. *Diversities, 13*(2), 23–37.

Kemp, C. (2009). Defining multilingualism. In L. Aronin & B. Hufeisen (Eds.), *The exploration of multilingualism* (pp. 11–26). Amsterdam: John Benjamins.

Kovelman, I., Baker, S. A., & Petitto, L.-A. (2008). Bilingual and monolingual brains compared: A functional magnetic resonance imaging investigation of syntactic processing and a possible "neural signature" of bilingualism. *Journal of Cognitive Neuroscience, 20*(1), 153–169. doi:10.1162/jocn.2008.20011

Kravchenko, A. V. (2007). Essential properties of language, or, why language is not a code. *Language Sciences, 29*(5), 650–671.

Labov, W. (1965). Linguistic research on the non-standard English of Negro children. In A. Dore (Ed.), *Problems and practices in the New York City Schools* (pp. 110–117). New York, NY: New York Society for the Experimental Study of Education.

Labov, W. (1970). The logic of non-standard English. In F. Williams (Ed.), *Language and poverty* (pp. 153–187). Chicago, IL: Rand McNally.

Labov, W. (1972). *Sociolinguistic patterns*. Philadelphia, PA: University of Pennsylvania Press.

Labov, W., Ash, S., & Boberg, C. (2006). *The atlas of North American English: Phonetics, phonology and sound change*. Berlin: Mouton de Gruyter.

Lewis, G., Jones, B., & Baker, C. (2012). Translanguaging: Developing its conceptualisation and contextualization. *Educational Research and Evaluation: An International Journal on Theory and Practice, 18*, 655–670 doi:10.1080/13803611.2012.718490

Liceras, J. M., Spradlin, K. T., & Fernández Fuertes, R. (2005). Bilingual early functional-lexical mixing and the activation of formal features. *International Journal of Bilingualism, 9*(2), 227–251.

Lillo-Martin, D., Müller, R., & Chen Pichler, D. (2016). The development of bimodal bilingualism: Implications for linguistic theory. *Linguistic Approaches to Bilingualism, 6*(6), 719–755.

Lindholm, K. J., & Padilla, A. M. (1978). Language mixing in bilingual children. *Journal of Child Language, 5*, 327–335.

Lipski, J. M. (1978). Code-switching and the problem of bilingual competence. In M. Paradis (Ed.), *Aspects of bilingualism* (pp. 250–264). Columbus, SC: Hornbeam Press.

Lipski, J. M. (2014). Spanish-English code-switching among low-fluency bilinguals: Towards an expanded typology. *Sociolinguistic Studies, 8*(1), 23–55. doi:10.1558/sols.v8i1.23

Lyons, J. (1981). *Language and linguistics: An introduction*. Cambridge, UK: Cambridge University Press.

Mackey, W. F. (1967). *Bilingualism as a world problem/Le bilinguisme, phenomene mondial*. Montreal: Harvest House.

MacSwan, J. (1999). *A minimalist approach to intrasentential code switching*. New York, NY: Garland Press.

MacSwan, J. (2000a). The architecture of the bilingual language faculty: Evidence from codeswitching. *Bilingualism: Language and Cognition, 3*(1), 37–54.

MacSwan, J. (2000b). The threshold hypothesis, semilingualism, and other contributions to a deficit view of linguistic minorities. *Hispanic Journal of Behavioral Sciences, 20*(1), 3–45.

MacSwan, J. (2004). Code switching and linguistic theory. In T. K. Bhatia & W. Ritchie (Eds.), *Handbook of bilingualism* (pp. 415–462). Oxford, UK: Blackwell.

MacSwan, J. (2005a). Codeswitching and generative grammar: A critique of the MLF model and some remarks on "modified minimalism." *Bilingualism: Language and Cognition, 8*(1), 1–22. doi:10.1017/s1366728904002068

MacSwan, J. (2005b). Comments on Jake, Myers-Scotton and Gross's response: There is no "matrix language." *Bilingualism: Language and Cognition, 8*(2), 277–284. doi:10.1017/s1366728905002312

MacSwan, J. (2013). Code switching and linguistic theory. In T. K. Bhatia & W. Ritchie (Eds.), *Handbook of bilingualism and multilingualism* (2nd ed., pp. 223–350). Oxford, UK: Blackwell.

MacSwan, J. (Ed.). (2014). *Grammatical theory and bilingual codeswitching.* Cambridge, MA: MIT Press.

MacSwan, J. (2016a). Codeswitching in adulthood. In E. Nicoladis & S. Montanari (Eds.), *Lifespan perspectives on bilingualism* (pp. 183–200). Washington, DC: American Psychological Association.

MacSwan, J. (2016b). Codeswitching and the timing of lexical insertion. *Linguistic Approaches to Bilingualism, 6*(6), 782–787.

MacSwan, J., & Colina, S. (2014). Some consequences of language design: Codeswitching and the PF interface. In J. MacSwan (Ed.), *Grammatical theory and bilingual codeswitching* (pp. 185–210). Cambridge, MA: MIT Press.

MacSwan, J., & Rolstad, K. (2005). Modularity and the facilitation effect: Psychological mechanisms of transfer in bilingual students. *Hispanic Journal of the Behavioral Sciences, 27*(2), 224–243.

Mahootian, S. (1993). *A null theory of code switching.* Doctoral dissertation, Northwestern University.

Mahootian, S. (1997). *Persian.* New York, NY: Routledge.

Makoni, S., & Makoni, B. (2010). Multilingual discourse on wheels and public English in Africa: A case for "vague linguistics." In J. Maybin & J. Swann (Eds.), *The Routledge companion to English language studies* (pp. 258–270). London: Routledge.

Makoni, S., & Pennycook, A. D. (2007). Disinventing and reconstituting languages. In S. Makoni & A. Pennycook (Eds.), *Disinventing and reconstituting languages* (pp. 1–41). Clevedon, UK: Multilingual Matters.

Martin-Beltrán, M. (2014). "What do you want to say?" How adolescents use translanguaging to expand learning opportunities. *International Multilingual Research Journal, 8*, 208–230.

Martínez, R. A. (2010). Spanglish as literacy tool: Toward an understanding of the potential role of Spanish-English code-switching in the development of academic literacy. *Research in the Teaching of English, 45*(2), 124–149.

Martínez, R. A., Hikida, M., & Durán, L. (2015). Unpacking ideologies of linguistic purism: How dual language teachers make sense of everyday translanguaging *International Multilingual Research Journal, 9*(2), 26–42. doi:10.1080/19313152.2014.977712

Martínez-Roldán, C. M. (2015). Translanguaging practices as mobilization of linguistic resources in a spanish/english bilingual after-school program: An analysis of contradictions. *International Multilingual Research Journal, 9*(2), 43–58.

Milian Hita, S. (2014). Codeswitching and the semantics-syntax interface: The role of aspectual features in constraining intrasentential codeswitching involving the verb. In J. MacSwan (Ed.), *Grammatical theory and bilingual codeswitching* (pp. 227–254). Cambridge, MA: MIT Press.

Milk, R. (1986). The issue of language separation in bilingual methodology. In E. Gracia & B. Flores (Eds.), *Language and literacy research in bilingual education* (pp. 67–86). Tempe, AZ: Center for Bilingual Education, Arizona State University.

Milk, R. (1990). Integrating language and content: Implications for language distribution in bilingual classrooms. In R. Jacobson & C. Faltis (Eds.), *Language distribution issues in bilingual schooling* (pp. 32–44). Clevedon, UK: Multilingual Matters.

Mishoe, M., & Montgomery, M. (1994). The pragmatics of multiple modal variation in North and South Carolina. *American Speech, 69*, 3–29.

Moll, L. C., Soto-Santiago, S., & Schwartz, L. (2013). Funds of knowledge in changing communities. In K. Hall, T. Cremin, B. Comber, & L. C. Moll (Eds.), *The Wiley Blackwell international handbook of research on children's literacy, learning and culture* (pp. 172–183). London: Wiley Blackwell.

Moro Quintanilla, M. (2014). The semantic interpretation and syntactic distribution of determiner phrases in Spanish-English codeswitching. In J. MacSwan (Ed.), *Grammatical theory and bilingual codeswitching* (pp. 213–226). Cambridge, MA: MIT Press.

Moschkovich, J. (2007). Using two languages when learning mathematics. *Educational Studies in Mathematics, 64*(2), 121–144.

Moyer, M. (1993). *Analysis of code-switching in Gibraltar.* Doctoral dissertation, Universidad Autonoma de Barcelona.

Müller, N., & Cantone, K. (2009). Language mixing in bilingual children: Codeswitching? In B. E. Bullock & A. J. Toribio (Eds.), *The Cambridge handbook of linguistic code-switching* (pp. 199–220). Cambridge, UK: Cambridge University Press.

Nava, N. (2009). Elementary teachers' attitudes and beliefs towards their students' use of code-switching in South Texas. *Lenguaje, 37*(1), 135–158.

Newmeyer, F. J. (1986). *The politics of linguistics.* Chicago, IL: The University of Chicago Press.

Newmeyer, F. J. (1988). *Linguistic theory in America* (2nd ed.). New York, NY: Academic Press.

Nguyen, H. H. (2012). The multilanguaging of a Vietnamese American in South Philadelphia. *Working Papers in Educational Linguistics, 27*(1), 65–85.

Nowak, L. (1972). Laws of science, theories, measurement. *Philosophy of Science, 39*, 533–548.

Nowak, L. (1992). The idealizational approach to science: A new survey. In J. Brzezin´ski & L. Nowak (Eds.), *Idealization III: Approximation and truth* (pp. 9–63). Amsterdam: Atlanta.

Oakes, J. (1985). *Keeping on track.* New Haven, CT: Yale University Press.

Otheguy, R., García, O., & Reid, W. (2015). Clarifying translanguaging and deconstructing named languages: A perspective from linguistics. *Applied Linguistics Review, 6*(3), 281–307. doi:10.1515/applirev-2015-0014

Otsuji, E., & Pennycook, A. (2011). Social inclusion and metrolingual practices. *International Journal of Bilingual Education and Bilingualism, 14*, 413–426.

Palmer, D. (2009). Code switching and symbolic power in a second grade two-way classroom: A teacher's motivation system gone awry. *Bilingual Research Journal, 32*(1), 42–59.

Palmer, D. K., & Martínez, R. A. (2013) Teacher agency in bilingual spaces: A fresh look at preparing teachers to educate Latino/a bilingual children. *Review of Research in Education, 37*, 269–297.

Palmer, D., Martínez, R., Henderson, K., & Mateus, S. (2014). Reframing the debate on language separation: Toward a vision for translanguaging pedagogies in the dual language classroom. *Modern Language Journal, 98*(3), 757–772.

Paradis, J., & Genesee, F. (1996). Syntactic acquisition in bilingual children: Autonomous or interdependent? *Studies in Second Language Acquisition, 18*, 1–25.

Paris, D. (2012). Culturally sustaining pedagogy a needed change in stance, terminology, and practice. *Educational Researcher, 41*(3), 93–97. doi:10.3102/0013189X12441244

Paulston, C. (1983). Second language acquisition in school settings. In W. Tikunoff (Ed.), *Compatibility of the SBIF features with other research and instruction for LEP students*. San Francisco, CA: Far West Laboratory for Educational Research and Development.

Pennycook, A. (2006). Postmodernism in language policy. In T. Ricento (Ed.), *An introduction to language policy: Theory and method* (pp. 60–67). London: Blackwell.

Pfaff, C. (1979). Constraints on language mixing: Intrasentential code-switching and borrowing in Spanish/English. *Language, 55*, 291–318.

Pinker, S. (1994). *The language instinct: How the mind creates language*. New York, NY: W. Morrow.

Poplack, S. (1978). Quantitative analysis of constraints on code-switching. In *Centro working papers*. New York: City University of New York, Centro de Estudios Puertorriquen˜os.

Poplack, S. (1981). The syntactic structure and social function of code-switching. In R. Durán (Ed.), *Latino language and communicative behavior* (pp. 69–92). Norwood, NJ: Ablex.

Ramirez, A. G., & Milk, R. D. (1986). Notions of grammaticality among teachers of bilingual pupils. *TESOL Quarterly, 20*(3), 495–513.

Rampton, B. (2007). Language crossing and redefining reality. In P. Auer (Ed.), *Codeswitching in conversation: Language, interaction and identity* (pp. 290–317). New York, NY: Routledge.

Reljić, G., Ferring, D., & Martin, R. (2014). A meta-analysis on the effectiveness of bilingual programs in Europe. *Review of Educational Research, 85*(1), 92–128. doi:10.3102/0034654314548514

Resnik, L., Asterhan, C. S. C., & Clarke, S. N. (Eds.). (2015). *Socializing intelligence through academic talk and dialogue*. Washington, DC: American Educational Research Association.

Reyes, I. (2004). Functions of code switching in schoolchildren's conversations. *Bilingual Research Journal, 28*(1), 77–98.

Riegelhaupt, F. (2000). Codeswitching and language use in the classroom. In A. Roca (Ed.), *Research on Spanish in the US* (pp. 204–217). Summerville, MA: Cascadilla Press.

Ritchie, W., & Bhatia, T. K. (2013). Social and psychological factors in language mixing. In T. K. Bhatia & W. Ritchie (Eds.), *Handbook of bilingualism* (pp. 375–390). Oxford, UK: Blackwell.

Robins, R. H. (1967). *A short history of linguistics*. Bloomington, IN: Indiana University Press.

Roeper, T. (1999). Universal bilingualism. *Bilingualism: Language and Cognition, 2*, 169–186.

Roeper, T. (2003). Multiple grammars, feature-attraction, pied-piping, and the question: Is AGR inside TP? In N. Müller (Ed.), *(In)vulnerable domains in multilingualism* (pp. 335–360). Amsterdam: Benjamins.

Roeper, T. W. (2011). Strict interfaces and three kinds of multiple grammars. In E. Rinkle & T. Kupisch (Eds.), *The development of grammar. Language acquisition and diachronic change* (pp. 205–228). Philadelphia, PA: John Benjamin.

Roeper, T. (2016). Multiple grammars and the logic of learnability in second language acquisition. *Frontiers in Psychology*, 7(14). doi:10.3389/fpsyg.2016.00014

Rolstad, K., Mahoney, K., & Glass, G. V. (2005). The big picture: A meta-analysis of program effectiveness research on English language learners. *Educational Policy, 19*, 572–594. doi:10.1177/0895904805278067

Ruíz, R. (1984). Orientations in language planning. *NABE: The Journal for the National Association for Bilingual Education, 8*(2), 15–34.

Sánchez, L. (2012). Convergence in syntax/morphology mapping strategies: Evidence from Quechua–Spanish code mixing. *Lingua, 122*(5), 511–528.

Sankoff, D., & Poplack, S. (1981). A formal grammar for code-switching. *Papers in Linguistics, 14*, 3–45.

Sayer, P. (2013). Translanguaging, TexMex, and bilingual pedagogy: Emergent bilinguals learning through the vernacular. *TESOL Quarterly, 47*, 63–88. doi:10.1002/tesq.53

Shin, S. J. (2005). *Developing in two languages: Korean children in America.* Clevedon, UK: Multilingual Matters.

Silva-Corvalán, C. (2014). *Bilingual language acquisition: Spanish and English in the first six years.* Cambridge, UK: Cambridge University Press.

Smith, P. H., & Murillo, L. A. (2015). Theorizing translanguaging and multilingual literacies through human capital theory. *International Multilingual Research Journal, 9*(2), 59–73. doi:10.1080/19313152.2014.985149

Soltero-González, L. (2009). Preschool Latino immigrant children: Using the home language as a resource for literacy learning. *Theory Into Practice, 48*(4), 283–289. doi:10.1080/00405840903192771

Soltero-González, L., & Butvilofsky, S. (2015). The early Spanish and English writing development of simultaneous bilingual preschoolers. *Journal of Early Childhood Literacy Research, 16*, 473–497. doi:10.1177/1468798415602050

Soltero-González, L., Escamilla, K., & Hopewell, S. (2011). Changing teachers' perceptions about the writing abilities of emerging bilingual children: Towards a holistic bilingual perspective on writing assessment. *International Journal of Bilingual Education and Bilingualism, 15*, 71–94. doi:10.1080/13670050.2011.604712

Soltero-González, L., Sparrow, W., Butvilofsky, S., Escamilla, K., & Hopewell, S. (2016). The effects of paired literacy instruction on the Spanish and English literacy outcomes of emerging bilingual children in grades first to third. *Journal of Literacy Research, 48*(1), 80–104.

Spolsky, B. (1998). *Sociolinguistics.* Oxford, UK: Oxford University Press.

Stenson, N. (2007). *Basic Irish: A grammar and workbook.* New York, NY: Routledge.

Timm, L. A. (1975). Spanish-English code-switching: El porqué and how-not-to. *Romance Philology, 28*, 473–482.

Toribio, A. J., & González-Vilbazo, K. E. (2014). Operator movement in English Spanish and German-Spanish codeswitching. In J. MacSwan (Ed.), *Grammatical theory and bilingual codeswitching* (pp. 87–118). Cambridge, MA: MIT Press.

Uriagereka, J. (2012). *Spell-out and the Minimalist Program.* Oxford, UK: Oxford University Press.

Valdes-Fallis, G. (1978). *Code switching and the classroom teacher. Language in education: Theory and practice 4.* Washington, DC: Center for Applied Linguistics.

Van Dulm, O. (2007). *The grammar of English-Afrikaans code switching: A feature checking account.* Utrecht: Netherlands Graduate School of Linguistics.

Van Dulm, O. (2009). English-Afrikaans intrasentential code switching: Testing a feature checking account. *Bilingualism: Language and Cognition, 12*(2), 193–212.

van Gelderen, E., & MacSwan, J. (2008). Interface conditions and codeswitching: AnF-movement analysis of pronouns and lexical DPs. *Lingua, 118*(6), 765–776.

Volterra, V., & Taeschner, T. (1978). The acquisition and development of language by bilingual children. *Journal of Child Language, 5*, 311–326.

Weinreich, U. (1953). *Languages in contact.* The Hague: Mouton.

Weisberg, M. (2007). Three kinds of idealization. *The Journal of Philosophy, 104*(12), 639–659.

Wentz, J. (1977). *Some considerations in the development of a syntactic description of code-switching.* Doctoral dissertation, University of Illinois, Urbana-Champaign.

Wentz, J., & McClure, E. (1977). Aspects of the syntax of the code-switched discourse of bilingual children. In F. J. Ingemann (Ed.), *1975 Mid-American Linguistics Conference papers.* Lawrence, KS: University of Kansas.

Williams, C. (1994). *Arfarniad o ddulliau dysgu ac addysgu yng nghyd-destun addysg uwchradd ddwyieithog* [An evaluation of teaching and learning methods in the context of bilingual secondary education]. Unpublished doctoral dissertation, University of Wales, Bangor, UK.

Wolfram, W. (1969). Linguistic correlates of social differences in the Negro community. *Georgetown Monograph Series on Languages and Linguistics, 22*, 249–257. Woolford, E. (1983). Bilingual code-switching and syntactic theory. *Linguistic Inquiry, 14*(5), 520–536.

Zentella, A. C. (1981). T'a bien, you could answer me en cualquier idioma: Puerto Rican codeswitching in bilingual classrooms. In R. P. Duran (Ed.), *Latino language and communicative behavior* (pp. 109–131). Norwood, NJ: Ablex.

Zentella, A. C. (1997). *Growing up bilingual: Puerto Rican children in New York.* Malden, MA: Blackwell.

9

ENGLISH LANGUAGE LEARNING IN GLOBALIZED THIRD SPACES

From Monocultural Standardization to Hybridized Translanguaging

David Hemphill and Erin Blakely***

*SAN FRANCISCO STATE UNIVERSITY; ** SANTA BARBARA CITY COLLEGE

Colonial Origins of Deficit-Based ELD Programs

The persistent view of English Language Learners (ELLs) as "at-risk" exemplifies the colonial logic behind many educational institutions and their presumed role in supporting "deprived" populations. "The objective of colonial discourse," Bhabha (1994) writes, "is to construe the colonized as a population of degenerate types . . . in order to justify conquest and to establish systems of administration and instruction" (p. 70). Tracked or remedial English Language Development (ELD) classes, tutoring, counseling, and parent education programs designed to "close the achievement gap" act as parts of this colonizing project.

In schools, resources are deployed to help non-native ELLs "catch up" to their native speaker peers. With the intention of maintaining the same standards for all, schools in the United States, for example, are required to provide remedial services to ensure that ELLs meet Common Core State Standards:

> [A] ll students should be held to the same high expectations outlined in the Common Core State Standards. This includes students who are English language learners . . . However, these students may require additional time, appropriate instructional support, and aligned assessments as they acquire both English language proficiency and content area knowledge
>
> *(CDE, 2015, p. 2).*

Standardized policies like the Common Core thus routinely classify ELLs as "at-risk" or in need of supplemental time and services. Under the guise of equity initiatives, ELLs are often then isolated in lower-level remedial classes, where their progress is measured in English-only tests that dismiss or ignore multilingual proficiencies.

The spread of the English language as the unquestioned global medium of business and intellectual exchange is one of the primary vehicles of contemporary colonialism. The worldwide domination of English is closely connected to its spread as a lingua franca for business and tourism, along with the spread of popular culture through music, films, and other forms of digital media. In a phenomenon Phillipson (1992) describes as linguistic imperialism, "the [global] dominance of English is asserted and maintained through the establishment and continuous reconstitution of structural and cultural inequities between English and other languages" (p. 47). These inequities among languages ensure that more resources are continuously allocated to English than to other languages, and benefit those who are proficient. English functions globally as a gatekeeper to higher levels of education and positions of power and prestige. Despite this colonial history, many educators and policymakers persist in viewing the spread of English as unquestionably "natural, neutral, and beneficial" (Pennycook, 1994).

The view that students must acquire standard, academic English contributes to a larger Western nation-building project. The very notion that there is a discrete language called English, bounded and pure, with a set grammar and vocabulary, is part of the legacy of nation-building (Anderson, 2008; Cummins, 2005; Creese & Blackledge, 2010). In codifying and linking "a language" with "a people," linguistic scholarship has played a role in developing the nation-state construct and in supporting global colonial expansion: "Named languages . . . are ideological constructions historically tied to the emergence of the nation-state in the 19th century, when the idea of autonomous languages . . . meshed with the differentiation of peoples in terms of spiritual essences" (Blommaert & Rampton, 2012, p. 10). The traditional idea of "a language" is, then, an ideological artifact that operates as a major component of modern governmentality (Blommaert & Rampton, 2012; Foucault, 1980; Hemphill & Blakely, 2015).

Many tactics of governmentality operate through both the construction of languages as bounded abstract systems and the seemingly neutral understanding of language acquisition as a linear process through which individuals develop specific cognitive competencies. These dominant constructions of language and language acquisition are based on positivism and structuralism in linguistics (Chomsky, 1975; Saussure, 1959). The consequent, dominant second language acquisition (SLA) research paradigm privileges the coding and quantifying of data and endorses the search for universal, underlying cognitive processes, rather than examining the contextual dimensions of language (Firth & Wagner, 1997).

The prevailing behaviorist, technocratic approaches in SLA research are promoted as the "only possible and valid scientific psychology . . . where the goals are taken as given and the problem is to find the most effective means of reaching the goal" (Kvale, 1976, p.107). Accordingly, ELD teachers are trained primarily in structural linguistic, "research-based" instructional practices that neglect social discursive approaches. ELD teachers thus rarely receive training on the historical role or colonizing functions of English and English language teaching in the world. The aims of technocratic research can only be oppressive, Kvale (1976) argues, as they are designed with the intent of "effectivizing the molding of human behavior in accordance with externally given ends, the prediction and control of the behavior of others" (p. 108).

Technocratic ELD "research-based" practices are based on a binary division between native and non-native English speakers that reifies and reduces both groups. Native and non-native speakers are viewed simplistically and homogeneously in most SLA research, as if there were clear-cut distinctions and uniformity among them. ELLs, for example, are classified as one subgroup in US national assessments. They are lumped together regardless of their socioeconomic status, race, nationality, immigrant status, prior exposure to language(s), community participation, or other social positions and identities.

SLA research focuses on native/non-native speaker identities as if they were the only identities that matter, rarely considering the range of other social identities. "The researcher's acts of othering, objectifying, patronizing, and judging further reduce the learner's social complexity" (Canagarajah, 2007, p. 929). Non-native speakers are further seen universally as subordinate to native speakers, who are assumed to have uniformly acquired complete fluency in their mother tongue. Firth and Wagner (1997) question the characterization of native speakers as homogeneously fluent, noting that: "How bilingualism, multilingualism, 'semi-lingualism', and (first) language loss relate to the concept of [native speakers] are in large measure ignored" (p. 292).

In addition to reifying and reducing the social complexity of native/non-native speakers, SLA research assumes that language learners respond uniformly, in predictable and patterned fashions, progressing through identical linear stages of second language acquisition. This is visible in the concept of "interlanguage," described by Larsen-Freeman and Long (1991) as "a continuum between the L1 [first language] and L2 [target language] along which all learners traverse" (p. 60). All interlanguage users are presumed to be in a transitional phase with underdeveloped skills and language, rather than users of their own distinct lingua franca. "Multilingual speakers," Canagarajah (2007) counters,

> are not moving toward someone else's target; they are constructing their own norms. It is meaningless to measure the distance of Lingua Franca English (LFE) speakers from the language of Anglo-American speakers, as LFE has no relevance to their [standard English] variety
>
> *(p. 927).*

Regular linguistic features of an interlanguage are termed "fossilizations" or "pragmatic failures." Yet such seemingly aberrant forms "may be deployed resourcefully and strategically, to accomplish social and interactional ends" (Firth & Wagner, 1997, p. 293).

It is likewise problematic to measure ELLs against a target of native fluency, as native speakers are erroneously assumed, in this paradigm, to have problem-free speech, devoid of repairs and misunderstandings. Repair sequences and misunderstandings are not aberrations, Firth and Wagner (1997) argue, but "integral parts of the progression of normal, conversational discourse, regardless of the social identities of the actors involved" (p. 295).

The predominant SLA model does not acknowledge the legitimacy and distinctness of users of English as a lingua franca language (Canagarajah, 2007; Brutt-Griffler, 2002; Seidlhofer, 2004). Yet English is used most often globally as a contact language by speakers of other languages for transnational communication. Speakers of English as a lingua franca are far greater in number than the traditionally understood native speakers. About 80 percent of global verbal exchanges in English do not involve native speakers, and frequently do not conform to the norms of standard Englishes. Kachru (1992) describes three circles or varieties of international English: an "Inner Circle" (Englishes that took shape and were spread across the world in colonial expansion from the UK to the US, Australia, Canada, and so forth); an "Outer Circle" (spread through imperial expansion in Asia and Africa); and an "Expanding Circle" (countries where English plays no historical or governmental role). The broad category of language varieties called English is thus increasingly shaped by both native and non-native speakers on a daily basis.

Recognizing that it is impossible to reconcile idealized native/non-native Englishes with the multilingualism and "superdiversity" of a transnational globalized world (Blommaert & Rampton, 2012), some sociolinguists have begun to work with the construct of a linguistic repertoire (Canagarajah, 2011; Creese & Blackledge, 2010; García, 2007). Instead of accepting the notion of a bounded speech community, they address how people take on different linguistic forms as they opt in and out of different groups, perform or play with linguistic signs of group belonging, and develop trajectories of group identifications. They employ the term "translanguaging" to argue that: for multilinguals, languages are not discrete and separated, but form an integrated system; multilingual competence emerges out of local practices where multiple languages are negotiated for communication; competence does not consist of separate competencies for each language, but a multicompetence; and proficiency is about hybrid repertoire building rather than total mastery of each and every language.

Despite this contemporary trend in sociolinguistic scholarship, a colonial hierarchy persists within schools privileging the dominant standard variety of English. School rankings of students' languages continue to construct hybrid varieties, such as Spanglish (Spanish and English) or Taglish (Tagalog and English), as inferior. The academic English language norms valued in schools include "precision in spelling, practice in handling abstract symbols, the ability to state explicitly the meaning of words" (Labov, 1972, p. 213). Though they are signals of "being literate," these middle-class norms, Labov argues, are not "better" for communicating, narrating experience, or reasoning.

Standardization and Commodification of Language

Colonization in schools occurs in large part through mandating a standardized and commodified "academic language," and devaluing other language varieties. Through standardization campaigns across the West, government controls have tightened and re-emphasized traditional, monolingual canons of knowledge in curriculum and assessment with "back-to-basics" campaigns to promote national cultural solidarity and unification. Standards-based educational reforms and campaigns to "close the achievement gap," often through English-only mandates, have led to conformity in content and a growing emphasis on culturally "neutral" basics. The result is what Skerrett (2008) calls a "monocultural restoration," leading to the loss in schools of many prior accommodations of cultural or linguistic diversity.

The spread of standardization campaigns across the West began in the late 1980s and early 1990s, when national educational reform movements in the UK, the US, Australia, and Canada moved toward marketization and accountability through:

- increased competition among schools, fueled by publication of test rankings
- paced and scripted curriculum
- political targets and timetables for delivering improved results
- "value-added" teacher assessments that sought to tie student test scores to individual teacher performance and merit-based pay
- sanctions, including involuntary teacher transfers, principal removal, and school closure ("reconstitution") for poor test performance
- (re)positioning of literacy coaches as compliance officers to enforce "curriculum fidelity"
- replacement of university-based professional learning with on-the-job, in-service training on government priorities and bureaucratic standards (Hargreaves & Shirley, 2009).

The standards-based curricula and testing regimes now dominant in Western public education were "organized scientifically for efficiency . . . casting teachers as managers of the process of producing student achievement scores" (Sleeter & Stillman, 2005, p. 44). Improving "performance indicators" and efficiency are now the codified, central aims of educational policy.

The predominant culture of assessment has led to the quantification of language skills and the accompanying notion that some people "possess" more or less language or literacy than others. The state-mandated California English Language Development Test (CELDT), for example, measures English language proficiency levels using a scoring rubric to label a student's overall performance as "beginning, early intermediate, intermediate, early advanced, or advanced." If students are classified as "Limited English Proficient (LEP)" they are enrolled in remedial programs or placed in a specialized track to receive supplemental ELD instruction. This placement often prevents access to the full curriculum and creates barriers to college entrance.

ELLs are frequently subjected to additional testing beyond regular literacy assessments, and are thus disproportionately affected by instructional practices that "teach to the test." ELLs in California, for instance, may even be required to report to their schools during the summer to take the CELDT, which determines their classification status and instructional grouping for the next school year. As a result, English language skills have become commodities with a presumed market value that teachers aim to transfer to students. "Rather than asking whose knowledge, language, and points of view are most worth teaching children, teachers and administrators are pressed to ask how well children are scoring on standardized measures of achievement" (Sleeter & Stillman, 2005, p. 44). "Under these conditions," writes Apple (1998),

> not only does education become a marketable commodity like bread and cars in which the values, procedures, and metaphors of business dominate, but its results must be reducible to standardized 'performance indicators'
> *(p. 25).*

Lyotard (1984) predicted that learning would begin to circulate along the same lines as money, instead of for its purported educational value. The pertinent distinction, Lyotard (1984) suggests, is "no longer . . . between ignorance and knowledge, but rather . . . between . . . units of knowledge exchanged in a daily maintenance framework ['payment knowledge'] . . . versus funds of knowledge dedicated to optimizing the performance of a project ['investment knowledge']" (p. 7). This exchange system is evidenced in the precise measurement of knowledge products and accountability structures now found in most schools.

Behind the standardization and commodification of knowledge in schools is the tacitly accepted belief that *learning is a product of teaching*: "[I]n school's official, institutionally fixed understanding, learning is normally regarded as a direct result of *teaching*, and since teaching is viewed as something that can be planned administratively, the learning processes of pupils automatically appear to be plannable as well" (Holzkamp, 2013, p. 118). This equation creates a technocratic school system that fixates on the administrative planning of "learning" under the assumption that the teacher's sole role is to provide students with uniform access to each measurable knowledge product.

In schools, learners are constructed as passive recipients of knowledge commodities which are constantly abstracted, isolated, and measured to rank student performance. In order to adhere to this system of measurement, schools must ensure that all students are exposed to a standardized curriculum in the same or comparable way. This accounts for schools' strict attendance policies, classroom management tactics to discipline students who are not visibly paying attention, and the near exclusive focus of teachers' planning time on developing concrete learning outcomes and techniques for producing them.

The specification of measurable learning outcomes gives the impression of precision and accountability, but, even when they are stated as simply as "will count to ten without errors," outcomes are difficult to measure precisely. Some students will perform this counting task easily, others hesitatingly. Yet they may count with or without understanding. "The illusion of measured learning," write Lave and McDermott (2002),

> makes substantial what is not and reifies it into numbers that align children within hierarchies that replicate injustices in the distribution of access and rewards . . . [I]n a system in which success is defined by failure of others, in a system in which everyone has to do better than everyone else, there is no way for everyone to achieve school success.
>
> *(p. 21)*

Defining learning as an individual's acquisition of taught skills has led to the near exclusive focus in schools on generating and specifying educational goals, learning outcomes, or objectives. Common learning objectives for ESL or ELD classes, for example, include precisely divided, decontextualized skills, such as:

1. Use count and non-count nouns with appropriate articles and quantifiers
2. Apply subject–verb agreement rules after nouns with phrasal modifiers
3. Recognize adjectival function and meaning of present and past participles
4. Recognize nominal function of infinitives and gerunds as subjects and objects
5. Recognize present perfect tense and adverbials denoting past to present time
6. Define and use specified modal verbs in present and past tense (EVC, 2015).

The foregoing competencies are required for students to be considered proficient English speakers, though many fluent native speakers of English would be unable to identify parts of speech or perform abstract grammatical tasks isolated from context. Acquiring these competencies also does not guarantee that a speaker will be considered fluent or proficient. "A person," notes Gee (1990),

> could be able to use a language perfectly and still not make sense (paradoxically put: a person could speak the language grammatically, use the language appropriately, and still get it 'wrong'). This is so because what is important is not just *how* you say it (how you *use* the grammar, that is, how you formulate a message given the context it is said in), but what *you are and* do when you say it
>
> *(pp. 139–140).*

Since language is negotiated by participants; what is inappropriate or intelligible in one interaction may differ entirely in another. The form language takes is thus always variable, "emerg[ing] out of and through interaction," and for that reason "it might well be that [it] never achieves a stable or even standardized form" (Meierkord, 2004, p. 129). "There is no meaning for form, grammar, or language ability outside the realm of practice. [Language] is not a product located in the mind of the speaker; it is a form of social action" (Canagarajah, 2007, p. 928).

Instead of reifying and commodifying language, distilling it artificially into separable skills and measuring individual progress in mastering standardized language skills, there is an area of scholarship—a multiliteracies approach—that treats learning and literacy as "part and parcel of, and inextricable from, specific social, cultural, institutional, and political practices. Thus, literacy is, in a sense, 'multiple'" (Gee, 1999, p. 356). A multiliteracies approach "argue[s] for a focus . . . on oral and written language as composed of diverse, closely interrelated 'tools' (mediating devices) for learning, development, and activity within concrete social practices" (Gee, 1999, p. 358; Cope & Kalantzis, 2000). From a multiliteracies perspective, the definition of a "text" includes "lifeworlds"—structured spaces, contexts, and discourse communities as texts to be read. With this broader view of what constitutes a text, recognizing and deciphering cultural, historical, ideological, spatial, and other dimensions become key parts of language practice and pedagogies.

ELD teachers are, however, afforded little if any time to investigate local conditions, student experiences, and contexts of students' everyday lives. Curriculum mandates, pacing guides, and test-driven curricula mean that teachers' professional development and evaluation are almost exclusively focused on fidelity to "research-based" practices that are presumed to promote skill acquisition. Teachers are evaluated on their adherence to curriculum standards and publishers' pacing guides, rather than the relevance of instruction to students or their social relations in practice.

As a result of standardization and commodification, ELD teacher preparation has in most instances become little more than marketing of approved products for instruction and remediation:

> The operational assumptions are that the right method, textually encoded into a particular commodity and then decoded and remediated into a normalized set of behaviors around the text/commodity, constitute an optimal educational practice and experience
>
> *(Luke, 2004, p. 1434).*

Educational research has largely been reduced to product testing of standards-aligned textbooks, instructional techniques, classroom management, and assessment systems. This focus on product testing results in the neglect of social relations. In contrast, meaning is not, Firth and Wagner (1997) argue, "an individual phenomenon . . . of private thoughts . . . transferred from brain to brain, but a social and negotiable product of interaction" (p. 290).

Learning as Identity-Making Practice

The current institutional arrangement of schools (timed lessons, decontextualized curricula, standardized testing) is based on the assumption that learning is "an isolated subject's secluded and parceled acquisition of a pre-given and secluded object of knowledge" (Dreier, 2008, p. 91). As a result of this conception of learning and the accompanying requisites to treat students uniformly and show fidelity to mandated standards, teachers are generally required to impede social relations during lessons. Efforts to curb student interactions or diversions, in order to focus exclusively on learning outcomes, mean that teachers often prompt students' evasive actions, contributing to the "mixture of stress, weariness, suspicion, pressure, bribery, resentment, and opportunism which constitutes the normality of everyday school life" (Holzkamp, 2013, p. 131). The artifacts of this are present in nearly every classroom, from behavior management systems that track and label students' "readiness to learn," to class points or "brain bucks" used to reward certain targeted and commodified actions. Along with these props come all of the identities produced by this mixture: worn-out teachers, poor staff retention, "problem" students, and the constant confusion of effort, obedience, skill, know-how, and achievement (Holzkamp, 2013).

To avoid these normalized and commodified artifacts of schooling and the colonial relations that underlie ELD instruction requires a reconceptualization of learning as identity-making social practice. Though almost all ELD instructional time, evaluations, and training are focused on "best practices" for producing commodified, measurable learning objectives, "the issue of conferring legitimacy," Lave and Wenger (1991) argue, "is more important than the issue of providing teaching" (p. 92). Rejecting the predominant individualistic and mechanistic view of learning, Lave and Wenger (1991) propose a situated learning theory that redefines learning as changing participation in communities of practice. Learning, in their view, is not confined to formal classroom settings but occurs as a part of everyday practice. "Learning, in the conceptualization that is made possible by notions of the constitutive everyday," writes Lave (2008), "is no longer viewed simply as a change in the autonomous subject's knowledge of an objective world. Learning is construed as the reconstruction of the way a subject is engaged in the world" (p. 43). In this reconfiguration, the main role for teacher education and educational research shifts from identifying the techniques that contribute to ELLs becoming more proficient on isolated measures of language skill, to considerations of both the historical constitution of everyday practices and, simultaneously, how subjects constitute themselves through their participation in practice (Lave, in press).

In line with situated learning theories, Holzkamp (2013) argues that learning cannot be administratively planned, sequenced, and delivered uniformly, as many educators assume. Learning trajectories, Dreier (2008) continues, are not linear, nor do they obey uniform mechanisms. Learning, he writes,

> is mostly a discontinuous process. When a learning issue or assignment emerges for the first time for a particular person or group of persons, they encounter it in a situated way in a particular context. They address and pursue it in a particular manner in that context depending on the particular setup of materials, co-participants, and possibilities and on their particular concerns in relation to that context
>
> *(pp. 86–87).*

These pursuits, Dreier (2008) adds, are "rarely finished in one learning situation and context" (p. 87). Instead of centering focus on the individual learner's mental processes and linear skill acquisition, situated learning theorists look at "fields of activity" (Lave, 1998) across the various social contexts of practice or "landscapes of learning" (Nielsen & Kvale, 2006). They investigate learning as an episodic process in which subjects are reconfigured, and at the same time reconfigure the production and reproduction of objects, texts, other persons, events, and institutions involved.

Similarly, expansive learning theories, based on the work of the Russian school of cultural-historical activity theory (Engeström & Sannino, 2010) and Bakhtin's (1981) theory of heteroglossia, offer a conceptualization of learning as discontinuous. They diversely conceive of learning as multi-voiced, distributed, or transformative expansions of social practice. Learning, in this conceptualization, involves boundary-crossing movements, often emerging from contradictions or historically evolving tensions: "contradictions are the driving force of transformation" (Engeström & Sannino, 2010, p. 5). Such transformations readily occur, Mørck (2010) argues, from boundary positions, where subjects collectively expand their action possibilities. Mørck (2010) investigates various dilemmas and double-binds that learners cannot resolve alone, but from which "joint cooperative actions can push a historically new form of activity into emergence" (Engeström, 1987, p. 165). "Traditionally," write Engeström and Sannino (2010), "we expect that learning is manifested as changes in the subject; i.e., in the behavior and cognition of the learners. Expansive learning is manifested primarily as changes in the object of the collective activity" (p. 8).

Applying situated and expansive learning theories, Danish and German critical psychologists are developing a form of "social practice" or "practice" research that investigates learning through analysis of how students intersubjectively conduct their everyday lives across multiple contexts (Dreier, 2008; Nielsen & Kvale, 2003; Mørck, 2011, 2010). This strand of research aims to understand how learners "become what they are in relations to the concrete material world" (Mørck & Huniche, 2006, p. 3). Lave (in press) calls further for research to take conflictual, contradictory relations and ask how they are produced in articulation with other such relations in practice, across contexts.

Acknowledging that identity construction and social context are inseparably a part of second language acquisition, Norton (2000) argues that SLA theory

> needs to develop a conception of identity that is understood with reference to larger . . . social structures which are reproduced in day-to-day social interaction . . . It is through language that a person negotiates a sense of self . . . and it is through language that a person gains access to—or is denied access to—powerful social networks that give learners the opportunity to speak.
>
> *(p. 5)*

Placed in remedial tracks, ELLs are often prohibited from the very social networks and everyday social practices that would enable them to develop "identities of mastery" (Lave & Wenger, 1991; Murrell, 2007). Valdés (2001), for example, tells the story of a young immigrant Latina student named Elisa, who works hard in middle school and high school to escape what Valdés calls the "ESL ghetto." She even changes school districts to register for mainstream, college-bound classes where her ESL record will not follow. When Elisa moves to another state, however, and takes the regular English placement test at a local community college, she is again told that she cannot take mainstream classes and will have to register for remedial ESL writing. As Valdés (2001) observes,

> The tiny flaws in [her written] English . . . were too much for the sensitivities of community college teachers. Elisa was told that she will not be eligible for enrollment in credit-bearing, college-level instruction in the regular English sequence until she finishes the sequence of ESL courses.
>
> *(p. 145)*

Educational institutions thus create and maintain identities, like ELL designations, through assessments and policies that aim narrowly to assimilate students and standardize learning outcomes and expectations. Yet learning the salient social divisions and identities of their social world is likely the main task that students engage in, both inside and outside the classroom. "This is an all-consuming job for children nearing adulthood, reason enough to explain why most curricular 'innovations' or teaching methods designed to improve teaching in classrooms have little effect and short lives" (Lave, 1996, p. 160).

Transnational Hybrid Identities

Identity is a process of articulation, argues Hall (1996), that entails discursive work and the marking of symbolic boundaries. It is neither an essential internal state nor the exclusive result of external discourse, as schools often assume, but instead is a hybrid process of intertwining categories, norms, and narratives over time. Learning or "growing up" involves a "hybridization pastiche process of stitching together an identity like trying on clothes, becoming your own hybrid, blending, shaping, and putting together something that's a range of cultures" (Luke qtd. in Besley, 2003, p. 170). Identity-making, especially for contemporary youth in a globalized era, "is about being between 16 or 18 different worlds . . . it's about navigating a sea of texts. Each one of these texts is trying to position you, sell you, define you" (Luke qtd. in Besley, 2003, p. 170). Thus identity development cannot be described solely in a linear way, where an essentialized adult, autonomous self slowly emerges. Identity, likewise, cannot solely be described by single labels of nation-state, ethnicity, or language. "Even when young people are not themselves traveling across national borders, or leaving their own bedrooms, they can find themselves, implicated within transnational networks" (Maira & Soep, 2005, p. xix).

Hybridity, or "how cultural forms and practices intermingle and traverse social boundaries," challenges notions of cultural purity, essential cultural features, or homogenous cultural identities (Lam, 2006, p. 217; Bhabha, 1994; Clifford, 1988). There is a need, writes Appadurai (1996), to reconceptualize the "landscape of group identity" to reflect current transnational conditions in which "groups are no longer tightly territorialized, spatially bounded, historically unselfconscious, or culturally homogenous" (p. 191), and to challenge the reductive manner of describing communities and languages as pure, stable, separable entities (native/non-native; ELL; at-risk; English).

Youth are particularly affected by globalizing forces of time and space compression (Harvey, 2000), as they rapidly construct, revise, and consume new identities based upon information they consume, create, and disseminate through multiple electronic devices and social media networks. Schools, however, remain tied to static systems. They have yet to respond, for example, to the mobility of many ELL families' labor migrations. Attendance policies punish ELL students who move seasonally or reside in multiple places, only sometimes allowing limited independent studies to accommodate these migrations.

Despite limited technology, resources, and access, educators are increasingly asked to teach new, "21st-century skills" to prepare students for the global economy and "global citizenship" (Zhao, 2009). These 21st-century curricula generally reflect a neoliberal perspective, celebrating the dominance of a single global market and the principles of liberal international trade (Shultz, 2007). Most of the 21st-century pedagogies adopted by schools accept neoliberal global expansion as a given, offering little to enable students to deconstruct patterns of inequality inherent in many globalization processes, or the hierarchies that privilege certain language practices over others. Though there is generally an absence of critical inquiry of North-South hierarchies (Shultz, 2007) in 21st-century skill-based instruction, some scholars and practitioners have begun rethinking the limitations of nation-state boundaries and single national languages, discourses, and cultures when considering how schools prepare students for a globalized world.

In the US, the Partnership for 21st Century Skills (2015) advocates a framework stressing: key subjects (3Rs and 21st-century themes of global awareness);

learning and innovation skills (critical thinking, communication, collaboration, and creativity); information, media, and technology skills; and life and career skills. The European Parliament and the Council of the European Union similarly identify key competences necessary for a fulfilling life in a globalizing knowledge society: communication in the mother tongue; communication in foreign languages; mathematical and basic competences in science and technology; learning to learn; social and civic competences; sense of initiative and entrepreneurship; and cultural awareness and expression (European Parliament, 2006).

Though identified as "at risk," ELL students often arrive in the classroom already functioning as global citizens with multilingual capacities and experiences of global interconnectedness. Through exposure to multiple media sources that offer differing accounts of current events, transnational students and ELLs generally are well positioned to gain the bifocality or "dual frame of reference" required in 21st-century critical thinking. Online access to news from another or home country may allow transnational students to see, for example, the gaps in coverage on the media from their host country. As one student comments about US news coverage: "Because on TV . . . They talk, but they don't give the whole chapter about what's going on in Ecuador . . . you want to read more about on the internet what's happening" (Lam & Rosario-Ramos, 2009, p. 184). The digital multiliteracy experiences of transnational students often take place outside the purview of the school and are thus rarely leveraged in the ELD classroom.

Despite 21st-century rhetoric to encourage global citizenship, most schools continue to construct and maintain language hierarchies that privilege standard, academic languages over any mixed language varieties, discouraging code-switching, mixing, or blending of languages. Many students enter school with a primary discourse composed of a hybrid mixture of languages that teachers find unacceptable. Even in the field of bilingual education, for instance, researchers and policymakers have traditionally argued that languages should be kept separate pedagogically. Instruction is expected to be carried out exclusively in the target language without recourse to L1, and translation between L1 and L2 is generally seen to have no place in teaching language or literacy. Even within dual language immersion models, practitioners are admonished to keep the two languages separate in what Cummins (2005) calls "two solitudes." Boundaries are erected around languages, mythically constructing multilingual students and teachers as "two monolinguals in one body" (Cummins, 2005).

Some sociolinguistic researchers (Canagarajah, 2011; Creese & Blackledge, 2010; García, 2007) question the possibility that learning can even take place one language at a time. Though it is infrequently elicited through conscious pedagogical strategies, translanguaging naturally occurs in schools and everyday practice. Specific knowledge and skills exhibited by students and teachers when translanguaging is used in the classroom may include: using bilingual label quests, repetition, and translation; engaging audiences; establishing identity positions that both oppose and support institutional values; annotating texts and providing greater access to the curriculum; and recognizing that languages do not fit into bounded entities—that all languages are needed to convey and negotiate meanings (Creese & Blackledge, 2010).

Translanguaging or code-switching among languages is rarely endorsed, however, in ELD classrooms. Thus, even in biliteracy programs designed to help students learn and maintain more than one language, teachers redirect, correct, or discipline children, enforcing a single, standard language. One teacher in a California PreK–8 Spanish-English biliteracy program describes, for instance, the constant effort and surveillance involved to ensure that her students do not speak Spanglish or mix languages:

> We show them we are switching languages by gesturing [turning an imagined knob at the temple]. We speak only one language for the whole lesson or the whole day and then switch. Students are not supposed to use the other language, but we hear them do it all the time. We have to correct them or they will use words like 'apushar'. We have to constantly remind them that the proper way to say it in Spanish is 'empujar'. We have to teach them academic language.
>
> *(Hemphill & Blakely, 2015, p. 141)*

"Words distorted by English," writes Anzaldúa (1999), "are known as anglicisms or pochismos" (p. 78). Anglicisms such as *bola* for ball, *carpeta* for carpet, *watchar* for watch, *parkiar* for park are, Anzaldúa (1999) argues, not incorrect, as teachers may assume, but are instead products of cultural realities and evolutions that reflect speakers' identities. Thus, trying to eradicate them from the classroom becomes an exclusionary act, promoting student alienation from the academic world: "In childhood we are told that our language is wrong. Repeated attacks on our native tongue diminish our sense of self . . . " (Anzaldúa, 1999, pp. 80–81). Language mixtures, Anzaldúa (1999) continues, are "not approved by any society":

> Chicano Spanish is considered . . . deficient, a mutilation of Spanish. But Chicano Spanish is not incorrect, it is a living language. For a people who are neither Spanish nor live in a country in which Spanish is the first language; for a people who live in a country in which English is the reigning tongue but who are not Anglo; for a people who cannot entirely identify with either standard (formal, Castilian) Spanish nor standard English, what recourse is left but to create their own language?
>
> *(p. 77)*

The problem with standard language and literacy rankings, Labov (1972) argues further, lies in teacher expectations, where progress in the early grades can be drastically impacted by a single random labeling, such as "below basic" or LEP.

This self-fulfilling prophecy is evident in the alienation of students with nonstandard language varieties from school and their disproportionate rates of academic failure. "[W]hen failure reaches such massive proportions," Labov (1972) writes,

> it seems . . . necessary to look at the social and cultural obstacles to learning and the inability of the school to adjust to the social situation . . . [Interventions are] designed to repair the child, rather than the school; to the extent that . . . [they are] based on this inverted logic . . . [they are] bound to fail. *(p. 232)*

The deficit theories that underlie school language and literacy assessments are "particularly dangerous," Labov (1972) contends, because they divert "attention away from real defects in our educational system to imaginary defects of the child . . . " (p. 202).

Third Spaces and Boundary Crossings

The hybrid ways ELLs make meaning, craft identities, and employ multiple literacies are not simply mixtures of established cultures and identities, but signs and meanings that are constantly appropriated, translated, rehistoricized, and read anew. Learning contexts, like student identities and languages, are hybrid productions. Instead of forcing students to operate within a bounded, standard academic language, allowing translanguaging or boundary crossings between discourses and practices can help expand students' learning as a social practice: "Utilizing multiple, diverse, and even conflicting mediational tools . . . promotes the emergence of third spaces, or zones of development, and thus expands learning" (Gutiérrez et al., 1999, p. 288). Bhabha (1994) echoes the call for attention to a "third space," or a hybrid space between established cultures, identities, and languages.

To illustrate how third spaces can develop and facilitate critical thinking, Lam (2004) offers a case study of Willis, a high-school ELL from Hong Kong. Willis spent years isolated in sheltered ELD classes, ignoring taunts about his thick accent. Instead of "mixing well" with either Asian immigrants or native English speakers, he finds his strongest identification with the characters in Japanese comics. From this third space, Willis critiques both US and Hong Kong cultural norms. He contrasts the Japanese plots to the static American comics, where superheroes defeat an endless string of "bad" guys. Likewise, he critiques the Hong Kong comics for their sloppy renderings and trendy plot lines.

Analyzing classroom interactions, Gutiérrez et al. (1999) note that there is typically an official interactional space including teacher-directed activities related to the standard curriculum, and an unofficial space comprised of "unauthorized side talk" and peer play. These "inappropriate" interactions are generally silenced, redirected, or disciplined. Gutiérrez et al. (1999) suggest that, by intentionally operating in the third space, teachers can expand students' engagement. The authors cite one example where a student makes a joke at his own expense during a class reading about the human body. "No wonder they call me bony," the student, Jorge, teases when students are asked to locate their spine. Rather than treat his comment as an unwelcome disruption, the teacher folds the student's comment into the class discussion. His comment, then,

> becomes part of the classroom text . . . Jorge . . . reemerges as expert in the official space as he answers the question that the teacher had been so intent on asking . . . His answer and the teacher's enthusiastic response co-constructs Jorge's identity as a knowing contributor. He is not simply the comical contributor; he is also a resource in the classroom
>
> *(Gutiérrez et al., 1999, pp. 299, 300).*

Instead of impeding social relations, in an intentionally developed, hybrid third space, student talk, translanguaging, jokes, slang, and emotions are re-scripted and included in the official class discussion, enabling students to bring their funds of knowledge (Moll, 1992; Yosso, 2005) into the curriculum: "Affective stances can not only be displayed, they are also welcome additions to classroom ethos and official knowledge" (Gutiérrez et al., 1999, p. 295).

Operating in a third space can help ELD teachers enable students to use the full potential of their linguistic repertoires. In this third space, "no single language . . . is privileged, and the larger linguistic repertoires of participants become tools for participating and making meaning in this new collaborative activity. In fact, these hybrid language practices . . . [can increase] the possibility of dialogue—and thus, interpretation" (Gutiérrez et al., 1999, p. 293). Use of the third space could include: using conflict as a starting place for negotiating and reorganizing lessons; drawing parallels between home and academic discourse; and accepting slang, humor, informal language, and mixed languages (like Spanglish or Taglish) in class discussions.

ELLs "deliberatively develop and deploy multiple literacies in their out-of-school lives to achieve personal, social, civic, and other goals" (Skerrett, 2012, p. 366). In contrast to the common assumption that screen time or consuming popular culture media are universally a waste of time, there is evidence that many forms of digital media (internet browsing, chatrooms, social media, video games, fan fiction) provide effective forums for expanding language and multiliteracies. Reading and writing fan fiction online, for instance, provides ELLs with access to affinity groups, as Skerrett (2012) observes:

> These youth composed and interacted in multiple genres and social registers, they offered sophisticated reviews and meta-analyses of fictions, they found opportunities for rhetorically conducting themselves as successful authors, and they enjoyed high levels of interactions with their online community.
>
> *(2012, p. 366)*

The hybridized positions most ELLs occupy between language communities are conceptualized as spaces where boundary crossing and expansive learning are readily possible, rather than deficit positions that ELD programs must remediate. Multilingual students are more successful, for example, than native speakers at decoding the meaning of unfamiliar lexical and grammatical items: "[Native speakers] had difficulties in such tasks as they did not bring skills and attitudes open to negotiation" (Canagarajah, 2007, p. 930). Given the variable and interactive nature of language in practice, acquisition should aim, Canagarajah (2007) argues, "towards versatility and agility, not mastery and control" (p. 932). "Acquisition," he adds, "is social practice, not separable mastery of knowledge, cognition, or form" (2007, p. 933).

It makes little sense, then, to compare proficiency to baseline data or to measure skills isolated from context, as currently mandated in ELD assessments. "We cannot speak of a target to be achieved," writes Canagarajah (2007), "when the speaker would be perfectly competent for communication at various levels of ability in different contexts" (p. 933). Instead of organizing standardized curricula and activities to build predictable grammatical skills, or to treat hypothesized language deficits, "activities," Mørck et al. (2013) argue, "should start with common engagement in an idea that can mobilize participants from different positions" (p. 95).

Instead of operating with deficit-based, native speaker models, decolonized ELD pedagogies would pay attention to the possibilities third spaces offer for expanding the boundary-crossing practices of students. These pedagogies would incorporate translanguaging and hybrid multiliteracies instead of trying to keep language bounded (insisting that students speak only one "pure" or "academic" language, one at a time). "Multilingualism," Canagarajah (2007) observes, "is at the heart of LFE's (Lingua Franca English) hybrid community identity and speaker proficiency" (p. 926). Breaking down the native/non-native binary, decolonized ELD pedagogies would recognize that all users of English as a lingua franca have "native" competence in the language variety they intersubjectively construct in each specific context of interaction.

Rather than focusing on standard "academic" English as the target of learning, in decolonized ELD pedagogies teachers would intentionally create third spaces for students, encouraging translanguaging and engagement with an evolving repertoire of codes. Decolonized pedagogies would break down the disciplinary and pedagogical boundaries that have long kept languages in hermetically sealed units. Instead of facilitating the acquisition and measurement of standardized, commodified English language skills, ELD instruction would become a matter of expanding the action possibilities for ELLs. Instead of focusing on the administrative planning of lessons, teachers' focus would shift toward the identity-making practices of their students and expanding their boundary crossings in multiple contexts of everyday lives.

References

Anderson, J. (2008). Towards integrated second language teaching pedagogy for foreign and community/heritage language in multilingual Britain. *Language Learning Journal, 36*, 79–89.

Anzaldúa, G. (1999). *Borderlands/La frontera: The new Mestiza*. San Francisco, CA: Aunt Lute Press.

Appadurai, A. (1996). *Modernity at large: Cultural dimensions of globalization*. Minneapolis, MN: University of Minnesota Press.

Apple, M. (1998). Are markets and standards democratic? *Educational Researcher, 27*(6), 24–28.

Bakhtin, M. (1981). *The dialogic imagination: Four essays*. Austin, TX: University of Texas Press.

Besley, A.C. (2003). Hybridized and globalized: Youth cultures in the postmodern era. *The Review of Education, Pedagogy, and Cultural Studies, 25*, 153–177.

Blommaert, J. & Rampton, B. (2012). Language and superdiversity. *MMG Working Paper*, (12–09).

Bhabha, H. K. (1994). *The location of culture*. New York: Routledge.

Brutt-Griffler, J. (2002). *World English: A study of its development*. Clevedon, UK: Multilingual Matters.

Canagarajah, S. (2007). Lingua franca English, multilingual communities, and language acquisition. *The Modern Language Journal, 91*, 923–939.

Canagarajah, S. (2011). Translanguaging in the classroom: Emerging issues for research and pedagogy. *Applied Linguistics Review, 2*(1), 1–28.

CDE. (2015). *California English Language Development Standards (Electronic Edition) Kindergarten Through Grade 12*. California Department of Education. http://www.cde.ca.gov/sp/el/er/documents/eldstndspublication14.pdf(accessed 9-20-15).

Chomsky, N. (1975). *The logical structure of linguistic theory*. New York: Plenum Press.

Clifford, J. (1988). *The predicament of culture: Twentieth-century ethnography, literature, and art*. Cambridge, MA: Harvard University Press.

Cope, B. & Kalantzis, M. (Eds. for the New London Group) (2000). *Multiliteracies: Literacy learning and the design of social futures*. London and New York: Routledge.

Creese, A. & Blackledge, A. (2010). Translanguaging in the bilingual classroom: A pedagogy for learning and teaching? *The Modern Language Journal, 94*(1), (Spring, 2010), 103–115.

Cummins, J. (2005). A proposal for action: Strategies for recognizing heritage language competence as a learning resource within the mainstream classroom. *The Modern Language Journal, 89*, 585–592.

Dreier, O. (2008). Learning in structures of social practice. In K. Nielsen, S. Brinkmann, C. Elmholdt, L. Tanggaard, P. Musaeus and G. Kraft (Eds.), *A Qualitative Stance*. Aarhus, Denmark: Aarhus University Press.

Engeström, Y. (1987). *Learning by expanding: An activity-theoretical approach to developmental research*. Helsinki, Finland: Orienta-Konsultit.

Engeström, Y. & Sannino, A. (2010). Studies of expansive learning: Foundations, findings, and future challenges. *Educational Research Review, 5*, 1–24.

European Parliament. (2006). Recommendation of the European Parliament and of the Council of 18 December 2006 on key competences for lifelong learning. *Official Journal of the European Union*, (2006/962/EC).

EVC. (2015). Evergreen Valley College: ESL 332 Learning Outcomes. http://www.evc-cit.info/language_arts/learning_outcomes/ESL/esl332.html (accessed 10-20-2015).

Firth, A. & Wagner, J. (1997). On discourse, communication, and (some) fundamental concepts in SLA research. *The Modern Language Journal, 81*(3) (Autumn, 1997), 285–300.

Foucault, M. (1980). In C. Gordon, (Ed.), *Power/Knowledge: Selected interviews and other writings, 1972–77.* New York: Pantheon Books.

García, O. (2007). Foreword. In S. Makoni and A. Pennycook (Eds.), *Disinventing and reconstituting languages* (pp. xi–xv). Clevedon, UK: Multilingual Matters.

Gee, J. P. (1990). *Social linguistics and literacies.* Bristol, PA: Falmer Press.

Gee, J. P. (1999). Critical issues: Reading and the New Literacy Studies: Reframing the National Academy of Sciences Report on Reading. *Journal of Literacy Research, 31*(3), 355–374.

Gutiérrez, K. D., Baquedano-López, P. & Tejeda, C. (1999). Rethinking diversity: Hybridity and hybrid language practices in the third space. *Mind, Culture, and Activity, 6*(4), 286–303.

Hall, S. (Ed.) (1996). *Representation: Cultural representations and signifying practices.* London: Sage Publications.

Hargreaves, A. & Shirley, D. L. (2009). *The fourth way: The inspiring future for educational change.* Thousand Oaks, CA: Corwin Press.

Harvey, D. (2000). Time-space compression and the postmodern condition. In D. Held and A. McGrew (Eds.), *The global transformations reader: An introduction to the globalization debate.* Cambridge, MA: Polity Press.

Hemphill, D. & Blakely, E. (2015). *Language, nation, and identity in the classroom: Legacies of modernity and colonialism in schooling.* New York: Peter Lang.

Holzkamp, K. (2013). *Psychology from the standpoint of the subject: Selected writings of Klaus Holzkamp.* London: Palgrave MacMillan.

Hussey, T. & Smith, P. (2002). The trouble with learning outcomes. *Active Learning in Higher Education, 3*(3), 220–233.

Kachru, B. B. (1992). World Englishes: Approaches, issues, and resources. *Language Teaching, 25*(1), 1–14.

Kvale, S. (1976). The psychology of learning as ideology and technology. *Behaviorism,* 4, 97–116.

Labov, W. (1972). *Language in the inner city: Studies in the Black English vernacular.* Philadelphia, PA: University of Pennsylvania Press.

Lam, W. S. E. (2004). Border discourses and identities in transnational youth culture. In J. Mahiri (Ed.), *What they don't learn in school: Literacy in the lives of urban youth.* New York: Peter Lang.

Lam, W. S. E. (2006). Chapter 6: Culture and learning in the context of globalization: Research directions. *Review of Research in Education, 30,* 213–237.

Lam, W. S. E. & Rosario-Ramos, E. (2009). Multilingual literacies in transnational digitally mediated contexts: An exploratory study of immigrant teens in the United States. *Language and Education, 23*(2), 171–190.

Larsen-Freeman, D. & Long, M. (1991). *An introduction to second language acquisition research.* London: Longman.

Lave, J. (1996). Teaching, as learning, in practice. *Mind, Culture, and Activity, 3*(3), 149–164.

Lave, J. (2008). Towards a social ontology of learning. In K. Nielsen, S. Brinkmann, C. Elmholdt, L. Tanggaard, P. Musaeus and G. Kraft (Eds.), *A Qualitative Stance.* Aarhus, Denmark: Aarhus University Press.

Lave, J. (2011). *Apprenticeship in critical ethnographic practice.* Chicago, IL: University of Chicago Press.
Lave, J. (in press). Situated learning: Historical process and practice. *BB Situated Learning Review.* (7-30-2014 draft).
Lave, J. & McDermott, R. (2002). Estranged labor learning. *Outlines: Critical Practice Studies, 4*(1), 19–48.
Lave, J. & Wenger, E. (1991). *Situated learning: Legitimate peripheral participation.* New York: Cambridge University Press.
Luke, A. (2004). Teaching after the market: From commodity to cosmopolitan. *The Teachers College Record, 106*(7), 1422–1443.
Lyotard, J. (1984). *The postmodern condition: A report on knowledge.* Minneapolis, MN: The University of Minnesota Press.
Maira, S. & Soep, E. (Eds.) (2005). *Youthscapes: The popular, the national, and the global.* Philadelphia, PA: University of Pennsylvania Press.
Meierkord, C. (2004). Syntactic variation in interactions across international Englishes. *English World-Wide, 25,* 109–132.
Moll, L. C., Amanti, C., Neff, D. & Gonzalez, N. (1992). Funds of knowledge for teaching: Using a qualitative approach to connect homes and classrooms. *Theory into Practice, 31,* 132–141.
Mørck, L. L. (2010). Expansive learning as production of community. *Yearbook of the National Society for the Study of Education, 109*(1), 176–191.
Mørck, L. L. (2011). Studying empowerment in a socially and ethnically diverse social work community in Copenhagen, Denmark. *Ethos: Journal of the Society for Psychological Anthropology, 39*(1), 115–137.
Mørck, L. L. & Huniche, L. (2006). Critical psychology in a Danish context. *Annual Review of Critical Psychology (Online),* (5).
Mørck, L. L., Hussain, K., Møller-Andersen, C., Ozupek, T., Palm, A. & Vorbeck, I. (2013).
Praxis development in relation to gang conflicts, Copenhagen, Denmark. *Outlines. Critical Practice Studies, 14*(2), 79–105.
Murrell, P. C. (2007). *Race, culture, and schooling: Identities of achievement in multicultural urban schools.* New York: Lawrence Erlbaum Associates.
Nielsen, K. & Kvale, S. (2006). The workplace: A landscape of learning. *Learning, Working, and Living.* Palgrave Macmillan, 119–135.
Norton, B. (2000). *Identity and language learning: Gender, ethnicity, and educational change.* Harlow, UK: Pearson Education.
Partnership for 21st Century Learning. (2015). *Framework for 21st century learning.* Retrieved October 19, 2015, from http://www.p21.org/storage/documents/P21_framework_0515.pdf.
Pennycook, A. (1994). *The cultural politics of English as an international language.* New York: Longman.
Phillipson, R. (1992). *Linguistic imperialism.* Oxford, UK: Oxford University Press.
Saussure, F. (1959). *Course in general linguistics.* New York: Columbia University Press.
Seidlhofer, B. (2004). Research perspectives on teaching English as a lingua franca. *Annual Review of Applied Linguistics, 24,* 209–239.
Shultz, L. (2007). Educating for global citizenship: Conflicting agendas and understandings. *The Alberta Journal of Educational Research, 53* (3), 248–258.
Skerrett, A. (2008). Racializing educational change: Melting pot and mosaic influences on educational policy and practice. *Journal of Educational Change, 9,* 261–280.

Skerrett, A. (2012). Languages and literacies in translocation: Experiences and perspectives of a transnational youth. *Journal of Literacy Research, 44*(4), 364–395.
Sleeter, C. & Stillman, J. (2005). Standardizing knowledge in a multicultural society. *Curriculum Inquiry, 35*(1), 27–46.
Valdés, G. (2001). *Learning and not learning English.* New York: Teacher's College Press.
Yosso, T. J. (2005). Whose culture has capital? A critical race theory discussion of community cultural wealth. *Race Ethnicity and Education, 8*(1), 69–91.
Zhao, Y. (2009). *Catching up or leading the way: American education in an age of globalization.* Alexandria, VA: ASCD.

10

MAPPING THE WEB OF FOREIGN LANGUAGE TEACHING AND TEACHER EDUCATION

Hatice Çelebi

UNIVERSITY OF MASSACHUSETTS AMHERST

Introduction

In this chapter I will focus on English foreign language (EFL) teaching and teacher education and discuss the ways worldwide English hegemony (Macedo, Dendrinos & Gounari, 2003) penetrates foreign language teacher education in countries where English is assumed to be key to the economic success of the nation and the economic wellbeing of its individuals. With this in mind, I would like to address the central formative elements of EFL teacher education and identity formation from a particular context, that of an insider from a country (Turkey) that may be considered as part of an "expanding circle" in reference to Kachru's (1985) concentric circles. It was in 2006 that Leech and Svartvik highlighted that this circle seemed to be "ever-expanding, strengthening the claims of English as the international language of today . . . and in the not too distant future, it will be appropriate to rename the 'Expanding Circle' the 'Expanded Circle'" (p. 5).

Phillipson (1992) draws on a distinction between "core" and "periphery" English-speaking countries. In the "core" are Britain, the United States, Canada, Australia, and New Zealand. In the periphery there are two types of countries: ones such as Japan and Norway, where English is used as an international link; and countries such as India, Nigeria, and Ghana, where English was imposed in colonial times and eventually became the language for intra-national communication. English, in this distinction, is placed at the center of the sociopolitical processes of imperialism, neo-colonialism, and global economic restructuring. This view analyzes the spread of English in relation to global inequality in terms of how it supplies positive development for the core countries and provides privileges to some people (primarily those in the "core") while being harmful in both obvious and subtle ways in the social, economic, and political spheres of the countries and people of the "periphery."

With the phenomenon of globalization, sociolinguists have been focusing on far-reaching implications of English hegemony for patterns of language use, linguistic change and variation, and its position as a lingua franca (Canagarajah, 2013; Cope & Kalantzis, 2000; García & Wei, 2014). They have also examined teaching methods and pedagogies in different genres, including discourses such as communicative language teaching, task-based learning, content and language-integrated learning (CLIL), computer mediated discourse, and, under the demands of the new capitalism shaped by globalization, the semiotic value of English (Breen & Candlin, 1980; Cameron, 2000; Czerniawska, 1998; Kramsch & Thorne, 2002; Tannen, 1984). Kramsch and Thorne (2002) review the gradual settling of "transmission of information" and communicative competence as the semiotic value of language in new times and, instead, propose a "ritual of engagement" (Tannen, 1984). The ritual of engagement focuses on sharing experiences, ideas, values, and sentiments rather than giving the language the value of a utilitarian economic exchange or considering language as a commodity. Critical studies have emerged covering many areas, including business and management. For instance, Czerniawska (1998) maintains that intensified global competition created a context for new managerial approaches that take language as a valuable commodity and a source for competition in the economic sector. One effect of this is the observed trend among employers who control and manage trivial details of employees' language and language use (Cameron, 2000; Du Gay, 1996), which takes away employee agency and creates an oppressive work environment that emphasizes the mechanics of the language rather than what was communicated.

A personal account highlights this trend of diminishing employee agency in the field of EFL teacher education while creating a hierarchical positioning with native/non-native speakers and reinforcing a "native speaker policy" (Phillipson, 1992). At the university in Turkey where I once worked we (the department faculty members) were asked to write a departmental report that summarized the two-year progress in the English Language Teaching (ELT) department. We were a group of academics and we prepared the report meticulously to submit to the board, which consisted only of the administrative faculty members, namely the vice-president and the deans, who were all native speakers of Turkish. After the board met we received an email from the dean asking that, from then on, the reports be first reviewed by a native speaker (of English, by implication) so that the text would not contain any spelling mistakes. In the report the word "assistant" was misspelled. Considering that a word processor would function like a native speaker of English in this case, a reconsideration of the responsibilities of the academy is called for. In the Foreword (p. x) of *A sanctuary of their own: Intellectual refugees in the academy* (Sassower, 2000), about "this landscape of technicist education," Macedo asks, "Can higher education institutions that function as cultural reproduction models create pedagogical spaces to prepare citizens who will be agents of change and who will be committed to invest in the life of the mind?"

The following sections provide an overview of the historical, socioeconomic, and sociopolitical dimensions that shape EFL teacher education and form the groundwork for my discussion on how English hegemony works to affect foreign language teacher education and create social, economic, and political inequalities for EFL teachers by othering them in Turkey and in other similar contexts (Derrida, 1973; Lacan, 1977; Lévinas, 1974; Said, 1978). I take an emic perspective and scrutinize two interrelated levels of the formative context that marginalizes foreign language teachers. The first level covers EFL and EFL teacher education as well as policy-related issues. The second level covers EFL teacher exchange-value discourse, along with EFL teacher education and teacher identity construction.

EFL Education

Today, Turkish national foreign language education policy mainly focuses on teaching English, but, until the 19th century, Western languages were not given much attention due to a focus on religious education and political interactions. Most foreign language education was Arabic, followed by French and German as the three foreign languages taught (Aygün, 2008; Sarıboğa-Alagöz, 2006). Turkey is one of the few monolingual nations that does not have a colonial past linked to Western nations (Bear, 1985). Nevertheless, its past offers a captivating picture. Yağmur (2001) describes it as follows:

> According to Ngugi (1994, cited in Alexander 1999: 39), in the African continent, the colonizing powers systematically undervalued the indigenous "people's culture, their art, dances, religions, history, geography, education, orature, and literature" and they deliberately elevated the languages of the colonizers. In the Ottoman case, as far as the Turkish language and people were concerned, there were no colonizing powers from outside that imposed a foreign language upon them, but it was their own rulers and intelligentsia that did so. Because of the widespread use of the Ottoman language in administration and education, the Turkish language was limited to daily communication. Over time, there appeared a huge gap between common folk and ruling classes. Intellectuals used the synthetic amalgam of Ottoman, and they distanced (rather alienated) themselves from the majority of people who spoke Turkish. Since Turkish was underrated as a means of scholarly writing, people came to believe that Turkish did not have adequate means and words for scientific work. As Alexander (1999) points out, there can be nothing more devastating than the underestimation of one's own mother tongue. In the case of Turkish, this wound was not inflicted by outside colonizing powers but by the Ottomans themselves.
>
> *(pp. 408–409)*

Despite the long history of teaching various foreign languages between the 10th and 19th centuries, literature covering the history of Turkish foreign language teacher education is limited because "the Turkish educational system does not seem to possess any well-formed approaches to foreign language teaching" (Nergis, 2011, p. 181).

In 1839 the Ministry of National Education (MONE) selected and sent talented young people to France to get their education in French and come back to teach it to young people. This attempt failed since the students sent to France did not have any controlled training (Tok, 2006). In the second half of the 18th century the Turkish government asked for help from the French government. As a result of this collaboration, Galatasaray Sultanisi was founded, which mainly taught French (the lingua franca at the time) as well as other languages with success (Tok, 2006). Bartu (2002) notes that, until the end of the 18th century, language was not considered a binding factor in Ottoman society in a nationalistic sense. Ortaylı (1983) states that the Turks were among the last groups to meet with nationalism, and Turkish as a symbol of national identity was accepted as the official language in the Ottoman Constitution with article 18 in December 1876 (Kuran, 1994). Prior to that time in Ottoman society, Arabic and Persian were the languages used as the medium of instruction, and French was used as a lingua franca (Bartu, 2002). In the second half of the 19th century, although it was decided that Turkish (rather than Arabic or Persian) was the official language, French took its place as the medium of instruction. The lack of materials in Turkish and a shortage of Turkish teachers exacerbated this situation (Demircan, 1988; Kuran, 1994). However, the issue of whether Turkish lacks the capacity to provide for education and scientific research still plays a role in the language policy debate (Sinanoğlu, 2000; Yücel, 1990).

In 1926 the first teacher education program was started to educate teachers of all disciplines. The program was later established as part of the Gazi Institute of Education, named after the founder of the Republic of Turkey, Gazi Mustafa Kemal Atatürk, in 1946. Departments of French in 1941, English in 1944, and German in 1947 were founded, with their three-year training periods increased to four years in 1978–1979. Between the 1950s and the 1980s the need for English language teachers increased. The number of students involved in immersion programs for education increased from 2,500 to 100,000 over the course of about 30 years. This created a great demand for English language teachers. A tendency to emphasize quantity over quality emerged. The number of English language teaching programs, as well as the number of students they accepted, also increased (Demircan, 2001). Offering alternative certification programs and recruiting teachers who did not graduate from departments of language pedagogy were two of the solutions, among others (Altundiş, 2006).

With a new law in 1982, the Higher Education Institution (HEI) and all other teacher educational institutions were transferred into existing university education faculties. The HEI is a central authority that "oversees the administrative and academic activities of the universities and coordinates the universities' activities with other government agencies" (Yıldırım & Ok, 2002, p. 262). Following this new law, reforms to teacher education were enacted (including foreign language teacher education), which increased the amount of practicum time. Programs were offered and steps were taken as constructive attempts to standardize and improve teacher education (Öztürk, 2005; Sağlam-Kürüm, 2005). However, in foreign language education programs the majority of the courses set by the HEI mainly comprised grammatical and structural knowledge of the language, and did not include courses concerning pedagogy or didactics (Salihoğlu, 2012). Between 1994 and 1999 the HEI began to restructure foreign language education with the help of the World Bank through a $23.1 million loan under the name of the World Bank-funded national education development project (NEDP) (Kavcar, 2002). The compulsory education period was raised from five to eight years, later causing teacher shortages. With the new restructuring, it was observed that there was a theoretical move from phonetics and grammatical structures towards more practice-based courses such as pedagogical grammar, discourse analysis, classroom-based curriculum, syllabus design, and testing (Altan, 1998). There were changes regarding the practicum, and MA programs with no thesis requirement were opened.

The restructuring was criticized: "Turkey has been pushed by international bodies to prepare an agenda for improving the quality of education and delivering compulsory education into mass in short term in 1996." (Tarman, 2010, p. 87). Changes in the practicum could not be implemented properly due to high student enrollment numbers of 4,000–6,000 (Salihoğlu, 2012). Kavcar (2002) lists 13 negative aspects of this restructuring, carried out by the restructuring committee. The first on this list was that, in addition to locals (Turkish faculty members), there were British and American "experts" from abroad who did not have sufficient background information about the teaching culture, conditions, and problems of the Turkish education system. He points out the systematic misjudgment in the decisions taken and delineates the negative effects the restructuring had for teachers of different disciplines. In sum, in the 1998–1999 academic year the practice component of pre-service teaching was increased, and teachers' competencies were defined (Ministry of Education, 2002). However, with the rapidly increasing population and a concern for expanding schooling, the teacher gap was filled with teachers who were not graduates of education faculties, and alternative solutions to the foreign language teacher shortfall were offered. In 2000 an agreement was signed between MONE and Anadolu University to start distance education phases in foreign language education to meet the urgent need. Later, studies raised questions as to whether the distance programs were effective in training foreign language education teachers (Özköse-Bıyık, 2007; Gültekin, 2006).

An alternative solution to training foreign language teachers has been training students through teaching certification programs. This means that undergraduate students of any discipline (for example, chemical engineering, mathematics, economics) of an English-medium university could become eligible to work as a foreign language teacher and be appointed in public schools after a short training of two semesters (Seferoğlu, 2004). One further alternative put into practice by MONE in 2000 was to appoint the graduates of English-medium programs in various fields of study as public-school teachers without any teaching certificate, resulting in "engineers, public administrators and so forth becoming English teachers in one day without any professional training at all" (Seferoğlu, 2004, p. 153). These "training" and certification processes starting in 2000 themselves devalued foreign language teaching, not just by instrumentalizing it but by implication, in that "anyone who has learned English can be a qualified English teacher." Additionally, in terms of quality, the idea that "anyone who speaks English can be an English teacher" resulted both in discontent with current foreign language teacher competencies and concerns and complaints about dissatisfied students, parents, and school administrators.

English is not one of the official languages of the nation; however, there is an increasing demand to have a working mastery of English since it is widely used in education and business. In the 2012–2013 academic year, with the enactment of a new law, 12 years of compulsory education were divided into three periods of four years (referred to as "4 + 4 + 4"), despite criticisms raised by education specialists (Finkel, 2012) and the nation's leading universities (Selvi, 2014). Although modifications have been made since that time, at present English education in public schools is introduced in the second grade with two hours of teaching per week, and continued with four hours in the fifth through eighth grades. In private schools, starting from the second grade, the number of hours of weekly English education may be as much as double that of public schools, reaching ten or more teaching hours. In terms of education at the tertiary level alone in 2016, there were around 190 public and private universities offering approximately 5,500 bachelor's degree programs, 1,500 (or around 28 percent) of which were instructed in English (ÖSYM Tablo 4, last updated in June 2016). This percentage was reported to be 18.5 percent of all bachelor's degree programs in 2013 (Arık & Arık, 2014). In these universities, newly registered students are required to complete an English-intensive preparatory year, after which they are expected to pass a proficiency exam at the end of the year in order to be able to start their departmental courses.

In terms of business, according to a July 2013 study based on data collected from the six most popular databases posting job vacancies, a working knowledge of English is required for more than 30 percent of jobs (British Council & TEPAV, 2013, p. 14). Based on the Quality of Life Surveys administered in collaboration with Eurofound in 2007, it was reported that the percentage of people in the Turkish workforce who agree that their level of English "well" affords them enhanced job prospects is 58 percent (cited in British Council & TEPAV, 2013, p. 15). These findings are especially noteworthy considering the fact that Turkey is the eighteenth largest economy in the world (World Bank Statistics, last updated in December 2016), and English is observed as a reform for academic internalization (Coleman,

2006) and upward mobility (Kirkpatrick, 2011). When this is the case, a systematic planning of foreign language teacher education that comes with a top-down acknowledgement of English foreign language teachers' role in shaping the economy is expected, and failing to bring English learners to a working knowledge of English is detrimental to the economies of knowledge and finance. However, whether this is how administrators, managers, and policy-makers deal with this planning is questionable.

Based on the results of Education First, the English Proficiency Index (EPI) ranks Turkey forty-third among forty-four countries (Koru & Akesson, 2011). The survey underlines Turkey's "very low proficiency" rank compared to its neighbors. There is a great deal of discontent with the "quality" of English language teaching across educational levels, from primary to tertiary. The most commonly reported obstacles are English language teachers' lack of knowledge about and competence in English, their traditional methodological approaches to teaching language, a lack of student motivation and interest in language learning, limited resources and technological equipment in classrooms, the number of hours students are exposed to English at schools and the age the exposure starts, and a shortage of English teachers. Studies reporting these obstacles in foreign language education do not shy away from relating them to foreign language teacher education; however, these studies do not analyze influential socioeconomic, sociopolitical, and cultural structures at the micro and macro levels. Both in private and public educational arenas, English language teachers are almost always scolded for their failure to bring the country to a desired level of English language competence. To change this state of affairs, foreign language teacher education programs have been structured and restructured constantly, taking "external expert" opinions, reports, models, curricula, materials, and resources into consideration. Phillipson (1992) argues, "Linguicism has taken over from racism as a subtler way of hierarchizing social groups in the contemporary world" (p. 241).

Following the overview of developments in foreign language teacher education based on the literature summarized above, I maintain that there is an observable tendency concerning foreign language teacher education in Turkey, which I describe as follows: the supremacy of English in education, accompanied by an increasing population, led the government to make decisions to apply immediate solutions to problems as they arose. The emphasis on teaching English and teaching in English created a situation where Turkey is insufficient in foreign language teacher education. This alone created a dependence on "core" countries (Phillipson, 1992) at times, while the causes of this dependence were not properly addressed by governmental or local solutions. In fact, it seems these so-called solutions only appeared to deepen the problems and cause more dependence, including financial dependence. The answer to why Turkey puts so much emphasis on teaching English and teaching in English seems to be grounded in an instrumentalist orientation highlighting national/individual economic development, but whether there is a proven causality between the two is still a valid question (see discussions about China in Feng, 2009; Hu, 2005; Niu & Wolff, 2005; Nunan, 2003).

EFL Teacher Education

Foreign language teacher education policy can be understood at the macro level as the national policies that determine the content of knowledge foundation courses in pre-service training or the number of practicum hours. It can also be understood at the micro level by referring to emerging social dynamics that determine teaching as a social practice; for example, teachers' agency in implementing macro-level policies. What shapes foreign language teacher education is closely linked to the practices and processes of language policy; i.e., creation, interpretation, and appropriation (Hornberger & Johnson, 2007) as well as the social context in which teachers are educated across the macro and micro levels.

A combination of macro and micro language policy analyses evokes the notion of "governmentality," proposed and reproduced by Foucault (1978 [2001]) and taken up by scholars focusing on language policy (e.g., Johnson, 2010; Pennycook, 1998, 2007). According to Foucault (1982), "government" does not merely refer to the government of the state. It also refers to a collection of multiple practices arising from self-governing that is enforced by the power that circulates within social institutions and communities: "the government of children, of souls, of communities, of families, of the sick . . . To govern, in this sense, is to structure the possible field of action of others" (Foucault, 1982, p. 790). In this sense, the emphasis is not on the state-driven, but on the contextual practices and discourses of self-governing. This theoretical approach is especially important for language policy analysis as well as foreign language teacher education policy analysis.

Tollefson (2000) explains that language policy refers to "a wide range of governmental and non-governmental actions designed to influence language acquisition and language use" (p. 13); one of its main purposes is "to manage language conflicts in multilingual situations" (p. 14), which is a "utopian dream of a single world language reducing language conflict" (p. 14). As research from language policy and planning (LPP) (Fishman, 1979; Haugen, 1983) moved towards critical language policy (CLP) (Tollefson, 2002, 2006; Watson-Gegeo & Gegeo, 1995) and the ethnography of language policy (ELP) (Hornberger & Johnson, 2007; Johnson, 2009), the theoretical framework of research in the topic has also shifted.

ELP studies embrace Foucault's (1982) notion of governmentality and emphasize the role of institutions and communities, policy-making agencies, and actors or "arbiters" (Johnson, 2010; Menken, 2008) in language policy-making processes. Along the same lines, I maintain that the theoretical tenets of ELP can be extended to foreign language education policy with the following premise: foreign language teacher education is determined by myriad language policy processes (creation, interpretation, and appropriation) that function at the macro and micro levels. Moreover, in a context where monolingual language policy is dominant, foreign language teacher education inevitably works to marginalize foreign language teachers through the complex workings of agencies or actors who are in power and are the authorities in knowledge construction and policy-making.

Monolingual policy is a one-language policy approach that serves the purpose of achieving economic success and political power rather than the exclusive use of language for communication. There are four main areas in which government agencies make decisions to form policies: medium of instruction, which languages will be taught, which languages teachers must know, and which languages will be used in public arenas such as courts, government offices, and voting (Tollefson, 2000). When non-governmental agencies and individual workplaces adopt a language policy similar to the government's, parallel practices concerning foreign language teacher education will be implemented and appropriated. Blommaert (1999, cited in McGroarty, 2010) suggests that, in order to examine the complexity of factors determining language policy, we need to scrutinize historicity, materialism, and verifiable reproducibility. On the same note, in this section I would like to comment upon two relatively recent baseline studies conducted by two agencies, the Economic Policy Research Foundation (referred to as TEPAV, with the Turkish acronym, due to its frequent use by international audiences), and the British Council (BC). I will briefly touch upon their proposed recommendations for foreign language education to form a case for a heuristic analysis of the discipline.

In November 2015 a report of a study conducted between March and April 2015 over a five-week period by BC and TEPAV (supported by HEI) was published. It explored two broad research questions: "What are the conditions in which pre- and in-sessional courses of English are offered in public and foundation universities in Turkey and how can these conditions be enhanced?" (British Council & TEPAV, 2015, p. 13). It examined English teaching in Turkey, using lesson observations, questionnaires, structured interviews, and focus groups. There were visits to 38 universities in 15 cities, surveys of 4,300 students and 400 teachers, observations of 65 classes, and interviews with 72 teachers and administrators. The report presented the problems and difficulties experienced in English language teaching in Turkish universities and proposed recommendations, some of which were interpreted and put into practice by HEI at the national level, to be implemented by all tertiary-level public and private universities in the country.

The 2015 study was a continuation of another study, which was also carried out by the same two institutions (TEPAV and BC). That study covered Turkish state schools at the primary, middle, high, and vocational school levels and analyzed the current state of English language teaching and learning in state schools. It was a large-scale study comprising 80 classes of English from 48 schools in different cities around Turkey; there were 87 interviews with teachers, and a survey of 1,394 parents/guardians and 19,380 students, conducted between February and July 2013.

Both the 2013 and 2015 reports are comprehensive and require a follow-up on whether the recommendations proposed by the reports have been put into practice, and a critical analysis of why a recommendation should not be carried out. For example, in the 2013 report it is recommended that a sustainable system of in-service training for English teachers should be developed and continuing professional development with an incentive scheme should be offered (BC & TEPAV, 2013, p. 54). The same recommendation has been repeated in the 2015 report (BC & TEPAV, 2015, p. 111):

> **Recommendation** *English teachers should have greater opportunities to access professional development as part of a quality assurance and accreditation scheme. In particular, training should be available in two vital areas:*
>
> a) **EAP/ESP:** All English teachers should undergo a short, intensive training programme in EAP/ESP, and some teachers in each university should be offered longer-term training such as that available by distance from some universities.
> b) **Teaching speaking skills**: All teachers should undergo training in techniques for incorporating student-student interaction at every stage of the lesson, with speaking integrated into every activity, regardless of the skill being practised. ELT publishers may offer such training as part of the package of materials sold to a university.

Referring to the 2015 study, Aydın (2016) comments, "Being the largest study carried out on Turkish higher education, there is no doubt that the results and the implications of the report will continue to be discussed in various contexts in the country" (p. 75), which I hope will be the case. Cooper (1989) developed a specific language planning question generated from decision-making theory in political science: "Who makes what decisions, why, how, under what conditions, and with what effect?" (p. 88). This heuristic approach is noteworthy for foreign language teacher education, particularly when such large-scale studies are conducted and recommendations are taken up to be turned into policies.

For instance, the dynamics regarding English teaching and the profile of teachers greatly differ in Turkey. For one thing, the systems concerning English language teacher recruitments for private and public schools are different. However, most studies reporting the obstacles in English language teaching or teacher professional development do not differentiate between the two. Private school administrators have their own approach to recruitment, which may include formal standardized interviews, testing basic and subject matter skills, observing actual teaching in real classrooms, or through demonstration teaching sessions. Public schools, on the other hand, only require teacher candidates to take a centralized exam, called KPSS (Selection Examination for Professional Posts in Public Organizations). KPSS has evolved from the problematic gap between "supply and demand." I use this phrase purposefully and ironically in order to draw attention to how neoliberal econometric metaphors affect the euphemistic level of discourse. Starting from June

2013, in this exam there are four sections a teacher candidate is tested from: general knowledge and ability (15 percent), general culture (15 percent), educational sciences (20 percent), subject knowledge (50 percent), responding to 290 multiple choice questions in 270 minutes in total in two sessions (morning and afternoon). Depending on the position vacancies for each teaching subject, the Ministry of Education announces the minimum scores to be appointed as a teacher for each teaching subject. As a result, the scenario whereby a teacher candidate who scores 99 out of 100 in KPSS is not recruited, while another candidate with a score of 17 gets appointed due to the shortage in numbers of teachers in different teaching subjects, is not rare (Kılıçkaya & Krajka, 2013, p. 99). The fact that Turkey puts such an emphasis on teaching English and in English creates a huge "market," which is, for English teachers, characterized by competition and a never-ending race for degrees and external certifications in order to work in private schools, and by perceived discrepancies and attitudes due to the centralized exam scores teachers get appointed with. Going back to Cooper's heuristic approach, unless language teacher education policies are scrutinized under five components (i.e., who makes what decisions, why, how, under what conditions, and with what effect at the national and international levels), foreign language teacher education will remain a subject of a discipline that cannot realize itself.

EFL Teacher Exchange-Value

The idea that language functions as a form of symbolic capital used in return for material capital and, as such, shapes social categories, identities, social relations, and economic conditions is not new (Bourdieu, 1977, 1982; Gal, 1989; Irvine, 1989). It is with this perspective that Heller (2010) maintains that language is part of what makes the social order and "we cannot abstract away from the value attached to linguistic forms and practices or from their links to all kinds of social activities and to the circulation of resources of all kinds that social order mediates" (p. 102). Interest in analyzing language as a commodity has recently increased since the monetary value of language is taking various forms that are now considered to be immediately exchangeable for material goods. In addition, a working-level knowledge of language seems to be the prerequisite to getting access to resources and being considered eligible to present other resources that one is required to have in different areas, such as education and business. Under the order of late capitalism and neo-colonialism, linguistic hegemony is managed against the background of the global market share and economy, which comes across as politically neutral and creates centrality of English in areas such as tourism, marketing and advertising, language teaching, translation, call centers, and performance art. These are seen as commodities and "as a resource to be produced, controlled, distributed, valued and constrained" (Heller, 2010, p. 108). Given such a state of linguistic materialism, one important question to ask is where the foreign language teacher stands in this global market with the exchange-value of what they do as a profession. Focusing on this question, I will argue that a paradoxical and artificial discourse has been dominating the teaching profession and the foreign language teacher profession. This discourse denies teachers' exchange-value, which creates an inequality by shaping the social order to push teachers down despite their role as knowledge and language workers, if we may awkwardly adopt these terms in order not to ignore the reality and its subtle contribution to a hegemonic, dominant ideology.

The Organization for Economic Co-operation and Development (OECD) publishes a series of books, OECD Insights (2007), written for public perusal. Chapter Two of the Insights entitled "Human Capital" is allocated to "The Value of People." The book introduces the chapter by touching upon elements of economic growth and points out that "[i]n the global knowledge economy, people's skills, learning, talents and attributes—their human capital—have become key to both their ability to earn a living and to wider economic growth" (p. 21). In this chapter, with the warning that economies do not necessarily have to grow, it is explained that there are four main elements of economic growth: land, labor or workers, the capital or the assets and money, and, lastly, enterprise or initiative to turn land into, for example, a business such as a factory.

The notion of human capital is closely related to the second factor, labor or workers. It is pointed out that, until the 20th century, economists understood labor as "worker as a mass." There were notable individual exceptions, such as Scottish economist Adam Smith in the 18th century. As stated in "Human Capital" (2017, p. 29), Smith believed that "workers' individual capabilities were a kind of capital—an asset just like a spinning wheel or a flour mill that could yield returns," and today it is widely agreed that human capital (i.e., the importance of people because of their abilities, knowledge, and competencies) is a key element to economic growth. As Hiver and Dörnyei (2015) maintain, "Clearly, finding and retaining the most effective teachers is an imperative for any society investing in its own continued future growth" (p. 1). Darling-Hammond (2005) summarized the situation around a decade ago in relation to the term "knowledge-based economy" and stated that most countries have made reforms in their teacher education systems, "recognizing that preparing accomplished teachers who can effectively teach a wide array of learners to high standards is essential to economic and political survival" (p. 237).

However, the discourse created by policy-makers around teachers in general, and similarly around English language teachers specifically, generates a value system that disregards teachers' role in the knowledge economy, which in turn marginalizes foreign language teachers by depriving them of financial and social status in society. Teachers are "the architects of society" (Hiver & Dörnyei, 2015) since they are in charge of raising the next generation of citizens. However, their symbolic role as architects has not been given the same importance and weight as the actual designers of buildings. The analogical comparison is far removed from the reality it is assumed to emerge from.

To illustrate in more concrete terms, according to the online database indeed.com, a design architect's average salary is $102,891 per year in the United States. This salary is estimated from 24,124 employees, users, and past and present job advertisements on the website over the past 12 months, dating from January 17, 2017 (indeed.com job vacancy database results for architects, 2017). The same database reports English as a Second Language (ESL) teachers' salary to be $46,115 per year, which is estimated from 3,374 employees, users, and past and present job advertisements during the same time period (indeed.com job vacancy database results for English as a Second Language teacher, 2017).

In addition to the relatively limited role of English foreign language teachers in the knowledge economy, reflected by their financial status, an evaluation of teachers that denies their role as economic facilitators of the knowledge-based economy has also been maintained. For example, Arne Duncan, (LinkedIn, 2015), the former Secretary of Education in the US Department of Education, commented on July 20, 2015, that "We are in the midst of a new era—one with more engaging lessons and creativity and innovation, which is bringing joy back into the classroom. For adults willing to stick with it, there simply could not be a better time to be a teacher." The same year, in Turkey, the Minister of National Education, Nabi Avcı, in his speech to celebrate Teachers' Day, noted that "Her öğretmen aynı zamanda bir değerler eğitimcisidir. Matematik, fizik, beden eğitimi öğretmeni de sınıf öğretmeni de aynı zamanda ve öncelikle bir mürebbi veya mürebbiyedir." (MEB Öğretmenler Günü, 2015), which translates as, "Every teacher is also a values educator. A math, physics, or physical education teacher and a classroom teacher is at the same time and in the first place a values educator" (translated by the author). As illustrated by these two examples, the profession has been frequently romanticized and mystified; teachers have been depicted with descriptions such as facilitators of engaging activities that potentially lead to learning, creativity, and joy, and as missionaries responsible for the transmission of values to the young generation. In the context of the knowledge economy, the total neglect of the ideas that teachers are "the architects of the future" as active producers of the knowledge economy and that the teaching profession is more than values transmission appears to form the evaluative discourse in the political, economic, and social milieu that the teaching profession is shaped by.

How such evaluative discourse denies teachers and foreign language teachers their social and financial status in society can be explained through the subtle workings of value priming. Until relatively recently, the main function of language was seen to focus on ideational, conceptual, or denotational meaning, and connotation was thought to be "lying outside the core meaning" (Backhouse, 1992, p. 297). However, even more recently, evaluation and evaluative prosody have become equally as important. Partington, Duguid, and Taylor (2013) point out that evaluation is "pervasive in practically all forms of linguistic communication" (p. 44). Stubbs (2001) maintains, "the whole point of an utterance may be to express the speaker's attitude, evaluation and point of view" (p. 198).

Describing evaluation is complex when applied to real-life contexts (Hunston, 2010), but the notion of evaluation can be taken in a dualistic, bi-nominal, and essentialist sense defined as "indication that something is good or bad" (Hunston, 2004, p. 157). The parameters of good or bad can extend to wider interrelated notations such as certainty/uncertainty, expectedness/unexpectedness, and praise/blame expressed overtly or covertly. "William and Mary got a divorce," "William divorced his wife, Mary," "Mary was divorced by William," and "William got a divorce" (Partington et. al 2013, p. 45) demonstrate different and relatively overt evaluations.

Evaluations are socially and psychologically meta-functional; while communicating their evaluations, speakers share their value system and express group belonging through sharing the same value system. In this way people construct and maintain relationships (Hunston & Thompson 2000). Partington et al. (2013) comment:

> Secondly, signalling evaluations both explicitly and implicitly can be used to direct, control and even manipulate the behaviour of others, generally to the advantage of the individual performing the evaluation (and this is where the social and individual functions of evaluation combine). Evaluation is the engine of persuasion. Speakers employ it to convince an audience of what should be seen as right and proper and what is not and that therefore the audience should conduct itself in a manner appropriate to the goal of achieving the former and eschewing the latter. Thus, as well as reflect, it can impose, overtly or covertly, a value system.
>
> *(p. 46)*

Hoey (2005) argues that (native) language users store words that they know in the context in which they have heard or read them, and through these *lexical primings* they build up a collection of words and phrases of context. When this theory of language is extended to social learning, it is proposed that, similar to lexical primings, value primings from previous contacts with other people are significant. They facilitate the "individual's ability with the in-group in the process of socialization" (Partington et al. 2013, p. 46), especially if the value primings come from people of "high status or affective significance" (p. 46), as exemplified by the comments from Duncan and Avcı. In light of the discussion in this section, I maintain that the context of the knowledge-based economy in which a working mastery of English is presumed to be a key to better financial prospects, and the paradoxical discourse that denies English language teachers their lucrative position in the economy, create a formative context that marginalizes foreign language teachers by romanticizing and mystifying their role in the knowledge society. The following section aims to lay out the historical and political context of the marginalization of foreign language teacher education, specifically in reference to foreign language education policy in Turkey.

EFL Teacher Identity Formation

> The identities we have, the stories we live by, tend to show different facets depending on the situations in which we find ourselves. This is no less true for teachers in their professional knowledge landscapes. Different facets, different identities, can show up, be reshaped and take on new life in different landscape settings. But . . . identities both have origins and change.
>
> *(Connelly & Clandinin, 1999, pp. 94–95)*

The above is cited in Nelson (2008, p. 207) who further comments, "[w]hen we intentionally form narratives of [these] experiences and inquire into them through a commitment to reflective practice, we are given the opportunity to identify the change, to consciously direct the change and thereby grow in confidence in the person we bring to our classroom" (pp. 207–208). I would like to build on the comment with a personal narrative for my discussion of foreign language teacher identity construction.

It was two years ago that I started teaching at a university education faculty in the (English) Foreign Language Education Department. I am a native speaker of Turkish and a non-native speaker of English, and I was given a faculty position to teach to prospective English language teachers, also native speakers of Turkish and non-native speakers of English. The day I was invited to sign my contract to teach in the department, I met the university president, who is also Turkish, a native Turkish speaker, and a non-native English speaker. As he handed over the contract for me to sign he congratulated me on my new job and, without further comment, said he did not believe that "Turkish people can teach English" (translated by the author). This informal comment is certainly not mundane, given the circumstances. It depicts "a story to live by" in a negative sense and raises questions about whether I can grow in confidence in the person I bring to the classroom. Foreign language teachers, educators, and student teachers all experience stories of this sort, which generate identity formation conflicts, perhaps more so than teachers of other disciplines due to the prevalent native/non-native speaker distinction.

Teachers' native/non-native status has been significant in the English as a Second Language (ESL) and English as a Foreign Language (EFL) fields because this identification functions as a determiner of certain privileges, such as getting better jobs (Clark & Paran, 2007; Mahboob, Uhrig, Newman & Hartford, 2004; Moussu & Llurda, 2008). Native English-speaking teachers (NESTs) are associated with "the ideal model" in terms of oral skills such as pronunciation, pragmatic skills, grammatical knowledge, and cultural background (Braine, 2010; Kirkpatrick, 2010; Wang, 2012). Although this perception has been challenged and has been, for instance, attributed to the "native speaking model" and described as the "native speaker fallacy" (Phillipson, 1992), the practice of favoring native speakers as language teachers seems to dominate the field (Canagarajah, 2005; Wang, 2012). It has been observed that the teaching strengths of NESTs and non-native English-speaking teachers (non-NESTs) are diverse, and each group contributes to the classroom differently. However, there is a gap in the research exploring the factors contributing to why non-NESTs are depicted as having one rigid identity (despite the diversity in the group [Huang, 2014; Park, 2012]) and the reasons why NESTs and non-NESTs might be preferred over the other. Research of this kind would inevitably refer to critical notions such as ideology, Eurocentric dominant values, linguistic imperialism and rights, and critical pedagogy along with the work of scholars such as Donaldo Macedo, Claire Kramsch, Robert Phillipson, Tove Skutnabb-Kangas, Bessie Dendrinos, and Alastair Pennycook, among others.

A significant body of literature exists arguing that learning to be a teacher and forming a teacher identity are as important as learning how to teach (Flores & Day, 2006; Hallman, 2015; Meijer, de Graaf & Meirink, 2011). Beauchamp and Thomas (2009, p. 184) emphasize that "the choice of teaching discipline may also affect identity, as disciplines may tend to have particular cultures of their own" (see Barty, 2004; Pennington, 2002; Varghese, Morgan, Johnston & Johnson, 2005). They point out that these cultures act as formative contexts, and exposure to these contexts results in confrontations with one's teacher identity. Such a case is evident in the discipline of teaching foreign language teachers, and more so when teachers themselves are originally learners and users of the foreign language they are teaching. Hiver and Dörnyei (2015) and Kelchtermans (2011) report the challenges that foreign language teachers encounter and call attention to the pressures they are exposed to. The source of challenges varies, arising from educational authorities, school managers, issues of accountability, increasing knowledge, and "command of the subject without the support mechanisms to do so; and demands from large groups of learners who not only pose academic challenges, but also import the turbulences of their personal lives into the social setting of school" (Hiver & Dörnyei, 2015, p. 2). The anxiety and conflict inherent in L2 teachers' work are reported to cause resistance to novelty, giving priority to survival rather than to pedagogic concerns, and serving as a defense mechanism against "the unusually high level" (Hiver & Dörnyei, 2015, p. 2) of stress (Kim, 2011; Littlewood, 2007; Olsen & Sexton, 2009; Tribble, 2012; Wedell, 2009).

How teacher identity is constructed and how it can be used to explore teacher development have both gained emphasis in the literature over the years (Olsen, 2008; Riopel, 2006; Sachs, 2005). According to Gee (2000), "identity" is "[b]eing recognized as a certain 'kind of person,' in a given context" (p. 99). It is shaped by the conditions and through opportunities supplied by the situational atmosphere (Bauman, 1996; Holland & Lave, 2001; Roth, 2004). It "serves as the repository of particular experiences in classrooms and schools, the site of thoughts, attitudes, emotions, beliefs and values" (Zembylas, 2003, p. 107). As such, construction of teacher identity is an ongoing process and happens through a continuous and changing process of formation (Akkerman & Meijer, 2011; Alsup, 2006; Varghese et al., 2005). Identity work has been scrutinized through the exploration of a variety of sources, such as personal experiences, self-awareness, self-observation and reflective teaching, and constructing "selves" (e.g., Bailey, Curtis & Nunan, 2001; Bukor, 2015; Cattley, 2007; Lamote & Engels, 2010). However, there is little evidence in the literature that foreign language teacher education programs include and offer core or elective courses where an issue as important as foreign language teacher identity formation is studied and explored. Grubbs, Jantarach and Kettem (2010) emphasize that factors leading to preferences "need to be examined carefully in terms of how extraneous variables might affect conclusions" (p. 573). Studies such as this edited volume provide an opportunity for a careful examination of such extraneous variables.

Conclusion

In this chapter I have explored the workings of English foreign language teaching and its trajectories in constructing subjectivities, categorizations, and social inequality in today's global market. I have tied this analysis to the historical, political, and economic conditions focusing on the symbolic and material mechanisms at work. My purpose has been to contribute to the "critical dialogue and political engagement" proposed by Kramsch in this volume, with an effort to participate in the process of decolonizing foreign language teaching, as suggested by the title of the volume. Tuck and Yang (2012) warn educators against using decolonization as a metaphor because "it turns decolonization into an empty signifier to be filled with any track towards liberation" (p. 7). They emphasize that what should be unsettling about decolonization is the history of "settler colonialism," which is a form of colonialism "in that settlers come with the intention of making a new home on the land, a homemaking that insists on settler sovereignty over all things in their new domain" (p. 5). Without critical dialogue and political engagement, I agree that decolonization as a metaphor creates an empty signifier since, quoting from Kramsch in this volume, "[t]here are no longer any clear-cut distinctions between colonizers and colonized." In the metaphor of decolonization in this volume, the hidden notion of "settlers" is not an empty filler but, rather, is a complex web of fine-grained symbolic and material mechanisms at work, which we should be able to map.

References

Akkerman, S. F. & Meijer, P. C. (2011). A dialogical approach to conceptualizing teacher identity. *Teaching and Teacher Education, 27*(2), 308–319.

Alsup, J. (2006). *Teacher identity discourses: Negotiating personal and professional spaces.* Mahwah, NJ: Routledge.

Altan, M. Z. (1998). A call for change and pedagogy: A critical analysis of teacher education in Turkey. *European Journal of Education, 33*(4), 407–417.

Altundiş, E. (2006). *İngilizce öğretmenlerinin eğitimsel kökenleri ve dil öğretiminde karşılaştıkları sorunlar (Kayseri ili örneği).* Unpublished master's dissertation, Erciyes University, Kayseri.

Arik, B. T. & Arik, E. (2014). The role and status of English in Turkish higher education. *English Today, 30*(04), 5–10.

Aydın, B. (2016). Professional development of language teachers in Turkey: Building the bridge between pre-service and in-service teacher training. *ELT Research Journal, 5*(2), 74–83.

Aygün, S. (2008). *Türkiye'de yabancı dil eğitimi ve Avrupa dilleri ortak çerçeve program.* Unpublished master's dissertation, Beykent University, Istanbul.

Backhouse, A. E. (1992). Connotation. *International encyclopedia of linguistics, 1*, 297–298.

Bailey, K. M., Curtis, A., Nunan, D. & Fan, D. (2001). *Pursuing professional development: The self as source* (Vol. 63, No. 59, p. 4). Boston, MA: Heinle & Heinle.

Bartu, H. (2002). Independence Or Development?: An Overview Of Turkey's Foreign Language Education Policies. *Sosyal Bilimler Dergisi 2002–2003*, 59–80.

Barty, L. (2004). Embracing ambiguity in the artefacts of the past: Teacher identity and pedagogy. *Canadian Social Studies, 38*(3), 3.

Bauman, Z. (1996). From pilgrim to tourist—Or a short history of identity. In S. Hall and P. du Guy (Eds.), *Questions of cultural identity* (pp. 18–36). London: Sage.

Bear, J. M. (1985). Historical factors influencing attitudes towards foreign language learning in Turkey. *Journal of Human Sciences of Middle East Technical University*, 1, 27–36.

Beauchamp, C. & Thomas, L. (2009). Understanding teacher identity: An overview of issues in the literature and implications for teacher education. *Cambridge Journal of Education, 39*(2), 175–189.

Blommaert, J. (1999). The debate is open. *Language ideological debates*, 1–38.

Braine, G. (2010). *Nonnative speaker English teachers: Research, pedagogy and professional growth.* New York: Routledge.

Breen, M. P. & Candlin, C. N. (1980). The essentials of a communicative curriculum in language teaching. *Applied Linguistics, 1*, 89.

Bourdieu P. (1977). The economics of linguistic exchanges. *Social Science Information, 16*(6), 645–68.

Bourdieu P. (1982). Ce que parler veut dire. Paris: Fayard.

British Council & TEPAV. (2013, November). *Turkey national needs assessment of state school English language teaching.* Retrieved from https://www.britishcouncil.org.tr/sites/default/files/turkey_national_needs_asses sment_of_state_school_english_language_teaching.pdf.

British Council & TEPAV. (2015). *The state of English in higher education in Turkey.* Ankara: Yorum Basın Yayın.

Bukor, E. (2015). Exploring teacher identity from a holistic perspective: Reconstructing and reconnecting personal and professional selves. *Teachers and Teaching, 21*(3), 305–327.

Cameron, D. (2000). Styling the worker: Gender and the commodification of language in the globalized service economy. *Journal of Sociolinguistics, 4*(3), 323–347.

Canagarajah, A. S. (Ed.) (2005). *Reclaiming the local in language policy and practice.* Mahwah, NJ: Lawrence Earlbaum Associates.

Canagarajah, A. S. (2013). *Literacy as translingual practice: Between communities and classrooms.* London: Routledge.

Cattley, G. (2007). Emergence of professional identity for the pre-service teacher. *International Education Journal, 8*(2), 337–347.

Clark, E. & Paran, A. (2007). The employability of non-native speaker teachers of EFL: A UK survey. *System, 35*, 407–430.

Coleman, J. A. (2006). English-medium teaching in European higher education. *Language Teaching, 39*(01), 1–14.

Connelly, F. M. & Clandinin, D. J. (Eds.) (1999). *Shaping a professional identity: Stories of educational practice.* New York: Teachers College Press.

Cooper, R. L. (1989). *Language planning and social change.* New York: Cambridge University Press.

Cope, B. & Kalantzis, M. (2000). *Multiliteracies: Literacy learning and the design of social futures.* London: Psychology Press.

Czerniawska, F. (1998). *Corporate speak: The use of language in business.* London: Macmillan.

Darling-Hammond, L. (2005). Teaching as a profession: Lessons in teacher preparation and professional development. *Phi Delta Kappan, 87*(3), 237–240.

Demircan, Ö. (1988). Dünden bugüne Türkiye'de yabancı dil [Foreign languages in Turkey from past to today]. Istanbul: Remzi Kitabevi.

Demircan, Ö. (2001). *Dünden bugüne Türkiye'de Yabancı Dil.* Istanbul: Remzi Kitabevi.

Derrida, J. (1973). *Speech and phenomena, and other essays on Husserl's theory of signs.* Chicago, IL: Northwestern University Press.

Du Gay, P. (1996). *Consumption and identity at work.* London: Sage.

Feng, A. (2009). English in China: Convergence and divergence in policy and practice. *AILA Review, 22*(1), 85–102.

Finkel, A. (2012, March). What's 4 + 4 + 4? *International Herald Tribune.* Retrieved from http://latitude.blogs.nytimes.com/2012/03/23/turkeys-education-reform-bill-is-about-playing-politicswith-pedagogy/.

Fishman, J. S. (1979). Bilingual education, language planning and English. *English World-Wide, 1*(1), 11–24.

Flores, M. A. & Day, C. (2006). Contexts which shape and reshape new teachers' identities: A multi-perspective study. *Teaching and Teacher Education, 22*(2), 219–232.

Foucault M. (1978) [2001]. Governmentality. In J. D. Faubion (Ed.), *Essential works of Foucault, 1954–1984: Power* (Vol. 3) (pp. 201–222). London: Penguin.

Foucault, M. (1982). The subject and power. *Critical inquiry, 8*(4), 777–795.

Gal, S. (1989). Language and political economy. *Annual Review of Anthropology*, 18, 345–67.

García, O. & Wei, L. (2014). *Translanguaging: Language, Bilingualism and Education.* London: Palgrave Macmillan.

Gee, J. P. (2000). Identity as an analytic lens for research in education. *Review of Research in Education, 25*, 99–125.

Grubbs, S. J., Jantarach, V. & Kettem, S. (2010). Studying English with Thai and native-speaking teachers. *Teachers and teaching: theory and practice, 16*(5), 559–576.

Gültekin, M. (2006). Using of distance education approach in teacher training: Anadolu University open education model. *The Turkish Online Journal of Educational Technology – TOJET, 5*(1), 101–116.

Hallman, H. L. (2015). Teacher as 'shape-shifter': Exploring the intersection of New Times and the teaching of English language arts. *Changing English, 22*(3), 282– 293.

Haugen, E. (1983). The implementation of corpus planning: Theory and practice. In J. Cobarrubias and J. A. Fishman (Eds.), *Progress in language planning* (pp. 269– 290). The Hauge: Mouton.

Heller, M. (2010). The commodification of language. *Annual Review of Anthropology, 39*, 101–114.

Hiver, P. & Dörnyei, Z. (2015) Language teacher immunity: A double-edged sword. *Applied Linguistics 2015*, 1–20.

Hoey, M. (2005). *Lexical priming: A new theory of words and language.* Stroud, UK: Psychology Press.

Holland, D. & Lave, J. (Eds.) (2001). *History in person: Enduring struggles, contentious practice, intimate identities*. Santa Fe, NM: School of American Research Press.
Hornberger, N. H. & Johnson, D. C. (2007). Slicing the onion ethnographically: Layers and spaces in multilingual language education policy and practice. *TESOL Quarterly*, 509–532.
Hu, G. (2005). Reforms of basic English-language education in China: An overview. *International Journal of Educational Reform, 14*(2), 140.
Huang, I. C. (2014). Contextualizing teacher identity of non-native-English speakers in US secondary ESL classrooms: A Bakhtinian perspective. *Linguistics and Education, 25*, 119–128.
Hunston, S. (2004). Counting the uncountable: Problems of identifying evaluation in a text and in a corpus. *Corpora and discourse, 9*, 157–188.
Hunston, S. (2010). *Corpus approaches to evaluation: Phraseology and evaluative language*. New York: Routledge.
Hunston, S. & Thompson, G. (Eds.) (2000). *Evaluation in text: Authorial stance and the construction of discourse*. Oxford, UK: Oxford University Press.
Indeed.com database: job vacancy results for architects (2017, April 9). Retrieved from https://www.indeed.com/salaries/Architect-Salaries.
Indeed.com database: job vacancy results for English as a second language teacher (2017, April 9). Retrieved from https://www.indeed.com/salaries/English-As-A-Second-Language-Teacher-Salaries?period=yearly.
Irvine J. (1989). When talk isn't cheap: language and political economy. *Am. Ethnol. 16*(2), 248–67.
Johnson, D. C. (2009). Ethnography of language policy. *Language Policy, 8*(2), 139–159.
Johnson, D. C. (2010). Implementational and ideological spaces in bilingual education language policy. *International Journal of Bilingual Education and Bilingualism, 13*(1), 61–79.
Kachru, B. B. (1985). Standards, codification, and sociolinguistic realm: The English language in the outer circle. In R. Quirk and H. G. Widdowson (Eds.), *English in the World* (pp. 11–30). Cambridge, UK: Cambridge University Press.
Kavcar, C. (2002). Cumhuriyet döneminde dal ögretmeni yetiştirme. *Ankara Üniversitesi Eğitim Bilimleri Fakültesi Dergisi, 35*(1–2), 1–14.
Kelchtermans, G. (2011). Vulnerability in teaching: The moral and political roots of a structural condition. In C. Day and J. C. K. Lee (Eds.), *New Understandings of Teacher's Work: Emotions and Emotional Change* (pp. 65–82). Netherlands: Springer.
Kılıçkaya, F. & Krajka, J. (2013). A review of language teacher selection and recruitment in Turkey and Poland. *International Journal of Research studies in language Learning, 2*(5), 93-104.
Kim, J. R. (2011). Influence of teacher preparation programmes on preservice teachers' attitudes toward inclusion. *International Journal of Inclusive Education, 15*(3), 355–377.
Kirkpatrick, A. (Ed.) (2010). *The Routledge handbook of world Englishes*. New York: Routledge.
Kirkpatrick, A. (2011). English as an Asian lingua franca and the multilingual model of ELT. *Language Teaching, 44*(02), 212–224.
Koru, S. & Akesson, J. (2011). Türkiye'nin İngilizce açığı. *Ankara: Türkiye Ekonomi Politikaları Araştırma Vakfı. 1*, 2012.
Kramsch, C. & Thorne, S. (2002). Foreign language learning as global communicative practice. In D. Block and D. Cameron (Eds.), *Language learning and teaching in the age of globalization* (pp. 83–100). London: Routledge.

Kuran, E. (1994). Türkiye'nin Batılılaşması ve Milli Meseleler. Türkiye Diyanet Vakfi Yayınları.
Lacan, J. (1977). Function and field of speech and language (1953). In A. Sheridan (Ed.), *Écrits: A selection* (pp. 30–113). London: Tavistock Publications.
Lamote, C. & Engels, N. (2010). The development of student teachers' professional identity. *European Journal of Teacher Education, 33*(1), 3–18.
Leech, G. N. & Svartvik, J. (2006). *English: One tongue, many voices.* Basingstoke, UK: Palgrave Macmillan.
Lévinas, E. (1974). Autrement qu'? tre, ou au-del? de l'essence. *The Hague: Martinus Nijhoff [Levinas, E.(1981). [Otherwise than being, or beyond essence. The Hague: Martinus Nijhoff] (Translated by A. Lingis).*
LinkedIn, (2015, November), Arne Duncan's post. Retrieved from https://www.linkedin.com/pulse/leading-from-classroom-arne-duncan.
Littlewood, W. (2007). Communicative and task-based language teaching in East Asian classrooms. *Language Teaching, 40*(3), 243–249.
Macedo, D., Dendrinos, B. & Gounari, P. (2003). *Hegemony of English.* Boulder, CO: Paradigm Publishers.
Mahboob, A., Uhrig, K., Newman, K. & Hartford, B. S. (2004). Children of a lesser English: Status of nonnative English speakers as college-level English as a second language teachers in the United States. In L. Kamhi-Stein (Ed.), *Learning and teaching from experience: Perspectives on nonnative English-speaking professionals* (pp. 100–120). Ann Arbor, MI: University of Michigan Press.
McGroarty, M. (2010). Language and ideologies. *Sociolinguistics and language education,* 3–39.
MEB Öğretmenler Günü, (2015, November 24). Retrieved from http://ankara.meb.gov.tr/www/baskent-ogretmenevinde-ogretmenler-gunu-kutlamasi/icerik/802.
Meijer, P. C., de Graaf, G. & Meirink, J. (2011). Key experiences in student teachers' development. *Teachers and Teaching: Theory and Practice, 17*(1), 115–129.
Menken, K. (2008). *English learners left behind: Standardized testing as language Policy.* Clevedon, UK: Multilingual Matters.
Moussu, L. & Llurda, E. (2008). Nonnative English speaking English language teachers: History and research. *Language Teaching, 41*(3), 315–348.
Nelson, C. D. (2008). Shifting teacher identities through inquiry into 'stories to live by' *Reflective Practice, 9*(2), 207–217.
Nergis, A. (2011) Foreign language teacher education in Turkey: A historical overview. *Procedia – Social and Behavioral Sciences Volume 15,* 181–185.
Niu, Q. & Wolff, M. (2005). Is EFL a modern Trojan horse? *English Today 84, 21*(4), 55–60.
Nunan, D. (2003). The impact of English as a global language on educational policies and practices in the Asia-Pacific region. *TESOL Quarterly, 37*(4), 589–613.
OECD Insights (2007). "Human Capital: How what you know shapes your life." OECD Publishing. Retrieved from https://www.oecd.org/insights/humancapitalhowwhatyouknowshapesyourlife.htm.
Olsen, B. (2008). How reasons for entry into the profession illuminate teacher identity development. *Teacher Education Quarterly,* Summer, 23–40.
Olsen, B. & Sexton, D. (2009). Threat rigidity, school reform, and how teachers view their work inside current education policy contexts. *American Educational Research Journal, 46*(1), 9–44.
Ortaylı, İ. (1983). İmparatorluğun En Uzun Yüzyılı, Hil Yayıncılık.

ÖSYM, Tablo 4. (2016, June 29). Retrieved from http://dokuman.osym.gov.tr/pdfdokuman/2016/OSYS/EKYER/TABLO-4_lisans04112016.pdf.

Özköse-Bıyık, C. (2007). A preliminary evaluation of the distance English language teacher training program (DELTTP) in Anadolu University, Turkey. *Turkish Online Journal of Distance Education, 8* (1), 143–162.

Öztürk, C. (2005). *Türkiye'de dünden bugüne öğretmen yetiştiren kurumlar.* Istanbul: MEB Yayınlar.

Park, G. (2012). "I Am Never Afraid of Being Recognized as an NNES": One Teacher's Journey in Claiming and Embracing Her Nonnative-Speaker Identity. *TESOL quarterly, 46*(1), 127-151.

Partington, A., Duguid, A. & Taylor, C. (2013). *Patterns and meanings in discourse: Theory and practice in corpus-assisted discourse studies (CADS)* (Vol. 55). Amsterdam: John Benjamins Publishing.

Pennington, M. C. (2002). Examining classroom discourse frames: An approach to raising language teachers' awareness of and planning for language use. *Language in Language Teacher Education*, 149–172.

Pennycook, A. (1998). *English and the discourses of colonialism.* London: Routledge. Pennycook, A. (2007). *Global Englishes and transcultural flows.* London: Routledge. Phillipson, R. (1992). *Linguistic imperialism.* Oxford, UK: Oxford University Press.

Riopel, M. C. (2006). *Apprendre à enseigner: Une identité professionelle à développer.* QC: Les Presses de L'Université Laval.

Roth, W. M. (2004). Identity as dialectic: Re/making self in urban school. *Mind, Culture, and Activity, 11*(1), 48–69.

Sachs, J. (2005). Teacher education and the development of professional identity: Learning to be a teacher. In P. Denicolo and M. Compf (Eds.), *Connecting policy and practice: Challenges for teaching and learning in schools and universities* (pp. 5–21). Oxford, UK: Routledge.

Sağlam, M. & Kürüm, D. (2005). Türkiye ve Avrupa Birliği ülkelerinde öğretmen eğitiminde yapsal düzenlemeler ve öğretmen adaylarn seçimi. *Milli Eğitim Dergisi*, 167, 53–70.

Said, E. (1978) [1995, 2001] *Orientalism: Western concepts of the Orient.* Delhi: Penguin.

Salihoglu, U. M. (2012). Pre-Service English Language Teacher Education: The Turkish Case. *Contemporary Online Language Education Journal, 2*(1), 151–168.

Sarıboğa-Alagöz, N. (2006). *Türkiye'deki ve Hollanda'daki İngilizce öğretmenliği programlarn karşılaştırılması.* Unpublished master's dissertation, Anadolu University, Eskişehir.

Sassower, R. (2000). *A sanctuary of their own: Intellectual refugees in the academy.* Lanham, MD: Rowman & Littlefield.

Seferoglu, G. (2004). A study of alternative English teacher certification practices in Turkey. *Journal of Education for Teaching, 30*(2), 151–159.

Selvi, A. F. (2014) The medium-of-instruction debate in Turkey: Oscillating between national ideas and bilingual ideals. *Current Issues in Language Planning*, (*15*)2, 133–152.

Sinanoğlu, O. (2000). Bye Bye Türkçe. Otopsi Yayınları.

Stubbs, M. (2001). *Words and phrases: Corpus studies of lexical semantics.* Oxford, UK: Blackwell Publishers.

Tannen, D. (1984). *Conversational style: Analyzing talk among friends.* Oxford, UK: Oxford University Press.

Tarman, B. (2010). Global perspectives and challenges on teacher education in Turkey. *International Journal of Arts & Sciences (IJAS), 3*(17), 78–96.

Tok, H. (2006). *Avrupa birliği ülkelerinde ve Türkiye'de uygulanan yabancı dil öğretimi programların karşılaştırılması*. Unpublished doctoral dissertation, İnönü University, Malatya.

Tollefson, J. (2000). Policy and ideology in the spread of English. In J. K. Hall and W. Eggington (Eds), *The sociopolitics of English language teaching* (pp. 7–21). Clevedon, UK: Multilingual Matters.

Tollefson, J. W. (Ed.) (2002). *Language policies in education: Critical issues*. Mahwah, NJ: Lawrence Erlbaum Publishers.

Tollefson, J. W. (2006). Critical theory in language policy. In T. Ricento (Ed.), *An introduction to language policy: Theory and method* (pp. 42–59). Oxford, UK: Blackwell.

Tribble, C. (Ed.) (2012). *Managing change in English language teaching: Lessons from experience*. London: British Council.

Tuck, E. & Yang, K. W. (2012). Decolonization is not a metaphor. *Decolonization: Indigeneity, Education & Society*, *1*(1),1–40.

Varghese, M., Morgan, B., Johnston, B. & Johnson, K. A. (2005). Theorizing language teacher identity: Three perspectives and beyond. *Journal of Language, Identity, and Education*, *4*(1), 21–44.

Wang, L. Y. (2012). Moving towards the transition: Non-native EFL teachers' perception of native-speaker norms and responses to varieties of English in the era of global spread of English. *Asian EFL Journal*, *14*(2), 46–78.

Watson-Gegeo, K. A. & Gegeo, D. W. (1995). Understanding language and power in the Solomon Islands: Methodological lessons for educational intervention. *Power and Inequality in Language Education*, 59–72.

Wedell, M. (2009). *Planning for educational change: Putting people and their contexts first*. London: Bloomsbury.

World Bank Statistics (2017, February 01). Retrieved from http://data.worldbank.org/data-catalog/GDP-ranking-table.

Yağmur, K. (2001). Languages in Turkey. *Multilingual Matters*, 407–428.

Yıldırım, A. & Ok, A. (2002). Alternative teacher certification in Turkey: Problems and issues. In R. G. Sultana (Ed.), *Teacher Education in the Mediterranean Region: Responding to the Challenges of Society in Transition* (pp. 259–275). New York: Peter Lang Inc.

Yücel, T. (1990). Yabancı dille öğretim. *Çağdaş Türk Dili, 30/31*, 884–888.

Zembylas, M. (2003). Emotions and teacher identity: A poststructural perspective. *Teachers and Teaching*, *9*(3), 213–238.

11

DECOLONIZING WORLD LANGUAGE EDUCATION

Toward Multilingualism

François Victor Tochon

THE DEEP INSTITUTE, UNIVERSITY OF WISCONSIN-MADISON

Critical Foreign Language Education, akin to critical literacy education (Freire & Macedo, 1997; Luke, 1997; Janks, 2000; Gottesman, 2016), is influenced by Critical Theory, the progressive movement started in Freire's Critical Pedagogy (1970, 1998). On the basis of a sociocultural theory of language, it raises the awareness of learners to the relationship between language and power and teaches how to handle this connection in a way that will empower minority learners. Along this line of thought, this chapter proposes a demonstration, in four points:

1) Critical to language education are the notions of status, hegemony, homogeneity, lingua franca, and language war. Furthermore, a few key languages not only support an agenda for international communication, they support globalization of capital, which represents a neo-colonial force in the sense that Foucault (1975) gave to this term, associating it with the colonization of the mind. This point relates to language market issues.
2) Language teachers have to question their role as proponents of an indoctrination system, with simplistic rules reducing languages to structures and standardized performance assessments for bureaucratic purposes. Bureaucracy is part of a dehumanizing agenda that treats humans like robots that must respond to well-specified goals. Bureaucracy hinders forms of emancipatory learning that could focus on proficiency and cross-cultural understanding. This point relates to the planned economies of schooling.
3) The necessary conditions to do any better do not seem to be met in today's schools; a peaceful evolution is required in world language education (WLE) to free teachers and students alike from industrial and technical thinking that supports forms of assessment which handicap creative learning and restrain the teacher's freedom to adapt the curriculum to every student.

4) Limiting views of schooling are currently criticized, but the unschooling trend is being revived by forces that capture children's minds with profitable tools in the name of online emancipation and differentiation through privatization. The emancipation work must focus on a change of mindset.

The following four sections focus on each of these points.

Criticizing Language Status, Hegemony, Homogeneity, Lingua Franca, War and Globalization

The perception that others represent a threat, which affects cross-cultural emotions, is being used to enforce language and culture hegemony, a wrong sense of linguistic homogeneity and status, and group supremacy. Historical ways to address such issues have been, on the one hand, international coalitions, the perpetuation of wars, and the imposition of lingua francas as hegemonic expressions of commonly accepted forms of cultural power, and, on the other hand, the spread of curricula for multilingualism, which can be considered another way to resolve language and culture wars (Skutnabb-Kangas, Phillipson, Mohanty & Panda, 2009). Thus, critical to language education are the notions of status, hegemony, homogeneity, lingua franca, and language war. Dominant languages support top-down globalization. Emergent trends suggest there would be a choice, either toward a world dominated by one or two hegemonic lingua francas or a pluralist world in which a variety of world languages could share power. This section addresses some component factors of this broad issue.

Language Status

"Language policy debates are always about more than language" (Ricento, 2006, p. 8). In the multidisciplinary and interdisciplinary field of language teacher education, curricula are viewed as influencing and being influenced by ideologies, values, and language identities, as well as international and market pressures (Phillips & Ochs, 2004). Language status, in particular, reflects the perceived social utility of a language, which is determined not only by market forces but also by the way specific cultural actors perceive and use language (Fishman, 2006). For example, a language policy may be intended to remove what is claimed to be an inferior or defective language; to provide access to an ostensibly "value-free" major language to lessen linguistic schisms in a nation-state; or to meet local demands for greater labor mobility. Language identity, political ideology, perceived labor markets, aesthetics, fashion, popular culture, and myths all become key components of language status. Language curricula in education are influenced by implicit purposes and values. Applied linguistics are linked to issues of social justice (Piller, 2016). Language status, in particular, as the perceived value of the social utility of a language, is influenced by culture and the way specific cultural actors see their language. The implicit purposes and values underlying language curricula and teacher education have an impact on school practices, and in turn affect a large number of children worldwide, the most sensitive time being in Grade K-3 when the language of the school is not the language the child uses at home.

Language Hegemony

Local languages and indigenous languages and cultures are disappearing around the planet because of systematic schooling in dominant languages (Fishman, 2006), which in itself deserves critical consideration in many countries. While laws and regulations protect the languages and cultures of minorities, those laws and regulations are not applied effectively, if at all. Suarez argues (2002) that hegemony is established through consent and persuasion, through leadership without force, its legitimacy being obtained on the basis of consensual rule (Gramci, 1971). "The United States often exerts its influence by maintaining hegemonic power structures that allow for a more subtle type of dominance (than British colonialism) that relies on both top-down institutional pressures and bottom-up choices by individuals who rationally wish to accrue the benefits that come with English fluency" (Harper, 2011, p. 517). Hegemony is instrumental in colonizing the mind to ways of conceiving life on Earth that support the idea that the market should take precedence over human choice. When the dominant ideology has been interiorized, it gives a sense of inevitability that characterizes the colonization of the mind. In contrast, we should aim at developing the multilingual mind (Dua, 2016).

Language Homogeneism

Language standardization and homogeneism emerged with the nationalistic movements that challenged various forms of imperialism, and it is a tool of language consolidation. The architects of nation building, in the terms of Blommaert and Verschueren (1998), planned for monoglotia. Furthermore, specific languages were chosen as units to define nations. Languages were associated with shared ideological loads that required homogeneity: "Traditional foreign language education was designed to produce cultural homogeneity rather than authentic cultural democracy. Although there has been great progress in diversifying foreign language education, it remains largely class based" (Macedo, 2014, p. 344). Language homogeneity is the result of human action, yet it does not always originate in deliberate design that may become coercive and unjust (Levy, 2003). Applied internationally, though, homogeneism creates an imaginary in which the world might converge into a universal embrace of English while thousands of languages fall into obsolescence.

Lingua Francas

The status of lingua franca is related to political and cultural prestige and financial power. Basically a lingua franca can be considered a language chosen for inter-ethnic and cross-cultural communication, and its choice is in the main determined by power and cultural capital. However, the term *lingua franca* is often used in ways that reinforce linguistic hegemony uncritically; for example, promoting global English as a "lingua frankensteinia" swallowing up national organisms (Phillipson, 2008): "The worldwide presence of English as a *lingua americana* is due to the massive economic, cultural and military impact of the USA. Labeling English as a *lingua franca,* if this is understood as a culturally neutral medium that puts every-one on an equal footing, entails not merely ideological dangers, it is simply false" (p. 250). The same could happen soon with Mandarin.

The role of official policy in developing a lingua franca appears minimal: "If the factors for lingua franca status are present, the language will spread. If not, there is no political action that can replicate them." (Wright, 2004, p. 134). The main issue is that, historically, lingua francas lead to linguicide (Skutnabb-Kangas & Phillipson, 2016). The worldwide community imagining of an English-using opening of all borders reinvents rituals and discourses that connect people through linguistic domination or hybridity; as Phillipson (2007) suggests, the agenda reflects metaphysical choices and a philosophy that underpins the type of world we wish to live in and the belief systems and values that guide us, such as consumerism and linguistic neo-imperialism. The promotion of English as a global language "militates against the ongoing use, and even existence, of minority languages" (May, 2006, p. 255). Harper (2011, p. 516) notes in this respect, "language policy scholars also forecast that the spread of English will result in the decline and extinction of many of the world's languages; current predictions state that between twenty percent and fifty percent of the estimated 6,800 natural languages in the world today will no longer exist at the end of the twenty-first century." What Harper could not anticipate was the forth-coming possible dominance of another language, yet whether the future global language is English or not does not change the issue.

Language Wars

Another area in which critical pedagogy finds legitimacy offers a counterweight to the move toward one world language, if this hegemonic attempt goes beyond propaganda and wishful thinking (Tochon, 2009). The change in denomination of foreign languages toward being labeled "world languages" goes along the lines of designating a number of world languages, namely those with more than a hundred million speakers, on which international communications would be based. Two critical conceptual movements around World English and English as a Lingua Franca (ELF) merged into a broad agreement, in the research community, that there will be World

Englishes (plural) and the lingua francas cannot be reified into one normative and exclusive variety (Kirkpatrick, 2007). Furthermore, it is now understood that the relative percentage of English speakers who speak English as a second language is roughly double that of the mother tongue speakers, which entails for L2 speakers the right to recreate the variety they believe to be the most conducive to international communication. This recently led even a fervent anti-imperialist author such as Phillipson (2010) to express some sympathy toward the nuanced and reconceptualized goals of ELF proponents, as the new norms might not emerge from Kachru and Bolton's (2006) inner circle but from a re-appropriation of the target language by the more peripheral circles. In this realm, the fields of language policy (LP) and now Language Education Policy (LEP[1]) continue to play a critical role of awakening. From a LEP viewpoint, a critical pedagogy is a form of awakening to the political role of language (language status, tests, pedagogies) in the oppression of minority societies and populations. Thus, in this respect, LEP knowledge as a field of study contributes to decolonizing the linguistic mindset.

World Languages and Globalization

Globalization does not only impact how languages are viewed worldwide, it has an effect on language, on language hierarchies, structures, and common uses, such as a general reorganization of the linguistic environment in globalizing societies, as illustrated in the Latinization of scripts. It also influences migration patterns and émigré communities worldwide. So-called free-market globalization has created "a dramatic growth in economic and social inequalities both within states and internationally" (Hobsbawn, 2007, p. 3). Phillipson (2006, pp. 351–352) translated Bourdieu's (2001) note on globalization:

> "Globalization" serves as a password, a watchword, while in effect it is the legitimatory mask of a policy aiming to universalize particular interests and the particular tradition of the economically and politically dominant powers, above all the United States, and to extend to the entire world the economic and cultural model that favors these powers most, while simultaneously presenting it as a norm, a requirement, and a fatality, a universal destiny, in such a manner as to obtain adherence or, at least, universal resignation.
>
> *(p. 84)*

Due to common views about the new lingua franca, some language education policy researchers adopt a legalist stand and posit that only the imposition of linguistic rights will help solve some of the challenges and concerns raised by globalization, such as genocide of linguistic minorities (Skutnabb-Kangas, 2000; Starkey, 2013). Other language policy researchers posit that the sociolinguistic challenge should not be addressed through an abstract essentialization of what languages entail, but through new ways of apprehending the phenomenon in its poly-linguaging (Jørgensen, 2008) to account for various repertoires that emerge in the name of the lingua franca but, nonetheless, vary greatly from region to region in their forms, genres, styles, and pronunciations. Thus redefined as a highly volatile process, the reorganizing of language repertoires under the spell of globalization may capture different forms of impact and ways of valuing the target language, which will affect its very coexistence and interchange capability in sociolinguistic environments. As globalization may serve local goals as well as global industries, its examination through the lens of multiplicity may make more sense, as it has explanatory power when analyzing the bites of the multiple head of the Hydra in its various locations. For example, the emergence of a Chinese English in Beijing may appear as a supervernacular with local indexicality (Kroon, Blommaert & Jie, 2013). Yet the notion that language is closely related to identity, and therefore eliminating minority languages through schooling characterizes one form of genocide as defined by the U.N. Convention, is a worthwhile demonstration (Toivanen & Saarikivi, 2016). Linguistic human rights are also instruments of decolonization opposing systemic hegemonic aggression.

Language Teachers Must Question Their Role: What About Pedagogies?

Having its roots in Trotskyism and the Frankfurt School of Sociology, Critical Theory challenges instrumental reason, its pretense to neutrality, reification, and naturalism, as any analysis of the social is imbued with subjective interpretation and ideological stands (Norton & Toohey, 2004). For Trotsky (1904), Critical Education depends on transnational community cooperation rather than institutional domination. It is active in education and orients pedagogy toward the interests of the low-income class, raising subjective consciousness, helping people gain an understanding of the objectives of social evolution to remove from its path, by its own organized strength, counter-evolutionary obstacles.

The Role Played by Language Education in the Agenda for Domination

- Separating the teaching of language and culture
- Struggling against bilingualism of the poor, emphasizing bilingualism of the elites (Kubota, 2014)
- Displacing minorities into the language and culture of the majority (Giroux, 2016)
- Limiting access to college and reducing funding for the poor
- Imposing controlled curricula and official knowledge (Apple, 1993)

In Tochon (2011) I offered a deconstruction of current paradoxes in the ways we tend to handle foreign language teaching (Skutnabb-Kangas & Phillipson, 2016).

> "Despite the discourse of value-free methods, today many scholars agree that methods cannot be separated from epistemology, and always have a moral and political dimension. Methods are not neutral endeavors: they proceed from specific worldviews . . . The insistence on methods being apolitical is a political stand. However—despite current hyper-rationalist formats—in many teacher education settings methodological fundamentalism is on its way out. Teaching languages involves interpersonal situations, complex and dynamic contexts and social differences produced by race, ethnicity, gender, sexual orientation, ability, linguistic status, money, power, and class. For the teacher, it is worth having multifold knowledge, multiple ways of knowing and interpreting situations, and adapting action within flexible methodologies."
>
> *(p. 13)*

Azocar (2005) observed American student teachers teaching Spanish and noted:

- Their reluctance to use Latin-American cooperative games and their preferred choices for American competitive games transferred to Spanish, thus normalizing language teaching into their own culture.
- Their refusal to express and teach socio-affective aspects of the Spanish culture.
- Their erasing of religious symbols as potentially inappropriate and promotional.

Azocar's study indicates how language teaching gets subordinated to imperatives of the dominant culture without this positioning being questioned or even seen by the student teachers. Most of them "are not able (or unwilling) to acknowledge themselves as cultural beings . . . Governmentality and colonization happen unconsciously and subtly" (Azocar, personal communication, January 8, 2006). The debate around culture tends to be depoliticized, normalized, and reduced to games, while issues such as cultural enminding are not addressed. The language and culture are conditioned and prepacked, Americanized within an acceptable format. The emphasis here is on the packaging of other cultures as being subservient to the dominant culture; culturally relevant pedagogy (Ladson-Billings, 2001). Learning otherness would require some anthropological insight of the self. Cultures have been objectified for the purpose of teaching, and their normalization processes are similar to other types of school normalizations (Valdman, 2001). Normalization is part of the colonizing process. In controlled environments, not only does it seem almost hazardous not to propose simplified views of other cultures for the purpose of teaching, it is impossible without distancing oneself *vis-à-vis* one's own culture and how it filters what one perceives in the cultures of others. Standardization supports preconceptions that may be detrimental to deeper learning. Some emancipation is required from teachers who want to address such issues as questioning the native language norm, language status, foreignness, attitudes, linguicism (language discrimination), and linguistic human rights (Kubota & Okuda, 2016).

Pedagogy of the Oppressed Has a Point

Freire was an avid reader of Leo Trotsky. Here are excerpts of a demonstration I made in 2015 (pages 302–305, slightly reworded):

> Transformational pedagogy inspired by Paolo Freire and deep pedagogy are related. Since the time Freire wrote Pedagogy of the Oppressed, the situation in the world has radicalized, particularly in the United States where the middle class has almost disappeared. The people who were previously in the middle of the spectrum on the salary scale are now representing the bottom 20%; 1% earn 358 times the mean salaries of the 99% (Norton & Ariely, 2011). One hundred and forty-seven financial companies direct 40% of the world's finances and have shares in roughly 1,500 partner companies that give them the decision-making power for 80% of the global financial resources (Vitali, Glattfelder & Battiston, 2011). Thus the situation now is that at least 85% of the world population are among the oppressed. Most of us are work slaves struggling for our survival in a system of constraints that makes our lives more and more unbearable. In search for a better definition of economy as a science to the service of humanity (Latouche, 2016), the current financial system is organized in a way that is detrimental to humanity at large and serves a superclass of criminal parasites (de Rivero, 2003; Rothkopf, 2008). We can observe a situation in which the flow of resources was diverted to go up on the pyramid of power rather than creating balanced exchanges. Money was decoupled from real value in a manner that a few printed paper money out of thin air and sold it with interests. Then, because of the created imbalance, between 2007 and 2016 the wealthy bailed themselves out to an amount close to 25 trillion dollars. The debt was attributed to the population at large, which may create generations of slave workers for the coming century, whose taxes will serve to pay the debt of the rich.

Thus today the contradiction that Freire described is at its maximum, to the point of disequilibrium. Such extraordinary imbalance in which the system is owned by a few who direct the world's transactions and decide austerity measures imposed on the whole population characterizes a situation of enslavement of humanity. Surveillance is constant. However, over time complex systems re-equilibrate themselves. When a system reaches a tipping point of imbalance, it suddenly reorganizes itself in a myriad of rebalancing moves from within, which may be about to happen.

This situation legitimates a pedagogy of social awakening, more than ever. As Freire feared, Education has become an instrument of oppression rather than liberation. The education systems are now top-down hierarchies, dialogue and democratic representation are less and less possible. In particular, the banking concept of education has reached its peak, as global standards are being imposed that target the development of the same outcomes for all rather than personalized inter-subjective and creative growth. Freire's generative themes are great transdisciplinary incentives for open project pedagogy, in which the students freely investigate what matters most in their lives . . .

In Freire's concept—which appears particularly in his letters to his niece Cristina when he reflects upon his life and work (see Letter Twelve, Araújo Freire & Macedo, 2000)—the relation of the student with the teacher is still hierarchical, as the teacher is fully in charge of the learner's awakening. The cultural circles are more than facilitated: they are initiated, guided and monitored. A deeper approach would be for study groups to become autonomous and that advisors become external, as facilitators, like peers in charge of feedback. In reducing the sense of hierarchy, such a deeper approach would achieve the goals of a pedagogy of the oppressed.

As long as school districts do not have much liberty to free the teachers from the bureaucratic duty of obedience to imposed forms of knowledge and our governments are the puppets of lobbies, education will be an instrument of oppression rather than liberation. It will be creating servile and dependent customers rather than creative citizens. This applies to many countries. For example, and in contrast, the purpose of pre-modern Chinese education was to acquire a language for deep understanding, actualizing ancient wisdom: language teaching was grounded in philosophy (Wu, 2014). Curricula were open and teachers were considered experts and wise enough to adapt master plans, contents and pacing to the needs of their students. Teachers were highly considered. Nowadays education focuses on the acquisition of objects, most teachers have a technical role in implementing the decision of others.

Freedom to learn is possible in situations under local control. However, governments dictate subject-matters, pacing and disciplinary programming, the forms of delivery and examinations targeting observable performance. This high-level top-down control implies a society of un-equals. This is the situation of schooling around the planet. The time is ripe for a Deep Turn. Accelerating a peaceful revolution within world languages education would generate a pedagogy of hope and deeper critical literacies.

A Peaceful Evolution is Required in World Language Education

The previous section has explored various struggles for a decolonizing pedagogy of languages and cultures that can be summarized as follows (Tochon, 2011):

> The standardization of methods reifies language education. Their principles are most often reduced to be taught out of context; such reductionism must be challenged, which should lead to challenges to native language supremacy, fossilization for the purpose of grammar teaching, issues of status and attitudes toward what is foreign;
>
> The struggle for a better recognition of local languages, including indigenous languages facing disappearance on the world stage because of killer languages such as, but not limited to, English;
>
> The struggle for a recognition of the rights of second language speakers to direct the language norms being taught in educational institutions, such as in ASEAN countries (Kirkpatrick, 2010);
>
> The struggle to deepening heritage learners' reading and writing proficiency in their own language as well as raising their comfort level in expressing themselves orally;
>
> The struggle for better recognition of the place of the learner, positing learners as curriculum builders in a critical and paradigmatic turning from institutional considerations to an interpersonal focus, relinquishing the idea of control in our educational institutions.

Hawkins and Norton (2009) offered a panorama of critical language teacher education. Their insights led them to recommend teachers to situate the nature of the programs and practices in their cultural and historical contexts, be responsive to learners in the form of reflexive and dialogical engagement, and focus on praxis through the integration of theory and practice. Like other educators, world language educators are supposed to work hard to reach and maintain high standards, while the standards system itself seems to have been created as a political, and a partly illusory, discourse. The application of competency standards is time-consuming in such a way that it cannot be properly achieved. Moreover, the indispensable resources that the most basic educational goals deserve are not provided. In the US, lacking funding, resources, political support and teachers, world language teaching risks disappearing from K-12 schools. In this context, is there hypocrisy in continuing business as usual when one notices that:

> The means are not provided to reach the ends that are required. Languages are taught in schools in a way that is less than satisfactory in terms of schedule, curriculum, variety, methods, efficiency, cultural impact, identity, and recognition. Children need life-related contents to manifest deep, long-term learning. They need to be in smaller groups, start to learn languages younger. The foreign language standards (5Cs), although offering an interesting framework, still may prevent larger, freer project-based approaches that would support a deeper understanding of cultures and of Otherness.
>
> The whole craze for accelerated language learning occurs in a financially fabricated warfare context[2]. While languages are and should be a

> unique entry into world peace, they become the main instruments for colonial snooping. Neo-imperialism uses the most counterintuitive instruments: force, intimidation, and corruption rather than knowledge, reliability, and accountability. It represses opposition and imposes obedience through decrees and statutory orders rather than creating harmony through consensual negotiation. It was thought it would be possible to communicate with China without Chinese, to forcefully persuade South American allies without any recognition of their languages and cultures. The results are at the opposite end of expectations. The most-spoken languages are not taught or valued, and the current language policies are at best characterized as "shooting themselves in the foot" (Lee & Marshall, 2001) and "shortsighted, counterproductive, even paranoid" (Stanton, 2005, p. 5). Overall, the logic of short-term efficiency negates proficiency, professionalism, diplomacy, and intelligence
>
> *(Tochon, 2011, p. 17).*

A peaceful evolution is required to free teachers and students alike from the bureaucratic mindset that transforms languages and cultures into prepacked, frozen chunks of knowledge that fit what a dehumanizing system can market.

Decolonizing Strategies . . .

In exploring the relations between dominant and minority groups, action must be context-sensitive and pragmatic in order to meet the present and remote needs of the speech communities concerned. Suarez's (2002) resistance strategy against linguistic hegemony requires acquiescence to such hegemony to reach proficiency in the dominant language and convince others of the importance of heritage language maintenance. She argues (p. 514) that minority groups can maintain their languages over time. Among the factors that support the maintenance of heritage languages are: the establishment of ethnic identity as well as supportive political and social attitudes (Frank, 1993); occupational and education mobility (Priestly, 1994); network-situated strategies of social reproduction (O'Riagain, 1994); native language use as a resistance to linguistic hegemony (Shannon, 1995); language as a symbol of a stigmatised ethnic group (Brankston & Henry, 1998); and modernization and the ethnolinguistic vitality of the language group (Yagmur, De Bot & Korzillus, 1999).

I derived from the contradictions analyzed a series of recommendations. As Lakoff (2002) suggests, every effort should be made to bring the decision-makers who have an "authoritative father," monological mindset—a form of hypocognition of their social role— to a more nurturing role. To make life more humane we need to work on identity, power for social healing, and the politics of the personal. The teacher has become a pawn within the hyper-capitalist chess game where all life is a paid-for experience (Rifkin, 2001). When problems arise they are fixed by specialists as you would fix an engine, leading to a view that lacks wholeness and induces dependency toward consumerist solutions. Western society partly prevents true connection with the children. Children cannot be touched, they are crowded in large groups, they are taught a technical approach to reality, and their interactions are engineered toward productivity and machines: computers, not people.

Teachers have to become transformative intellectuals and critical pedagogists. With the goal of awareness-catching, the teacher may act as a social healer (Tochon, 2004). A number of scholars have developed such a conceptualization inspired by the translation of Freire's works (Araújo Freire & Macedo, 2000; Giroux, 2016; McLaren, 2006) in the field of languages, such as Tollefson (1995), Benesch (2001), Pennycook (2001), Reagan (2005a) and Osborn (2006)[3]. Basically, the teacher's knowledge and experience need to be valued and recognized.

Teaching self and otherness is part of teaching culture and language. Accessing another culture is an identity-building process. Interactions need to be biographically situated. Beliefs about ontology and reality, as well as social positioning, play a huge role in the perception and stance *vis-à-vis* the other language and culture. Thus methods should become more embodied and personal, and lead to a reflection on one's potentially discriminatory identity processes. The search for a grand cultural narrative and its prototypes — somewhat stereotypical — should be replaced by local, small-scale attempts at developing projects fitted to specific experiences and goals. Dealing with cultures equates with dealing with identity processes and entering a dialogue with others (Tracy, 2002).

The teaching of languages is going through a legitimating crisis. Kumaravadivelu (2003) emphasizes the need for raising cultural consciousness. He stresses language skills integration, social relevance, and negotiated interaction as well as intuitive heuristics and post-method pedagogy. Reflective strategies are but a first step in the move toward a deeper approach to language teaching. The second step is to recognize the politics of pedagogy: that the classroom is a politicized space. Its tensions and contradictions characterize teaching and explain the teacher's eclecticism. The socially situated teacher invites students to take stands vis-à-vis knowledge and cultures, discourses, and power. Involving participants and experiences from indigenous as well as international communities can be as important as choosing the right interactional structures to frame classroom exchanges. What is the legitimacy of teaching strategies and cultural generalizations *in abstracto*? There is no clear window into the moving dynamics of cultures. Cultures are socially layered. Any gaze at the culture of others is filtered through epistemic lenses imbued with language, race, ethnicity, class, and gender. The typical outsider looking at otherness also tends to ignore subtle differences within the target culture and language.

Languages are related to crucial issues that young people know well, such as naming and labeling, discriminating, disempowering, categorizing, stage setting, discursive sexting, internet searching, arguing and persuading, group belonging, and achieving and reconceptualizing (Thomas & Wareing, 1999). Students should be actively involved in learning. They should be provided with examples as they build awareness of these aspects, aiming for a more humane version of cosmopolitanism (Ikeda, 2010; Obelleiro, 2012). The Foucaultian concept of "colonization of the mind" should be understood in practice (Scheurich & Bell McKenzie, 2005). Teaching a language is not a matter of grammar. Part of it is related with a clash of identities. There should be a focus on culturally situated meanings. The decolonizing of FLE as a discipline might impact other disciplines as well. The first, and key, step is to help students reflecting on their own culture. The second step is to provide opportunities to get involved with other cultures. They need prolonged and repeated immersion experiences, week- and month-long stays where the language is used in authentic life situations. This is a deeply beneficial way for students to frequent the target language and feel at home within the other culture. Cultural equality, rationales for the fear and acceptance of difference, communication across cultures, and the advantages of national multiculturalism should be discussed. Collaboration across complementary bilingual programs could be organized transnationally. Immersion could be lived on-site with the help of local bilinguals, such as staying with local families who speak the language at home.

Critical Conclusion

This chapter emphasized the need for cross-cultural communication through multilingualism. It also emphasized the complexity of language and culture situations and their ramifications for power struggles, as language is capital. Critical analyses may help in deciphering the underlying power games that impose shallow learning, supplant other cultures, and do not lead to proficiency nor shared understanding among people. Decolonizing foreign language education may help transform it as an instrument of decolonization itself. In this way it may be useful to apply criticism to critical trends as well. Be critical of the absence of criticism in places where one would think it would have its genuine bed. Also be critical of criticism: it reinforces polarization and may lead to dogmatism and indoctrination. Emancipation theories are sometimes used to control people through polar ideologies that keep them busy with belief struggles.

According to his acquaintances, Freire's bedside book was Leo Trotsky's. There are sound aspects to Trotsky's idea of self-criticism to promote continuous change. Ironically, permanent revolution was actually the idea of Alexander Parvus, Trotsky's adviser whose role was to devise wars for profit, a hypothesis that still has explanatory power in the analysis of the situation in the Middle-East (Karaömerlioglu, 2004). Parvus made a fortune frequenting Young Turks and actively setting the stage for Kemalism and Bolshevism (Pößneck, 1997). A few international actors prepared a form of globalization in which their elite minority would have worldly control through political ideologies, religion, and omnipresent surveillance. A higher-level decolonization of the mind is required here.

> Rather than conclude that such distressing trends follow intrinsically from an "aggressive" and "sociopathic" human nature, reasonable observers should likely associate the outgrowth of these tendencies with the dominance of the capitalist system, for, as Oxfam noted in a January 2014 report, the richest 85 individuals in the world possess as much wealth as a whole half of humanity—the 3.5 billion poorest people—while just 90 corporations have been responsible for a full two-thirds of the carbon emissions generated since the onset of industrialisation. As these staggering statistics show, then, the ecological and climatic crises correspond to the extreme concentration of power and wealth produced by capitalism . . .
>
> *(Sethness, 2014, p. 1).*

It is not that on top of the world structure there is a good-guy bad-guy struggle. There are power factions struggling for their expansion or their survival, using the tools of propaganda, political persuasion, finance, and religion to gather followers. For language teachers who are critically aware, the decolonizing of the mind and emancipation are about thinking out of the monocultural and monolingual box and educating students for a multilingual mind that is not subservient to the "globish" system of reason (Popkewitz, 2016) but prioritizes local and mutual connections.

Notes

1 See the informative website of the International Network for Language Education Policy Studies: http://www.languageeducationpolicy.org.

2 Due to the increased requirements for electronic accountability, the teacher education system seems to race out of control and, to get up to speed, students need to sacrifice their balance, their health, and go heavily into debt. Many are bound to the economic banking system for up to twenty years (if you include grace periods, deferments, debt consolidations, and refinancing of their loans) without any chance to end this nightmare with personal bankruptcy.

3 Reagan (2005b) notes that a large section of "Pedagogy of the Oppressed" (Freire, 1970) on the role of spirituality has been censored, which tells much on the sanitization of foreign works. So much for cultural untranslatability. Moreover, in the English version of Freire's book the only excerpt in French—a quote from Sartre—has been recreated from English and is syntactically wrong and meaningless.

Disclosure

Professor Tochon is President of Deep University International, a Section 509(a)(2) charity.

References

ACTFL/AATF/AATG/AATSP (1996). *Standards for Foreign Language Learning: Preparing for the 21st Century*. Yonkers, NY: National Standards in Foreign Language Education Project.

Apple, M. W. (1993). *Official knowledge. Democratic Education in a conservative age.* New York: Routledge.

Araújo Freire, A. M. & Macedo, D. (2000). *The Paulo Freire Reader.* New York: Cotinuum.

Azocar, A. (2005, December). *Research on Spanish Elementary Education: An Alternative Perspective using Post-Colonial Interpretations.* Madison, WI: University of Wisconsin-Madison, School of Education, Spanish for All Program.

Benesch, S. (2001). *Critical English for academic purposes: theory, policy and practice.* Mahwah, NJ: Lawrence Erlbaum.

Blommaert, J. & Vershueren, J. (1998). *Debating diversity: Analyzing the discourse of tolerance.* New York: Routledge.

Bourdieu, P. (2001). Contre-Feux 2: Pour un mouvement social européen. 84 Paris: Raisons d'agir.

Brankston, C. & Henry, J. (1998). The silence of the Gators: Cajun ethnicity and intergenerational transmission of Louisiana French. *Journal of Multilingual and Multicultural Development,* 19, 1–23.

Dua, H. R. (2016). Multilingual Mind, Multi-competence and Conceptual Metaphor. In S. Pattanayak, C. Pattanayak and J. Bayer (Eds), *Multilingualism and Multiculturalism: Perceptions Practices and Policy* (pp.114–129). Delhi: Orient BlackSwan.

Fishman, J. A. (2006). Language policy and language shift. In T. Ricento (Ed.), *An introduction to language policy: Theory and method* (pp. 311–328). Malden, MA: Blackwell.

Foucault, M. (1975). *Surveiller et punir.* Paris: Gallimard.

Frank, D. (1993). Political, religious, and economic factors affecting language choice in Saint Lucia. *International Journal of the Sociology of Language, 102,* 39–56.

Freire, P. (1970). *Pedagogy of the Oppressed.* New York: Continuum.

Freire, P. (1998). *Pedagogy of Freedom: Ethics, Democracy, and Civic Courage.* Lanham, MD: Rowman & Littlefield.

Freire, P. & Macedo, D. (1997). *Pedagogy of the City.* New York: Continuum.

Giroux, H. A. (2016). *Disposable Youth: Racialized Memories, and the Culture of Cruelty.* New York: Routledge.

Gottesman, I. (2016). *The Critical Turn in Education: From Marxist Critique to Poststructuralist Feminism to Critical Theories of Race.* New York: Routledge.

Gramci, A. (1971). *Selections from the Prison Notebooks. Quintin Hoare and Geoffrey Nowell Smith.* New York: International.

Harper, S. M. (2011). Counting the Costs of a Global Anglophonic Hegemony: Examining the Impact of U.S. Language Education Policy on Linguistic Minorities Worldwide. *Indiana Journal of Global Legal Studies, 18*(1), 515–538.

Hawkins, M. & Norton, B. (2009). Critical language teacher education. In A. Burns and J. Richards (Eds.), *Cambridge guide to second language teacher education* (pp.30– 39). Cambridge, UK: Cambridge University Press.

Hobsbawn, E. (2007). *Globalization, Democracy and Terrorism.* London: Little Brown.

Ikeda, D. (2010). *Soka education: For the happiness of the individual.* Santa Monica, CA: Middleway Press.

Janks, H. (2000). Domination, Access, Diversity and Design: a synthesis for critical literacy education. *Educational Review, 52*(2), 175–186.

Jørgensen, J. N. (2008). Poly-lingual languaging around and among children and adolescents. *International Journal of Multilingualism, 5*(3), 161–176.

Kachru, B. & Bolton, K. (2006). *World Englishes: critical concepts in linguistics.* New York: Routledge.

Karaömerlioglu, M. A. (2004). Helphand-Parvus and his Impact on Turkish Intellectual Life, *Middle Eastern Studies, 40*(6), pp.145–165.

Kirkpatrick, A. (2007). *World Englishes: Implications for International Communication and English Language Teaching.* Cambridge, UK: Cambridge University Press.

Kirkpatrick, A. (2010). *English as a Lingua Franca in ASEAN: a multilingual model.* Hong Kong: Hong Kong University Press.

Kroon, S., Blommaert, J. & Jie, D. (2013). Chinese and globalization. In J. Duarte and I. Gogolin (Eds.), *Linguistic Superdiversity in Urban Areas. Research Approaches.* New York: John Benjamins.

Kubota, R. (2014). The Multi/Plural Turn, Postcolonial Theory, and Neoliberal Multiculturalism: Complicities and Implications for Applied Linguistics. *Applied Linguistics, 2014,* 1–22.

Kubota, R., & Okuda, T. (2016). Confronting Language Myths, Linguicism and Racism in English Language Teaching in Japan. In P. Bunce, R. Phillipson, V. Rapatahana and R. Tupas (Eds), *Why English? Confronting the Hydra* (pp.77–87). Bristol, UK: Multilingual Matters.

Kumaravadivelu, B. (2003). *Beyond methods. Macrostrategies for language teaching.*

New Haven, CT: Yale University Press.

Ladson-Billings, G. (2001). *Crossing over to Canaan.* San Francisco, CA: Jossey-Bass.

Lakoff, G. (2002). *Moral politics. How liberals and conservatives think.* Chicago, IL: University of Chicago Press.

Latouche, S. (2016). *L'invention de l'économie* (Inventing Economy). Paris: Albin Michel.

Lee, R. H. & Marshall, D. F. (2001). "Shooting themselves in the foot": consequences of English Only supporters "going to law". In R. Duenas Gonzalez and I. Melis (Eds), *Language ideologies. Critical perspectives of the Official English Movement.* Vol. 2. History, Theory, and Policy (pp. 171–190). Mahwah, NJ: Lawrence Erlbaum.

Levy, J. T. (2003). Language rights, literacy, and the Modern State. In W. Kymlicka and A. Patten (Eds.), *Language Rights and Political Theory* (pp. 230–249). Cambridge, MA: Oxford University Press.

Luke, A. (1997). Critical approaches to Literacy. In D. Corson (Ed.), *Encyclopedia of Language and Education.* Amsterdam: Kluwer.

Macedo, D. (2014). Decolonizing Foreign Language Education: An Afterword. In F. V. Tochon, *Help Them Learn a Language Deeply: The Deep Approach to World Languages and Cultures* (pp. 339–348). Blue Mounds, WI: Deep University Press.

May, S. (2006) Language Policy and Minority Rights. In T. Ricento (Ed.), *An Introduction to Language Policy: Theory and Method* (pp. 255–272). Malden, MA: Blackwell.

McLaren, P. (2006). *Rage and Hope: Interviews on War, Imperialism, and Critical Pedagogy.* New York: Peter Lang, Counterpoints: Studies in the Postmodern Theory of Education.

Morin, E. (1964). *Introduction à une politique de l'Homme* (Introduction to Politics of the Human). Paris: Seuil.

Norton, B. & Toohey, K. (2004). *Critical pedagogies and language learning.* Cambridge, UK: Cambridge University Press.

Norton, M. I., & Ariely, D. (2011). Building a better America – One Wealth Quintile at a Time. Perspectives on Psychological Science, 6(1), 9–12. Retrieved from: http://www.people.hbs.edu/mnorton/norton%20ariely%20in%20press.pdf or http://people.duke.edu/~dandan/Papers/Other/BuildingBetterAmerica.pdf.

Obelleiro, G. (2012). A moral cosmopolitan perspective on language education. *Critical Inquiry in Language Studies, 9*(1–2), 33–59.

O'Riagain, P. (1994). Language maintenance and language shift as strategies of social reproduction. *Journal of Multilingual and Multicultural Development, 15*, 179–198.

Osborn, T. A. (2006). *Teaching world languages for social justice. A sourcebook of principles and practices.* Mahwah, NJ: Lawrence Erlbaum.

Pennycook, A. (2001). *Critical applied linguisics. A critical introduction.* Mahwah, NJ: Lawrence Erlbaum.

Phillips, D. & Ochs, K. (2004). Researching policy borrowing: Some methodological challenges in comparative education. *British Educational Research Journal, 30*(6), 773–784.

Phillipson, R. (2006). Language policy and language imperialism. In T. Ricento (Ed.), *An Introduction to Language Policy: Theory and Method* (pp. 346–361). Malden, MA: Blackwell.

Phillipson, R. (2008). Lingua franca or lingua frankensteinia? English in European integration and globalisation. *World Englishes, 27*(2), 250–267.

Phillipson, R. (2010). *Linguistic Imperialism Continued.* New York: Routledge.

Piller, I. (2016). *Linguistic Diversity and Social Justice. An Introduction to Applied Sociolinguistics.* Cambridge, MA: Oxford University Press.

Popkewitz, T. (2016). *The "Reason" of Schooling: Historicizing Curriculum Studies, Pedagogy, and Teacher Education.* New York: Routledge.

Pößneck, E. (1997). *Lenin als Kontrahent von Parvus im Jahr 1917.* Schkeuditz : GNN-Verlag.

Priestly, T. (1994). Effects of educational and social mobility on language maintenance, language attitudes and language structure: The case of Sele in Carinthia. *Journal of Multilingual and Multicultural Development, 15,* 199–217.

Reagan (2005a). *Critical questions, critical perspectives: Languages and the second language educator.* Greenwich, CT: Information Age, Contemporary Language Studies in Education.

Reagan, T. (2005b, September). *Critical theory, globalization and international language education.* University Lecture Series. University of Wisconsin-Madison. September 16, 2005.

Ricento, T. (2006). *An introduction to language policy: Theory and method.* Malden, MA: Blackwell.

Rifkin, J. (2001). *The age of access. The new culture of hypercapitalism where all of life is a paid-for experience.* New York: Penguin Putnam.

Rivero (de), O. (2003). *The myth of development. Non-viable economies of the 21st century.* New York: Zed Books, Global Issues.

Rothkopf, D. (2008). *Superclass: The Global Power Elite and the World They Are Making.* New York: Farrar, Straus and Giroux.

Scheurich, J. J. & Bell McKenzie, K. (2005). Foucault's methodologies: archaeology and genealogy. In N. K. Denzin and Y. S. Lincoln (Eds), *The Sage handbook of qualitative research* (4th edition) (pp. 841–868). Thousand Oaks, CA: Sage.

Sethness, Javier (2014). Noam Chomsky: Ecology, Ethics, Anarchism. Alternet, April 3, 2014. Retrieved from: http://www.alternet.org/economy/noam-chomsky-ecology-ethics-anarchism.

Shannon, S. (1995). The hegemony of English: A case study of one bilingual classroom as a site of resistance. *Linguistics and Education, 7,* 175–200.

Skutnabb-Kangas, T. (2000). *Linguistic genocide in education – or worldwide diversity and human rights?* Mahwah, NJ: Lawrence Erlbaum.

Skutnabb-Kangas, T. & Phillipson, R. (2016). *Language Rights.* London: Routledge.

Skutnabb-Kangas, T, Phillipson, R., Mohanty, A. K. & Panda, M. (2009). *Social Justice through Multilingual Education.* Bristol, UK: Multilingual Matters.

Stanton, D. C. (2005). On linguistic human rights and the United States 'Foreign' Language crisis. *ADFL Bulletin, 36*(2), 5–13.

Starkey, H. (2013). Human rights (including linguistic human rights). In C. A. Chapelle (Ed.), *Encyclopedia of Applied Linguistics.* New York: Wiley-Blackwell. DOI: 10.1002/9781405198431.wbeal0517.

Suarez, D. (2002). The paradox of linguistic hegemony and the maintenance of Spanish as a heritage language in the United States. *Journal of Multilingual and Multicultural Development, 23*(6), 512–530.

Thomas, L. & Wareing, S. (1999). *Language, society and power.* New York: Routledge.

Tochon, F. V. (2004). Le nouveau visage de l'enseignant expert (The New Face of the Expert Teacher). *Recherche et Formation, 47*, 89–103.

Tochon, F. V. (2009). The Key to Global Understanding: World Languages Education. Why Schools Need to Adapt. *Review of Educational Research. 79*(2), 650–682.

Tochon, F. V. (2011). Reflecting on the paradoxes of foreign language teacher education: a critical system analysis. *Porta Linguarum, 15*, 7–24.

Tochon, F. V. (2015). *Help them learn a language: Why We Need a Deep Approach to World Languages and Cultures.* Blue Mounds, WI: Deep University Press.

Toivanen, R. & Saarikivi, J. (2016). *Linguistic genocide or superdiversity? New and old language diversities.* Bristol, UK: Multilingual Matters.

Tollefson, J. W. (1995). *Power and inequality in language education.* Cambridge, UK: Cambridge University Press.

Tracy, K. (2002). *Everyday talk. Building and reflecting identities.* New York: Guilford.

Trotsky, L. (1904). *Nashi Politicheskiya Zadachi* (On our political tasks, transcribed by A. Lehrer). New Park.

Valdman (2001, October). *The notion of the pedagogical norm in instructed SLA.* Presentation made at the 4th Pacific Second Language Research Forum. University of Hawaii at Manoa.

Vitali, S., Glattfelder, J. B. & Battiston, S. (2011). *The network of global control.* Zurich, CH: ETH Zurich, System Designs. Retrieved from: http://arxiv.org/PS_cache/arxiv/pdf/1107/1107.5728v2.pdf.

Wright, S. (2004). *Language Policy and Language Planning.* New York: Palgrave Macmillan.

Yagmur, K., De Bot, K. & Korzillus, (1999). Language attrition, language shift and ethnolinguistic vitality of Turkish in Australia. *Journal of Multilingual and Multicultural Development, 20*, 51–69.

INDEX

Page numbers in *italics* refer to figures.